THE FEMINIST CARE TRADITION
IN ANIMAL ETHICS

T0204410

THE FEMINIST CARE TRADITION IN ANIMAL ETHICS

A Reader

EDITED BY

Josephine Donovan and Carol J. Adams

Columbia University Press New York

Columbia University Press

Publishers Since 1893

New York   Chichester, West Sussex

Copyright © 2007 Columbia University Press

All rights reserved

Library of Congress Cataloging-in-Publication Data

The feminist care tradition in animal ethics : a reader /

edited by Josephine Donovan and Carol J. Adams.

p. cm.

Includes bibliographical references and index.

ISBN 978-0-231-14038-6 (cloth : alk. paper)

ISBN 978-0-231-14039-3 (pbk. : alk. paper)

1. Animal welfare—Moral and ethical aspects.

2. Animal rights.   3. Feminist theory.

I. Donovan, Josephine, 1941–   II. Adams, Carol J.   III. Title.

HV4708.F36   2007

179'.3—dc22   2007023258

Columbia University Press books are printed on
permanent and durable acid-free paper.

Printed in the United States of America

Designed by Audrey Smith

Contents

The Feminist Care Tradition in Animal Ethics

Introduction

JOSEPHINE DONOVAN AND
CAROL J. ADAMS

The Feminist Care Tradition in Animal Ethics: A Reader collects in one volume the leading articles in the feminist ethic-of-care tradition in animal ethics. Part I includes many of the chapters that appeared in our earlier volume on the subject, *Beyond Animal Rights: A Feminist Caring Ethic for the Treatment of Animals* (1996), while part II incorporates articles on new theoretical developments in feminist animal care ethics that appeared subsequent to the publication of that anthology and, in most cases, were written in response to it.

This introduction provides an overview of the feminist ethic-of-care tradition and summarizes other contemporary approaches to animal ethics, including feminist analyses that do not rely on ethic-of-care theory, in order to point up some of the ways the ethic-of-care perspective differs from the others. We are aware of the complex problems inherent in using the word *animals* but find none of the alternatives (*other animals, nonhumans*) satisfactory. We will use the common word *animal* while recognizing, of course, that humans are animals, too, and that anthropocentrism drives the inclusion of other species under that label.

Feminist ethic-of-care theory originally derived from Carol Gilligan's celebrated *In a Different Voice* (1982), which identifies a women's "conception of morality" that is "concerned with the activity of care . . . responsibility and relationships," as opposed to a men's "conception of morality as fairness," which is more concerned with "rights and rules" (19). Gilligan calls the feminine conception "a morality of responsibility," in contrast to the masculine "morality of rights," which emphasizes "separation rather than connection" and focuses more on the autonomy of the individual than on her context and relationships (19). In analyzing one woman subject's response to a hypothetical, Gilligan extrapolates that it implies a morality that is concerned with "sustaining connection . . . keeping the web of relationships intact" (59). Whereas the masculine concern with rights, rules, and an abstract ideal of justice tends often to seem like "a math problem with humans" (28), the feminine approach offers a more flexible, situational, and particularized ethic.

Gilligan's book was soon followed by several others, notably Nel Noddings's *Caring* (1984) and Sara Ruddick's *Maternal Thinking* (1989), which further explore the idea of a women's caring ethic. And numerous other works criticize and/or refine aspects of Gilligan's theory (see, especially, Kittay and Meyers 1987; Cole and Coultrap-McQuin 1992; Larrabee 1993; Tong 1993; Tronto 1993).

In general, the feminist care ethic thus has rejected abstract, rule-based principles in favor of situational, contextual ethics, allowing for a narrative understanding of the particulars of a situation or an issue. As with feminism in general, care theory resists hierarchical dominative dualisms, which establish the powerful (humans, men, whites) over the subordinate (animals, women, people of color). Some ecofeminist writers have, in fact, regarded as definitional to patriarchy men's control over women, animals, and nature (French 1985).

Many theorists have recognized that the hierarchical dominative dualism that characterizes patriarchal thought took an especially deadly turn in the early modern era, when it was powerfully rearticulated in Cartesian objectivism, which divided the world into mind and matter. As matter was assumed to be lifeless and without energizing spirit (unlike in much premodern thinking, which is animist), it was held to be of lesser value than mind, spirit, or reason. In this viewpoint, which undergirds much modern thinking about animals, animals are reduced to mere things, machine-like automatons lacking inner spirit, sensitivity, or feelings. As Thomas Kelch (chapter 9, this volume) points out, it is this view that supports the current common law conception of animals as property.

The feminist ethic of care regards animals as individuals who do have feelings, who can communicate those feelings, and to whom therefore humans have moral obligations. An ethic of care also recognizes the diversity of animals—one size doesn't fit all; each has a particular history. Insofar as possible, attention must be paid to these particularities in any ethical determination concerning them.

Attention is a key word in feminist ethic-of-care theorizing about animals. Attention to the individual suffering animal but also—and this is a critical difference between an ethic-of-care and an "animal welfare" approach—attention to the political and economic systems that are causing the suffering. A feminist ethic-of-care approach to animal ethics offers a *political* analysis. As Joan Tronto points out in *Moral Boundaries* (1993), an ethic of care necessarily entails political theory and analysis (esp. chap. 6). Unlike traditional welfare approaches, with which animal care theory is sometimes confused, which deal with one animal at a time and fail to critique or oppose the system responsible, ethic-of-care theory insists that these causal systems be addressed. As Catharine MacKinnon notes, we are for "caring and empathy while never letting power off the hook" (chapter 13, this volume).

In short, the feminist care approach recognizes the importance of each individual animal while developing a more comprehensive analysis of her situation. Unlike "welfare" approaches, therefore, the feminist care tradition in animal ethics includes a political analysis of the reasons why animals are abused in the first place. This analysis arises from feminist theory, incorporating an understanding of the economic and political aspects of animal abuse. It also contains a political analysis of the care tradition—specifically, how it became associated (and so denigrated by this association) with women.

Ideological systems often screen humans from animals' harm and suffering by offering rationalizations that legitimize those harms, as a number of theorists—notably, in this volume, Brian Luke (chapter 5), Kenneth Shapiro (chapter 6), and Carol J. Adams (chapter 8) as well as Luke (1995)—have emphasized. Men especially, Luke and Shapiro note, are socialized from an early age by our "sex-species system" (Adams, chapter 8) to consider sympathy and compassion for animals as unmanly and feminine (Luke 1997, 1998), one aspect of a more general derision of compassion in society at large, as discussed by Adams in "The War on Compassion." Moreover, harm done to animals is rendered invisible for most people, as Luke notes, by massive ideological screening that shields them from the suffering animal in the laboratory or slaughterhouse. Unless these ideological systems are countered and invalidated, little progress will be made in ending animal exploitation and abuse.

Some ethic-of-care theorists emphasize that our attention be directed as well to what the animals are telling us—rather than to what other humans are telling us about them. Josephine Donovan (chapter 16, this volume) calls for a renewed emphasis on dialogue with animals, learning their communication systems, reading their body language phenomenologically, and taking these communication seriously in our ethical decisions.

Such attentiveness—to the individual animal, to the differences between animals and ourselves, and to controlling systems—requires effort, courage, and discipline. It is not easy to go against dominant systems, to break through ideological obfuscation, and to see and hear the suffering that is in reality endemic, extensive, and ubiquitous. But if animal abuse is to be seriously reduced and eliminated, such attentiveness is required of all who care about animals.

Some have suggested that the ethic-of-care approach is weakened by its apparent moral relativism. While certain authors in this collection do allow for flexibility in ethical decision making (see, especially, Curtin, chapter 3; Slicer, chapter 4; Garbarino, chapter 10; Clement, chapter 12; Gruen, chapter 14), we believe that certain core principles support an ethic-of-care approach. It is wrong to harm sentient creatures unless overriding good will result *for them*. It is wrong to kill such animals unless in immediate self-defense or in defense of those for whom one is personally responsible. Moreover, humans have a moral obligation to care for those animals who, for whatever reason, are unable to adequately care for themselves, in accordance with their needs and wishes, as best the caregivers can ascertain them and within the limits of the caregivers' own capacities. Finally, people have a moral duty to oppose and expose those who are contributing to animal abuse.

While theorizing about what is now called animal ethics dates back to antiquity (Sorabji 1993), the issue began to receive renewed attention in the last quarter of the twentieth century. In the contemporary discussion, several philosophical approaches have emerged in addition to the feminist ethic-of-care perspective. They include animal rights theory, stemming from the liberal political tradition; deep ecology theory; Marxism; and phenomenology.

Animal rights theory, developed largely by Tom Regan and Peter Singer, dominated the debate in its early phases, whereas the others have come to the fore in recent years. Regan (1983) has extended the Enlightenment notion of natural rights—that every person is entitled to be treated with dignity, as an end, not a means—to adult mammals, indeed to all "subjects of a life" (243). Singer (1975), writing in the utilitarian tradition, argues that rights be extended to all sentient creatures, all who can experience pain and pleasure; such creatures' interest in not being mistreated has to be included in any moral calculation about their fates (8, 18).

Feminist care theorists—especially, in this volume, Marti Kheel (chapter 1), Josephine Donovan (chapter 2), Deane Curtin (chapter 3), Brian Luke (chapter 5), and Cathryn Bailey (chapter 15)—have questioned certain premises of the animal rights position. One problem is that rights theory was developed in the seventeenth and eighteenth centuries, the so-called Age of Reason, and reflects its rationalist roots, relying on a mechanistic ontology of territorial atomism. It envisages a society of rational, autonomous, independent agents whose territory or property is entitled to protection from external agents (other people and the government). The founding documents of the United States presumed these rights holders, or "persons," to be white, male property owners. Women, slaves, and the propertyless were excluded from the category of personhood and therefore had no civic rights.

Animal rights theorists have maintained, in effect, that animals are entitled to be considered "persons" before the law and to have rights like those enjoyed by human persons—that is, the basic right to have their territory (their selves, their bodies, their space) held inviolate from unwarranted human intrusions and/or abuse. To sustain their claim, they have had to argue that animals are, in many respects, similar to humans, that they are autonomous individuals with an intelligence that corresponds to human reason (this is Regan's [1983] position; Singer [1975], as noted, argues that sentience rather than rationality be the basis on which "rights" or moral status be granted).

Here, then, is the second difficulty with the application of rights theory to animals: it requires an assumption of similarity between humans and animals, eliding the differences. In reality, animals are only with considerable strain appropriable to Cartesian man. Curtin (chapter 3, this volume), for example, questions whether moral status should depend on an identity of features or interests. MacKinnon (chapter 13, this volume) similarly rejects the "like-us" approach, noting that granting rights to animals inasmuch as they resemble humans fails to see animals on their own terms, just as a strict "equal rights" approach to the law fails to recognize the differences between men's and women's situations and status and, therefore, often does not address women's unique realities and issues.

The third difficulty in applying rights theory to animals lies in the ontology that underlies rights discourse. It presumes a society of equal autonomous agents, who require little support from others and need only that their space be protected from others' intrusions. Animals are not equal to humans; domestic animals, in particular, are for the most part dependent on humans for survival—a situation requiring an ethic that recognizes this inequality. Rights theory has, in fact, been criticized by feminists when applied to humans because its vision of the equal, autonomous individual (male) ignores the network of supporting persons (usually female) who enable his autonomy—that is, who raise him, feed him, clothe him, and so forth. In short, rights theory disregards the fact that most humans and animals operate within interdependent support systems and provides no obligation to care for those who are unable to live autonomously.

The fourth problem with the rights approach is that it devalues, suppresses, or denies the emotions. Thus a major aspect of the human–animal connection—love—is not encompassed. Since the exclusion of the emotional response is a major reason why animal abuse and exploitation continue, it seems contradictory for animal defense advocates to also claim (as Regan [1983] and Singer [1990] have done) that feelings are an inappropriate basis for ethical treatment.

Finally, the rights approach (as well as utilitarian interest theory) tends to be abstract and formalistic, favoring rules that are universalizable or judgments that are quantifiable. Many ethical situations, however, including those involving animals, require a particularized, situational response—one that considers context and history, the relational web that Gilligan (1982) describes—that may not be universalizable or quantifiable.

The second major approach to animal ethics that developed in the later twentieth century is that of "deep ecology." Derived largely from Aldo Leopold's notion of the "land ethic" in *A Sand County Almanac* (1949), it proposes a "biotic right"; that is, nature, conceived as a "biotic community," has the right to exist apart from human interests (Devall and Sessions 1984; Nash 1989:70–71). Under this theory, the rights and interests of individuals (whether human, animal, or tree) are subordinated to the needs of the community. Regan (1983) has criticized this view as "environmental fascism" (362). Feminists also have criticized deep ecology for its sexist assumptions, its covert hierarchism (wild animals are privileged over domestic), and its ethical neglect of individual suffering (see, especially, Kheel, chapter 1, this volume; 1990).

While there has been little Marxist theorizing about animals (Benton 1988, 1993; Sanbonmatsu 2005), it remains in our view a promising approach yet to be fully developed. Perhaps the most cogent work to date is Barbara Noske's *Humans and Other Animals* (1989). Rearticulating Marxist concern about reification and commodification, Noske argues for a "resubjectification of animals" (168) who are commodified as objects under capitalist industrialism–factory farming, which she labels the "Animal Industrial Complex" (14–29). Donovan (chapter 16, this volume) deploys Hungarian Marxist Georg Lukács's "standpoint theory" to argue that animals' subjective standpoint needs to be articulated as a point of resistance to the production process in which they are slaughtered.

While feminists have long criticized Marxist theory for its neglect of women, they do share with Marxists and critical theorists a political perspective. As noted, ethic-of-care feminists in the area of animal ethics have been especially vocal in their insistence on a political analysis and generally share the Marxist critique of capitalist industrialism and globalization.

Phenomenologists who advocate a "shift away from 'seeing from outside,'" as practiced in modern science, "to a 'sensing from within'" (109)— as noted by Elizabeth A. Behnke (1999)—have, as in the Marxist approach, advocated a recognition of the subjectivity of animals, an awareness of aliveness within bodily presence. Behnke and other theorists included in H. Peter Steeves's collection *Animal Others* (1999), as well as Ralph Acampora (1995) and Kenneth Shapiro (1989), have pioneered this direction in animal ethics.

In their concern with interspecies communication and recognition of animal subjectivity, feminist ethic-of-care theorists find much in the phenomenological approach that is compatible with their views. However, unless informed by a political analysis, phenomenology risks remaining purely descriptive without a prescription of how to improve the lives it describes.

In our collection *Animals and Women* (1995), we identify three feminist positions on the question of the status of animals:

- Rejection of the idea of a link between feminism and animal ethics
- Acceptance of the idea
- Silence on the subject

The first approach, the most familiar, supported by theorists like Simone de Beauvoir in *The Second Sex* (1949), negates the ancient association between women and animals, arguing that women are not like animals, but are distinctly human. In seeking to affirm women's rationality, these theorists, beginning with Mary Wollstonecraft in *A Vindication of the Rights of Woman* (1792), denied women's "animality" in order to affirm their humanity and entitlement to basic rights. We hypothesized that this emphasis on severing the connection between women and animals may have been a necessary phase in the transformation of cultural ideology.

Already in the nineteenth century, however, British animal welfare activists, such as Anna Kingsford and Frances Power Cobbe, questioned this approach. Both theorists and activists, they identified connections between invasions of women's bodies and vivisection of animals. In her important book *The Old Brown Dog* (1985), Coral Lansbury describes how Cobbe "was always aware of the connections between vivisection, pornography, and the condition of women" (129). Lansbury also suggests that English suffragists, many of whom had been subjected to torturous forced feeding during hunger strikes in prison, identified with vivisected animals as a result of that experience: "Every dog or cat strapped down for the vivisector's knife reminded them of their own condition" (82). In reviewing Henry Salt's book *Animal Rights* (1892), for a working-class, feminist newspaper of the 1890s, Edith Ward (1892) argued that "the case of the animal is the case of the woman." She explained that the

> similitude of position between women and the lower animals, although vastly different in degree, should insure from the former the most unflinching and powerful support to all movements for the amelioration of the conditions of animal existence. What, for example, could be more calculated to produce brutal wife-beaters than long practice of savage cruelty towards the other animals? And what, on the other hand, more likely to impress mankind with the necessity of justice for women than the awakening of the idea that justice was the right of even an ox or a sheep? (41)

As with the animal defense movement of the late twentieth and early twenty-first centuries, women were the majority of members of British antivivisection societies at the end of the nineteenth century. Donovan suggests that late-eighteenth-century sentimentalism—which she links to "women's increasing participation in cultural life"—"paved the way intellectually for the animal protection movement of the nineteenth century" (chapter 2, this volume).

Similarly, the civil rights and anti–Vietnam War movements in the 1960s paved the way for the resurgence of the feminist movement in the late 1960s. By the early 1970s, before the publication of Peter Singer's *Animal Liberation* in 1975, feminists were establishing theoretical and activist connections with animal issues. Early writings, such as those of Constantia Salamone (1973, 1982) in feminist newspapers of the day, including New York's *Majority Report*, and Carol Adams (1975, 1976) in *The Lesbian Reader* (an anthology of writings from *Amazon Quarterly*) and *Second Wave* (a Boston-based feminist journal), articulate a uniquely feminist position on the status of animals: that their mistreatment is traceable to a patriarchal culture. This argument not only links the status of women to that of animals, but also argues that animal activism requires a feminist analysis and feminism requires an analysis that addresses the status of animals.

The second approach we identified, therefore—that developed by radical and cultural feminists—recognized the link between the oppression of women and that of animals and identified the patriarchal roots of their subjugation. Cultural feminists then began looking to women's traditional culture for alternative values, and it is from this perspective that the ethic-of-care approach emerged.

In the radical feminist tradition, besides Carol Adams's *The Sexual Politics of Meat* (1990), early writings that emphasize the connection between the oppression of women and of animals under patriarchal domination include Andrée Collard's *Rape of the Wild* (1988). Focusing on animal experimentation and hunting, Collard uses animals as a window into the death-oriented values of patriarchal society, both because she is deeply concerned for animals' well-being "and partly because man's treatment of them exposes those values in the crudest, most undisguised form" (2). Susanne Kappeler's *The Pornography of Representation* (1986) implicitly links the status of women and the status of animals as objects whose role is to subjectify men. In "Speciesism, Racism, Nationalism . . . or the Power of Subjectivity" (1995), Kappeler makes her insight explicit, while extending it to explain how a hierarchical culture structured on race, gender, and species operates. As did Salamone and Adams in the 1970s, Norma Benney, in "All of One Flesh" (1983), identifies historical and contemporary connections between women and animals, points out that it is "the *female* animal which is the most exploited" (146), and notes that the antivivisection movement was led by women. She proposes that feminists, in their efforts to overthrow patriarchy, must become "aware of the suffering of non-humans" (151); otherwise, feminists will misunderstand the concept of liberty: "It is neither fair nor just to claim freedom for ourselves, without at the same time claiming freedom for the creatures which share the planet with us, who are cruelly oppressed from birth to death by patriarchal attitudes and systems, and who do not have women's power to organize themselves" (142). Jane Meyerding (1982) also has contributed a radical feminist analysis, identifying patriarchal hierarchy as not only dividing people from one another, but also separating them "from other animals, planets, and the earth itself" (15).

We, the editors, endorse a unified radical and cultural feminist approach to animal issues, repositioning the ethic of care within the political perspective of the radical feminist tradition.

In *An Unnatural Order* (1997), Jim Mason argues that all human oppression originated in the domestication and subsequent oppression of animals. Mason coined the term *misothery* (from the Greek words for *hatred/contempt* and *animal*) to denote speciesist derogation of animals, which he views as parallel to *misogyny*: hatred of and contempt for women (163–64). The theory that the oppression of women, animals, and other subjugated groups is interrelated has proved to have practical implications—for instance, creating alliances between battered women's shelters and veterinarians to ensure that animal companions also receive shelter from batterers. In "Woman-Battering and Harm to Animals" (1995), Carol Adams, after identifying the ways in which batterers harm animals and how harm to animals enables the batterer to control the battered woman, explores the implications for feminist theory: "Gender is an unequal distribution of power; interconnected forms of violence result from and continue this inequality. In a patriarchy, animal victims, too, have become feminized. A hierarchy in which men have power over women and humans have power over animals, is actually more appropriately understood as a hierarchy in which men have power over women, (feminized) men, *and* (feminized) animals" (80).

The application of the insight that the victims of violent abuse share a form of oppression and its implications for the social sciences can be found in several books. Randall Lockwood and Frank R. Ascione's *Cruelty to Animals and Interpersonal Violence* (1998) collects a variety of articles that provide literature reviews and discuss applications (including the issue of reporting animal abuse and watching for animal abuse in a family as a sign of possible child abuse). Amy Fitzgerald's *Animal Abuse and Family Violence* (2005) examines the social construction and abuse of animals, and summarizes a research project that discovered through in-depth interviews with several women that animal abusers control women: not only through their behavior toward animals, but also by purchasing animals and subsequently forcing the women to "give them up" to animal shelters. Fitzgerald also notes how the anthropocentric nature of the social sciences limits their ability to recognize and respond to the reality and implications of multiple forms of abuse. Clifton P. Flynn's (1999, 2000a, 2000b) work in sociology also situates animals within the study of family violence, arguing that the failure to do so affects the well-being of both companion animals and family members. In all these studies, one chilling fact stands out: the power of an abuser increases the more the human victim cares about the fate of the nonhuman victim (see also Adams 1994).

The application of the feminist recognition of interrelated oppressions as it pertains to violent abuse is represented in this volume by the work of James Garbarino (chapter 10). In 2006, partly as a result of these writings, Maine passed a law that allows judges to include companion animals in protection orders for spouses and partners who leave abusive relationships.

In another area that studies interconnected forms of violence, Piers Beirne (1997, 1998, 2004) critiques the anthropocentric nature of criminology, especially as it has labeled and defined bestiality, which he shows to be a highly inadequate term for the sexual violation of animals. He proposes that the term be "Animal Sexual Assault." Karen Davis's *More than a Meal* (2001) shows how both wild and domestic turkeys are subject to human sexual violence. What Davis has attempted for turkeys—the recognition of their worth as individual beings—Susan E. Davis and Margo Demello, in *Stories Rabbits Tell* (2003), provide for rabbits: challenging their social construction: "Words about women and rabbits—like 'dumb bunny' and 'cunt'—belittle and degrade women and rabbits simultaneously. And the very success of the Playboy Bunny—a creature that is half rabbit and half woman, after all—reveals a male penchant for a very chilling notion of female sexuality: one that is bound in notions of prey, childishness and submissiveness, on the one hand, and unbridled lust, fertility and even witchery on the other" (312).

In *Animals and Women*, we identify a third feminist approach to animal ethics: silence—that is, ignoring the issue. Lynda Birke (1994), a biologist who wrote the first book on the construction of the animal in biological science from a feminist perspective, draws on feminist critiques of modern science to highlight the speciesism in both the biological construction of animals and the feminist critiques that ignore the situation of animals. Rejecting biological determinist arguments as arising from an impoverished understanding of the natural world, Birke identifies the problem that the "silent approach" causes in biology: in their critique of science, feminists reject biological determinism for women but accept the notion for animals. Essentially, if women are not "hard-wired," why, then, believe that other animals are? Does the biological critique end at the species boundary? Can not the "biological" itself be regarded as culturally constructed?

We feel that feminists who ignore the realities of the perception of animals in science and other fields not only are exhibiting limited and warped vision, but also are failing to see the linkages among the oppressions noted earlier and, by their silence, are allowing enormous suffering to continue unaddressed.

Recently, however, new feminist approaches to animal ethics have emerged that, although they do not fall under the ethic-of-care umbrella, deserve notice. They include postmodernist, certain ecofeminist, and Aristotelian approaches.

Although feminist postmodernism, like care theory, rejects the Enlightenment-based rights theory, generally speaking the postmodernist exigency to deconstruct coherent political assertion leaves it a problematic approach to animal ethics. Nevertheless, Donna Haraway's writings, probably the best-known feminist postmodernist approach to animals, although flawed from an ethic-of-care perspective, have made important contributions. Haraway's (1988) identification of racist and sexist narratives in primate studies offers invaluable insight into the social construction of primatology. Yet, while Haraway in *The Companion Species Manifesto* (2003), which examines on a personal level interspecies relationships (specifically with dogs), acknowledges the "scandal of the meat-producing 'animal industrial complex'" (34)—drawing on Noske's (1989) analysis—she apparently continues to endorse meat eating (40).

A recent article in a postmodernist vein that successfully deconstructs naturalized binaries such as human/animal, which are routinely used to legitimize animal abuse, is Maneesha Deckha's "The Salience of Species Difference for Feminist Theory" (2006). Deckha is able to employ a deconstructionist method without losing sight of the underlying power relations that enable animal exploitation.

Some ecofeminist writers, particularly Karen J. Warren (1987, 1990) and Val Plumwood (1993, 1995, 2002), also have addressed the question of animal ethics. While contributing enormously to the analysis of the patriarchal roots of environmental exploitation, each is willing to sacrifice individual animals to the "holistic" context. Plumwood's celebrated

"Human Vulnerability and the Experience of Being Prey" (1995) describes her own near-death in the mouth of a crocodile. She posits that the absence of the experience of being prey may, in recent centuries, have contributed to the growth of hubris in humans, who have forgotten the vulnerability and humility that such an experience necessarily renders. Plumwood developed a critique of ecofeminist writings that fail to acknowledge that all beings are potential prey.

In *Environmental Culture* (2002), Plumwood extends her theory, proposing a "dialogical interspecies ethic" (167–95) that would seem to be consistent with an ethic of care; however, her argument that humans can "conceive [of nonhumans] both as communicative others and as food" (157) is obviously incompatible with a care ethic which requires that humans heed what the "communicative others" are telling them—invariably that they do not want to be killed and eaten. David Eaton (2002) provides the most thorough response to Plumwood's theorizing against feminist vegetarians.

Sheri Lucas (2005) offers a similar critique of Kathryn Paxton George's views on feminist vegetarianism. Antivegetarian arguments such as George's and Plumwood's are inconsistent with a feminist ethic of care, because those who care about animals obviously do not destroy and consume them. Two ecofeminist theorists whose writings are generally consistent with an ethic of care are Lori Gruen (1993, 1994, 1996, 2001, chapter 14, this volume) and Greta Gaard (1993, 1994, 1997, 2001, 2003; see also Gaard and Gruen 1993; Gruen and Gaard 1995). Their antispeciesism distinguishes them from such contextual ecofeminist writers as Warren and Plumwood. Through a focus on vegetarianism, Gruen integrates an ecofeminist approach to animals with an ethic of care. Gaard (2003) provides a synthesis of feminist and vegetarian approaches to animals.

Tracing her theory to Aristotle, Martha Nussbaum (2004) argues that contractarian and utilitarian approaches, as well as compassion-based ethics, are inadequate to the task of "recognizing a wide range of types of animal dignity, and of corresponding needs for flourishing" (300). She proposes instead a "capabilities approach" to animal ethics, which urges that all individuals be allowed to thrive to the greatest extent that their capabilities permit.

In rejecting compassion-based ethics, such as the ethic of care, Nussbaum (2004) notes, "The emotion of compassion involves the thought that another creature is suffering significantly, and is not (or not mostly) to blame for that suffering. It does not involve the thought that someone is to blame for that suffering" (301). As noted earlier, however, the feminist ethic-of-care tradition in animal ethics, like feminist theory in general, insists on seeking the cause for the suffering—that is, attributing blame. Indeed, the care theory we advocate goes beyond compassion to include caring enough to find out who is causing the harm and stopping it. As Tronto (1993) points out, the assumption that care has to be apolitical is false (166–70). Also, unlike Nussbaum's capabilities approach, care theory attends to those who are not flourishing or who cannot.

Evelyn Pluhar, in "Legal and Moral Rights of Sentient Beings and the Full Personhood View" (2006), another contribution to animal ethics, argues that "any beings capable of caring about what happens to them, even if it is only in the simple sense of wanting pain to stop, are fully morally significant" (278). She adds that "it is enormously unlikely that any sentient being will not care about what next happens to him or her," and thus it is "highly probable that the class of sentient beings is coextensive with the class of morally significant beings" (278). In *Beyond Prejudice* (1995), she argues for the moral significance of mammals, which thus should be granted basic moral rights, and suggests that the benefit of the doubt be extended to nonmammalian species, such as reptiles, amphibians, and fishes. By 2006, updating her formulation, she determined that as the latter "can care about what happens to them [, they] should, therefore, be extended basic and equal moral rights" (278). Thus, although not operating within the ethic-of-care tradition, Pluhar has come to conclusions compatible with its tenets.

In concluding, we find it significant that two of the most influential thinkers of our time—Jacques Derrida and J. M. Coetzee—have adopted (without labeling it as such) a feminist ethic-of-care approach to the treatment of animals. In "The Animal that Therefore I Am" (2002), Derrida states, "No one can deny the suffering, fear or panic, the terror or fright that humans witness in certain animals" (396). He adds, "Everybody knows what terrifying and intolerable pictures a realist painting could give to the industrial, mechanical, chemical, hormonal, and genetic violence to which man has been submitting animal life for the past two centuries" (395). Derrida predicts that "a war [is] being waged, the unequal forces of which could one day be reversed, between those who violate not only animal life but even and also this sentiment of compassion and, on the other hand, those who appeal to an irrefutable testimony to this pity" (397). He admits that the images prompted by his language might be "pathetic" but proposes that they open up the issue of pathos. Derrida's point was, in fact, made by feminist animal activist Anna Kingsford in the nineteenth century. Her heightened language, however, resulted in accusations that she was hysterical about the issue of animal abuse, and therefore her view was largely dismissed. But Derrida asserts that the mistreatment of animals is a scandal that is worth getting hysterical about and defends the emotional approach to animal ethics. A further discussion of aspects of Derrida's views may be found in Adams's "The War on Compassion."

In *The Lives of Animals* (1999), Coetzee, who was awarded the Nobel Prize for Literature in 2003, has presented his perspective through a female persona, Elizabeth Costello (for a fuller discussion, see Donovan 2004). Costello proposes that what is needed to end the massive human exploitation and abuse of animals, which she compares with the Holocaust, is an awakening of moral awareness, which requires a kind of visceral empathy for the suffering of others: "The horror of the death camps [and by extension, slaughterhouses] is that the killers refused to think themselves into the place of their victims. . . . In other words, they closed their hearts. The heart is the seat of a faculty, *sympathy,* that allows us to share at times the being of another" (34).

We offer this collection in the hope that people may learn to open their hearts to animals, while keeping their minds alert to the systemic causes of their suffering, and thus move toward ending once and for all the unspeakable abuse that currently exists.

REFERENCES

Acampora, Ralph. 1995. "The Problematic Situation of Post-Humanism and the Task of Recreating a Symphysical Ethos." *Between the Species* 11, nos. 1–2:25–32.

Adams, Carol J. 1975. "The Oedible Complex: Feminism and Vegetarianism." In *The Lesbian Reader*, ed. Gina Covina and Laurel Galana, 145–52. Oakland, Calif.: Amazon.

——. 1976. "Vegetarianism: The Inedible Complex." *Second Wave* 4, no. 4:36–42.

——. 1990. *The Sexual Politics of Meat: A Feminist-Vegetarian Critical Theory.* New York: Continuum.

——. 1994. "Bringing Peace Home: A Feminist Philosophical Perspective on the Abuse of Women, Children, and Pet Animals." *Hypatia: A Journal of Feminist Philosophy* 9, no. 2:63–84.

——. 1995. "Woman-Battering and Harm to Animals." In *Animals and Women: Feminist Theoretical Explorations*, ed. Carol J. Adams and Josephine Donovan, 55–84. Durham, N.C.: Duke University Press.

Adams, Carol J., and Josephine Donovan, eds. 1995. *Animals and Women: Feminist Theoretical Explorations.* Durham, N.C.: Duke University Press.

Behnke, Elizabeth A. 1999. "From Merleau-Ponty's Concept of Nature to an Interspecies Practice of Peace." In *Animal Others: On Ethics, Ontology, and Animal Life*, ed. H. Peter Steeves, 93–116. Albany: State University of New York Press.

Benney, Norma. 1983. "All of One Flesh: The Rights of Animals." In *Reclaim the Earth: Women Speak Out for Life on Earth*, ed. Léonie Caldecott and Stephanie Leland, 141–50. London: Women's Press.

Benton, Ted. 1988. "Humanism = Speciesism: Marx on Humans and Animals." *Radical Philosophy* 50:4–18.

——. 1993. *Natural Relations: Ecology, Animal Rights, and Social Justice.* London: Verso.

Beirne, Piers. 1997. "Rethinking Bestiality: Towards a Concept of Interspecies Sexual Assault." *Theoretical Criminology* 1, no. 3:317–40.

——. 1998. "For a Nonspeciesist Criminology: Animal Abuse as an Object of Study." *Criminology* 37, no. 1:117–48.

——. 2004. "From Animal Abuse to Interhuman Violence? A Critical Review of the Progression Thesis." *Society and Animals* 12, no. 1:39–65.

Birke, Lynda. 1994. *Feminism, Animals, and Science: The Naming of the Shrew.* Buckingham, Eng.: Open University Press.

Coetzee, J. M. 1999. *The Lives of Animals.* Ed. Amy Gutmann. Princeton, N.J.: Princeton University Press.

Cole, Eve Browning, and Susan Coultrap-McQuin, eds. 1992. *Explorations in Feminist Ethics: Theory and Practice.* Bloomington: Indiana University Press.

Collard, Andrée, with Joyce Contrucci. 1988. *Rape of the Wild: Man's Violence Against Animals and the Earth.* London: Women's Press.

Davis, Karen. 2001. *More than a Meal: The Turkey in History, Myth, Ritual, and Reality.* New York: Lantern Books.

Davis, Susan E., and Margo Demello. 2003. *Stories Rabbits Tell: A Natural and Cultural History of a Misunderstood Creature.* New York: Lantern Books.

Deckha, Maneesha. 2006. "The Salience of Species Difference for Feminist Theory." *Hastings Women's Law Journal* 17, no. 1:1–38.

Derrida, Jacques. 2002. "The Animal that Therefore I Am (More to Follow)." *Critical Inquiry* 28:369–418.

Devall, Bill, and George Sessions. 1984. *Deep Ecology: Living as if the Planet Mattered.* Salt Lake City: Smith.

Donovan, Josephine. 2004. "'Miracles of Creation': Animals in J. M. Coetzee's Work." *Michigan Quarterly Review* 43, no. 1:78–93.

Donovan, Josephine, and Carol J. Adams, eds. 1996. *Beyond Animal Rights: A Feminist Caring Ethic for the Treatment of Animals.* New York: Continuum.

Eaton, David. 2002. "Incorporating the Other: Val Plumwood's Integration of Ethical Frameworks." *Ethics and the Environment* 7, no. 2:153–80.

Fitzgerald, Amy. 2005. *Animal Abuse and Family Violence: Researching the Interrelationships of Abusive Power.* Mellen Studies in Sociology, vol. 48. Lewiston, N.Y.: Mellen.

Flynn, Clifton P. 1999. "Exploring the Link Between Corporal Punishment and Children's Cruelty to Animals." *Journal of Marriage and the Family* 61: 971–81.

——. 2000a. "Why Family Professionals Can No Longer Ignore Violence Toward Animals." *Family Relations* 49, no. 1:87–95.

——. 2000b. "Woman's Best Friend: Pet Abuse and the Role of Companion Animals in the Lives of Battered Women." *Violence Against Women* 6, no. 2:162–77.

French, Marilyn. 1985. *Beyond Power: On Women, Men, and Morals.* New York: Summit.

Gaard, Greta, ed. 1993. *Ecofeminism: Women, Animals, Nature.* Philadelphia: Temple University Press.

——. 1994. "Milking Mother Nature: An Ecofeminist Critique of rBGH." *The Ecologist* 24, no. 6:1–2.

——. 1997. "Women, Animals, and an Ecofeminist Critique." *Environmental Ethics* 18, no. 4:440–43.

——. 2001. "Ecofeminism on the Wing: Perspectives on Human–Animal Relations." *Women & Environments* 52–53:19–22.

——. 2003. "Vegetarian Ecofeminism: A Review Essay." *Frontiers* 23, no. 3:117–46.

Gaard, Greta, with Lori Gruen. 1993. "Ecofeminism: Toward Global Justice and Planetary Health." *Society and Nature* 2, no. 1:1–35.

Gilligan, Carol. 1982. *In a Different Voice: Psychological Theory and Women's Development*. Cambridge, Mass.: Harvard University Press.

Gruen, Lori. 1993. "Dismantling Oppression: An Analysis of the Connection Between Women and Animals." In *Ecofeminism: Women, Animals, Nature*, ed. Greta Gaard, 60–90. Philadelphia: Temple University Press.

——. 1994. "Toward an Ecofeminist Moral Epistemology." In *Ecological Feminism*, ed. Karen J. Warren, 120–38. New York: Routledge.

——. 1996. "On the Oppression of Women and Animals." *Environmental Ethics* 18, no. 4:441–44.

——. 2001. "Beyond Exclusion: The Importance of Context in Ecofeminist Theory." In *Land, Value, Community: Callicott and Environmental Philosophy*, ed. Wayne Ouderkirk and Jim Hall, 219–26. Albany: State University of New York Press.

Gruen, Lori, and Greta Gaard. 1995. "Comment on Kathryn Paxton George's 'Should Feminists Be Vegetarians?'" *Signs: Journal of Women in Culture and Society* 21, no. 1:230–41.

Haraway, Donna. 1988. *Primate Visions*. New York: Routledge.

——. 2003. *The Companion Species Manifesto: Dogs, People, and Significant Otherness*. Chicago: Prickly Paradigm Press.

Kappeler, Susanne. 1986. *The Pornography of Representation*. Minneapolis: University of Minnesota Press.

——. 1995. "Speciesism, Racism, Nationalism . . . or the Power of Scientific Subjectivity." In *Animals and Women: Feminist Theoretical Explorations*, ed. Carol J. Adams and Josephine Donovan, 320–52. Durham, N.C.: Duke University Press.

Kheel, Marti. 1990. "Ecofeminism and Deep Ecology: Reflections on Identity and Difference." In *Reweaving the World: The Emergence of Ecofeminism*, ed. Irene Diamond and Gloria Feman Orenstein, 128–37. San Francisco: Sierra Club Books.

Kittay, Eva Feder, and Diana T. Meyers, eds. 1987. *Women and Moral Theory*. Totowa, N.J.: Rowman & Littlefield.

Lansbury, Coral. 1985. *The Old Brown Dog: Women, Workers and Vivisection in Edwardian England*. Madison: University of Wisconsin Press.

Larrabee, Mary Jeanne, ed. 1993. *An Ethic of Care: Feminist and Interdisciplinary Perspectives*. New York: Routledge.

Leopold, Aldo. 1949. *A Sand County Almanac, and Sketches Here and There*. New York: Oxford University Press.

Lockwood, Randall, and Frank R. Ascione. 1998. *Cruelty to Animals and Inter-*

personal Violence: Readings in Research and Application. West Lafayette, Ind.: Purdue University Press.

Lucas, Sheri. 2005. "A Defense of the Feminist-Vegetarian Connection." *Hypatia: A Journal of Feminist Philosophy* 20, no. 1:150–77.

Luke, Brian. 1995. "Taming Ourselves or Going Feral? Toward a Nonpatriarchal Metaethic for Animal Liberation." In *Animals and Women: Feminist Theoretical Explorations*, ed. Carol J. Adams and Josephine Donovan, 290–319. Durham, N.C.: Duke University Press.

——. 1997. "A Critical Analysis of Hunters' Ethics." *Environmental Ethics* 19:25–44.

——. 1998. "Violent Love: Hunting, Heterosexuality, and the Erotics of Men's Predation." *Feminist Studies* 24:627–55.

Mason, Jim. 1997. *An Unnatural Order: Why We Are Destroying the Planet and Each Other*. New York: Continuum. [Reissued 2005 as *An Unnatural Order: The Roots of Our Destraction of Nature*. New York: Lantern.]

Meyerding, Jane. 1982. "Feminist Criticism and Cultural Imperialism (Where does one end and the other begin)." *Animals' Agenda*, November–December, 14–15, 22–23.

Nash, Roderick Frazier. 1989. *The Rights of Nature: A History of Environmental Ethics*. Madison: University of Wisconsin Press.

Noddings, Nel. 1984. *Caring: A Feminine Approach to Ethics and Moral Education*. Berkeley: University of California Press.

Noske, Barbara. 1989. *Humans and Other Animals: Beyond the Boundaries of Anthropology*. London: Pluto Press. [Reissued 1997 as *Beyond Boundaries: Humans and Animals*. Montreal: Black Rose Books.]

Nussbaum, Martha C. 2004. "Beyond 'Compassion and Humanity?': Justice for Nonhuman Animals." In *Animal Rights: Current Debates and New Directions*, ed. Cass Sunstein and Martha C. Nussbaum, 299–320. Chicago: University of Chicago Press.

Pluhar, Evelyn. 1995. *Beyond Prejudice: The Moral Significance of Human and Nonhuman Animals*. Durham, N.C.: Duke University Press.

——. 2006. "Legal and Moral Rights of Sentient Beings and the Full Personhood View." *Organization & Environment* 19, no. 2:275–78.

Plumwood, Val. 1993. *Feminism and the Mastery of Nature*. London: Routledge.

——. 1995. "Human Vulnerability and the Experience of Being Prey." *Quadrant*, March, 29–34.

——. 2002. *Environmental Culture: The Ecological Crisis of Reason*. London: Routledge.

Regan, Tom. 1983. *The Case for Animal Rights*. Berkeley: University of California Press.

Ruddick, Sara. 1989. *Maternal Thinking: Toward a Politics of Peace*. Boston: Beacon Press.

Salamone, Constantia. 1973. "Feminist as Rapist in the Modern Male Hunter Culture." *Majority Report: The Women's Newspaper*, October.

———. 1982. "The Prevalence of the Natural Law Within Women: Women and Animal Rights." In *Reweaving the Web of Life: Feminism and Nonviolence*, ed. Pam McAllister, 364–75. Philadelphia: New Society.

Sanbonmatsu, John. 2005. "Listen, Ecological Marxist! (Yes, I said *Animals!*)." *Capitalism Nature Socialism* 16, no. 2:107–14.

Shapiro, Kenneth. 1989. "Understanding Dogs Through Kinesthetic Empathy, Social Construction, and History." *Anthrozoös* 3, no. 3:184–95.

Singer, Peter. 1975. *Animal Liberation*. New York: Avon.

Sorabji, Richard. 1993. *Animal Minds and Human Morals: The Origins of the Western Debate*. Ithaca, N.Y.: Cornell University Press.

Steeves, H. Peter, ed. 1999. *Animal Others: On Ethics, Ontology, and Animal Life*. Albany: State University of New York Press.

Tong, Rosemarie. 1993. *Feminine and Feminist Ethics*. Belmont, Calif.: Wadsworth.

Tronto, Joan C. 1993. *Moral Boundaries: A Political Argument for an Ethic of Care*. New York: Routledge.

Ward, Edith. 1892. Review of *Animal Rights*, by Henry Salt. *Shafts*, November 19.

Warren, Karen J. 1987. "Feminism and Ecology: Making Connections." *Environmental Ethics* 9, no. 1:3–20.

———. 1990. "The Power and the Promise of Ecological Feminism." *Environmental Ethics* 12, no. 2:125–46.

The War on Compassion

CAROL J. ADAMS

In our lifetime, what was not supposed to happen "ever again"—genocide—has instead happened again and again. As Samantha Power shows in *A Problem from Hell* (2002), her study of genocide in the twentieth century, the perception of genocide is all in the framing. Governments acting against a minority want the violence to be perceived as civil war or tribal strife, as quelling unrest and restoring order, as a private matter that does not spill over into the international community. Other governments weigh their own national interests against the needs of those being killed.

After watching the movie *Hotel Rwanda* and as I began reading *A Problem from Hell*, among the many disturbing questions that surfaced for me, besides the obvious one—How could we have let this happen?—was the question, How can we get people to care about animals when they do not even care when people are being killed?

But as this question came to mind, I realized that it was the wrong one because it accepts a hierarchy of caring that assumes that people first have to care about other people before they care about animals and that these

This chapter was first presented as The Paul O'Neill Lecture at Transylvania University in Lexington, Kentucky, May 2005.

caring acts are hostile to each other. In fact, violence against people and that against animals is interdependent. Caring about both is required.

While I could not read about genocide without thinking about the other animals and what humans do to them, I am sophisticated enough to know that this thought is experienced as an offense to the victims of genocide. However, I am motivated enough to want to ask more about the associations I was thinking about and sensing because *human* and *animal* are definitions that exist in tandem, each drawing its power from the other in a drama of circumscribing: the animal defining the human, the human defining the animal. As long as the definitions exist through negation (human is this, animal is not this, human is not that, animal is that—although what is defined as human or animal changes), the inscription of *human* on something, or the movement to be seen as human (for example, Feminism is the radical notion that women are human), assumes that there is something fixed about humanness that "humans" possess and, importantly, that animals do not possess. Without animals showing us otherwise, how do we know ourselves to be human?

Despite all the efforts to demarcate the human, the word *animal* encompasses human beings. We are human animals; they, those we view as not-us, are nonhuman animals.

Discrimination based on color of skin that occurs against those above the human–animal boundary is called *racism*; when it becomes unspeakably murderous, it is called genocide. Discrimination by humans that occurs against those below the human–animal boundary is called *species-ism*; when it becomes murderous, it is called meat eating and hunting, among other things. The latter is normalized violence. Is it possible that species-ism subsumes racism and genocide in the same way that the word *animal* includes humans? Is there not much to learn from the way normalized violence disowns compassion?

When the first response to animal advocacy is, How can we care about animals when humans are suffering? we encounter an argument that is self-enclosing: it re-erects the species barrier and places a boundary on compassion while enforcing a conservative economy of compassion; it splits caring at the human–animal border, presuming that there is not enough to go around. Ironically, it plays into the construction of the world that enables genocide by perpetuating the idea that what happens to human animals is unrelated to what happens to nonhuman animals. It also fosters a fallacy: that caring actually works this way.

Many of the arguments that separate caring into deserving/undeserving or now/later or first those like us/then those unlike us constitute a politics of the dismissive. Being dismissive is inattention with an alibi. It asserts that "this does not require my attention" or "this offends my sensibility" (that is, "We are so different from animals, how can you introduce them into the discussion?"). Genocide, itself, benefits from the politics of the dismissive.

The difficulty that we face when trying to awaken our culture to care about the suffering of a group that is not acknowledged as having a suffering that matters is the same one that a meditation such as this faces: How do we make those whose suffering does not matter, matter?

False Mass Terms

All of us are fated to die. We share this fate with animals, but the finitude of domesticated animals is determined by us, by human beings. We know when they will die because we demand it. Their fate, to be eaten when dead, is the filter by which we experience their becoming "terminal animals."

The most efficient way to ensure that humans do not care about the lives of animals is to transform nonhuman subjects into nonhuman objects. This is what I have called the structure of the absent referent (Adams 2000:51). Behind every meal of meat is an absence: the death of the nonhuman animal whose place the meat takes. The absent referent is that which separates the meat eater from the other animal and that animal from the end product. Humans do not regard meat eating as contact with another animal because it has been renamed as contact with *food*. Who is suffering? No one.

In our culture, *meat* functions as a mass term (Quine 1960:99; Adams 1994:27), defining entire species of nonhumans. Mass terms refer to things like water or colors; no matter how much of it there is or what type of container it is in, water is still water. A bucket of water can be added to a pool of water without changing it. Objects referred to by mass terms have no individuality, no uniqueness, no specificity, no particularity. When humans turn a nonhuman into "meat," someone who has a very particular, situated life, a unique being, is converted into something that has no individuality, no uniqueness, no specificity. When five pounds of meatballs are added to a plate of meatballs, it is more of the same thing; nothing is changed. But taking a living cow, then killing and butchering that cow, and finally grinding up her flesh does not add a mass term to a mass term and result in more of the same. It destroys an individual.

What is on the plate in front of us is not devoid of specificity. It is the dead flesh of what was once a living, feeling being. The crucial point here is that humans transform a unique being, and therefore not the appropriate referent of a mass term, into something that is the appropriate referent of a mass term.

False mass terms function as shorthand. *They* are not like *us*. Our compassion need not go there—to their situation, their experience—or, if it does, it may be diluted. Their "massification" allows our release from empathy. We cannot imagine ourselves in a situation where our "I-ness" counts for nothing. We cannot imagine the "not-I" of life as a mass term.

To kill a large number of people efficiently, the killers succeed when they have made the people they are targeting into a mass term. Philip Gourevitch (1998), writing of the genocide in Rwanda, explains: "What distinguishes genocide from murder, and even from acts of political murder that claim as many victims, is the intent. The crime is wanting to make a people extinct. The idea is the crime. No wonder it's so difficult to picture. To do so you must accept the principle of the exterminator, and see not people, but *a people*" (202).

Gourevitch says that "the idea is the crime." The victims are seen as a mass term by their oppressors: "not people, but *a people*." When a group is regarded as *a people*, not as being composed of individual people, certain conventions of thought and stereotypes take over. The claim is made that the people can be defined as a group, through racial, ethnic, or species characteristics: in Germany in the 1930s and 1940s, what Jews are like and what Jews do; in Rwanda in the 1950s and forward, what Tutsis are like and what Tutsis do. These characteristics heighten the idea of their existence as being a threat to others or as being dirty. Then the false characteristics become fixed through their existence as a metaphor.

The presumptions and mistakes of racial biology reiterate similar presumptions and mistakes in "species" biology. Humans think they can know "cows" or "birds" and use adjectives drawn from this assumption: *cowlike, birdbrain*. Susanne Kappeler (1995) observes that

Western theories of racism attained proper "scientific" status in the nineteenth and twentieth centuries in the guise of medicine, psychiatry, eugenics, anthropology, demography, and so forth. They stand in direct continuity with the theories that categorize nonhuman animals in species, and living beings into humans, animals, and plants—categories modeled on the paradigms of the natural sciences. These included attempts to establish classifications of "kinds" of people based on "typical" data—be it measurements of bodies and body parts, genetic data, or behavioral features. (327)

Gourevitch (1998) writes, "The idea is the crime," seeing *a people*, not people. One explanation for the appalling indifference of those of us who live in the United States and Great Britain to mass killings is that we, like their oppressors, may see the targeted victims as a mass term. When people are not experienced in their individuality, their deaths may not feel immediate. During the genocide in Rwanda, one American officer explained the calculations they were doing: "one American casualty is worth about 85,000 Rwandan dead" (quoted in Power 2002:381).

The "massification" of beings permits the dilution, the diminution of our attention. The more of a mass term they become, the less concern they need provoke. It is like an hourglass: the sands of our compassion drain into the bottom. How do we flip the hourglass? How do we revive or awaken compassion?

Mass terms are linked to subjects being diminished. In their diminishment, as I pointed out in *The Sexual Politics of Meat* (2000), all that is left for them is to become metaphors for others.

According to Robert Pogue Harrison, in *The Dominion of the Dead* (2005), what we do with our dead is what supposedly demarcates us as humans. We bury them. The dead influence us through the laws they bequeathed to us and the cultural and physical institutions we inherit from them. Everywhere we turn, we experience "the foundational authority of the predecessor" (ix). For the moment, I will not argue with Harrison's presumption that humans are *necrocratic* and nonhumans are not. (Elephants' grieving processes are elaborate.) But, after genocides or fratricides like the Civil War, the survivors dig up the bodies buried in mass graves, as in Rwanda or Gettysburg, and try to reassert through separate burials each one's individuality against the annihilation of the mass term. We cannot undo the act of genocide—the dead are dead—but we can undo part of the idea that allows genocide, the use of mass terms, by asserting the individual and maintaining our ties to the dead as individuals.

And this is a basic difference; meat eaters bury animals in their own bodies. When nonhuman living beings are converted conceptually into false mass terms to enable their conversion into products, we come to believe that their deaths do not matter to themselves. Animals are killed because they are false mass terms, but they die as individuals—as a cow, not as beef; as a pig, not as pork. Each suffers his or her own death, and this death matters a great deal to the one who is dying.

"Treated like animals"

In the face of the knowledge that genocide has happened in our lifetime—not only once, but repeatedly—and that countries such as the United States and institutions such as the United Nations failed to respond—with Rwanda, the United States was reduced to parsing the difference between "acts of genocide" and genocide—the questions arise: Why didn't we respond? Why didn't we care?

Several forms of explanation have been offered, which Power details in *A Problem from Hell* (2002) and which are discussed later. One important reason Power notes for peoples' apparent indifference, especially during the Holocaust, is disbelief: "The notion of getting attacked for being (rather than for doing) was too discomfiting and too foreign to process readily" (36).

Animals are killed daily for *being* rather than for *doing*; they may be killed because they are "just animals." Humans are not supposed to be killed because they are "a people." Moreover, it is humans who do the "doing" to animals. Human beings may be killed for doing (doing wrong, presumably, but not for doing wrong to animals). When humans are killed for being rather than for doing, the "beingness" attributed to them is often animal-like.

Many favorable descriptions of human beings emphasize doing rather than being. Humans use their intelligence; nonhumans are instinctive. Humans love; nonhumans mate. Humans cultivate friendships; nonhumans exhibit "affiliative behavior." Humans are humane, cultivated, and refined; nonhumans are beasts and brutal (Dunayer 2001). When someone says, "I was treated like an animal," he or she means, "I was treated as though I had no feelings, as though I was not alive." We have created institutions that reinforce the contention that animals *are*, not that animals *do*. Karen Davis (2005) observes that "seeing animals in industrialized settings such as factory farms encourages the view that animals are inherently passive objects whose only role in life is to serve the human enterprise" (31). When someone says, "I was treated like an animal," he or she means, "I was reduced to literal existence. I could not do; I was done to."

How are people made less human? Two of the most predictable ways are to define them as false mass terms and to view them as animals. Acts of violence that include animalizing language transform people into false mass terms, since animals already exist in that linguistic no-man's-land of lacking a recognizable individuality. When someone says, "I was treated like an animal," he or she means, "I was treated as though I were not an individual." Conditions for violence flourish when the world is structured hierarchically, in a false Darwinian progression that places humans at the top:

Humans
Subhumans
Animals
Insects
"Material" nature; Earth, "dirt"

The farther down the great chain of being a creature is placed, the lower the barriers to violence. When someone says, "I was treated like an animal," he or she means, "I was made vulnerable to violence by being moved down on the species ladder." This is reflected in the epigraph, a quote from Adolf Hitler, to the first book of Art Spiegelman's *Maus: A Survivor's Tale* (1986): "The Jews are undoubtedly a race, but they are not human" (quoted in De Angelis 2005). Leo Kuper writes in *Genocide* (1983): "The animal world has been a particularly fertile source of metaphors of dehumanization." People designated as animals "have often been hunted down like animals" (88). Or exterminated like insects.

When a group is deemed not human, oppressors have several options for establishing just who they see the group members as. For the hierarchy that places humans at the top is more complicated than the one I presented earlier:

Humans
Subhumans
The devil[1]
Primates other than humans
Mammals other than primates
    Predators
        Top carnivores[2]
        Carnivores

1. The devil (a human–animal being) walks upright, has the facial characteristics of a human, but has horns, hoofs, and a tail.
2. The top carnivores are those that eat carnivores—for example, birds of prey, tigers, and white sharks.

Prey (herbivores: four-legged, two-legged)
"Vermin" (rats, mice)
Reptiles (snakes)
Insects ("pests")
  Spiders
  Cockroaches
  Ants
"Material" nature; Earth, "dirt"

Using propaganda campaigns, genocidal governments reinforce the idea of being, rather than of doing: Hitler considered the Jews to be sub-human and vermin; the Hutus in control in Rwanda regarded the Tutsis as cockroaches (*inyenzi*) or the devil. When genocidal governments rename humans as animals, they reinforce the ladder of human superiority by pushing some people off it. So when someone says, "I was treated like an animal," he or she is standing on the human ladder and looking down, to those who have never been on the top rung.

The Original Oppression

Human society takes from the oppression of animals its structures and treat-ment of people. Although we often fail to see the literal origins of human institutions, as Keith Thomas (1983) and Jim Mason (1997), among others, established decades ago, all forms of oppression can be traced to the treat-ment of animals by humans. Domestication became the pattern for social subordination; predation, the pattern for killing and extermination.

It is the nature of the burnt offering (the literal meaning of the word *holocaust*) of animals to disappear—whether consumed by fire or by human beings. The literal disappeared, but it became the form and function of an unequal human society's treatment of people.

When Theodor Adorno states, "Auschwitz begins wherever someone looks at a slaughterhouse and thinks: they're only animals" (quoted in Patterson 2002:53), he is saying that the structure of human inequality begins in the abattoir. But some claim that there is a difference: domesti-cated/enslaved animals have been brought into existence by humans and have life so humans can take it, whereas people threatened by genocide already exist, and the genocidal impulse is to completely eliminate them. Nonexistence for human beings is their elimination as a specific group, ethnicity, or race; nonexistence for animals, according to this reasoning, is never being born in the first place. But the genocidal impulse, when considered, helps us see that this distinction is a fallacy. It assumes that speciesism is not an aspect of genocide and that racism is not a form of speciesism.

At least one writer believes that "the breeding of animals first produced the concepts of 'race' and of 'pure blood'" (Jean-Pierre Digard, quoted in Sax 2000:83). Speciesism has always been a tool of colonialism, creating a hierarchy of skin color and group characteristics. Kappeler (1995) observes that politics is zoology by another name: "the very point of categorization is to create discriminating *identities*, 'types' of people allegedly sharing the same (typical) feature(s), thus to justify their social and political roles . . . and invalidate their rights as individuals"(330).

The category "human being" is stratified:

RACE CONTINUUM	"EVOLUTIONARY" CONTINUUM
Whites	Civilized
	"Beastlike" (peasants, farm workers)
Nonwhites	Primitive (pretechnological, indigenous, aboriginal)
	Hunters and herders
	Gatherers and farmers

European colonizers evaluated indigenous peoples according to their relationship with animals and the land. They assumed that those who controlled and killed animals were more advanced than those who tilled fields. One of the demarcations of the evolutionary status of a culture was whether it was dependent on animal protein. Thus a hierarchy descends from Western meat eaters to pretechnological hunters to gatherers.

Consider how the Belgians imposed a hierarchy in Rwanda. Gourevitch (1998) notes that whether Hutus and Tutsis were descended from different peoples, they "spoke the same language, followed the same religion, intermarried and lived intermingled, without territorial distinctions, on the same hills, sharing the same social and political culture in small chiefdoms" (47–48). But still there was a distinction. Tutsis were herders, and Hutus were cultivators: "This was the original inequality: cattle are a more valuable asset than produce, and although some Hutus owned cows while some Tutsis tilled the soil, the word Tutsi became synonymous with a political and economic elite" (48).

Racism recapitulates speciesism. The category "human being" is stratified by speciesism; the hierarchy imposed by colonialism mirrors that of humans over nonhumans:

RACE CONTINUUM	SPECIES CONTINUUM
Whites (civilized)	Humans/top carnivores imagery
Primitive (pretechnological, indigenous, aboriginal, and targets of genocide)	Primates other than humans
	Mammals
	Herbivores
	"Vermin"
	Reptiles
	Insects

The race continuum not only recapitulates the species continuum, but draws its strength in categorization from it.

Immigrants are also regarded, derogatorily, as animals. In an analysis of language used to discuss Latinos in newspapers, animal metaphors were found to be the predominant imagery. Researchers found metaphors of immigrants as animals that were lured, pitted, or baited; animals that can be attacked and hunted; animals that can be eaten; pack animals; and rabbits, needing to be ferreted out (Santa Ana 2002:82–94). For example, American citizens give birth, but immigrants "drop their babies." Santa Ana writes, "The ontology of IMMIGRANT AS ANIMAL can be stated concisely: Immigrants correspond to citizens as animals correspond to humans" (86). Thus another hierarchy can be posed:

Human	Not human
Member of human society	Outsider or other
Citizen	Immigrant

According to Kappeler (1995),

Classification is neither neutral, being put to political use only "thereafter," nor is it objective: it is itself an act of social and political discrimination and thus the expression of the subjectivity of power. What is said to be a quality of the object is in fact a difference construed in relation to an implicit norm constituted in the classifying subject. Racism and sexism as political practices construct *another* race and *another* sex, a race of "others" and a sex of "others."   (338)

The concept of "other" requires a normative someone or someones who are not other; who are the measure by which otherness is established; to whom otherness might move closer or farther away, but who do not themselves depart from the normative nature of their beingness. This "otherness" ratifies the primacy of those against whom otherness is defined.

Activist and scholar Karen Davis (2005) reminds us that from a chicken's experience, the human hand is the cruelest thing she will know (47). With Davis's insight in mind, consider this formative conversation in the history of genocide in the twentieth century: when Raphael Lemkin, who coined the word *genocide*, was studying linguistics, he asked his professor why Mehmed Talaat, the person responsible for "the killing by firing squad, bayoneting, bludgeoning, and starvation of nearly 1 million Armenians" (Power 2002:1), was not prosecuted for what he had done. His professor told Lemkin that there was no law under which Talaat could be arrested. The professor explained, "'Consider the case of a farmer who owns a flock of chickens,' he said, 'He kills them and this is his business. If you interfere, you are trespassing'" (Power 2002:17). Perhaps one reason we did not respond to the genocides of the twentieth century is that we had learned to tolerate a hierarchical world in which killing is accepted.

I recently heard from a feminist animal rights scholar, who wrote:

I live 6 miles up the road from one of the largest slaughterhouses in the nation. Nobody in this little town blinks an eye as each day semi-trailer after semi-trailer crammed full of living entities streams down Main Street carrying cows to their brutal executions. Got behind one of these horrors the other day. The stench was overpowering, but what really got me was the bumper sticker: EAT BEEF: The West Wasn't Won on Salad.

The triumphalism of such contemporary declarations should remind us that when anxiety asserts itself about the place of animals in our hierarchical world, it is never asserting itself only about animals.

Why Don't We Care?

Jacques Derrida's "The Animal that Therefore I Am" (2002) identifies the most egregious actions humans have taken against other animals (including subsuming them all under the category "animal"): "Everybody knows what terrifying and intolerable pictures a realist painting could give to the industrial, mechanical, chemical, hormonal, and genetic violence to which man has been submitting animal life for the past two centuries" (395). He assumes that such a description may be "pathetic"—that is, evoking sympathy. Derrida argues that for the past few centuries, we have waged a campaign against compassion that allows factory farms and other horrors to continue. He calls it the "war on pity." Such a campaign instantiates objectification: both the objectification of the animals who become mass terms and the objectification of feelings, so they fail to be heeded in making decisions about the fate of terminal animals. If genocide requires the turning of humans into animals, the war on pity provides the institutional framework for not caring about what happens to someone labeled "animal."

Derrida (2002) says that

> no one can deny the *unprecedented* proportions of this subjection of the animal. . . . No one can deny seriously, or for very long, that men do all they can in order to dissimulate this cruelty or to hide it from themselves, in order to organize on a global scale the forgetting or misunderstanding of this violence that some would compare to the worst cases of genocide (there are also animal genocides: the number of species endangered because of man takes one's breath away). (394)

There, even he says it: what is happening to animals some "would compare to the worse cases of genocide." He adds,

> One should neither abuse the figure of genocide nor consider it explained away. For it gets more complicated here: the annihilation of certain species is indeed in process, but it is occurring through the organization and exploitation of an artificial, infernal, virtually interminable survival, in conditions that previous generations would have judged monstrous, outside of every supposed norm of a life proper to animals that are thus exterminated by means of their continued existence or even their overpopulation. (394)

Samantha Power (2002) offers several explanations to begin the discussion of why apathy prevails over caring: we lack the imagination needed to reckon with evil, and it is hard to even imagine evil. It is assumed that people act rationally. American policy makers discovered that, counter to the presumptions of diplomacy, "rational people" can be gratuitously violent (with Derrida I might add, such a discovery was made by animal activists centuries ago). The failure to protest is interpreted as indifference, and those who do care do not have the political strength to change policy. The killing is reinterpreted, deflecting attention from the culprits. The national interest, or so it is thought, prevents intervention. Being attacked for *being* rather than *doing* seems unbelievable.

But now we can add to Power's list. The ability to objectify feelings, so they are placed outside the political realm, is another reason people have not cared. Submission to authority requires such objectification—indeed, rewards it. Not only do people learn that feelings do not matter, but even the awareness of feelings is lost within the objectifying mind-set. As a result, people may become afraid to care, which requires that they have the courage to break from the normalizing ideological screen that has posited that "it's okay if it's an *x*, but not a *y*."

The war on compassion has resulted in a desire to move away from many feelings, especially uncomfortable ones. As a result, fear, which is an understandable response to a new experience—say, that of encountering a snake or a spider—becomes the justification for killing a snake or a spider. If feelings were not objectified, we might have developed the ability to interact with the fear, to respect it and the being who is causing it, rather than try to destroy both the feeling and the being.

The war on compassion has caused many people to think that it is futile to care. They are unable, imaginatively, to see how their caring will change anything. They experience a passivity inculcated by current political situations as well as by the media. They lack the imagination not to believe that something terrible might be done, but that the something terrible that is happening can be undone.

The war on compassion, further, has caused people to fear that beginning to care about what happens to animals will destroy them because the knowledge is so overwhelming. They prefer not to care rather than to face the fragility, at the least, or the annihilation of the caring self, at the most extreme, that they suspect arises from caring. But caring does not make people more fragile or annihilate them. In fact, through caring, individuals not only acquire new experiences and skills that accompany these experiences, but also discover that they are part of a network that can sustain them even when caring evolves into grief for what is happening.

Finally, the war on compassion has caused people to believe that they have to help humans first. As long as we treat animals as animals, as long as we accept that there is the category "animals," both the treatment and the concept will legitimize the treatment of humans like animals. Derrida (2002) hypothesized that the "war on pity" was passing through a critical phase. It may have begun when animal activists proclaimed that "if it's not okay for a y, it's not okay for an x," and in that proclamation began the process of overcoming the divisions between not only the x's (animals) and the y's (humans), but also compassion and the political realm.

ACKNOWLEDGMENTS

I thank the O'Neill Lecture Committee and the O'Neill family for inviting me to present new work under the auspices of the lectureship. I thank Josephine Donovan for her editing of the original lecture.

REFERENCES

Adams, Carol J. 1994. *Neither Man nor Beast: Feminism and the Defense of Animals*. New York: Continuum.

———. 2000. *The Sexual Politics of Meat: A Feminist-Vegetarian Critical Theory*, 2nd ed. New York: Continuum.

Davis, Karen. 2005. *The Holocaust and the Henmaid's Tale: A Case for Comparing Atrocities*. New York: Lantern Books.

De Angelis, Richard. 2005. "Of Mice and Vermin: Animals as Absent Referent in Art Spiegelman's *Maus*." *International Journal of Comic Art* 7, no. 1:230–49.

Derrida, Jacques. 2002. "The Animal that Therefore I Am (More to Follow)." *Critical Inquiry* 28:369–418.

Dunayer, Joan. 2001. *Animal Equality: Language and Liberation*. Derwood, Md.: Ryce.

Gourevitch, Philip. 1998. *We Wish to Inform You that Tomorrow We Will Be Killed with Our Families: Stories from Rwanda*. New York: Farrar, Straus and Giroux.

Harrison, Robert Pogue. 2005. *The Dominion of the Dead*. Chicago: University of Chicago Press.

Kappeler, Susanne. 1995. "Speciesism, Racism, Nationalism . . . or the Power of Scientific Subjectivity." In *Animals and Women: Feminist Theoretical Explorations*, ed. Carol J. Adams and Josephine Donovan, 320–52. Durham, N.C.: Duke University Press.

Kuper, Leo. 1983. *Genocide: Its Political Use in the Twentieth Century*. New Haven, Conn.: Yale University Press.

Mason, Jim. 1997. *An Unnatural Order: Why We Are Destroying the Planet and Each Other*. New York: Continuum. [Reissued 2005 as *An Unnatural Order: The Roots of Our Destruction of Nature*. New York: Lantern.]

Patterson, Charles. 2002. *Eternal Treblinka: Our Treatment of Animals and the Holocaust*. New York: Lantern Books.

Power, Samantha. 2002. *"A Problem from Hell": America and the Age of Genocide*. New York: HarperPerennial.

Quine, Willard Van Orman. 1960. *Word and Object*. Cambridge, Mass.: MIT Press.

Santa Ana, Otto. 2002. *Brown Tide Rising: Metaphors of Latinos in Contemporary American Public Discourse.* Austin: University of Texas Press.

Sax, Boria. 2000. *Animals in the Third Reich: Pets, Scapgoats, and the Holocaust.* New York: Continuum.

Spiegelman, Art. 1986. *Maus: A Survivor's Tale.* Book 1, *My Father Bleeds History.* New York: Pantheon.

Thomas, Keith. 1983. *Man and the Natural World.* New York: Pantheon.

PART I

Foundational Articles, 1985–1996

CHAPTER I

ॐ

The Liberation of Nature
A Circular Affair

MARTI KHEEL

> The new understanding of life must be systemic and interconnected. It cannot be linear and hierarchical, for the reality of life on earth is a whole, a circle, an interconnected system in which everything has its part to play and can be respected and accorded dignity.
> —Elizabeth D. Gray[1]

Introduction

Over the last twenty years feminist thought has shed a radically new light on many fields of inquiry. One of the most recent areas to receive the benefit of such illumination has been that of our society's attitudes toward nature. During this same time period, a voluminous body of literature has emerged in a new field of philosophy called "environmental ethics."[2] The writers in this field (predominantly men) have shown little or no interest in the feminist literature. In the following, I attempt to redress this neglect and to show that feminist thought can, indeed, shed significant light on this important new area of study.

Central to feminist thought has been a critique of Western dualistic thinking. Western dualistic thought sees the world in terms of static polarities—"us and them," "subject and object," "superior and inferior," "mind and body," "animate and inanimate," "reason and emotion," "culture and nature." All

This chapter was first published in *Environmental Ethics* 1985, vol. 7, no. 2. © 1985 by Marti Kheel. Revised for Josephine Donovan and Carol J. Adams, eds., *Beyond Animal Rights* (New York: Continuum, 1996). Published by permission of the author and *Environmental Ethics*.

such dualities have two characteristics in common: (1) the first half of the duality is always valued more than the other, and (2) the more valued half is always seen as "male" and the less valued half as "female." The Western dualistic worldview can be traced back to early Greek philosophy and the Jewish and Christian religions, being reinforced in the 1600s by the increasingly mechanistic worldview of modern science.[3] The result of this long history of dualistic thinking has been the ruthless exploitation of women, animals, and all of nature. In place of dualistic thinking feminists have posited a holistic vision of reality in which everything is integrally interconnected and thus part of a larger "whole." Thus, whereas dualistic thought has perceived the world through a "spatial metaphor (up-and-down),"[4] these feminists have seen diversity within a larger whole. The recent findings of quantum physics have reaffirmed this feminist vision. They have verified in the world of matter what many people have experienced in the world of spirit—namely, the oneness of the universe.

Thus, we learn from quantum physics that atoms instead of being hard and indestructible consist, instead, of vast regions of space in which extremely small particles move. At the subatomic level, we are told, matter consists of very abstract entities that have a dual aspect: "Depending on which way the experiments are performed, they appear sometimes as particles, sometimes as waves."[5] The Taoist notion that everything is in flux, and that the only constant is change, turns out to have a solid grounding in the world of matter. Thus, we learn that "subatomic particles do not exist with certainty at definite places, but rather show 'tendencies to exist,' and atomic events do not occur with certainty at definite times and in definite ways, but rather show 'tendencies to occur.'"[6] Consequently, we can never predict an atomic event with certainty; we can only say how likely it is to happen. As Fritjof Capra puts it, "Quantum theory forces us to see the universe not as a collection of physical objects, but rather as a complicated web of relations between the various parts of a unified whole."[7]

Hierarchical Thought Within Environmental Ethics

THE DUALISTIC HERITAGE

By contrast with the holistic vision set forth by both feminists and quantum physicists, the goal of much of the literature in environmental ethics has been the establishment of hierarchies of value for the different parts of nature. It is assumed that hierarchy is necessary to aid us in making moral choices in our interactions with nature. Conflict is taken for granted; it is assumed that one part of nature must always win, while another must always lose. Thus, in a real sense, the field of environmental ethics perpetuates the tradition of dualistic thought.[8]

HOLISM

The concept of hierarchy finds two major forms of expression in the literature. One form is expressed through the ongoing debate over whether individual beings or the larger concept of "the whole" (or the "biotic community") should be given moral preference. Some "animal liberationists"[9] argue that it is the individual who must be considered over the whole, whereas many "holists" argue that it is the good of the whole that must take precedence. Many holists will protest that theirs is a nonhierarchical paradigm in that everything is viewed as an integral part of an interconnected web. However, holists such as Aldo Leopold and J. Baird Callicott clearly indicate that the interconnected web does, indeed, contain its own system of ranking.[10] Such writers have dispensed with the system of classification that assigns value to a being on the basis of its possession of certain innate characteristics, only to erect a *new* form of hierarchy in which individuals are valued on the basis of their relative contribution to the good of the whole (that is, the biotic community).

According to Callicott, the "good of the community as a whole, serves as a standard for the assessment of the relative value and relative ordering of its constitutive parts and therefore provides a means of adjudicating the often mutually contradictory demands of the parts considered separately for *equal* consideration."[11] At the top of Callicott's scale are rare and endangered species: "*Specimens* of rare and endangered species, for example, have a *prima facie* claim to preferential consideration from the perspective of the land ethic."[12] At the bottom of Callicott's hierarchy of value are domestic animals: "Environmental ethics sets a very low priority on domestic animals as they very frequently contribute to the erosion of the integrity, stability, and beauty of the biotic communities into which they have been insinuated."[13] Callicott goes so far as to posit a mathematical equation by which the value of an individual being may be gauged: "The preciousness of individual deer, as of any other specimen, is inversely proportional to the population of the species."[14] To eliminate any doubt concerning his views on equality, he adds that "the land ethic manifestly does not accord equal moral worth to each and every member of the biotic community."[15]

There is a sense in which the three different camps to which Callicott refers in the field of environmental ethics may be seen to reflect three different political positions: monarchists, liberals, and totalitarians.[16] The "ethical humanists," as Callicott has labeled them, may be viewed as the monarchists, with their insistence on ranking certain individuals (namely, humans) as being the most worthy individuals (that is, the aristocrats). As in a true monarchy, status is conferred by one's birth into a particular "class" or in this case "species." The "animal liberationists," on the other hand, may be seen as the free enterprise liberals arguing for extension of rights to individual beings within a competitive framework. Status is conferred on the basis of merit and does not necessarily follow rigid division by species. No concern for the whole (as in the "state" or the "biotic community") is manifested, since it is felt that a respect for the rights of the individual being is all that is necessary to achieve a just society. Finally, the "holists," such as Callicott and Leopold, may be compared to totalitarians, with their insistence on the subordination of the individual to the greater good of the collective whole.

Callicott perceives an analogy between the holist concept of the good of the biotic community and Plato's totalitarian conception of the good of the society as a whole. In an attempt to differentiate his own views, however, he goes on to reprimand Plato for the "temerity to insist that the good of the whole transcends individual claims," asserting that "moral problems involving individual human beings in a political context are very different from moral problems pertaining to a different whole."[17] This assertion, however, does not explain why one set of moral rules should apply to nature, while another applies to society. To dichotomize reality in such a manner is simply to accept the existing divisions of our society which views itself as separate from (and, in fact, opposed to) nature, rather than simply an extension of it. Callicott thus fails to show how his ideas differ in their implications from those of Plato.

Ironically, Callicott's "holism" may be seen to have much in common with utilitarianism. In both systems, the individual is treated as a means for the attainment of a greater end. In the former case, that which is good is judged by the standard of the biotic community, whereas in the latter case, it is gauged by the happiness of the greatest number. Although the content of the hierarchy varies, the structure remains the same. Both systems of thought also share the problem inherent in any scheme that claims the ability to compare the relative value of such abstractions as "happiness" or the "biotic good"—that is, who should establish such values and how?

INDIVIDUAL RIGHTS

The other form of hierarchical thought within environmental ethics is reflected in the attempt by both "ethical humanists" and "animal liberationists" to establish the relative values of the individual parts of nature. In this endeavor various criteria are proposed such as "sentience," "consciousness," "rationality," "self-determination," "interests." A being that possesses one of these characteristics is said to have "intrinsic value" or the right to "moral consideration," whereas a being without them is said to lack these. A large part of this literature consists of debating which beings possess these characteristics—that is, arguing whether divisions should occur along the lines of species or whether some overlap may exist. Ironically, although many of these writers feel that they are arguing against notions of hierarchy, the vast majority simply remove one set of hierarchies only to establish another. Thus, many writers on the subject of animal liberation may raise the status of animals to a level that warrants our moral concern only to exclude other parts of nature, such as plants and trees. Thus, Bernard Rollin, who clearly feels that animals merit our ethical consideration, emphatically states that "in and of itself, the physical environment has no interests in life and is, therefore, not a direct object of moral concern."[18]

Some animal liberationists have attempted to expand the notion of rights arguing for the concept of the inherent value of individual beings. Even these writers, however, often fail to overcome the concept of hierarchy. Thus, according to Tom Regan, beings are deserving of rights if they can have a life that is "better or worse for them, independently of whether they are valued by anyone else."[19] But if we were, as Regan suggests, to accord rights or value only to those beings that can have a life that is better or worse for them, our current understanding of the word *life* would exclude from direct moral consideration such parts of nature as streams, mountains, and air.

Regan seems to show some concern over this limitation. In his words:

> But limiting the class of beings that have inherent value to the class of living beings seems to be an arbitrary decision and one that does not serve well as a basis for an environmental ethic. . . . If I am right, the development of what can properly be called an environmental ethic requires that we postulate inherent value in nature.[20]

Outside of this important reference, however, Regan has failed to argue for the inherent value of all of nature. What has, perhaps, hindered him from so doing is the belief that this notion necessarily precludes a valuing of the individual parts of nature. The holist camp, by contrast, is convinced that a valuing of the individual for itself will somehow detract from a valuing of the whole. Both schools of thought are trapped within the dualistic mindset. Neither can see that moral worth can exist *both* in the individual parts of nature *and* in the whole of which they are a part. It is reliance on reason as the sole arbiter in our dealings with nature that makes the two schools of thought appear distinct. But these positions are not polar opposites, nor even part of a "triangular affair" (each position representing one extreme of a triangle, as Callicott argues). If we allow for an element of feeling in our interactions with nature, the positions represented by these camps dissolve into different points on a circle. No point may, thus, be said to be more important than any other. The liberation of nature is, in fact, a circular affair.

A vision of nature that perceives value both in the individual and in the whole of which it is a part is a vision that entails a reclaiming of the term *holism* from those for whom it signifies a new form of hierarchy (namely, a valuing of the whole over the individual). Such a vision asks us to abandon the dualistic way of thinking that sees value as inherently exclusive (that is, the belief that the value of the whole cannot also be the value of the individual). It invites us to see value not as a commodity to be assigned by isolated rational analysis, but rather as a living dynamic that is constantly in flux. If we can believe the findings of quantum physics, ecology, and the spiritual experiences of many individuals, we can agree with the holists that the nature of reality is, indeed, a web of interconnections, a circle or a "whole." What most holists seem to forget, however, is that the whole consists of individual beings—beings with emotions, feelings, and inclinations—and that these, too, are part of the whole. To rely on rational analysis alone to determine what the good of the whole might be is to ignore the reality of such feelings as well as their expression in particular circumstances.

The concept of holism I am advocating here does not view the "whole" as composed of discrete individual beings connected by static relationships that rational analysis can comprehend and control. Rather, I am proposing a concept of holism that perceives nature (much like the new physics perceives subatomic particles) as comprising individual beings that are part of a *dynamic* web of interconnections in which feelings, emotions, and inclinations (or energy) play an integral role. Just as quantum physics cannot predict atomic events with certainty at exact times and specific places, so too we cannot postulate that one species or one individual is of greater or lesser value than another. The attempt to formulate universal, rational rules of conduct ignores the constantly changing nature of reality. It also neglects the emotional-instinctive or spontaneous component in each particular situation, for in the end, emotion cannot be contained by boundaries and rules; in a single leap it can cross over the boundaries of space, time, and species. It is, I feel, the failure of most writers within environmental ethics to recognize the role of emotion that has perpetuated within the environmental ethics literature the dualistic thinking so characteristic of Western society.

Reason versus Emotion in Environmental Ethics

THE RULE OF REASON

Most of the literature within the field of environmental ethics may be seen as an attempt to establish rationally both hierarchies of value and universal rules of conduct based on such values. Most such literature presumes that reason alone will tell us which beings are of greatest value and, thus, what rules of conduct should govern our interactions with them. Singer refers to this idea when he states, "Ethics requires us to go beyond 'I' and 'you' to the universal law, the universalizable judgment, the standpoint of the impartial spectator or ideal observer or whatever we choose to call it."[21]

Interestingly, the field of environmental ethics is an outgrowth of two movements that were (and are) highly charged emotionally—that is, the animal rights and environmental movements. Significantly, the members (mostly women)[22] of the early animal rights movement were often labeled "animal lovers" or "sentimentalists" in an attempt to belittle their concerns. But, as James Turner points out, "animal lovers were not ashamed to admit that their campaign to protect brutes from abuse was more the result of sentiment than of reason."[23]

With the publication of Peter Singer's *Animal Liberation*, the animal liberation movement took a new direction. It was assumed that one of the reasons for the failure of the earlier movement was its appeal to emotion, rather than hard, logical, well-reasoned arguments. The new movement for animal rights (as well as environmental ethics) proudly grounds itself in rationality. As Peter Singer states, "Nowhere in this book, however, do I appeal to the reader's emotions where they cannot be *supported by reason*."[24]

Elsewhere Singer elaborates, "Ethics does not demand that we eliminate personal relationships and partial affections, but it does demand that when we act we assess the moral claims of those affected by our actions *independently of our feelings for them*."[25] Dieter Birnbacher echoes this same idea when he states, "To be classed as moral, a norm must not express the contingent preferences of a certain individual or of a certain group, but must be issued from an interpersonal, *impartial* point of view and claim to be *rationally justifiable* to everyone."[26] In a similar vein, Paul W. Taylor states, "I hold that a set of moral norms (both standards of character and rules of conduct) governing human treatment of the natural world is a *rationally grounded* set if and only if, first, commitment to those norms is a practical entailment of adopting the attitude of respect for nature as an ultimate moral attitude, and second, the adopting of that attitude on the part of all *rational agents* can itself be *justified*."[27]

The appeal to reason in ethics has a long philosophical tradition. One of its most notable proponents was Kant, who felt that an action was moral only if it was derived from a rationally grounded conception of the universally right or morally correct course of action. Kant went so far as to maintain that no action that springs from a natural inclination can have moral worth. Although most modern-day philosophers do not elevate reason to quite such heights, most still feel that any appeal to emotion is tantamount to having no argument at all.

THE LIMITS OF REASON

Although the literature in environmental ethics relies predominantly on the use of rational arguments, references to the limitations of rationality still manage to insinuate themselves. The frequent reference to an idea being "intuitive," "counterintuitive," or "reasonable" is, at least, a partial recognition of the significance of intuition or nonrational thought in moral decisions. Less frequent are direct references to the limitations of reason, as in the statement by Alistair S. Gunn: "It may be that an environmental ethic involves a return to intuitionism, perhaps even a quasi-religious philosophical idealism."[28] In a similar vein, Tom Regan states, "How then, are we to settle these matters. I wish I knew. I am not even certain that they can be settled in a rationally coherent way, and hence the tentativeness of my closing remarks."[29]

Although often not explicitly stated, a significant portion of the literature does, in fact, rely on appeals to intuition or emotion. The argument from "marginal cases" (that is, "defective humans")[30] is, perhaps, the most notable example of this occurrence. The argument from "marginal cases" concludes that if we do not wish to treat a marginal human being in a particular manner, there is no ethically defensible reason for treating at least some animals in a similar fashion. The proponents of this argument rely on our "intuition" or "feeling" that such behavior toward humans is wrong. Thus, Regan states, "Let us agree that there are certain immoral ways of treating (say) marginal beings; for example, suppose we agree that it is morally wrong to cause them gratuitous pain or arbitrarily to restrict them in their ability to move about as they will."[31] Why we should accord "marginal human beings," or even "nonmarginal human beings," such rights is never established. The limitations of rational argument may, in fact, make it impossible to prove rationally why *anyone* or *anything* should have rights. Again, we fall back on the need to recognize and affirm the significance of feeling in our moral choices.

Rational arguments are also often used in the literature in emotionally selective ways. Thus, many writers fail to follow their arguments to their "rational" conclusion when this appears to be counterintuitive. It could be argued, for example, that the rational or logical extension of the arguments of the two major camps within environmental ethics would be to advocate the ultimate extinction of the human species. Callicott, for example, maintains that value distinctions should be established by ascertaining the importance of an organism to the stability of the biotic community. However, it is not at all clear that human beings contribute in any positive way to such stability, and a great deal of evidence suggests the reverse. In the words of James D. Hefferman, "If the integrity, stability, and beauty of the biotic community is the *summum bonum*, the best thing we can do is to find some ecologically sound way of disposing of the human race or at least drastically reducing the human population."[32] Similarly, it could be argued that the utilitarian goal of the minimization of suffering and pain could be most successfully implemented if human beings were thoughtful enough to become extinct.

The call to reason is also used by other writers as a means of learning our "natural place" within nature. Such writers argue that by understanding our "natural place" within nature we can learn what our moral actions should be. But, one might ask, why should *is* imply *ought*? Why should our natural place within nature dictate what it *should* be? To my knowledge, no philosopher to date has answered this question with a convincing "rational" argument, and I suspect that none will. Pragmatic arguments about how we will destroy all life on Earth unless we find our natural place within nature cannot persuade those who have no regard for life to begin with. Only those who *feel* their connection to all of nature to begin with will take an interest in its continuation. In more ways than one, the liberation of nature is a circular affair.

Dissolving the Dichotomies

What seems to be lacking in much of the literature in environmental ethics (and in ethics in general) is the open admission that we cannot even begin to talk about the issue of ethics unless we admit that we care (or feel something). And it is here that the emphasis of many feminists on personal experience and emotion has much to offer in the way of reformulating our traditional notion of ethics. Although this may appear at first to support the stereotypical divisions of our society that associate men with rationality and women with emotion, the emphasis on feeling and emotion does not imply the exclusion of reason. Rather, a kind of unity of reason and emotion is envisioned by many feminists.[33] As Carol McMillan puts it, "to contrast thought and emotion by assuming that the latter is devoid of all cognition is to miss one of its crucial features."[34] Similarly, Mary Midgley states that "feeling and action are essential elements in morality, which concentration on thought has often made philosophers overlook. . . . In general, feelings, to be effective, must take shape as thought, and thoughts, to be effective must be powered by suitable feelings."[35] In the words of Sara Ruddick, "intellectual activities are distinguishable but not separable from disciplines of feeling. There is a unity of reflection, judgment and emotion."[36] Robin Morgan has used the term *unified sensibility* to describe this fusion of feeling and thought. In her words:

> How often have feminists called . . . for the "peculiar blend of feeling and ratiocination" in our battles against the patriarchal dichotomization of intellect and emotion! It is the insistence on the connections, the demand for synthesis, the refusal to be narrowed into desiring less than everything—that is so much the form of metaphysical poetry and of metaphysical feminism. The unified sensibility.[37]

How, then, are we to attain such a "unified sensibility"? The difficulty lies in conceiving of something as alien to our usual conception of hierarchy and rules as what is proposed. The problem of unifying our own nature is compounded further when we, ourselves, are removed from the rest of nature. Emotion easily divides from reason when we are divorced from the immediate impact of our moral decisions. A possible step, therefore, in striving to fuse these divisions is to experience directly the full impact of our moral decisions. If we *think*, for example, that there is nothing morally wrong with eating meat, we ought, perhaps, to visit a factory farm or slaughterhouse to see if we still *feel* the same way. If we, ourselves, do not want to witness, let alone participate in, the slaughter of the animals we eat, we ought, perhaps, to question the morality of indirectly paying someone else to do this on our behalf. When we are physically removed from the direct impact of our moral decisions—that is, when we cannot see, smell, or hear their results—we deprive ourselves of important sensory stimuli, which may be important in guiding us in our ethical choices.

Feminists have often emphasized the importance of personal experience in political and other seemingly impersonal matters. Its importance for ethical decisions is equally vital. This is, perhaps, the most practical implication of a feminist ethic: that we must involve ourselves as directly as possible in the *whole* process of our moral decisions. We must make our moral choices a circular affair.

Elizabeth Dodson Gray also highlights the importance of direct experience in moral decision-making through an analogy with the situation faced by parents in making decisions about their children. In her words:

> The point is that we parents continually find some ground for making our decisions, grounds other than ranking our children in some hierarchy of their worth. What we perceive instead is that our children have differing needs, differing strengths, differing weaknesses. And occasions differ too. It is upon the basis of some convergence of all these factors that we make our decisions. And our decisions are always made within the overriding imperative that we seek to preserve the welfare of each of them as well as the welfare of the entire family.[38]

Carol McMillan adds weight to this notion by her statement:

> The whole search in philosophy for universals, substances, essences, is a symptom of this preoccupation with the methods of science, of the craving for generality and the contemptuous attitude toward the

particular case. . . . A refusal to grant that action based on natural inclination may sometimes be a legitimate way of responding to a moral difficulty obscures not only the nature of a moral difficulty but also the nature of goodness.[39]

In her book *In a Different Voice*, Carol Gilligan argues that the emphasis on particularity and feeling is a predominantly female mode of ethical thought. As she puts it:

The moral imperative that emerges repeatedly in interviews with women is an injunction to care, a responsibility to discern and alleviate the real and recognizable trouble of this world. . . . The reconstruction of the dilemma in its contextual particularity allows the understanding of cause and consequence which engages the compassion and tolerance repeatedly noted to distinguish the moral judgments of women.[40]

Men, on the other hand, she states, develop a sense of morality in which "relationships are subordinated to rules (stage four) and rules to universal principles of justice (stages five and six)."[41] According to Gilligan, "the rights conception of morality that informs [Lawrence] Kohlberg's principled level (stages five and six) is geared to arriving at an objectively fair or just resolution to moral dilemmas upon which all rational persons could agree."[42]

The problems entailed in implementing a female mode of ethical thought within a patriarchal society are obvious. With men building bigger and better bombs, rapidly depleting our natural resources, and torturing millions of animals in laboratories, one rightly worries what a particular individual's natural inclination might be. As Sara Ebenreck puts it, "If the answer to how to treat a tree or a field is dependent on what the person 'hears intuitively' from the field or tree, then—as John Kultgen points out—we must be open to the possibility that some people will hear a message which is 'rape us, despoil us, enslave us.'"[43]

It needs to be said in this context that men may respond in different ways to the call to ground our ethics in practical experience. Clearly, men do have a greater propensity toward violence as can be seen by their greater involvement in such violent activities as wars, violent crime, hunting, trapping, and the like. Whether this propensity is biological or environmental or a combination of both is still an unanswered question. Whatever else we may conclude from this difference, however, it is difficult to escape the conclusion that in our dealings with nature, men have much to learn from women. Indeed, many men, including Buckminster Fuller, Lionel Tiger, and Lyall Watson, have concluded that "the only hope may be to turn the world over to women."[44]

Most nonhumans seem instinctively to take only what they need from the environment to survive. If humans ever had such an ability, we seem to have lost it.[45] The further divorced human beings are from this instinct or sensibility that nonhuman animals have, the more we seem to require rationality to act as its substitute. Interestingly, Aldo Leopold suggests that "ethics are possibly a kind of community instinct in-the-making."[46] Perhaps, then, we are fortunate in that the human capacity to destroy life, to ravage the Earth, and to otherwise wreak havoc on the world around us coexists with yet another capacity—namely, the capacity to question our right to do so.

It is only when our instincts have failed us that we turn to such concepts as rights. Thus, it is not surprising that the idea of individual rights and natural law emerged during the civil war in England, a time of great social upheaval.[47] The notion of *rights* can, in fact, be conceived of only within an antagonistic or competitive environment. The concept of competition is inherent in the very definition of rights. As Joel Feinberg states, "To have a right is to have a claim to something *against* someone."[48] The concept of rights is, thus, inherently dualistic. Unfortunately, however, we do live in a dualistic society where competition is a fact of life. The concept of rights in an expanded form to include all of nature thus sometimes may be a necessary tactical device within our current society.

Conclusion

Feminist spirituality has shown us how the concept of a patriarchal religion, which views God as a male figure of authority in the sky telling us how we should think or feel, does not speak to the needs of those who feel that their spirituality flows from within. In a similar vein, it may be argued, the concept of ethics as a hierarchical set of rules to be superimposed upon the individual does not address the needs of those people (perhaps, mostly women) who feel that their morality or inclinations toward nature reside within themselves.

For such people, an environmental ethic might be described in the words of Elizabeth Dodson Gray:

Some day, perhaps, we shall have an identity that can enjoy the earth as friend, provider and home. When that happens, we will know that when the earth hurts, it will hurt us. Then, the environmental ethic will not just be in our heads but in our hearts—in the nerve endings of our sensitivity.[49]

With such a sensitivity we could perhaps then dispense with the rigid, hierarchical rules of the past. If guidelines were to exist at all, they might simply flow from the desire to minimize human interference with the rest of nature.

In its highest form this sensitivity is, perhaps, simply love, for it is love that unifies our sensibilities and connects us with all of life. As Starhawk puts it:

Love connects; love transforms. Loving the world, for what it is and our vision of what it could be, loving the world's creatures (including ourselves), caring for the stream, picking up the garbage at our feet, we can transform. We can reclaim our power to shape ourselves and our world around us.[50]

This sensitivity—the "unified sensibility"—cannot, however, be developed on only an abstract, rational plane any more than I can learn to love someone that I have never seen. It is a sensitivity that must flow from our direct involvement with the natural world, and the actions and reactions that we bring about in it. If such direct involvement is often not a possibility for many of us, this does not mean that we should abandon the attempt to achieve the sensitivity described. Although in our complex, modern society we may never be able to fully experience the impact of our moral decisions (we cannot, for example, directly experience the impact that eating meat has on world hunger),[51] we can, nonetheless, attempt as far as possible to experience emotionally the knowledge of this fact.

What does all of this mean for environmental ethics as a field of study? How might the field of environmental ethics be changed by a recognition of the importance of feeling and emotion and personal experience in moral decision-making? For one thing, writers in environmental ethics might spend less time formulating universal laws and dividing lines, and spend more time using reason to show the limitations of its own thought. They might, for instance, show how seemingly "rational" rules and ideas are, in fact, based on distinct feelings. Few of us, for example, would relinquish the idea that we, as humans, are more important than a stone. Yet, by showing that such a thought is based, in fact, on a feeling and that it cannot be justified by rational thought alone, we may be able to detach from our egos long enough to see that we are, indeed, all part of a whole of which no part may rationally be said to be more important than another. Currently, those with power in our society use rationality as a means of enforcing their own morality. If it could also be shown that such rationality is, in fact, derived from particular feelings, we could then begin to genuinely assess those feelings and the morality that flows from them.

Environmental theorists also might begin to talk more openly about their experiences and feelings, and their relevance to their ideas and actions. Rather than spending time trying to find a moral dividing line within nature, they might, instead, examine their own internal divisions (such as that between reason and emotion). In order to unite these dualities within themselves they might then attempt as far as possible to experience in practice the full implications of their own moral theories. In a similar vein, an appeal to their readers' emotions and sympathies might be considered more relevant in an argument for moral vegetarianism than an appeal to reason.

Finally, environmental ethics might become more willing to recognize that the most fundamental questions about nature and the universe cannot, in the end, be answered rationally. Such an admission may not leave us with the sense of resolution and control that so many of us seem to hunger for, but it may, on the other hand, bring us closer to a feeling of the wonder of the universe and, perhaps, as a consequence, a greater appreciation of all of life.

ACKNOWLEDGMENTS

The author thanks Lene Sjerup, Steve Sapontzis, Marcia Keller, Darlaine Gardetto, and Peter Radcliffe for their encouragement and helpful comments.

NOTES

1. Elizabeth Dodson Gray, *Green Paradise Lost* (Wellesley, Mass.: Roundtable, 1979), 58.

2. Throughout this chapter, I have used the generally accepted term *environmental ethics* to refer to the literature on the ethics of our treatment of animals as well as nature more generally. My own preference is for the term *nature ethics*, since it more clearly implies the inclusion of human beings within its parameters.

3. According to Carolyn Merchant, *The Death of Nature: Women, Ecology, and the Scientific Revolution* (San Francisco: Harper & Row, 1980), the worldview that saw nature as a living organism composed of interdependent parts was replaced in the 1600s by a mechanistic worldview that saw nature as an inanimate object operating much like a machine.

4. Gray, *Green Paradise Lost*, 58.

5. Fritjof Capra, *The Tao of Physics* (New York: Bantam Books, 1983), 55.

6. Ibid., 120.

7. Ibid., 124.

8. Although hierarchical thought is not dualistic in the sense of referring necessarily to only two values on a given scale, it may be seen as dualistic in the sense of always judging the value of a given being as more or less than that of another, rather than simply perceiving diversity. Hierarchical thought is also dualistic in its design, its major purpose being to assign rights to some and exclude them to others. In these ways hierarchical thought may be seen as a major expression of dualistic thinking.

9. I prefer the term *animal liberationist* to Callicott's humane moralist. My definition of this camp, however, is broader than Callicott's, which refers only to the utilitarian school.

10. Callicott has subsequently softened his earlier position in an attempt to achieve a reconciliation between liberation and environmental ethics. See "Animal Liberation and Environmental Ethics: Back Together Again," in *In Defense of the Land Ethic: Essays in Environmental Philosophy* (Albany: State University of New York Press, 1989), 49–59.

11. J. Baird Callicott, "Animal Liberation: A Triangular Affair," *Environmental Ethics* 2 (1980): 324–25.

12. Ibid., 325.

13. Ibid., 337.

14. Ibid., 326.

15. Ibid., 327.

16. According to Callicott, there are three major camps within the environmental ethics literature. These are the "humane moralists," the "ethical humanists," and the "ethical holists." The three camps are said to represent three separate poles of a triangle. See Callicott, "Animal Liberation," 315–16, 324–25.

17. Ibid., 329.

18. Bernard Rollin, *Animal Rights and Human Morality* (Buffalo, N.Y.: Prometheus, 1981), 63.

19. Tom Regan, *All that Dwell Therein* (Berkeley: University of California Press, 1982), 71.

20. Ibid., 202–3.

21. Peter Singer, *Practical Ethics* (New York: Cambridge University Press, 1979), 11.

22. The animal rights movement emerged from the humane movements of both England and the United States. According to Sydney Coleman, women made up such a large part of the humane movement that "were the support of the women of America suddenly withdrawn, the large majority of societies for the prevention of cruelty to children and animals would cease to exist" (*Humane Society Leaders in America* [Albany, N.Y.: American Humane Association, 1924], 178).

23. James Turner, *Reckoning with the Beast* (Baltimore: Johns Hopkins University Press, 1980), 33.

24. Peter Singer, *Animal Liberation* (New York: Avon Books, 1975), xi. Italics added.

25. Singer, *Practical Ethics*, 11.

26. Dieter Birnbacher, "A Priority Rule for Environmental Ethics," *Environmental Ethics* 4 (1980): 14.

27. Paul W. Taylor, "The Ethics of Respect for Nature," *Environmental Ethics* 3 (1981): 197.

28. Alistair S. Gunn, "Why Should We Care About Rare Species?" *Environmental Ethics* 2 (1980): 203.

29. Regan, *All that Dwell Therein*, 202–3.

30. See, for example, Singer, *Practical Ethics*, and Regan, *All that Dwell Therein*.

31. Regan, *All that Dwell Therein*, 119.

32. James D. Heffernan, "The Land Ethic: A Critical Appraisal," *Environmental Ethics* 4 (1982): 243.

33. Some of the ideas of Eastern religions also address the false division between reason and emotion. As Capra points out (*Tao of Physics*), the notion

of "enlightenment" (the awareness of the "unity and mutual interrelation of all things") is "not only an intellectual act, but is an experience which involves the whole person and is religious in its ultimate nature." The feminist notion of a "unified sensibility" may differ primarily from this notion of enlightenment in that feminists place less emphasis on withdrawal from the world (as in the inward activity of meditation) and more on a full participation in it.

34. Carol McMillan, *Women, Reason and Nature* (Princeton, N.J.: Princeton University Press, 1982), 28.

35. Mary Midgley, *Heart and Mind* (New York: St. Martin's, 1981), 12, 4.

36. Sara Ruddick, "Maternal Thinking," *Feminist Studies* 6, no. 2 (1980): 348.

37. Robin Morgan, "Metaphysical Feminism," in *The Politics of Women's Spirituality*, ed. Charlene Spretnak (Garden City, N.Y.: Anchor, 1982), 387.

38. Gray, *Green Paradise Lost*, 148.

39. McMillan, *Women, Reason and Nature*, 28.

40. Carol Gilligan, *In a Different Voice: Psychological Theory and Women's Development* (Cambridge, Mass.: Harvard University Press, 1982), 100.

41. Ibid., 18. According to Lawrence Kohlberg, children undergo six stages of moral development, the sixth stage representing a fully mature moral being. Unfortunately, Kohlberg's study was based on interviews with boys only and ignores the significance and value of the different way in which women develop morally.

42. Ibid., 21–22.

43. Sara Ebenreck, "A Partnership Farmland Ethic," *Environmental Ethics* 5 (1983): 40.

44. Laurel Holliday, *The Violent Sex* (Guerneville, Calif.: Blue Stocking, 1978), 171.

45. Exceptions to this generalization may, perhaps, be found among certain tribal peoples.

46. Aldo Leopold, *A Sand County Almanac, and Sketches Here and There* (Oxford: Oxford University Press, 1966), 36.

47. Raymond Polin, "The Rights of Man in Hobbes and Locke," in *Political Theory and the Rights of Man*, ed. D. D. Raphael (Bloomington: Indiana University Press, 1967), 16–26; S. F. Sapontzis, "The Value of Human Rights," *Journal of Value Inquiry* 12 (1978): 210–24.

48. Joel Feinberg, "The Rights of Animals and Unborn Generations," in *Responsibilities to Future Generations*, ed. Ernest Partridge (Buffalo, N.Y.: Prometheus, 1980), 139.

49. Gray, *Green Paradise Lost*, 85.

50. Starhawk, *Dreaming the Dark* (Boston: Beacon, 1982), 44.

51. Meat eating has been implicated by a number of writers as a major contributor to world hunger. It is estimated that 80 to 90 percent of all grain

grown in America is used to feed animals, that seventeen times as much land is used as the amount needed to plant grains such as soybeans, and that "if we ate half as much meat, we could release enough food to feed the entire 'developing world'" (Barbara Parham, *What's Wrong with Eating Meat?* [Denver: Ananda Marga, 1979], 38; see also John Robbins, *Diet for a New America* [Walpole, N.H.: Stillpoint, 1987]).

CHAPTER 2

෨ぺ

Animal Rights and Feminist Theory

JOSEPHINE DONOVAN

Peter Singer prefaces his ground-breaking treatise *Animal Liberation* (1975) with an anecdote about a visit he and his wife made to the home of a woman who claimed to love animals, had heard he was writing a book on the subject, and so invited him to tea. Singer's attitude toward the woman is contemptuous: she had invited a friend who also loved animals and was "keen to meet us. When we arrived our hostess's friend was already there, and . . . certainly was keen to talk about animals. 'I do love animals,' she began . . . and she was off. She paused while refreshments were served, took a ham sandwich, and then asked us what pets we had." Singer's point is not only to condemn the woman's hypocrisy in claiming to love animals while she was eating meat but also to dissociate himself from a sentimentalist approach to animal welfare. Speaking for his wife as well, he explains:

> We were not especially "interested in" animals. Neither of us had ever been inordinately fond of dogs, cats, or horses. . . . We didn't

This chapter was first published in *Signs: Journal of Women in Culture and Society* 1990, vol. 15, no. 2. © 1990 by The University of Chicago. All rights reserved. Published by permission of the author and *Signs*.

"love" animals.... The portrayal of those who protest against cruelty to animals as sentimental, emotional "animal lovers" [has meant] excluding the entire issue ... from serious political and moral discussion.[1]

In other words, he fears that to associate the animal rights cause with "womanish" sentiment is to trivialize it.[2]

Singer's concerns about the image and strategies of animal rights activists are shared by another major contemporary theorist of animal rights, Tom Regan. In his preface to *The Case for Animal Rights* (1983) Regan stresses that "since all who work on behalf of the interests of animals are ... familiar with the tired charge of being 'irrational,' 'sentimental,' 'emotional,' or worse, we can give the lie to these accusations only by making a concerted effort not to indulge our emotions or parade our sentiments. And that requires making a sustained commitment to rational inquiry."[3] In a later article Regan defends himself against charges of being hyperrational by maintaining that "reason—not sentiment, not emotion—reason compels us to recognize the equal inherent value of ... animals and ... their equal right to be treated with respect."[4] Regan's and Singer's rejection of emotion and their concern about being branded sentimentalist are not accidental; rather, they expose the inherent bias in contemporary animal rights theory toward rationalism, which, paradoxically, in the form of Cartesian objectivism, established a major theoretical justification for animal abuse.

Women animal rights theorists seem, indeed, to have developed more of a sense of emotional bonding with animals as the basis for their theory than is evident in the male literature. Mary Midgley, for example, another contemporary animal rights theorist, urges, "What makes our fellow beings entitled to basic consideration is surely not intellectual capacity but emotional fellowship." Animals, she notes, exhibit "social and emotional complexity of the kind which is expressed by the formation of deep, subtle, and lasting relationship."[5] Constantia Salamone, a leading feminist animal rights activist, roundly condemns the rationalist, masculinist bias of current animal rights theory.[6] In the nineteenth century, women activists in the antivivisection movement, such as Frances Power Cobbe, viewed as their enemy the "coldly rational materialism" of science, which they saw as threatening "to freeze human emotion and sensibility.... Antivivisection ... shielded the heart, the human spirit, from degradation at the hands of heartless science."[7]

Yet Singer's anecdote points up that one cannot simply turn uncritically to women as a group or to a female value system as a source for a humane relationship ethic with animals. While women have undoubtedly been less guilty of active abuse and destruction of animals than men (Virginia Woolf observes in *Three Guineas*: "The vast majority of birds and beasts have been killed by you; not by us"),[8] they nevertheless have been complicit in that abuse, largely in their use of luxury items that entail animal pain and destruction (such as furs) and in their consumption of meat. Charlotte Perkins Gilman, an animal welfare crusader as well as a feminist, criticized such hypocrisy decades before Singer in her "A Study in Ethics" (1933). Condemning women's habit of wearing "as decoration the carcass of the animal," Gilman remarks the shocking inconsistency that

> Civilized Christian women, sensitive to cruelty, fond of pets, should willingly maintain the greatest possible cruelty to millions of harmless little animals. . . . Furs are obtained by trapping. Trapping means every agony known to an animal, imprisonment, starvation, freezing, frantic fear, and pain. If one woman hung up or fastened down hundreds of kittens each by one paw in her backyard in winter weather, to struggle and dangle and freeze, to cry in anguish and terror that she might "trim" something with their collected skins . . . she would be considered a monster.[9]

Recognizing that such problems are involved in women's historical relationship with animals, I believe that cultural feminism, informed by an awareness of animal rights theory, can provide a more viable theoretical basis for an ethic of animal treatment than is currently available.

Contemporary animal rights theory includes two major theoretical approaches, one based on natural rights theory and the other on utilitarianism. The major theoretician for the natural rights position is Tom Regan, whose primary statement appears in *The Case for Animal Rights*. In this lengthy, impressive, but sometimes casuistical document Regan argues that animals—in particular, adult mammals—are moral entities who have certain inalienable rights, just as humans do, according to the natural rights doctrine enunciated in the eighteenth century (particularly by Locke).[10]

Regan builds his case primarily by refuting Kant, who had stipulated in his second formulation of the Categorical Imperative that "man and generally any rational being *exists* as an end in himself, *not merely as a means,"* that rational beings possess *"absolute worth,"* and that therefore they are entitled to treatment as ends.[11] It is on the basis of their rationality that humans are identified by Kant and other Enlightenment thinkers as moral agents who are therefore entitled to such natural rights as to be treated as ends.

In the articulation of Locke and the framers of the U.S. Declaration of Independence and Constitution not all humans were in fact considered sufficiently rational as to be considered "persons" entitled to rights: only white, male property holders were deemed adequately endowed to be included in the category of personhood. Indeed, much of the nineteenth-century women's rights movement was devoted to urging that women be considered persons under the Constitution.[12] Here as elsewhere in Western political theory women and animals are cast together. Aristotle, for example, linked women and animals in the *Nicomachean Ethics* by excluding them from participation in the moral life. As Keith Thomas points out, the centuries-long debate over whether women have souls paralleled similar discussions about the moral status of animals.[13]

In building his case for animal rights, Regan extends the category of those having absolute worth or inherent value to include nonrational but still intelligent nonhuman creatures. He does this by elaborating the distinction between moral agents (those who are capable of making rational, moral judgments) and moral patients (those who cannot make such formulations but who are nevertheless entitled to be treated as ends). This is contrary to Kant, who maintains that "animals . . . are there merely as a means to an end. That end is man."[14]

Regan makes his case by countering Kant's theory that human moral patients (that is, those who are severely retarded, infants, or others unable to reason) need not be treated as ends. This to Regan is unacceptable. Therefore, if one accepts both moral agents and moral patients as entitled to the basic respect implied in the notion of rights, Regan argues, it follows that nonhuman moral patients (animals) must be included in the category of those entitled to be treated as ends. To argue otherwise is speciesist; that is, it arbitrarily assumes that humans are worth more than other life-forms. Speciesism is a concept borrowed from feminist and minority group theory. It is analogous to sexism and racism in that it privileges one group (humans, males, whites, or Aryans) over another.[15] Regan, therefore, maintains an absolutist deontological nonconsequentialist position; treating animals as ends is, he insists, a moral duty. It is a matter of justice, not kindness.[16]

Although Regan rejects Kant's determination of rationality as the basis for entry into the "kingdom of ends," he specifies that those who have "inherent value" must have a subjective consciousness (be "subject of a life") and/or have the kind of complex awareness found in adult mammals.[17] This criterion leaves open the question of severely retarded humans, humans in irreversible comas, fetuses, even human infants. Regan's criterion in fact privileges those with complex awareness over those without.[18] Therefore, though it rejects Kantian rationalism, Regan's theory depends on a notion of complex consciousness that is not far removed from rational thought, thus, in effect, reinvoking the rationality criterion. I do not quarrel with the idea that adult mammals have a highly developed intelligence that may be appropriated to human reason; rather I question the validity of the rationality criterion. Regan's difficulty here stems in part, it seems, from natural rights theory, which privileges rationalism and individualism, but it may also reflect his own determined exclusion of sentiment from "serious" intellectual inquiry.

From a cultural feminist point of view, the position developed by utilitarian animal rights theorists is more tenable in this regard because it dispenses with the higher-intelligence criterion, insisting instead on the capacity to feel—or the capacity to suffer—as the criterion by which to determine those who are entitled to be treated as ends.

The utilitarian position in animal rights theory has been developed principally by Peter Singer. Indeed, it is his admirable and courageous book *Animal Liberation* that largely galvanized the current animal rights movement. Singer's central premise derives from a key passage in Jeremy Bentham's *Introduction to the Principles of Morals and Legislation* (1789). During a high tide of the natural rights doctrine, the French Revolution, Bentham wrote:

> The day *may* come when the rest of the animal creation may acquire those rights which never could have been withholden from them but by the hand of tyranny. . . . It may one day come to be recognized that the number of the legs, the villosity of the skin, or the termination of the *os sacrum* are reasons . . . insufficient for abandoning a sensitive being to the same fate. What else is it that should trace the insuperable line? Is it the faculty of reason, or perhaps the faculty of discourse? But a full-grown horse or dog is beyond comparison a more rational, as well as a more conversable animal than an infant of a day, or a week, or even a month, old. But suppose the

case were otherwise, what would it avail? The question is not, Can they *reason?* nor, Can they *talk?* but, *Can they suffer?*[19]

A similar passage occurs in Rousseau's *Discourse on the Origin of Inequality* (1755). It seems in part to be a rejoinder to the Cartesian view of animals as machines (discussed below):

> We may put an end to the ancient disputes concerning the participation of other animals in the law of nature; for it is plain that, as they want both reason and free will, they cannot be acquainted with that law; however, as they partake in some measure of our nature in virtue of that sensibility with which they are endowed, we may well imagine they ought likewise to partake of the benefit of natural law, and that man owes them a certain kind of duty. In fact, it seems that, if I am obliged not to injure any being like myself, it is not so much because he is a reasonable being, as because he is a sensible being.[20]

Thus, both Bentham and Rousseau advocate that natural rights, or entrance into Kant's kingdom of ends, be accorded to creatures who can feel. Their assumption is that the common condition that unites humans with animals is sensibility, the capacity to feel pain and experience pleasure.

The utilitarian position proceeds from this premise to establish that if a creature is sentient, it has interests that are as equally worthy of consideration as any other sentient creature's interests when humans make decisions about their well-being. In Singer's words, "The capacity for suffering and enjoyment is *a prerequisite for having interests.*"[21] A stone, for example, does not have interests in the question of being kicked because it cannot suffer, whereas a mouse does have such interests because she can experience pain as a result. "If a being suffers," Singer maintains, "there can be no moral justification for refusing to take that suffering into consideration. . . . The principle of equality requires that its suffering be counted equally with the like suffering . . . of any other being." In short, "pain and suffering are bad and should be prevented or minimized, irrespective of the race, sex, or species of the being that suffers."[22] This is the essence of the utilitarian animal rights position.

Utilitarian animal rights theory has the virtue of allowing some flexibility in decision-making, as opposed to Regan's absolutist stance that no animal's suffering is justifiable under any circumstances. As a utilitarian, Singer insists, for example, that an awareness of consequences can and should influence the evaluation of an individual's fate in any given situation. This leads him to admit that "there could conceivably be circumstances in which an experiment on an animal stands to reduce suffering so much that it would be permissible to carry it out even if it involved harm to the animal . . . [even if] the animal were a human being."[23] Elsewhere he says that if the suffering of one animal would have the result of curing all forms of cancer, that suffering would be justifiable.[24] Singer's basic position is that "similar interests must count equally, regardless of the species of the being involved. Thus, if some experimental procedure would hurt a human being and a pig to the same extent, and there were no other relevant consequences . . . it would be wrong to say that we should use the pig because the suffering of the pig counts less than the suffering of a human being."[25]

Therefore, although Singer also uses the term "animal rights," his modifications take it even farther from traditional natural rights doctrine than do Regan's reconceptions. It is not a matter of political rights of a rational citizen, such as the right to free speech or to vote, nor is it the right of an intelligent creature to be treated as an end (in Kantian terms). Rather it is the right of a sentient creature to have its interests in remaining unharmed considered equally when weighed against the interests of another sentient creature.[26]

Singer's insistence that animals have interests equal to humans makes his argument as morally compelling as Regan's contention that animals have rights. Nevertheless, there are some weaknesses in the utilitarian position. One is that a precise value standard for decision-making or weighing of interests is not provided, which allows unacknowledged prejudices to intrude. Second, it requires a quantification of suffering, a "mathematization" of moral beings, that falls back into the scientific modality that legitimates animal sacrifice. Thus, while it recognizes sensibility or feeling as the basis for treatment as a moral entity, the utilitarian position remains locked in a rationalist, calculative mode of moral reasoning that distances the moral entities from the decision-making subject, reifying them in terms of quantified suffering. Just as the natural rights theory proposed by Regan inherently privileges rationality, Singer's utilitarianism relapses into a mode of manipulative mastery that is not unlike that used by scientific and medical experimenters to legitimate such animal abuses as vivisection. It is for this reason that we must turn to cultural feminism for alternative theory.

Cultural feminism has a long history. Even during feminism's "first wave," thinkers otherwise as diverse as Margaret Fuller, Emma Goldman, and Charlotte Perkins Gilman articulated a critique of the atomistic individualism and rationalism of the liberal tradition.[27] They did so by proposing a vision that emphasized collectivity, emotional bonding, and an organic (or holistic) concept of life. In *Woman in the Nineteenth Century* (1845), for example, Fuller argued that the "liberation" of women and their integration into public life would effect a feminization of culture, which would mean a reign of "plant-like gentleness," a harmonic, peaceful rule, an end to violence of all kinds (including, she specifies, the slaughter of animals for food) and the institution of vegetarianism (substituting, she urges, "pulse [beans] for animal food").[28] Gilman put forth a similar vision in her utopian novel *Herland* (1915). Indeed, in addition to Fuller and Gilman there is a long list of first-wave feminists who advocated either vegetarianism or animal welfare reform, including Mary Wollstonecraft, Harriet Beecher Stowe, Lydia Maria Child, Elizabeth Blackwell, Elizabeth Stuart Phelps Ward, Victoria Woodhull, Elizabeth Cady Stanton, the Grimké sisters, Lucy Stone, Frances Willard, Frances Power Cobbe, Anna Kingsford, Caroline Earle White, and Agnes Ryan.[29]

In the second wave of feminist theory there were a few articles specifically linking feminism with animal rights: for example, Carol Adams's articles on vegetarianism and Constantia Salamone's piece in *Reweaving the Web of Life* (1982).[30] A number of other works linked feminism more generally with ecology, such as those by Susan Griffin, Carolyn Merchant, Rosemary Radford Ruether, Marilyn French, Paula Gunn Allen, Chrystos, and Ynestra King.[31]

From the cultural feminist viewpoint, the domination of nature, rooted in postmedieval, Western, male psychology, is the underlying cause of the mistreatment of animals as well as of the exploitation of women and the environment. In her pathbreaking study, *The Death of Nature: Women, Ecology, and the Scientific Revolution*, Carolyn Merchant recognizes that "we must reexamine the formation of a world view and a science that, by reconceptualizing reality as a machine rather than a living organism, sanctioned the domination of both nature and women."[32]

Critiques of the logical fallacies inherent in the epistemology of science are not new. Wittgenstein demonstrated the tautological nature of the analytic judgment in his *Tractatus* in 1911, indeed, a point Hume made in the *Enquiry Concerning Human Understanding* in 1748; but it was the critique offered by Max Horkheimer and Theodor Adorno in their *Dialectic of Enlightenment* (1944) that first made the connection between what

Husserl called the "mathematization of the world,"[33] and the derogation of women and animals.[34]

The scientific or experimental method converts reality into mathematical entities modeled on the physical universe, which, as seen in Newton's laws, is cast in the image of a mechanism that operates according to fixed repetitions. No distinction is made between life-forms such as human and animal bodies, which are seen as machines in the Cartesian view, and non-life-forms such as rocks.

Horkheimer and Adorno argue that the imposition of the mathematical model upon reality reflects a psychology of domination. "In [scientific] thought, men distance themselves from nature in order thus imaginatively to present it to themselves—but only in order to determine how it is to be dominated." Using the term *enlightenment* to refer to the scientific viewpoint, they note that "enlightenment is as totalitarian as any system"; it operates "as a dictator toward men. He knows them in so far as he can manipulate them."[35]

The pretensions of universality of scientific knowledge and the generalizing character of the machine metaphor mean that differences and particularities are erased, subdued, dominated: "In the impartiality of scientific language, that which is powerless has wholly lost any means of expression."[36] As Max Scheler noted, "Those aspects which cannot be represented in the chosen symbolic language of mathematics . . . are assigned a fundamentally different status: they belong to the realm of the 'subjective' and 'unscientific.'"[37] Thus, all that is anomalous—that is, alive and nonpredictable—is erased or subdued in the Newtonian/Cartesian epistemological paradigm. The anomalous and the powerless include women and animals, both of whose subjectivities and realities are erased or converted into manipulable objects—"the material of subjugation"[38]—at the mercy of the rationalist manipulator, whose self-worth is established by the fact that he thus subdues his environment. "Everything—even the human individual, not to speak of the animal—is converted into the repeatable, replaceable process, into a mere example for the conceptual models of the system."[39]

Horkheimer and Adorno conclude that this scientific epistemology is an ideological form that is rooted in the material conditions of social domination—particularly that of men over women. In "their nauseating physiological laboratories" scientists "force [information] from defenseless [animals]. . . . The conclusion they draw from mutilated bodies [is that] . . . because he does injury to animals, he and he alone in all creation voluntarily functions. . . . Reason . . . belongs to man. The animal . . . knows only irrational terror."[40] But the scientist feels no compassion for or empathy with his victims because "for rational beings . . . to feel concern about an irrational creature is a futile occupation. Western civilization has left this to women . . . [through] the division of labor imposed on her by man."[41]

The association of the postmedieval split between reason and the emotions with the division of labor and in particular with the rise of industrial capitalism is a well-developed thesis, particularly among Marxist theorists. Eli Zaretsky, in *Capitalism, the Family and Personal Life* (1976), suggests that the reification of public life occasioned by alienated industrial labor meant personal relationships were relegated to the private sphere: "The split in society between 'personal feelings' and 'economic production' was integrated with the sexual division of labour. Women were identified with emotional life, men with the struggle for existence."[42]

Women's connection with economic life has been nearly universally "production for use" rather than "production for exchange"—that is, their labor has prepared material for immediate use by the household rather than for use as a commodity for exchange or for monetary payment. Such a practice, theorists have argued, tends to create a psychology that values the objects of production emotionally in a way that alienated production for exchange cannot. Since in the capitalist era it is largely women who engage in use-value production, it may be a basis for the relational, contextually oriented epistemology that contemporary theorists ascribe to Western women.[43] The relegation of women, emotions, and values to the private sphere, to the margins, allowed, as Horkheimer, Adorno, and others have noted, masculine practices in the public political and scientific sphere to proceed amorally, "objectively," without the restraint of "subjective" relational considerations, which are in any event elided or repressed by the dominant disciplines.

Like Carolyn Merchant, Horkheimer and Adorno recognize that the witchhunts of the early modern period were symptomatic of the new need to erase and subdue anomalous, disorderly (and thus feminine) nature. Horkheimer and Adorno consider that the eradication of witches registered "the triumph of male society over prehistoric matriarchal and mimetic stages of development" and "of self-preserving reason . . . [in] the mastery of nature."[44] Merchant suggests witches represent that aspect of nature that did not fit into the orderly pattern of the mathematical paradigm; they therefore were seen as dangerously rebellious: "Disorderly woman, like chaotic nature, needed to be controlled."[45]

Merchant notes that Bacon, one of the formulators of the experimental method, used the analogy of a witch inquisition to explain how the scientist manipulates nature in order to extract information from it. He wrote: "For you have but to follow it and as it were hound nature in her wanderings, and you will be able when you like to lead and drive her afterward to the same place again."[46] The image of nature as a female to be dominated could not be more explicit.

The mathematical paradigm imposed the image of the machine on all reality. It was Descartes who most fully developed the idea that nonmental life-forms function as machines, which some of his followers (La Mettrie, e.g., in *L'homme machine*) carried to its extreme. Tom Regan critiques the Cartesian view at length in *The Case for Animal Rights*;[47] it is clear that the notion of animals as feelingless, unconscious robots (which Rousseau, among others—see above—rejected) legitimated (and continues to legitimate) atrocious scientific experimentation. One early anonymous critic of Descartes noted:

> The [Cartesian] scientists administered beatings to dogs with perfect indifference and made fun of those who pitied the creatures as if they felt pain. They said the animals were clocks; that the cries they emitted when stuck were only the sound of a little spring that had been touched, but that the whole body was without feeling. They nailed the poor animals up on boards by their four paws to vivisect them to see the circulation of the blood which was a great subject of controversy.[48]

In "The Cartesian Masculinization of Thought" Susan Bordo describes Cartesian objectivism as an "aggressive intellectual 'flight from the feminine.'"[49] "The 'great Cartesian anxiety' [seen especially in the *Meditations*] is over separation from the organic female universe of the Middle Ages and the Renaissance. Cartesian objectivism [is] a defensive response to that separation anxiety."[50] In the process "the formerly female earth becomes inert *res extensa*: dead, mechanically interacting nature. . . . 'She' becomes 'it'—and 'it' can be understood. Not through sympathy, of course, but by virtue of the very *object*-ivity of 'it.'"[51]

Natural rights theory, likewise an expression of Enlightenment rationalism, similarly imposes a machine grid upon political and moral reality. Recent feminist theorists have criticized the neutral and objective pretenses of the liberal theoretical tradition for leaving out the anomalous context in which events occur, inscribing them instead in an abstract grid that distorts or ignores the historical environment. For example, Catharine A. MacKinnon has criticized the traditional liberal interpretation of U.S. constitutional law for its neutral approach to justice. She urges that we "change one dimension of liberalism as it is embodied in law: the definition of justice as neutrality between abstract categories," for this approach ignores the "substantive systems"—that is, the real conditions in which the abstractions operate. MacKinnon therefore rejects, to use her example, the idea that "strengthening the free speech of the Klan strengthens the free speech of Blacks."[52] This thesis is invalid, she maintains, because it equates "substantive powerlessness with substantive power"[53] through the use of a mechanistic conceptual model. Thus, MacKinnon, like the cultural feminists discussed below, rejects the "mathematizing" elisions of Enlightenment rationalism in favor of a view that "sees" the environmental context. Had the vivisectionists described above allowed this epistemological shift, they presumably would have "seen" the pain—the suffering and emotions—of the animals, which the machine abstraction through which they were viewing them ignored.

Unfortunately, contemporary animal rights theorists, in their reliance on theory that derives from the mechanistic premises of Enlightenment epistemology (natural rights in the case of Regan and utilitarian calculation in the case of Singer) and in their suppression/denial of emotional knowledge, continue to employ Cartesian, or objectivist, modes even while they condemn the scientific practices enabled by them.

Two of the earliest critics of Cartesian mechanism were women: Margaret Cavendish, the Duchess of Newcastle (1623–73), and Anne Finch, Lady Conway (1631–79). Finch emphatically rejected the Cartesian view; she felt that animals were not "composed of 'mere fabric' or 'dead matter,' but had spirits within them 'having knowledge, sense, and love, and divers other faculties and properties of a spirit.'"[54] Cavendish, an untutored genius, challenged Descartes directly. She met him while she and her husband were in exile in France in the 1640s, and she later exchanged letters with him about his *Treatise on Animals*. In one of his letters, dated November 23, 1646, he is prompted by her to defend his notion of animals as machines: "I cannot share the opinion of Montaigne and others who attribute understanding or thought to animals."[55]

As Keith Thomas (in *Man and the Natural World*) recognizes, Cavendish was one of the first to articulate the idea of animal rights.[56] Her biographer, Douglas Grant, notes: "Her writings . . . constantly illustrate her sensibility to nature [and] its creatures: how she felt for 'poor Wat,' the hunted hare . . .

the stag; her pity for their unnecessary sufferings making her speak out in a century when cruelty to animals was all too common."[57] "As for man, who hunts all animals to death on the plea of sport, exercise, and health," she asked, "is he not more cruel and wild than any bird of prey?"[58]

The resistance of Finch and Cavendish to the impositions of early modern science were not isolated accidents, I propose. Indeed, if we accept Michel Foucault's contention that the ascendancy of the scientific disciplines and their attendant institutions was a historical process of colonization that intensified through the postmedieval period, reaching a height in the late nineteenth century, we must read Finch's, and Cavendish's critiques as an early feminist resistance to a process that inevitably meant the destruction of women's anomalous worlds. The suppression of women's social realities effected by the pseudoscientific medical theories (especially those of the sexologists) of the late nineteenth century was the final stage in what Foucault has labeled the *médicalisation de l'insolite*—the medicalization of the anomalous.[59] This process itself involved the social imposition of sexologist paradigms analogous to the scientific imposition of the mathematical machine paradigm on all living forms.

Perhaps this is why many women of the period seem to have felt a kinship to animals. Both were erased (at best) or manipulated (at worst) to behave in accordance with paradigms imposed by the rationalist lords—whether vivisectors or sexologists. Women in fact became the primary activists and energizers of the nineteenth-century antivivisection movement, which should be seen, I propose, as one manifestation of a counterhegemonic resistance undertaken by women against the encroachments of the new disciplines. Just as sexologists anatomized women's world "of love and ritual," "entomologizing" it (to use Foucault's term) into various species and subspecies of deviance, so vivisectors turned animal bodies into machines for dissection.

In her study of the nineteenth-century English antivivisection movement, *The Old Brown Dog*, Coral Lansbury argues that women activists thus identified with the vivisected dog: "Every dog or cat strapped down for the vivisector's knife reminded them of their own condition." It was an image of dominance. Indeed, pioneer woman doctor Elizabeth Blackwell saw ovarectomies and other gynecological surgery as an "extension of vivisection." For the suffragists, "the image of the vivisected dog blurred and became one with the militant suffragette being force fed in Brixton Prison."[60]

The dominance over nature, women, and animals inherent in this scientific epistemology, which requires that the anomalous other be forced into ordered forms, may be rooted in the Western male maturation process that requires men to establish their autonomous identity against the maternal/feminine. Hanna Fenichel Pitkin's recent analysis of the psychological development of Machiavelli, a prototypical formulator of post-medieval secularism, is most instructive in this regard. She reveals that "Machiavelli's writings show a persistent preoccupation with manhood."[61] "If *virtù* [manliness] is Machiavelli's favorite quality, *effeminato* . . . is one of his most frequent and scathing epithets."[62] In *The Prince* Machiavelli asserts that a leader rules "either by fortune or by ability (*virtù*)."[63] *Virtù* implies manipulative rationality and a certain macho willingness to exert military control. *Fortuna,* on the other hand, represents the nonrational, that which is unpredictable, all that is other to the exertion of rational control and masculine domination. In another celebrated passage in *The Prince* Machiavelli asserts: "Fortune is a woman and in order to be mastered she must be jogged and beaten."[64]

In an unfinished poem that treats the Circe legend, Machiavelli opposes the world of women, nature, and animals to the civilized world of public order, the world of men. Pitkin notes that Circe is seen as a witch who has the power to turn men into beasts; much is made by Machiavelli of the "contrast between her feminine, natural world, and the world of men which is political and the product of human artifice. . . . Juxtaposed to the masculine world of law and liberty [is] the forest world where men are turned into animals and held captive in permanent dependence."[65] "Male culture," therefore, "symbolizes control over nature."[66]

Pitkin concludes, "Civilization . . . history, culture, the whole *vivere civile* that constitute the world of adult human autonomy are . . . male enterprises won from and sustained against female power—the engulfing mother . . . women as the 'other.' . . . The struggle to sustain civilization . . . thus reflects the struggle of boys to become men."[67] In "Gender and Science" (1978) Evelyn Fox Keller similarly argues that the autonomy and objectivity of the male scientist reflect the basic dissociation from the feminine affective world required in the male maturation process.[68]

Beyond this ontogenetic theory is the phylogenetic thesis developed by Rosemary Radford Ruether that patriarchal civilization is built upon the historical emergence of a masculine ego consciousness that arose in opposition to nature, which was seen as feminine. Sexism, she notes, is rooted in this "'war against the mother,' the struggle of the transcendent ego to free itself from bondage to nature."[69] Developing the existentialist notion of the transcendent masculine *pour soi,* and the immanent feminine *en soi*, Ruether urges (thereby rejecting Simone de Beauvoir's thesis in *The Second Sex*) that the continual cultural attempt to transcend the feminine is what has led to our present ecological and moral crisis.

The fundamental defect in the "male ideology of transcendent dualism" is that its only mode is conquest. "Its view of what is over against itself is not that of the conversation of two subjects, but the conquest of an alien object. The intractability of the other side of the dualism to its demands does not suggest that the 'other' has a 'nature' of her own that needs to be respected and with which one must enter into conversation. Rather, this intractability is seen as that of disobedient rebellion." Thus, "patriarchal religion ends . . . with a perception of the finite cosmos itself as evil in its intractability" to technological, scientific progress.[70]

In *Beyond Power* (1985) Marilyn French argues that "patriarchy is an ideology founded on the assumption that man is distinct from the animal and superior to it. The basis for this superiority is man's contact with a higher power/knowledge called god, reason, or control. The reason for man's existence is to shed all animal residue and realize fully his 'divine' nature, the part that *seems* unlike any part owned by animals—mind, spirit, or control."[71] French sees a sadomasochism inherent in this cultural impulse to mutilate or kill off the animal/feminine in the self. According to French, patriarchal society has reached a frightening impasse: "Our culture, which worships above all else the power to kill, has reached the point of wishing to annihilate all that is 'feminine' in our world."[72]

Recent cultural feminist theorists have identified alternative epistemological and ontological modes that must, I believe, replace the mode of sadomasochistic control/dominance characteristic of patriarchal scientific epistemology. Ruether, for example, urges the development of new ways of relating to nature and to nonhuman life-forms. "The project of human life," she says, "must cease to be seen as one of 'domination of nature.' . . . Rather, we have to find a new language of ecological responsiveness, a reciprocity between consciousness and the world systems in which we live and move and have our being."[73] In *Sexism and God-Talk* (1983) Ruether suggests that human consciousness be seen not as different from other life-forms but as continuous with the "biomorphic" spirit inherent in other living beings:

> Our intelligence is a special, intense form of . . . radial energy, but it is not without continuity with other forms; it is the self-conscious or "thinking dimension" of the radial energy of matter. We must

respond to a "thou-ness" in all beings. This is not romanticism or an anthropomorphic animism that sees "dryads in trees," although there is truth in the animist view. . . . We respond not just as "I to it," but as "I to thou," to the spirit, the life energy that lies in every being in its own form of existence. The "brotherhood of man" needs to be widened to embrace not only women but also the whole community of life.[74]

Ruether calls for "a new form of human intelligence," one based on a relational, affective mode popularly called "right-brain thinking," which moves beyond the linear, dichotomized, alienated consciousness characteristic of the "left-brain" mode seen in masculinist scientific epistemology. Linear, rationalist modes are, Ruether enjoins, "ecologically dysfunctional."[75] What is needed is a more "disordered" (my term—if order means hierarchical dominance) relational mode that does not rearrange the context to fit a master paradigm but sees, accepts, and respects the environment.

In *The Sacred Hoop: Recovering the Feminine in American Indian Traditions* (1986), Paula Gunn Allen finds in those traditions attitudes toward nature that are quite different from the alienation and dominance that characterize Western epistemology and theology. God and the spiritual dimension do not transcend life but rather are immanent in all life-forms. All creatures are seen as sacred and entitled to fundamental respect. Allen, herself a Laguna Pueblo–Sioux, recalls that "when I was small, my mother often told me that animals, insects, and plants are to be treated with the kind of respect one customarily accords to high-status adults." Nature, in her culture, is seen "not as blind and mechanical, but as aware and organic." There is "a seamless web" between "human and nonhuman life."[76]

Rather than linear, hierarchical, mechanistic modes, Allen proposes a return to the achronological relational sensibility characteristic of her people. Recognizing that "there is some sort of connection between colonization and chronological time," Allen observes:

Indian time rests on a perception of individuals as part of an entire gestalt in which fittingness is not a matter of how gear teeth mesh with each other but rather how the person meshes with the revolving of the seasons, the land, and the mythic reality that shapes all life into significance. . . . Women's traditional occupations, their arts and crafts, and their literatures and philosophies are more often accretive than linear, more achronological than chronological, and more dependent on harmonious relationships of all elements within a field of perception than western culture in general. . . . Traditional peoples perceive their world in a unified-field fashion.[77]

In her study of contemporary women's art, *Women as Mythmakers* (1984), Estella Lauter identified the contours of a new myth that involves women and nature. "Many of these artists accept the affinity between woman and nature as a starting point—in fact, creating hybrid images of woman/animal/earth until the old distinctions among the levels in the Great Chain of Being seem unimportant."[78] Recognizing Susan Griffin's *Woman and Nature* (1978) as prototypical, Lauter detects in contemporary women's literature and art "an image of relationships among orders of being that is extremely fluid without being disintegrative."[79]

In these works, boundaries between the human world and the vegetable and animal realm are blurred. Hybrid forms appear: women transform into natural entities, such as plants, or merge with animal life. Lauter finds "surprising numbers of women" poets have a "high degree of identification with nature, without fear and without loss of consciousness." Many of these artists have revalidated ancient mythic figures that emblematize aspects of women's relationship with nature: Demeter/Kore, Artemis/ Diana, Daphne, Circe. The earth is seen not as "dead matter to be plundered, but wounded matter from which renewal flows. The two bodies, women's and earth's, are sympathetic."[80]

The women artists and the feminist theorists cited here point to a new mode of relationship; unlike the subject-object mode inherent in the scientific epistemology and the rationalist distancing practiced by the male animal rights theorists, it recognizes the varieties and differences among the species but does not quantify or rank them hierarchically in a Great Chain of Being. It respects the aliveness and spirit (the "thou") of other creatures and understands that they and we exist in the same unified field continuum. It appreciates that what we share—life—is more important than our differences. Such a relationship sometimes involves affection, sometimes awe, but always respect.

In "Maternal Thinking" Sara Ruddick urges that a maternal epistemology, derived from the historical practice of mothering—that is, caring for an other who demands preservation and growth—can be identified. She calls it a "holding" attitude, one that "is governed by the priority of keeping over acquiring, of conserving the fragile, or maintaining whatever is at hand and necessary to the child's life." Ruddick contrasts the "holding" attitude to "scientific thought, as well as . . . to the instrumentalism of technocratic capitalism." Maternal practice recognizes "excessive control as a liability," in sharp distinction to scientific modes of manipulation.[81]

The maternal ethic involves a kind of reverential respect for the process of life and a realization that much is beyond one's control. Citing Iris Murdoch and Simone Weil as her philosophical predecessors, Ruddick calls this an ethic of humility. It is an attitude that "accepts not only the facts of damage and death, but also the facts of the independent and uncontrollable, developing and increasingly separate existences of the lives it seeks to preserve." Ruddick calls such an attitude "attentive love," the training to ask, "What are you going through?"[82] Were vivisectionists to ask such a question, we would not have vivisection.

In a recent article Evelyn Keller draws similar distinctions to Ruddick's in her observations of Nobel prize winner Barbara McClintock's "feminine" scientific practice (which contrasts so markedly to the aggressive manipulation of nature proposed by Bacon, seen at its worst in laboratory animal experimentation). McClintock believes in "letting the material speak to you," allowing it to "tell you what to do next." She does not believe that scientists should "impose an answer" upon their material, as required in the mathematical paradigm of traditional scientific epistemology; rather, they should respond to it and retain an empathetic respect for it.[83] It is interesting that numerous women scientists and naturalists who have worked with and observed animal life for years—such as Jane Goodall, Dian Fossey, Sally Carrighar, Francine Patterson, Janis Carter—exhibit this ethic implicitly: a caring, respecting attitude toward their "subjects."[84]

Finally, Carol Gilligan's *In a Different Voice* (1982) suggests that a feminine ethic is one rooted in a "mode of thinking that is contextual and narrative rather than formal and abstract."[85] What she names a "morality of responsibility" is in direct contrast to the "morality of rights" seen in Regan's animal rights theory. In the former, a feminine mode, "morality and the preservation of life are contingent upon sustaining connection . . . [and] keeping the web of relationships intact." She contrasts this with the "rights" approach (which is seen in her study as more characteristically masculine) that relies upon "separation rather than connection," and on a "formal logic" of hierarchically ranged quantitative evaluations.[86]

Gilligan, Ruddick, Lauter, Allen, Ruether, and French all propose an ethic that requires a fundamental respect for nonhuman life-forms, an ethic that listens to and accepts the diversity of environmental voices and the validity of their realities. It is an ethic that resists wrenching and manipulating the context so as to subdue it to one's categories; it is nonimperialistic and life affirming.

It may be objected that this ethic is too vague to be practicable in decisions concerning animals. My purpose here, however, is not to lay out a specific practical ethic but, rather, to indicate ways in which our thinking about animal/human relationships may be reoriented. Some may persist: suppose one had to choose between a gnat and a human being. It is, in fact, precisely this kind of either/or thinking that is rejected in the epistemology identified by cultural feminism. In most cases, either/or dilemmas in real life can be turned into both/ands. In most cases, dead-end situations such as those posed in lifeboat hypotheticals can be prevented. More specifically, however, it is clear that the ethic sketched here would mean feminists must reject carnivorism; the killing of live animals for clothing; hunting; the trapping of wildlife for fur (largely for women's luxury consumption); rodeos; circuses; and factory farming; and that they must support the drastic redesigning of zoos (if zoos are to exist at all) to allow animals full exercise space in natural habitats; that they should reject the use of lab animals for testing of beauty and cleaning products (such as the infamous "LD-50" and Draize tests) and military equipment, as well as psychological experimentation such as that carried out in the Harlow primate lab at the University of Wisconsin; that they should support efforts to replace medical experiments by computer models and tissue culture; that they should condemn and work to prevent further destruction of wetlands, forests, and other natural habitats. All of these changes must be part of a feminist reconstruction of the world.

Natural rights and utilitarianism present impressive and useful philosophical arguments for the ethical treatment of animals. Yet, it is also possible—indeed, necessary—to ground that ethic in an emotional and spiritual conversation with nonhuman life-forms. Out of a women's relational culture of caring and attentive love, therefore, emerges the basis for a feminist ethic for the treatment of animals. We should not kill, eat, torture, and exploit animals because they do not want to be so treated, and we know that. If we listen, we can hear them.

ACKNOWLEDGMENT

This article is dedicated to my great dog Rooney (1974–87), who died as it was being completed but whose life led me to appreciate the nobility and dignity of animals.

NOTES

1. Peter Singer, *Animal Liberation* (New York: Avon, 1975), ix–x. Throughout this chapter, I use the shorthand term *animal rights theory* to refer to any theorizing about humane treatment of animals, regardless of its philosophical roots. I would like to acknowledge the contribution of Gloria Stevenson, who introduced me to the concept of animal rights years ago, and my dog Jessie.

2. In the *Ethics* Spinoza remarked that opposition to animal slaughter was based on "superstition and womanish pity" rather than on reason, as cited in Mary Midgley, *Animals and Why They Matter* (Athens: University of Georgia Press, 1983), 10. This is the kind of charge that disconcerts Singer.

3. Tom Regan, *The Case for Animal Rights* (Berkeley: University of California Press, 1983), xii.

4. Tom Regan, "The Case for Animal Rights," in *In Defense of Animals*, ed. Peter Singer (New York: Blackwell, 1985), 24.

5. Mary Midgley, "Persons and Non-Persons," in *In Defense of Animals*, ed. Singer, 60.

6. Constantia Salamone, Xeroxed form letter, July 1986.

7. James Turner, *Reckoning with the Beast: Animals, Pain and Humanity in the Victorian Mind* (Baltimore: Johns Hopkins University Press, 1980), 101, 103. Roswell C. McCrea, *The Humane Movement: A Descriptive Survey* (1910; reprint, College Park, Md.: McGrath, 1969), 117, notes that sentimentalism versus rationalism as a basis for animal rights theory was an issue in the nineteenth-century animal rights campaign: "As a rule humane writings [and] work are based on a 'faith' rather than any rationalistic scheme of fundamentals. The emotional basis is a common one, and the kind treatment of animals is assumed to be a thing desirable in itself." The exception was the Humanitarian League under Henry Salt, which tried to place "humane principles on a consistent and rational basis." It was based "not merely on a kindly sentiment, a product of the heart rather than of the head." However, Frances Power Cobbe and other women theorists of the time were not afraid to privilege the heart. For an introduction to their ideas, see Coral Lansbury, *The Old Brown Dog: Women, Workers, and Vivisection in Edwardian England* (Madison: University of Wisconsin Press, 1985).

8. Virginia Woolf, *Three Guineas* (1938; reprint, New York: Harcourt, Brace, 1963), 6. Woolf's note to this passage indicates she had done some research on the issue.

9. Charlotte Perkins Gilman, "A Study in Ethics" (Schlesinger Library, Radcliffe College, Cambridge, Mass., 1933, typescript; published by permission of the Schlesinger Library). It must be noted that the women criticized by Singer and Gilman are guilty of sins of omission rather than commission; they are not actively conducting atrocities against animals. Their failure is due to ignorance and habit, traits that are presumably correctable through moral education. In this article I focus mainly on the rationalist ideology of modern science because it is the principal contemporary legitimization of animal sacrifice and because its objectifying epistemology, which turns animals into "its," has become the pervasive popular view of animals, thus legitimizing other forms of animal abuse such as factory farming.

10. Despite his accent on rigorously rational inquiry, Regan throughout uses the term *counterintuitive* as a kind of escape clause whenever deductive reason per se proves inadequate. An example of where Regan's argument becomes (to me at least) illogical is his lifeboat hypothetical where he maintains that with four normal adult humans and one dog, it is the dog that must be sacrificed. His reasoning here suggests an unacknowledged hierarchy with humans still at the top. See Regan, *Case for Animal Rights*, 324–25. See also Peter Singer's critique in "Ten Years of Animal Rights Liberation," *New York Review of Books*, January 17, 1985, 46–52, esp. 49–50, and "The Dog in the Lifeboat," *New York Review of Books*, April 25, 1985, 57.

11. Immanuel Kant, "Theory of Ethics," in *Kant Selections*, ed. Theodore M. Greene (New York: Scribner, 1927), 308–9.

12. See further discussion in Josephine Donovan, *Feminist Theory: The Intellectual Traditions of American Feminism*, rev. ed. (New York: Continuum, 1992), 5–7.

13. Keith Thomas, *Man and the Natural World: A History of the Modern Sensibility* (New York: Pantheon, 1983), 43. For further thoughts on the "cultural symbolism" that links women and animals, see Midgley, *Animals and Why They Matter*, 78–79.

14. Immanuel Kant, "Duties to Animals and Spirits," as cited in Regan, *Case for Animal Rights*, 177.

15. Ibid., 155; the term *speciesist* was coined, according to Regan, by Richard D. Ryder in *Victims of Science* (London: Davis-Poynter, 1975). See also Singer, *Animal Liberation*, 7, 9.

16. Regan, *Case for Animal Rights*, 280.

17. Ibid., 243.

18. Ibid., 77, 247, 319.

19. Jeremy Bentham, *Introduction to the Principles of Morals and Legislation*

(1789), in *The English Philosophers from Bacon to Mill*, ed. Edwin A. Burtt (New York: Modern Library, 1939), 847, n. 21.

20. Jean-Jacques Rousseau, *The Social Contract and Discourse on the Origin and Foundation of Inequality Among Mankind*, ed. Lester G. Crocker (New York: Washington Square, 1967), 172. See also Midgley, *Animals and Why They Matter*, 62.

21. Singer, *Animal Liberation*, 8.

22. Ibid., 8, 18.

23. Peter Singer and Tom Regan, "The Dog in the Lifeboat: An Exchange," *New York Review of Books*, April 25, 1985, 57. It should be noted that however much Regan and Singer disagree in theory, in practice their positions are similar: each opposes animal experimentation, exploitation of animals for food and clothing, factory farming, trapping, hunting, rodeos, and circuses.

24. Singer, "Ten Years of Animal Rights Liberation," 48.

25. Ibid.

26. Peter Singer, "Ethics and Animal Liberation," in *In Defense of Animals*, ed. Singer, 1–10. Historically, utilitarianism developed as part of the wave of sentimentalism that emerged in late-eighteenth-century Europe, which paved the way intellectually for the animal protection movement of the nineteenth century. See Turner, *Reckoning with the Beast*, 31–33, and Thomas, *Man and the Natural World*, 173–80. Of course, women's increasing participation in cultural life in the eighteenth century undoubtedly contributed to the emergence of sentimentalism and to the growing empathy for animals seen in Bentham's and Rousseau's statements.

27. For a full discussion, see Donovan, *Feminist Theory*, 31–63. The other major theoretical tradition that one might wish to turn to for alternative ideas about human relationship with the natural world is Marxism; however, as Isaac D. Balbus perceptively points out in *Marxism and Domination: A Neo-Hegelian, Feminist, Psychoanalytic Theory of Sexual, Political, and Technological Liberation* (Princeton, N.J.: Princeton University Press, 1982), Marxism is rooted in a philosophy of domination. Marx indeed saw human identity as formed through labor that manipulates an objectified physical world. Balbus turns instead to Hegel, who urged that "all substance is subject," that is, motivated by a specific teleology, but all subjects are not identical (285). "Neither instrumental reason nor mere intuition or feeling but rather a new form of instrumental, empathic reason will guide the interactions between humans and the world on which they depend" (286). Such a "postobjectifying consciousness" (285) will emerge, Balbus believes, when new child-rearing practices are developed that intervene in the present male maturation process, which requires the development of enmity for the mother. Thus, Balbus turns in the latter part of his book to neo-Freudian cultural feminist theory—specifically that developed by Dorothy Dinnerstein—to substantiate his position.

28. Margaret Fuller, *Woman in the Nineteenth Century* (1845; reprint, New York: Norton, 1971), 113.

29. Mary Wollstonecraft, *A Vindication of the Rights of Woman* (1792; reprint, Baltimore: Penguin, 1975), 291–92, and *Original Stories from Real Life* (London: J. Johnson, 1788); Harriet Beecher Stowe, "Rights of Dumb Animals," *Hearth and Home*, January 2, 1869, 24; Elizabeth Blackwell, *Essays in Medical Sociology* (London: Longmans Green, 1909); Elizabeth Stuart Phelps Ward, "Loveliness: A Story," *Atlantic Monthly*, August 1899, 216–29, "'Tammyshanty,'" *Woman's Home Companion*, October 1908, 7–9, *Trixy* (Boston: Houghton Mifflin, 1904), *Though Life Do Us Part* (Boston: Houghton Mifflin, 1908), and various articles on vivisection; Frances Power Cobbe, *The Modern Rack* (London: Swann, Sonnenshein, 1899), and *The Moral Aspects of Vivisection* (London: Williams & Margater, 1875); Anna Bonus Kingsford, *The Perfect Way in Diet*, 2d ed. (London: Kegan, Paul, Trench, 1885), and *Addresses and Essays on Vegetarianism* (London: Watkins, 1912). Woodhull, the Grimké sisters, Stone, and Willard are mentioned by various sources as being vegetarian, and Child as being concerned with animal protectionism. See Singer, *Animal Liberation*, 234. Elizabeth Griffith, in her biography *In Her Own Right* (New York: Oxford University Press, 1984), 34–35, notes that Elizabeth Cady Stanton followed the Grahamite (largely vegetarian) regime in her youth, following the practices of the Grimkés. Ruth Bordin, in *Frances Willard: A Biography* (Chapel Hill: University of North Carolina Press, 1986), 122, says Frances Willard believed that flesh-eating was "savagery" and that the "enlightened mortals of the twentieth century [would] surely be vegetarians." Indeed, there is an interesting connection between the nineteenth-century temperance and humane movements. In 1891 the WCTU in Philadelphia (probably under the aegis of Mary F. Lovell) developed a "Department of Mercy" dedicated to antivivisectionism. According to Turner, *Reckoning with the Beast*, 94, it was virulently antiscience. In *Letters of Lydia Maria Child* (1883; reprint, New York: Negro Universities Press, 1969), Child says she is a member of the SPCA and supports the humane movement. She stresses the close kinship between animals and humans as her rationale (letter of 1872, 213–14). Caroline Earle White was a leading animal protectionist in nineteenth-century Philadelphia; she wrote numerous articles on the subject. Much of Agnes Ryan's material is unpublished in the Schlesinger Library in Cambridge. It includes an "animal rights" novel, *Who Can Fear Too Many Stars?* Charlotte Perkins Gilman wrote numerous articles on animal issues, including "The Beast Prison," *Forerunner*, November 1912, 128–30, and "Birds, Bugs and Women," *Forerunner*, May 1913, 131–32. A further useful reference on women in the U.S. nineteenth-century animal welfare movement is Sydney H. Coleman, *Humane Society Leaders in America* (Albany, N.Y.: American Humane Association, 1924).

30. Carol J. Adams, "The Oedible Complex: Feminism and Vegetarian-

ism," in *The Lesbian Reader*, ed. Gina Covina and Laurel Galana (Oakland, Calif.: Amazon, 1975), 145–52, and "Vegetarianism: The Inedible Complex," *Second Wave* 4, no. 4 (1976): 36–42; Constantia Salamone, "The Prevalence of the Natural Law: Women and Animal Rights," in *Reweaving the Web of Life: Feminism and Nonviolence*, ed. Pam McAllister (Philadelphia: New Society, 1982), 364–75. See also the articles by Janet Culbertson, Cynthia Branigan, and Shirley Fuerst in "Special Issue: Feminism and Ecology," *Heresies*, no. 13 (1981); Joan Beth Clair (Newman), "Interview with Connie Salamone," *Woman of Power*, no. 3 (1986): 18–21; Andrée Collard, "Freeing the Animals," *Trivia*, no. 10 (1987): 6–23; Karen Davis, "Farm Animals and the Feminine Connection," *Animals' Agenda*, January–February 1988, 38–39, which provides an important feminist critique of the macho vein in the ecology movement; and Andrée Collard, with Joyce Contrucci, *Rape of the Wild: Man's Violence Against Animals and the Earth* (Bloomington: Indiana University Press, 1989). Alice Walker also embraced the animal rights cause in the 1980s. See her "Am I Blue?" *Ms.*, July 1986, in *Through Other Eyes: Animal Stories by Women*, ed. Irene Zahava (Freedom, Calif.: Crossing, 1988), 1–6, and Ellen Bring, "Moving Toward Coexistence: An Interview with Alice Walker," *Animals' Agenda*, April 1988, 6–9.

More recent works include Deborah Slicer, "Your Daughter or Your Dog? A Feminist Assessment of the Animal Research Issue" (chapter 4, this volume); Carol J. Adams, *The Sexual Politics of Meat: A Feminist-Vegetarian Critical Theory* (New York: Continuum, 1990), and *Neither Man nor Beast: Feminism and the Defense of Animals* (New York: Continuum, 1994); and Greta Gaard, ed., *Ecofeminism: Women, Animals, Nature* (Philadelphia: Temple University Press, 1993).

31. Susan Griffin, *Woman and Nature: The Roaring Inside Her* (New York: Harper & Row, 1978); Carolyn Merchant, *The Death of Nature: Women, Ecology, and the Scientific Revolution* (San Francisco: Harper & Row, 1980); Rosemary Radford Ruether, *New Woman/New Earth: Sexist Ideologies and Human Liberation* (New York: Seabury, 1975), and *Sexism and God-Talk: Toward a Feminist Theology* (Boston: Beacon, 1983); Marilyn French, *Beyond Power: On Women, Men, and Morals* (New York: Summit, 1985); Paula Gunn Allen, *The Sacred Hoop: Recovering the Feminine in American Indian Traditions* (Boston: Beacon, 1986); Chrystos, "No Rock Scorns Me as Whore," in *This Bridge Called My Back: Writings by Radical Women of Color*, ed. Cherríe Moraga and Gloria Anzaldúa (Watertown, Mass.: Persephone, 1981), 243–45; Ynestra King, "Feminism and the Revolt of Nature," *Heresies*, no. 13 (1981): 812–16.

32. Merchant, *Death of Nature*, xviii.

33. As cited in Colin Gordon, afterword to *Power/Knowledge: Selected Interviews and Other Writings, 1972–1977*, by Michel Foucault (New York: Pantheon, 1980), 238.

34. Max Horkheimer and Theodor F. Adorno, *Dialectic of Enlightenment* (1944; reprint, New York: Herder & Herder, 1972).

35. Ibid., 39, 24, 9.

36. Ibid., 23.

37. As cited in William Leiss, *The Domination of Nature* (New York: Braziller, 1972), 111. Sandra Harding, *The Science Question in Feminism* (Ithaca, N.Y.: Cornell University Press, 1986), 124, similarly observes that "it is the scientific subject's voice that speaks with general and abstract authority; the objects of inquiry 'speak' only in response to what scientists ask them, and they speak in the particular voice of their historically specific conditions and locations."

38. Horkheimer and Adorno, *Dialectic*, 84.

39. Ibid.

40. Ibid., 245.

41. Ibid., 248; see also 14, 21.

42. Eli Zaretsky, *Capitalism, the Family and Personal Life* (New York: Harper, 1976), 64.

43. Nancy C. M. Hartsock, *Money, Sex and Power: Toward a Feminist Historical Materialism* (New York: Longman, 1983), 152, 246. On use-value production, see Karl Marx, *Capital*, in *Karl Marx: Selected Writings*, ed. David McLellan (Oxford: Oxford University Press, 1977), 422–23. See Harding, *Science Question in Feminism*, 142–61, for a useful summary of what she calls "feminist standpoint epistemologies." They are rooted, she notes, in the assumption derived from Hegel's notion of the master/slave consciousness that "women's subjugated position provides the possibility of a more complete and less perverse understanding" (26). Women's historical experience of silence, of being in the "slave" position vis-à-vis the "master" may provide a basis for empathy with other silenced voices, such as those of animals.

44. Horkheimer and Adorno, *Dialectic*, 249.

45. Merchant, *Death of Nature*, 127.

46. Ibid., 168.

47. Regan, *Case for Animal Rights*, 3–33.

48. Ibid., 5.

49. Susan Bordo, "The Cartesian Masculinization of Thought," *Signs: Journal of Women in Culture and Society* 11, no. 3 (1986): 439–56, esp. 441.

50. Ibid.

51. Ibid., 451.

52. Catharine A. MacKinnon, "Pornography, Civil Rights, and Speech," *Harvard Civil Rights/Civil Liberties Law Review* 20, no. 1 (1985): 4.

53. Ibid., 15. See also Donovan, *Feminist Theory*, 2–3, 28–30.

54. [Anne Finch], *The Principles of the Most Ancient and Modern Philosophy* (1690), as cited in Merchant, *Death of Nature*, 260.

55. René Descartes, *Philosophical Letters*, trans. and ed. Anthony Kenny (Oxford: Oxford University Press, 1957), 44.

56. Thomas, *Man and the Natural World*, 128, 170, 173–74, 280, 293–94.

57. Douglas Grant, *Margaret the First* (Toronto: University of Toronto Press, 1957), 44.

58. Ibid., 124. The principal sources of Margaret Cavendish's writings on animal rights are her *Poems and Fancies* (1653; 2d ed., 1664), *Philosophical Letters* (1664), and *The World's Olio* (1655). Her empathetic imagination extends to plant life, to which she also imputes a form of consciousness (see esp. "Dialogue *between* an Oake, *and a* Man *cutting him downe*," in *Poems and Fancies*).

59. Michel Foucault, *La Volonté de savoir*, vol. 1 of *Histoire de la sexualité* (Paris: Gallimard, 1976), 61 (my translation). For studies of female sexual deviance as defined by nineteenth-century sexologists, see George Chauncey, Jr., "From Sexual Inversion to Homosexuality: Medicine and the Changing Conceptualization of Female Deviance," *Salmagundi* 58–59 (1982/1983): 114–45, and Lillian Faderman, "The Morbidification of Love Between Women by Nineteenth-Century Sexologists," *Journal of Homosexuality* 4, no. 1 (1978): 73–90.

60. Lansbury, *Old Brown Dog*, 82, 89, 24.

61. Hanna Fenichel Pitkin, *Fortune Is a Woman: Gender and Politics in the Thought of Niccolò Machiavelli* (Berkeley: University of California Press, 1984), 125. Pitkin's analysis relies on the work of "object-relations" neo-Freudian feminists such as Nancy Chodorow, Dorothy Dinnerstein, and Jane Flax.

62. Ibid., 25.

63. *Niccolò* Machiavelli, *The Prince and Selected Discourses*, ed. Daniel Donno (New York: Bantam, 1966), 13.

64. Ibid., 86–87.

65. Pitkin, *Fortune Is a Woman*, 124, 128.

66. Ruether, *Sexism and God-Talk*, 76.

67. Pitkin, *Fortune Is a Woman*, 230.

68. Evelyn Fox Keller, "Gender and Science" (1978), in *Discovering Reality: Feminist Perspectives on Epistemology, Metaphysics, Methodology, and the Philosophy of Science*, ed. Sandra Harding and Merrill B. Hintikka (Dordrecht: Reidel, 1983), 187–205, esp. 197. Hunting is, of course, the quintessential rite of passage in the male maturation process. As Barbara A. White notes in *The Female Novel of Adolescence* (Westport, Conn.: Greenwood, 1985), 126–27, "many initiation stories [involve] a hunt [where] the protagonist destroys a 'feminine principle.'" Numerous feminist theorists have connected hunting with male dominance. See Charlotte Perkins Gilman, *His Religion and Hers* (1923; reprint, Westport, Conn.: Hyperion, 1976), 37–38. A more recent scholarly study is Peggy Reeves Sanday, *Female Power and Male Dominance: On the Origins of Sexual Inequality* (Cambridge: Cambridge University Press, 1981), 66–69, 128–30.

69. Ruether, *New Woman/New Earth*, 25.

70. Ibid., 195–96.

71. French, *Beyond Power*, 341.

72. French, *Beyond Power*, 523. Lansbury, *Old Brown Dog*, chap. 7, recognizes the inherent connection between vivisection and sadomasochistic pornography and, indeed, analyzes a number of late-nineteenth-century works of pornography that include scenes of vivisection.

73. Ruether, *New Woman/New Earth*, 83.

74. Ruether, *Sexism and God-Talk*, 87.

75. Ibid., 89–90. See also Gina Covina, "Rosy Rightbrain's Exorcism/Invocation," in *Lesbian Reader*, ed. Covina and Galana, 90–102.

76. Allen, *Sacred Hoop*, 1, 80, 100, see also 224.

77. Ibid., 154, 243, 244.

78. Estella Lauter, *Women as Mythmakers: Poetry and Visual Art by Twentieth-Century Women* (Bloomington: Indiana University Press, 1984), 18. A separate study could be written on animals in women's fiction. In a number of works, animals are used to avenge injuries done to women; for example, Edith Wharton, "Kerfol" (1916), in *The Collected Short Stories of Edith Wharton*, ed. R. W. B. Lewis (New York: Scribner, 1968), 282–300, and Sylvia Plath, "The Fifty-ninth Bear" (1959), in *Johnny Panic and the Bible of Dreams* (New York: Harper & Row, 1979), 105–14. In others, the woman–animal identification is explicit. See Mary Webb, *Gone to Earth* (fox) (1917; reprint, New York: Dalton, 1974); Radclyffe Hall, *The Well of Loneliness* (fox) (New York: Covice, Freed, 1929); Ellen Glasgow, *The Sheltered Life* (ducks) (Garden City, N.Y.: Doubleday Doran, 1932); Zora Neale Hurston, *Their Eyes Were Watching God* (mule) (1937; reprint, Urbana: University of Illinois Press, 1978); Willa Cather, *A Lost Lady* (woodpecker) (New York: Knopf, 1923); and Hariette Arnow, *Hunter's Horn* (fox) (New York: Macmillan, 1949). In many of Glasgow's novels, the animal–woman connection is a central issue. See Josephine Donovan, *The Demeter-Persephone Myth in Wharton, Cather, and Glasgow* (University Park: Pennsylvania State University Press, 1989), esp. chap. 5. In many works by women, animals are women's closest companions, and often there is a kind of psychic communication between them (especially when the women are witches). See Annie Trumbull Slosson, "Anna Malann," in *Dumb Foxglove and Other Stories* (New York: Harper, 1898), 85–117; Mary E. Wilkins (Freeman), "Christmas Jenny," in *A New England Nun and Other Stories* (New York: Harper, 1891), 160–77; Sarah Orne Jewett, "A White Heron," in *The Country of the Pointed Firs*, ed. Willa Cather (1925; reprint, Garden City, N.Y.: Anchor, 1956), 161–71; Virginia Woolf, "The Widow and the Parrot: A True Story," in *The Complete Shorter Fiction of Virginia Woolf*, ed. Susan Dick (San Diego: Harcourt Brace Jovanovich, 1985), 156–63; Rose Terry (Cooke), "Dely's Cow," in *How Celia Changed Her Mind and Selected Stories*, ed. Elizabeth Ammons (New Brunswick, N.J.: Rutgers University Press, 1986), 182–95; and Susan Glaspell,

"A Jury of Her Peers," in *American Voices/American Women*, ed. Lee R. Edwards and Arlyn Diamond (New York: Avon, 1973), 359–81. Sarah Grand's *The Beth Book* (1897; reprint, New York: Dial, 1980) and various works by Elizabeth Stuart Phelps Ward (n. 29) are explicitly antivivisectionist. See Lansbury, *Old Brown Dog*, for further works in this area. Flannery O'Connor exposed the male hubris involved in hunting in "The Turkeys," in *Complete Stories* (New York: Farrar, Straus and Giroux, 1971), 42–53. Other significant works include Colette, *Creatures Great and Small*, trans. Enid McLeod (London: Secker & Warburg, 1951); Virginia Woolf, *Flush: A Biography* (London: Hogarth, 1923); and May Sarton, *The Fur Person* (1957; reprint, New York: New American Library, 1970). See also Zahava, ed., *Through Other Eyes*. Ellen Moers, in *Literary Women* (Garden City, N.Y.: Doubleday, 1977), 260, notes "a rich untapped field remains to yield a fortune in scholarly dissertations, and that is the animals in the lives of literary women. George Sand had a horse . . . named Colette; Christina Rossetti had the wombat; Colette had all those cats; Virginia Woolf was positively dotty about all sorts of animals. But it is their dogs who will serve the purpose best—Elizabeth Barrett's spaniel named Flush; Emily Dickinson's 'dog as large as myself.'" The most promising recent theoretical approach to the issue of women's connection with animals is that proposed by Margaret Homans in *Bearing the Word: Language and Female Experience in Nineteenth-Century Women's Writing* (Chicago: University of Chicago Press, 1986). Using Lacanian theory, Homans urges that women and nature are linked as "the absent referent" in patriarchal discourse. Her discussion of Heathcliff's sadistic treatment of birds in *Wuthering Heights* is especially suggestive. She observes that Cathy's aim is "to protect nature from figurative and literal killing at the hand of androcentric law" (78).

I further elaborate on Homans's analysis in "Ecofeminist Literary Criticism: Reading the Orange," *Hypatia: A Journal of Feminist Philosophy* 11, no. 2 (1996): 161–84. See also Marian Scholtmeijer, "The Power of Otherness: Animals in Women's Fiction," in *Animals and Women: Feminist Theoretical Explorations*, ed. Carol J. Adams and Josephine Donovan (Durham: N.C.: Duke University Press, 1995), 231–62.

79. Lauter, *Women as Mythmakers*, 19.

80. Ibid., 177, 174.

81. Sara Ruddick, "Maternal Thinking," *Feminist Studies* 6, no. 2 (1980): 350–51. See also her *Maternal Thinking: Toward a Politics of Peace* (Boston: Beacon, 1989).

82. Ruddick, "Maternal Thinking," 351, 359.

83. Evelyn Fox Keller, "Feminism and Science," *Signs: Journal of Women in Culture and Society* 7, no. 3 (1982): 599.

84. Jane Goodall, *In the Shadow of Man* (Boston: Houghton Mifflin, 1971), and *The Chimpanzees of Gombe: Patterns of Behavior* (Cambridge, Mass.: Harvard University Press, 1986); Dian Fossey, *Gorillas in the Mist* (Boston: Houghton

Mifflin, 1983); Sally Carrighar, *Home to the Wilderness* (Boston: Houghton Mifflin, 1973). See Eugene Linden, *Silent Partners* (New York: Times, 1986), on Patterson and Carter. Janis Carter spent eight years trying to reintroduce Lucy, a chimpanzee who had learned sign language, to the wild in West Africa. She tells her moving story in "Survival Training for Chimps," *Smithsonian*, June 1988, 36–49. Goodall has sharply condemned the treatment of chimpanzees in American laboratories. See her "A Plea for the Chimps," *New York Times Magazine*, May 17, 1987. Also of interest is Cynthia Moss, *Elephant Memories: Thirteen Years in the Life of an Elephant Family* (New York: Morrow, 1988), and Sue Hubbell's relationship with her bees, seen in *A Country Year: Living the Questions* (New York: Random House, 1986).

85. Carol Gilligan, *In a Different Voice: Psychological Theory and Women's Development* (Cambridge, Mass.: Harvard University Press, 1982), 19. For a further discussion of the ethic proposed in cultural feminist theory, see Donovan, "The New Feminist Moral Vision," in *Feminist Theory*, 171–86.

86. Gilligan, *In a Different Voice*, 59, 19, 73. Another important work that develops a cultural feminist ethic is Nel Noddings, *Caring: A Feminine Approach to Ethics and Moral Education* (Berkeley: University of California Press, 1984). Unfortunately, however, while Noddings believes the caring ethic she endorses is enhanced by a celebratory attitude toward the female domestic world, which includes, she notes, "feeding the cat," she nevertheless specifically rejects the main tenets of animal rights theory, including not eating meat. It is clear that her "caring" ethic extends only to humans; the arbitrariness of her position can only be attributed to an unexamined speciesism. Nodding's book, while admirable in other ways, is weakened by this bias, thereby illustrating how feminist theory must be informed by animal rights theory if we are to avoid the hypocrisies and inconsistencies of the tea-ladies condemned by Singer (for Noddings evinces affection for her pets even while endorsing carnivorism [154]).

For a further discussion, see the dialogue between Noddings and Donovan in *Signs: Journal of Women in Culture and Society* 16, no. 2 (1991): 418–25.

CHAPTER 3

༁

Toward an Ecological Ethic of Care

DEANE CURTIN

Introduction

Suddenly the animal rights movement is gaining the attention of the popular press as it never has before. Its hold on the public's attention may be
due to the fact that, while its proposals are viewed as radical, it responds to
what have become core intuitions in our culture about the basic project of
moral theory: the establishment of human or natural rights. But as rights
are expanded to new domains, particularly as this expansion has begun to
interact with feminist conceptions of morality, the question arises whether
the language of rights is the best conceptual tool for exploring distinctively
feminist insights about ecological ethics.

Ecofeminism is the position that "there are important connections—
historical, experiential, symbolic, theoretical—between the domination
of women and the domination of nature."[1] It argues that the patriarchal
conceptual framework that has maintained, perpetuated, and justified
the oppression of women in Western culture has also, and in similar
ways, maintained, perpetuated, and justified the oppression of nonhuman

This chapter was first published in *Hypatia: A Journal of Feminist Philosophy* 1991, vol.
6, no. 1. © 1991 by Deane Curtin. Published by permission of the author.

animals and the environment. This chapter affirms that perspective, but it raises questions about the best way to express from an ecofeminist position the moral connection between human and nonhuman animals.

Karen Warren has raised the issue of how to express ecofeminist moral insights in beginning to develop "ecofeminism as a feminist and environmental ethic."[2] She notes that a feminist ethic is pluralist and it may use rights language "in certain contexts and for certain purposes." But she says, and I agree, that ecofeminism "involves a shift *from* a conception of ethics as primarily a matter of rights, rules, or principles predetermined and applied in specific cases to entities viewed as competitors in the contest of moral standing" to an ethic that "makes a central place for values of care, love, friendship, trust, and appropriate reciprocity—values that presuppose that our relationships to others are central to our understanding of who we are."[3]

I think Warren raises the critical issue. If ecofeminism is going to make good on its claim that there are important conceptual connections between the domination of nature and the domination of women, and furthermore, that since there are these connections, an environmental ethic is incomplete if it does not take into account feminist ethical perspectives, the rights model must be examined for whether it is conceptually the best way of expressing ecofeminist insights.

I believe that the language of rights is not the best way to express ecofeminist insights, and that a better approach can be found in a politicized ethic of care. I shall consider the animal rights project and its conceptual limitations for feminists (and for ecofeminists in particular), I then briefly rehearse some of the feminist arguments concerning an alternative ethic of care. Finally, I extend a politicized version of that ethic to an ecologically based feminist ethic for the treatment of animals. Here I will be particularly interested in the ways feminism and ecology are connected through our relations to what we are willing to count as food.[4]

Feminism and Animal Rights

There are two quite different views that have gone under the label of a rights-based ethics. I focus on these because they have dominated discussions of animal rights. I make no claim within the context of this chapter, however, that these two alternatives exhaust the possibilities for a rights-based ethics. My more limited point is to choose the two approaches that have played the most central role in the animal rights literature and argue that they cannot be understood as expressing distinctively feminist insights. The first, which has not proven very sympathetic to the interests of animals, I call the exchange-value alternative. The second, which has been regarded as more promising, I call the cross-species identity alternative.

A version of the exchange-value alternative has been defended by Alan White. A right, he says, "is something which can be said to be exercised, earned, enjoyed, or given, which can be claimed, demanded, asserted, insisted on, secured, waived, or surrendered. . . . A right is related to and contrasted with a duty, an obligation, a privilege, a power, a liability."[5] To be capable of having a right, he argues, is to be a subject capable of being spoken about in "the full language of rights." It follows, according to White, that only persons can have rights because only persons can be spoken about in the full language of rights. Infants, the unborn, the comatose are still persons, or potential persons, so "they are logically possible subjects of rights to whom the full language of rights can significantly, however falsely, be used."[6] By contrast, White contends, nonhuman animals cannot exercise a right, nor can they recognize a correlative obligation.[7]

Jan Narveson has put the case against extending rights to animals bluntly. He insists that we recognize the rights of other beings only in contexts where we stand to gain from such recognition in the long run, and we observe rights relationships only with those who are capable of entering into and keeping an agreement. "Humans," he says, "have nothing generally to gain by voluntarily refraining from (for instance) killing animals or 'treating them as mere means,'"[8] nor are animals capable of making and sustaining agreements.

If we judge whether rights should be extended to new conceptual domains on the basis of considerations suggested by Narveson, nonhuman animals are excluded. Animals, in this view, are to be used according to the self-interest of human beings. If there are any moral strictures on the treatment of animals, they are based on whether certain practices offend the moral sensibilities of those who do possess rights. Nonhuman animals possess no rights themselves.

The second approach to rights depends not on exchange value but on the cross-species identity of certain rights-making characteristics. James Rachels's procedure depends on selecting clear cases in which humans can be said to have rights. He then asks whether there are relevant differences between humans and other animals that would justify refusing to ascribe the right possessed by the human to the nonhuman. If no difference is found, the right is said to be possessed by all animals that are identical in that respect, not just humans.

In some cases, Rachels finds that there are relevant differences. A right to exercise freedom of religion cannot be extended to other animals; the right to liberty can be. He asserts, "The central sense of Freedom is that in which a being is free when he or she is able to do as he or she pleases without being subject to external constraints on his or her actions."[9] This definition of liberty based on doing whatever one wishes without external constraints applies across species. The caged tiger in the zoo is not free; the tiger in the "wild" is.

In a similar vein, Tom Regan has argued that "inherent value . . . belongs equally to those who are the experiencing subjects of a life."[10] He emphasizes that this is a theory about the inherent value of "individuals" and that "reason—not sentiment, not emotion—reason compels us to recognize the equal inherent value of these animals and, with this, their equal right to be treated with respect."[11] According to this second approach to animal rights, then, nonhuman animals may have some, but not all, rights enjoyed by human animals.

Both of these approaches to animal ethics (particularly the cross-species identity approach since that has been regarded as the more likely alternative) make a number of assumptions that can be challenged if one's goal is to provide an ecofeminist ethic. My intention is not so much to make these arguments here as to rehearse positions that have been argued for elsewhere as a means of placing the present discussion in context.

First, it can be argued that views such as Rachels's and Regan's are too narrow to express feminist insights[12] because they allow us to recognize only those rights-making characteristics that nonhuman animals have in virtue of being in some way *identical* to humans. Rachels has granted, for example, that by his procedure of establishing animal rights on the basis of whether nonhuman animals are like humans, we are theoretically denied access to rights that other animals may possess uniquely.[13] (In fact, I am not sure what one could do to elucidate what this claim *means*, given that we cannot, in principle, know what the criteria for such rights would be.) Rachels's procedure recognizes only identity of interests, not diversity. Similarly, Regan's criterion for possession of inherent value picks out a common denominator in virtue of which humans and nonhumans are identical. But many of the interests an ecological ethic may have rest precisely on the differences between humans and other animals.

The assumption that moral status depends on identity of interests has been challenged by some feminists.[14] A feminist ethic tends to be pluralistic in its intention to recognize heterogeneous moral interests. It sees the attempt to reduce moral claims to identity of interests as one strand in a moral fabric that has tended to exclude women's voices. If ecofeminism is to make the claim that there are important conceptual connections between ecology and feminism, it should question whether a feminist ecological ethic is best expressed through the extension of rights to nonhuman animals on the basis of their partial identity to human beings.

The second concern about the compatibility of ecofeminism with the rights approach is that the rights approach to treatment of animals is formalistic. It is committed to the idea that equal treatment based on a criterion of cross-species identity is the central concept of morality where this is defined as treatment that is neutral with respect to context. It recommends a decision procedure by which those beings that have rights can be separated from those that do not. Its aspirations are universalistic. Feminist approaches to ethics, however, tend to be not only pluralistic but contextual.[15] They tend to be based on actual interests in the narrative context of lived experiences.[16]

Third, the rights approach does not express feminist moral insights because it is inherently adversarial. As Joel Feinberg has said, "To have a right is to have a claim *to* something *against* someone."[17] Though conflict certainly may arise over a feminist understanding of morality, it does not begin from a theoretical assumption of conflict. Rather, a feminist understanding is more likely to be based in a pluralistic context that is dialogical and seeks mutual accommodation of interests.[18]

Fourth, connected to a dialogical understanding of ethics, feminist moral thought tends to reconceptualize personhood as relational rather than autonomous.[19] Whereas the rights approach requires a concept of personhood that is individualistic enough to defend the sphere in which the moral agent is autonomous, feminist approaches to ethics tend to see moral inquiry as an ongoing process through which persons are defined contextually and relationally.

Fifth, whereas the rights approach has tended to argue that ethical judgments are objective and rational, and do not depend on affective aspects of experience, this has been questioned by feminist critics partly on the grounds that the conception of the purely rational is a myth, and partly on the grounds that this myth has tended to marginalize the experiences of women by portraying them as personal rather than moral.[20] Following the work of Carol Gilligan, many feminists suggest that an ethic of care is better able to express the connection between reason and feeling found in women's moral discourse.

Finally, as a result of the emphasis on the rational in traditional moral theory, feminist insights concerning the body as moral agent have been missed. But as some feminist philosophers have argued, the identification of woman with body has been one pretext on which women's lives have been marginalized.[21]

These six considerations suggest, then, that the rights approach as applied to the treatment of animals is not a very promising route for establishing a feminist ecological ethic. In a world where the language of rights is the common moral currency, there may be contexts in which it would be helpful for feminists to present the case for moral treatment of animals in terms of rights. However, I would argue that there is nothing distinctively feminist about this approach. If one accepts that there is a deep ideological connection between the oppression of nature and the oppression of women in Western culture, one must look to a distinctively feminist understanding of oppression.

A Politicized Ethic of Caring For

A source for much of the feminist literature on women's psychological and moral development is Carol Gilligan's *In a Different Voice*.[22] Whereas the rights approach tends to emphasize identity of moral interests, formalistic decision procedures, an adversarial understanding of moral discourse, personhood as autonomous, and a valorization of the nonbodily aspects of personhood, Gilligan's research indicates that women's moral experiences are better understood in terms of recognition of a plurality of moral interests, contextual decision-making, nonadversarial accommodation of diverse interests, personhood as relational, and the body as moral agent. Furthermore, an ethic of care has an intuitive appeal from the standpoint of ecological ethics. Whether or not nonhuman animals have rights, we certainly can and do care for them. This includes cases where we regularly experience care in return, as in a relationship with a pet, as well as cases where there is no reciprocity, as in the case of working to preserve natural habitats. It even seems possible to say we can care for nonsentient beings. Karen Warren has written about two attitudes one can bring to mountain climbing. One seeks to dominate and conquer the mountain; the other seeks to "climb respectfully with the rock." One can care for the rock partly *because* it is "independent and seemingly indifferent to my presence."[23]

Whereas an ethic of care does have an intuitive appeal, without further development into a political dimension Gilligan's research may be turned against feminist and ecofeminist objectives. First, if not politicized, an ethic of care can be used to privatize the moral interests of women. In contrast to the rights model, which seeks to cordon off "my" territory over which I have control, the caring-for model may often suggest that the interests of others should, in certain contexts, come before one's own, and that knowing what to do in a particular situation requires empathetic projection into another's life. Putting the other in front of oneself can easily be abused. The wife who selflessly cares for her husband, who cares only about himself, is only too well known.

In a society that oppresses women, it does no good to suggest that women should go on selflessly providing care if social structures make it all too easy to abuse that care. The injunction to care must be understood as part of a radical political agenda that allows for development of contexts in which caring for can be nonabusive. It claims that the relational sense of self, the willingness to empathetically enter into the world of others and care for them, can be expanded and developed as part of a political agenda so that it may include those outside the already established circle of caring for. Its goal is not just to make a "private" ethic public but to help undercut the public/private distinction.

An ethic of care that is not politicized can be localized in scope, thereby blunting its political impact. Caring for resists the claim that morality depends on a criterion of universalizability, and insists that it depends on special, contextual relationships. This might be taken to mean that we should care for the homeless only if our daughter or son happens to be homeless. Or it might mean that persons in dominant countries should feel no need to care for persons in dominated countries. Or it might mean that we should care only for those of the same species.

As part of a feminist political agenda, however, caring for can remain contextualized while being expanded on the basis of feminist political insights. To take a political example, one of the sources of the oppression of women in countries like India is that deforestation has a disproportionate effect on women whose responsibilities usually include food preparation. A common sight in these countries is village women walking farther every year in search of safe water and fuel for food. In such contexts, the destruction of the environment *is* a source of women's oppression.[24] The point here is not that there is a single cause of women's oppression, or that in countries like India women's oppression is always ecologically based.

There are problems like the euphemistically termed "kitchen accident" in which women are burned to death by husbands who are disappointed with the dowry. I am arguing that, in the mosaic of problems that constitute women's oppression in a particular context, no complete account can be given that does not make reference to the connection between women and the environment. Caring for women in such a context includes caring for their environment. A distinctively feminist understanding of community development in countries like India may, then, provide a common context of related (though not identical!) interests that would connect women in the United States with women and the environment in India.

A distinction can be drawn between caring *about* and caring *for* that helps clarify how caring can be expanded. Caring about is a generalized form of care that may have specifiable recipients, but it occurs in a context where direct relatedness to specific others is missing. For example, feminist perspectives may lead one to a sense of connection between oneself and the plight of women in distant locations. But if one has not experienced the condition of women in India, for example, and more than that, if one has not experienced the particular conditions of women in a specific village in a specific region of India, caring remains a generalized caring about. As an element in a feminist political agenda, such caring about may lead to the kinds of actions that bring one into the kind of deep relatedness that can be described as caring for: caring for particular persons in the context of their histories.

Similar comments may be made about classic environmental issues. By reading about the controversy surrounding logging of old-growth forests, one might come to care about them. But caring for is marked by an understanding of and appreciation for a particular context in which one participates. One may, for example, come to understand the issue partly in terms of particular trees one has become accustomed to looking for on a favorite hike, trees that one would miss given changes in logging regulations. With these political and ecological considerations in mind, I conclude that an ethic of care can be expanded as part of a feminist political agenda without losing its distinctive contextual character. It can resist privatization and localization, retaining the contextualized character that is distinctive of caring for.

Another possible problem with a politicized ethic of care is the contention, argued for notably by Nel Noddings, that caring for can only be elucidated conceptually through the idea of reciprocity. If this is correct, it would be difficult to extend a politicized version of caring for to contexts of community development or to nonhuman animals where reciprocity is either inappropriate or impossible. It would also constitute an important similarity to the exchange-value theory of rights.

Noddings argues that "the caring relation . . . requires . . . a form of *responsiveness* or *reciprocity* on the part of the cared-for" to be a complete act of caring for.[25] Though she notes some cases where this may occur with nonhuman animals, she doubts in general whether our relations with animals do reach such a stage of completion in reciprocity. She doubts, therefore, whether we can really be said to care for nonhuman animals.

I find Noddings's requirement of reciprocity unconvincing. Reciprocity is important in certain contexts of caring for—those Noddings takes as her principal examples, such as caring education—because in those contexts we are looking for a response that indicates that caring has had the desired effect. But I regard these as special cases that become dangerous to feminist moral interests if generalized. Many of the contexts of caring for that an ecofeminist might be especially interested in are precisely those in which reciprocity cannot be expected. It seems quite possible that a feminist political consciousness may lead one to care for women in a Dalit village in India. But it would be dangerous to suggest that such caring for requires reciprocity. Is it really caring for if something is expected in return? We ought to distinguish the *contextualization* of caring for (the requirement that all caring for has a determinant recipient) from the *localization* of caring for, which resists the expansion of caring for to the oppressed who are geographically remote from us, or to nonhuman nature.

In summary, ecofeminist philosophy seeks not only to understand the condition of women but also to use that understanding to liberate women and nature from the structures of oppression. In achieving a new sense of relatedness of the kind that feminist and ecofeminist political philosophy can provide, one is enabled to enter into caring-for relationships that were not available earlier. One may come to see, for example, that the white, middle-class American woman's typical situation is connected with— though not identical to—the condition of women in oppressed countries. Caring for can also be generated by coming to see that one's life (unknowingly) has been a cause of the oppression of others. The caring-for model does not require that those recipients of our care must be "equal" to us. Neither does it assume they are not equal. It is based on developing the capacity to care, not the criterion of equality. The resultant caring for may lead to a new sense of empowerment based on cultivating the willingness to act to empower ourselves and others.

Contextual Moral Vegetarianism[26]

In this section I provide an example of a distinctively ecofeminist moral concern: our relations to what we are willing to count as food. Vegetarianism has been defended as a moral obligation that results from rights that nonhuman animals have in virtue of being sentient beings.[27] However, a distinctively ecofeminist defense of moral vegetarianism is better expressed as a core concept in an ecofeminist ethic of care. One clear way of distinguishing the two approaches is that whereas the rights approach is not inherently contextual (it is the response to the rights of all sentient beings),[28] the caring-for approach responds to particular contexts and histories. It recognizes that the reasons for moral vegetarianism may differ by locale, by gender, as well as by class.

Moral vegetarianism is a fruitful issue for ecofeminists to explore in developing an ecological ethic because in judging the adequacy of an ethic by reference to its understanding of food one draws attention to precisely those aspects of daily experience that have often been regarded as beneath the interest of philosophy. Plato's remark in the *Gorgias* is typical of the dismissive attitude philosophers have usually had toward food. Pastry cooking, he says, is like rhetoric: both are mere "knacks" or "routines" designed to appeal to our bodily instincts rather than our intellects.[29]

Plato's dismissive remark also points to something that feminists need to take very seriously—namely, that a distinctively feminist ethic, as Susan Bordo and others argue, should include the body as moral agent. Here too the experience of women in patriarchal cultures is especially valuable because women, more than men, experience the effects of culturally sanctioned oppressive attitudes toward the appropriate shape of the body. Bordo has argued that anorexia nervosa is a psychopathology made possible by Cartesian attitudes toward the body at a popular level. Anorexics typically feel alienation from their bodies and the hunger "it" feels. Bordo quotes one woman as saying she ate because "my stomach wanted it"; another dreamed of being "without a body." Anorexics want to achieve "absolute purity, hyperintellectuality and transcendence of the flesh."[30]

Kim Chernin's account of her eating disorder in *The Obsession* brings out her discovery that her disorder was not caused by food but by a dysfunctional sense of herself as a person. To overcome her obsession "requires, in whatever form is appropriate, the evolution and expression of self."[31]

She is returned to a healthy understanding of her *self* when she overcomes her estrangement from her *body*, when she accepts her body as her self: "My body, my hunger, and the food I give to myself, which have seemed like enemies to me, now have begun to look like friends."[32] Health returns when she is able to move from a Cartesian alienation from her body to a reconception as unified sensibility, a body/mind acting in unison.

Chernin's experience is extremely important philosophically. Her eating disorder is not so much a dysfunctional relation to food as it is a dysfunctional sense of personhood that shows itself through food. Specifically, it shows itself through her inability to accept herself as body, which prevents her from having a healthful relationship to food. Once she accepts herself as body, however, she is able, for the first time, to enter into a direct and healthful relationship to food.

Much can be learned from Chernin's acceptance of herself as body and of the food that becomes her body. Though experiences like Chernin's do not imply vegetarianism,[33] they do imply an openness to the reality of the way our relations to what we will count as food shape one's sense of personhood, and how one understands one's relations to others. Through accepting the possibility that our relations to food can define who we are, one comes to see the choice of what will count as food as a moral choice that reflects who one is and as an ontological commitment to the way the world will be ordered by that choice.

Taking these experiences of women seriously as expressive of what it means to be healthy, it is possible to see that our relations to food provide a philosophically interesting context that highlights the fact that personhood is bodily and relational. It develops in a social context. Just as men have typically been socialized in the agora, women have typically been socialized in the kitchen, and not just any kitchen, but a particular context with particular oral traditions including certain kinds of foods and certain methods of food preparation and presentation.[34] The kitchen has been an oppressive context for women, but it has also been a context of sociability and solidarity among women.

Another reason moral vegetarianism is an issue of particular interest to ecofeminists is that, as Carol Adams has vividly demonstrated in *The Sexual Politics of Meat*, there are important connections through food between the oppression of women and the oppression of nonhuman animals.[35] Typical of the wealth of evidence she presents are the following: the connection of women and animals through pornographic representations of women as "meat" ready to be carved up, for example, in "snuff" films; the fact that language masks our true relationship with animals, making them "absent referents" by giving meat words positive connotations ("That's a meaty question"; "Where's the beef?"), while disparaging nonflesh foods ("Don't watch so much TV! You'll turn into a vegetable"); men, athletes and soldiers in particular, are associated with red meat and activity ("To have muscle you need to eat muscle"), whereas women are associated with vegetables and passivity ("ladies' luncheons" typically offer dainty sandwiches with no red meat).

As a "contextual moral vegetarian," I cannot refer to an absolute moral rule that prohibits meat eating under all circumstances. There may be some contexts in which another response is appropriate. Though I am committed to moral vegetarianism, I cannot say that I would never kill an animal for food. Would I not kill an animal to provide food for my son if he were starving? Would I not generally prefer the death of a bear to the death of a loved one? I am sure I would. The point of a contextualist ethic is that one need not treat all interests equally as if one had no relationship to any of the parties.

Beyond personal contextual relations, geographical contexts may sometimes be relevant. The Ihalmiut, for example, whose frigid domain makes the growing of food impossible, do not have the option of vegetarian cuisine. The economy of their food practices, however, and their tradition of "thanking" the caribou for giving its life are reflective of a serious, focused, compassionate attitude toward the "gift" of a meal.

In some cultures violence against nonhuman life is ritualized in such a way that one is present to the reality of one's food. The Japanese have a Shinto ceremony that pays respect to the insects that are killed during rice planting. Tibetans, who as Buddhists have not generally been drawn to vegetarianism, nevertheless give their own bodies back to the animals in an ultimate act of thanks by having their corpses hacked into pieces as food for the birds.[36] Cultures such as these have ways of expressing spiritually the idea "we are what we eat," even if they are not vegetarian.

If there is any context, on the other hand, in which moral vegetarianism is completely compelling as an expression of an ethic of care, it is for economically well-off persons in technologically advanced countries. First, these are persons who have a *choice* of what food they want to eat; they have a choice of what they will *count* as food. Morality and ontology are closely connected here. It is one thing to inflict pain on animals when climate offers no other choice. But in the case of killing animals for human consumption where there is a choice, this practice inflicts pain that is completely unnecessary and avoidable. The injunction to care, considered as an issue of moral and political development, should be understood to include the injunction to eliminate needless suffering wherever possible, and particularly the suffering of those whose suffering is conceptually connected to one's own. It should be understood as an injunction that includes the imperative to rethink what it means to be a person, connected with the imperative to rethink the status of nonhuman animals. An ecofeminist perspective emphasizes that one's body is oneself, and that by inflicting violence needlessly, one's bodily self becomes a context for violence. One becomes violent by taking part in violent food practices. The ontological implication of a feminist ethic of care is that nonhuman animals should no longer count as food.

Second, most of the meat and dairy products in these countries do not come from mom-and-pop farms with little red barns. Factory farms are responsible for most of the six billion animals killed for food every year in the United States.[37] It is curious that steroids are considered dangerous for athletes, but animals who have been genetically engineered and chemically induced to grow faster, and come to market sooner, are considered to be an entirely different issue. One would have to be hardened to know the conditions factory-farm animals live in and not feel disgust concerning their treatment.[38]

Third, much of the effect of the eating practices of persons in industrialized countries is felt in oppressed countries. Land owned by the wealthy that was once used to grow inexpensive crops for local people has been converted to the production of expensive products (beef) for export. Increased trade of food products with these countries is consistently the cause of increased starvation. In cultures where food preparation is primarily understood as women's work, starvation is primarily a women's issue. Food expresses who we are politically just as much as bodily. One need not be aware of the fact that one's food practices oppress others in order to be an oppressor.

From a woman's perspective, in particular, it makes sense to ask whether one should become a vegan, a vegetarian who, in addition to refraining from meat and fish, also refrains from eating eggs and dairy products. Since the consumption of eggs and milk has in common that it exploits the reproductive capacities of the female, vegetarianism is not a gender-neutral issue.[39]

To *choose one's diet* in a patriarchal culture is one way of politicizing an ethic of care. It marks a daily, bodily commitment to resist ideological pressures to conform to patriarchal standards, and to establishing contexts in which caring for can be nonabusive.

Just as there are gender-specific reasons for women's commitment to vegetarianism, for men in a patriarchal society moral vegetarianism can mark the decision to stand in solidarity with women. It also indicates a determination to resist ideological pressures to become a "real man." Real people do not need to eat "real food," as the American Beef Council would have us believe.

Conclusion

Research on an ethic of care provides a very important beginning for an ecofeminist ethic, but it runs the risk of having its own aims turned against it unless it is regarded as part of a political agenda that consciously attempts to expand the circle of caring for. Ecofeminism is in a position to accomplish this expansion by insisting that the oppression of women, the oppression of the environment, and the oppressive treatment of nonhuman animals are deeply linked. As one kind of feminism it can emphasize that personhood is embodied, and that through the food which becomes our bodies, we are engaged in food practices that reflect who we are. Ecofeminism is also in a position to offer a politicized ethic that promises liberation from the forms of oppression that link women and the environment.

NOTES

1. Karen Warren, "The Promise and Power of Ecofeminism," *Environmental Ethics* 12, no. 2 (1990): 126.

2. Ibid., 138.

3. Ibid., 141, 143.

4. In attempting to work out a conception of morality that is consistent with ecofeminism, I am conscious of speaking as a man about the experiences of women. I do not intend to speak *for* women, but as a man who believes men as well as women can learn from the testimony of women's experiences. I believe, for example, that men can learn something important about what it means to be a person by listening to women speak about anorexia nervosa. This is not meant to deny that there are important gender differences in the ways women and men experience food.

5. Alan White, "Why Animals Cannot Have Rights," in *Animal Rights and Human Obligations*, 2d ed., ed. Tom Regan and Peter Singer (Englewood Cliffs, N.J.: Prentice-Hall, 1984), 119–21, as excerpted from Alan White, *Rights* (Oxford: Oxford University Press, 1989), 120.

6. White, "Why Animals Cannot Have Rights," 120.

7. Ibid., 121.

8. Jan Narveson, "A Defense of Meat Eating," in *Animal Rights and Human Obligations*, ed. Regan and Singer, 193; originally published as "Animal Rights Revisited," in *Ethics and Animals*, ed. Harlan B. Miller and William H. Williams (Clifton, N.J.: Humana, 1983), 45–59.

9. James Rachels, "Why Animals Have a Right to Liberty," in *Animal Rights and Human Obligations*, ed. Regan and Singer, 125.

10. Tom Regan, "The Case for Animal Rights," in *Animal Rights and Human Obligations*, ed. Regan and Singer, 112.

11. Ibid., 113.

12. Feminist insights into ethics are those that can be seen as arising from and expressing the conditions of women's moral lives. While there is a broad range of views that have been advanced by feminist ethicists, there are also patterns of agreement. In what follows, I am suggesting that these patterns of agreement are sufficiently well developed to call into question the conceptual link between ecofeminist ethics and the language of rights.

13. Rachels, "Why Animals Have a Right to Liberty," 124.

14. See Marilyn Frye, "In and Out of Harm's Way: Arrogance and Love," in *The Politics of Reality* (Trumansburg, N.Y.: Crossing, 1983), 66–72, for the distinction between arrogant and loving perception; María Lugones, "Playfulness, 'World'-Travelling, and Loving Perception," *Hypatia: A Journal of Feminist Philosophy* 2, no. 2 (1987): 3–19, on the distinction between unity,

which erases difference, and solidarity, which recognizes difference; and Seyla Benhabib, "The Generalized and the Concrete Other: The Kohlberg–Gilligan Controversy and Feminist Theory," in *Feminism as Critique: On the Politics of Gender*, ed. Seyla Benhabib and Drucilla Cornell (Minneapolis: University of Minnesota Press, 1987), 77–95, where she describes the rights approach as "monological" (91) in its inability to recognize the moral "other."

15. See Iris Marion Young, "Impartiality and the Civic Public: Some Implications of Feminist Critiques of Moral and Political Theory," in *Feminism as Critique*, ed. Benhabib and Cornell, 57–76, where she connects deontological theories with what Adorno called the logic of identity which "eliminate(s) otherness" by denying "the irreducible specificity of situations and the difference among moral subjects" (61).

16. Not all feminists would agree that a feminist ethics should be inherently contextual. Susan Moller Okin has argued that the rights perspective can include both the requirement of universalizability and empathetic concern for others. She proposes that the rights approach can be contextualized; thus she doubts whether there is a "different voice" in morality. I question whether she has succeeded in showing this, however, since her suggestion that the rights perspective requires us "to think from the point of view of everybody, of every 'concrete other' whom one might turn out to be" still entails "*equal* concern for others" (Susan Moller Okin, "Reason and Feeling in Thinking About Justice," in *Feminism and Political Theory*, ed. Cass R. Sunstein [Chicago: University of Chicago Press, 1990], 32, 34, italics added). This is still not fully compatible with the care perspective, which allows that a particular context of caring may include caring that is *un*equal. Even if contextualized, a rule-based ethic still proceeds by finding cross-situational identity. There is a difference between contextualizing a rule-governed theory, and a theory that is inherently contextualized. I therefore tend to side with those who argue that there is a distinctively feminist ethic of care that cannot be reduced to the justice perspective. In fact, I would be sympathetic to a position that is even more pluralistic than the alternatives of rights or care. Charles Taylor argues that there are moral perspectives based on personal integrity, perfection, and liberation ("The Diversity of Goods," in *Utilitarianism and Beyond*, ed. Amartya Sen and Bernard Williams [Cambridge, Mass.: Harvard University Press, 1982], 133). These may not be reducible either to rights or care. I would suggest that an ecofeminist ethics of care is most appropriately developed in dialogue with what Taylor calls the liberation orientation rather than the rights orientation. I intend to do this by arguing in the next section that the care perspective needs to be politicized.

17. Joel Feinberg, "The Rights of Animals and Unborn Generations," in *Responsibilities to Other Generations*, ed. Ernest Partridge (Buffalo, N.Y.: Prometheus, 1980), 139.

18. Benhabib and Cornell, eds., *Feminism as Critique*, sec. 4.

19. Ann Ferguson, "A Feminist Aspect Theory of the Self," in *Women, Knowledge, and Reality: Explorations in Feminist Philosophy*, ed. Ann Garry and Marilyn Pearsall (Boston: Unwin Hyman, 1989), 93–107; Lugones, "Playfulness, 'World'-Travelling, and Loving Perception"; Deane Curtin, "Dogen, Deep Ecology and the Ecological Self," *Environmental Ethics* 16, no. 2 (1994): 195–213.

20. Alison Jaggar, "Love and Knowledge: Emotion in Feminist Epistemology," in *Gender/Body/Knowledge: Feminist Reconstructions of Being and Knowing*, ed. Alison M. Jaggar and Susan R. Bordo (New Brunswick, N.J.: Rutgers University Press, 1989), 139–43.

21. Susan Bordo, "The Body and the Reproduction of Femininity: A Feminist Appropriation of Foucault," in *Gender/Body/Knowledge*, ed. Jaggar and Bordo, 13–33.

22. See Eva Feder Kittay and Diana T. Meyers, eds., *Women and Moral Theory* (Totowa, N.J.: Rowman & Littlefield, 1987), and Sunstein, ed., *Feminism and Political Theory*, for useful collections of papers illustrating the influence of Gilligan's research. Owen Flanagan and Kathryn Jackson, "Justice, Care, and Gender: The Kohlberg–Gilligan Debate Revisited," in *Feminism and Political Theory*, ed. Sunstein, 37–52, give a helpful overview of the large body of literature on this subject. They point out several changes that might be helpful to Gilligan's theory. For example, whereas she depicts the alternative between a rights perspective and a care perspective in terms of a gestalt shift, Flanagan and Jackson argue that this does not accurately represent the shift that occurs between the two perspectives. A gestalt shift, such as the duck–rabbit, only allows the image to be seen as either a duck or a rabbit. But research suggests that most people can see a particular moral situation from the perspective of either rights or care, but that one of these perspectives is regarded as more important, and the distinction in importance tends to be gender-based, women emphasizing care, men emphasizing rights (Flanagan and Jackson, "Justice," 38–40). This suggests the two perspectives are psychologically, not inherently, mutually exclusive, although one may find contexts in which the perspectives do conflict.

23. Warren, "Promise and Power of Ecofeminism," 135.

24. An excellent source is Vandana Shiva, *Staying Alive: Women, Ecology, and Development* (London: Zed, 1988). See, particularly, her account of the Chipko movement (67–77), which began when women in the Himalayan foothills literally hugged trees that were sacred to them to spare them from deforestation. The movement has grown into a full-scale human development project.

25. Nel Noddings, *Caring: A Feminine Approach to Ethics and Moral Education* (Berkeley: University of California Press, 1984), 150.

26. By this term, I intend to indicate a distinction between vegetarianism based on considerations of health and vegetarianism based on moral considerations.

27. Tom Regan, *The Case for Animal Rights* (Berkeley: University of California Press, 1983), 330–53.

28. Regan calls the animal's right not to be killed a prima facie right that may be overridden. Nevertheless, his theory is not *inherently* contextualized.

29. Plato, *Gorgias*, in *Plato: The Collected Dialogues of Plato, Including the Letters*, ed. Edith Hamilton and Huntington Cairns (Princeton, N.J.: Princeton University Press, 1961), 245.

30. Susan R. Bordo, "Anorexia Nervosa as the Psychopathology of Popular Culture," in *Feminism and Foucault: Reflections on Resistance*, ed. Irene Diamond and Lee Quinby (Boston: Northeastern University Press, 1988), 94–95.

31. Kim Chernin, *The Obsession: Reflections on the Tyranny of Slenderness* (New York: Harper & Row, 1981), 12.

32. Ibid., 8.

33. Vegetarianism, which can be understood as an expression of health, is also commonly tried by anorexics in their attempt to "transcend the flesh."

34. See Lisa Heldke, "Recipes for Theory Making," *Hypatia: A Journal of Feminist Philosophy* 3, no. 2 (1988): 15–30, for a detailed account of the oral traditions of the kitchen, including recipe swapping.

35. Carol J. Adams, *The Sexual Politics of Meat: A Feminist-Vegetarian Critical Theory* (New York: Continuum, 1990), 1.

36. This practice is also ecologically sound, since it saves the enormous expense of firewood for cremation.

37. Adams, *Sexual Politics of Meat*, 6.

38. John Robbins, *Diet for a New America* (Walpole, N.H.: Stillpoint, 1987). It should be noted that in response to such knowledge, some reflective non-vegetarians commit to eating range-grown chickens but not those grown in factory farms.

39. I owe this point to a conversation with Colman McCarthy.

༖

CHAPTER 4

Your Daughter or Your Dog?

A Feminist Assessment
of the Animal Research Issue

DEBORAH SLICER

John Stuart Mill said that "every great movement must experience three stages: ridicule, discussion, adoption."[1] What is popularly called the animal rights movement is a significant contemporary social movement. And while this movement continues to take its undeserved share of ridicule, it has, for the most part, advanced beyond that first stage and into the second, discussion. There is even some encouraging evidence that its recommendations are being adopted by a significant number of people who are becoming vegetarians; buying "cruelty-free" toiletries, household products and cosmetics; refusing to dissect pithed animals in biology classes or to practice surgery on dogs in medical school "dog labs"; and rethinking the status of fur.

In the academy, a busy decade or more of writing and debate has coincided with a decade of intense social activism. A vast amount of literature in this area has been written by utilitarian theorist Peter Singer, rights theorist Tom Regan, and those who are responding to them.

Singer's and Regan's arguments share a number of features, and I refer

This chapter was first published in *Hypatia: A Journal of Feminist Philosophy* 1991, vol. 6, no. 1. © 1991 by Deborah Slicer. Published by permission of the author.

to those collectively as the Singer–Regan approach.[2] I begin by outlining this approach in section I. In section II, I draw from recent ecofeminist critiques of ecological ethics, especially of deep ecology, to explain how, similarly, the Singer–Regan approach neglects context and concrete individuals, how it overestimates the scope of principles and discounts our affective responses in moral life. In section III, I discuss the use of live animals in biomedical research. Researchers constantly tell us that we must choose between "us" (human beings) and "them" (animals), between our daughters and our dogs. They tell us it is either medical progress via the current, virtually unchecked rate and standards of animal sacrifice, or else a return to the Dark Ages. I think that both this characterization *and* the Singer–Regan characterization of the issue are dangerously misleading, for reasons I explain in that section. Throughout the paper, I try to make clear why animal rights issues, including the research one, are feminist issues, and I will make clearer the connections between some recent ecofeminist work and animal rights issues.[3]

I want to say that I have the utmost respect for both Singer and Regan as committed and inspiring activists and as academicians who have worked very hard to give these issues credibility in a discipline disposed toward dismissing them either as nonissues or as "pop" philosophy. Even though our scholarship differs, what we ultimately hope to accomplish for the several billion animals who are destroyed on this planet each year by and for the sake of human beings is the same.

I

Singer and Regan question traditional criteria that are offered as necessary and sufficient conditions for an entity's being owed moral consideration—moral personality, an ability to enjoy the "higher" pleasures—on the grounds that such criteria exclude certain human "marginal" cases, for example, infants, the severely mentally disabled, the very senile, and the comatose. Their approach is to search for what R. G. Frey (1980) has called a "lowest common denominator," a capacity or characteristic that is common to both the "normal" and the problematic human cases. The criterion they settle on is the capacity to have "interests."

Singer and Regan give basically the same account of these interests. In *The Case for Animal Rights*, Regan argues that at least mammalian animals, one year old or older, have both "preference" and "welfare" interests, which can be either frustrated or enhanced. By "preference" interests, Regan means "those things that an individual is *interested* in, those things he likes, desires, wants or, in a word, prefers having, or, contrariwise, those things he dislikes, wants to avoid or, in a word, prefers not having" (Regan 1983:87). By "welfare" interests, he means those things that are *in* an individual's interests, something that would benefit an individual (Regan 1983:88). Of course an individual may or may not be interested in what is in that individual's interests.

Wishing to avoid the problem of so-called marginal cases, Regan says that individuals with preference interests have inherent value and that this value is marked by certain minimal rights, the most basic of which is the right to "treatment that is respectful of the kind of value they have, and all are owed this treatment equally; in particular, individuals who have inherent value are not to be treated as if they were mere 'receptacles' of valuable experiences" (Regan 1983:277).[4] Singer says that sentient beings have interests, much like Regan's preference interests, in, at least, avoiding painful experiences and acquiring pleasurable ones. Possessing such interests entitles an individual to have those interests given due weight in a utilitarian calculation.

As many critics have noted, a great deal hinges on the lowest common denominator argument, an argument that appeals to the rationalist's penchant for parsimony and logical consistency. It insists that we choose an essential—that is, a necessary and sufficient—criterion of moral considerableness and that we apply it consistently to bring a vast array of both human and nonhumans equally into the moral fold. Failure to give animals the moral consideration they are due is "speciesist," a moral wrong similar to racism and sexism. To paraphrase Singer, speciesism is an irrational bias toward members of one's own species and against members of other species (Singer 1977:7).

According to Singer, a utilitarian calculation of both the animal and human pleasures and sufferings that result from such practices as flesh eating, product testing, biomedical research and education, and recreational hunting will in the vast majority of cases weigh in favor of the animals. According to Regan, these various practices violate an animal's right to respectful treatment, that is, we do not treat them in ways consistent with the recognition of their equal possession of inherent value. Instead, we treat them as receptacles of intrinsic value (e.g., pleasure), lacking any value of their own.

II

Singer's and Regan's arguments are recognizable offshoots of what some feminists, following Carol Gilligan's (1982) analysis, call the "justice tradition" in moral and political philosophy.[5] Here, I will focus on how such theories misrepresent our moral relations with animals rather than with other human beings.

1. Essentialism

Singer and Regan, like their mentors the utilitarians and Kant, respectively, have an "essentialist" view of the moral worth of both human beings and animals. This means that they propose a single capacity—the possession of interests—for being owed moral consideration. It is clear that they believe this condition is a sufficient one for being owed such consideration. And while they do not say specifically that possessing such interests is *necessary*, Singer and Regan *treat* the possession of preference interests as a necessary condition. For example, the lowest common denominator argument, which is central to their respective attempts to bring animals into the moral fold equally with human beings, is sound only if possessing interests is treated as necessary. Both writers say that those who do not possess interests are, at best, problematic. And both Singer and Regan condone sacrificing those without interests for the sake of those who do possess them.[6]

Essentialism is objectionable for a number of reasons. First, it renders inessential and unimportant certain relationships—familial relationships or friendships, for example—that do seem essential and important to many of the rest of us (Francis and Norman 1978). Second, as some feminist writers have noted, essentialism strips an individual of his or her "specific history, identity, and affective-emotional constitution" (Walker 1989:18). Specifically, animal rights theories reduce individuals to that atomistic bundle of interests that the justice tradition recognizes as the basis for moral considerableness. In effect, animals are represented as beings with the *kind of capacity* that human beings most fully possess and deem valuable for living a full *human* life.

Several ecofeminists, including Marti Kheel (chapter 1, this volume), Jim Cheney (1987), and Karen Warren (1990), have noted something very much like essentialism, or at least a certain arrogance underlying essentialism, in the environmental ethics literature, especially among deep ecologists.[7] Both Kheel and Warren show how such arrogance leads to hierarchical and dualistic thinking. Jim Cheney agrees with Ariel Kay Salleh, who claims that, as Cheney puts it, attempts by deep ecologists "to overcome human (really masculine) alienation from nature fail in the end because they are unable to overcome a masculine sense of the self and the kinds of ethical theory that go along with this sense of self" (Cheney 1987:121). I agree with Cheney, who points out that some deep ecologists fail to recognize and respect the integrity of the "other," of animals and nonsentient nature, when they describe their relationship to nature in terms of nature being a part of *them*, when they merely expand "the self to *include* that in relationship to which it feels alienated" (Cheney 1987:121). Cheney describes this metaphorically as a "megalomaniacal pond sucking up all the water of the world and becoming itself an ocean" (Cheney 1987:124).

In contrast to this "megalomaniacal" view, as Karen Warren discusses her first rock-climbing experiences she compares a potentially "arrogant" relationship with the rock—as invasive, as conqueror, as coercive—with a climber's "loving" relationship. She says of the latter:

> One recognizes the rock as something very different, something perhaps totally indifferent to one's own presence, and finds in that difference joyous occasion for celebration. One knows "the boundary of the self," where the self—the "I," the climber—leaves off and the rock begins. There is no fusion of two into one, but a complement of two entities *acknowledged* as separate, different, independent, yet *in relationship*; they are in relationship *if only* because the loving eye is perceiving it, responding to it, noticing it, attending to it. (Warren 1990:137)

Singer and Regan extend the moral community to include animals on the basis of sameness. They do not acknowledge, much less celebrate, differences between humans and other animals. This sort of self-centric importance, this assimilation of the other into the sameness of self, the "fusion of two into one" and the "erasure of difference," as Warren puts it, is central to the concept of arrogance that Marilyn Frye (1983) and Iris Murdoch (1970) have previously articulated.

Warren's loving attention to the rock's difference, independence, indifference did not result in her antipathy or moral apathy with regard to the rock. Instead, she says, "I felt an overwhelming sense of gratitude for what it offered me—a chance to know myself and the rock differently, to appreciate unforeseen miracles like the tiny flowers growing in the even tinier cracks in the rock's surface, and to come to know a sense of *being in relationship* with the natural environment. . . . I felt myself *caring* for this rock" (Warren 1990:135).

There is no reason why animals' differences, independence, indifference cannot be grounds for caring, for relationships characterized by such ethically significant attitudes as respect, gratitude, compassion, fellow or sisterly feeling, and wonder. Such animal ethologists as Jane Goodall (1971) have practiced for decades what Warren (1990), who is indebted to Marilyn Frye (1983), calls "loving attention." Goodall and other women (some of them feminist) scientists have suggested that such an attitude and its practice are not only appropriate moral attitudes with regard to the subjects they are studying but an epistemologically fruitful one as well (e.g., see Keller 1983).

Both Warren and Kheel note how arrogant essentialism re-creates moral hierarchies and dualistic thinking in ways that "establish inferiority and subordination" (Warren 1990:129).[8] Marti Kheel puts the point like this: "Ironically, although many of these writers feel that they are arguing against notions of hierarchy, the vast majority simply remove one set of hierarchies only to establish another. Thus, many writers on the subject of animal liberation may raise the status of animals to a level that warrants our moral concern only to exclude other parts of nature, such as plants and trees" (chapter 1, this volume:43). And there is even a pecking order among those in the upper echelons (among those who possess interests) of the hierarchy. Singer and Regan say that in dire cases, when we must choose between animal and human life, the life of the human, because it has more valuable potential experiences, takes priority.[9]

Central to an ecofeminist analysis of patriarchy is the claim that such value hierarchies, which categorize women, animals, and nonsentient nature on the same devalued side of the dualism, serve to oppress women along with nature in a vast array of similar ways.[10] Unfortunately, like many of the deep and certainly the "shallow" ecologists, Singer's and Regan's analyses do not cut deeply enough into our culture's objectionable use of these dualistic hierarchies. In fact, their "liberation" theories only perpetuate such thinking.

2. CONTEXT AND PRINCIPLES

A second feature of the justice tradition that has received attention is the propensity among those working in that tradition to characterize moral situations generally and abstractly and at the expense of contextual detail. What is lost in this kind of characterization of moral life or of a moral dilemma are historical, social, economic, familial, and other details that seem crucial to an assessment of a situation, a decision, or a character. Singer and Regan give us such delimited descriptions, and these descriptions allow them to formulate general, prescriptive principles that are applicable to similarly and superficially described situations. The use of such principles is a third feature of the Singer–Regan approach that I discuss.

As noted in section I, for Singer and Regan the animal research issue and the vegetarian issue are described similarly as situations in which animals' interests, given the strict and impartial consideration they are due, override human interests in eating them or in using them as experimental subjects. And the reasons our desires are overridden—because animals' desires are stronger or their rights given priority by an adjudicatory principle of justice that we have all decided on—should be recognized as good reasons by anyone capable of following a logical inference.

At least since Gilligan, a central task of feminist moral criticism has been to assess the role, proper status, and nature of principles in moral life. Some ecofeminists have raised similar questions about principles in reviewing work by deep ecologists and in deciding whether there is a place for principles in their own theories.[11] It is often said that general principles are too legalistic and abstract to be helpful in resolving unique, highly context-laden, nongeneralizable situations and that a "principled morality" leaves no room for virtue and affection.[12] While these writers do not eschew the use of principles entirely, they do reject any morality that worships principles while neglecting such things as virtue or the affections. I agree with these writers, and I object to the way rights and utilitarian principles are often presented to us in classrooms, textbooks, and scholarly books and articles as our only "reasonable" options. This is objectionable because if these are our only options, then we must sometimes disregard what our imaginations or hearts or the simple facts are telling us, in order to articulate situations, some of them very uncooperative, in a way that fits these principles and their corresponding conceptual

frameworks. Singer's and Regan's awkward attempts to articulate interspecies moral relations using these standard theories and conceptual
frameworks exemplify this point.

What principles we articulate and ultimately choose to rely on are relevant to a very complex web of "beliefs, feelings, modes of expression, circumstances and more, arranged in characteristic ways and often spread
out over time" (Walker 1989:18). In an essay on bioregional narrative, Jim
Cheney suggests that we "extend these notions of context and narrative
outward so as to include not just the human community, but also the
land, one's community in a larger sense." Moreover, "for a genuinely contextualist ethic to include the land . . . the land must *speak* to us; we must
stand in *relation* to it; it must *define* us, and we it" (Cheney 1989:128–29).
I should think that this concept of "the land" would entail sentient nature.
And because we not only are *defined by* but also *define* this relationship—
not in terms of static and essentialist necessary and sufficient conditions
but in contextually rich and evolving terms—we will have opportunities
to evaluate and alter aspects of the relationship when certain features of it
(our arrogance and our waste, for example) are brought forcefully to our
attention, and we may well want to recommend some of these alternatives universally.

Recently, Karen Warren articulated eight "boundary conditions"—necessary conditions that "delimit the territory of a piece without dictating what
the interior . . . looks like"—of any feminist ethic and of any ecofeminist
ethic. One of those conditions states that a feminist ethic or an ecofeminist
ethic cannot be naturist—that is, cannot condone the oppressive domination of sentient and nonsentient nature—or contribute to any other "'-ism'
which presupposes and advances a logic of domination." Warren defines
a "logic of domination" as "a structure of argumentation which leads to a
justification of subordination" (Warren 1990:128). This "logic" entails a
value system that designates "subordinates" and their "inferior" characteristics or capacities. A second condition holds that any theory should be
fluid, in process, changing over time, and emerging out of "concrete and
alternative descriptions of ethical situations." A third requires that feminist ethics must give a place to "values typically unnoticed, underplayed,
or misrepresented in traditional ethics" and will do so while recognizing a
role for traditional values (Warren 1990:139–40).

These boundary conditions are also relevant to any critique of the animal rights literature and to attempts to reconceptualize our moral relationships with and obligations to the animals with whom Singer and Regan

are concerned. I have already discussed how Singer and Regan retain an unfortunate "logic of domination" in their respective theories. Their atemporal, abstract, and acontextual characterizations of issues, of the values at stake, and of appropriate resolutions grossly oversimplify some of these highly complex issues, including, as I show in section III, the research one. Such characterizations also oversimplify our actual and potential relationships with and responses to animals, depriving us of opportunities to respond to and make responsible choices about the enormous cost to other sentient life of such intimate and routine practices involving, for example, what we eat, the bath soap and shampoo that we use, and the pills that we take for a headache or to prevent a pregnancy.

3. THE AFFECTIONS

Peter Singer says that he does not "love" animals, that he has "argued" his case, "appealing to reason rather than to emotion or sentiment . . . because reason is more universal and more compelling in its appeal" (Singer 1977:255). Regan says that we should make "a concerted effort not to indulge our emotions or parade our sentiments. And that requires making a sustained commitment to rational inquiry" (Regan 1983:xii).

A fair number of critics, after and long before Carol Gilligan, have said that such faith in the rational and universal force of principles at the expense of our emotional responses is naive, based on an insensitivity to our actual moral psychology and a Western and perhaps masculinist contempt for our emotions, which are considered "womanish." Critics have shown how this rationalist ideal fails to account for what motivates us in many of our personal relations, where love, or friendship, or the affections, for example, often are, and should be, a (or the) predominant motive.[13] Singer and Regan follow the tradition that polarizes reason and the emotions and that privileges reason when the two conflict.

There is no pat formula for deciding when our affective responses have a place, or how much weight they should have, in resolving dilemmas affecting either personal or public relations. For the most part, deciding when and to what extent our affective responses are appropriate and helpful involves entering into a particular narrative. Probably there are situations, even involving personal relations, that call for the use of some maxim that is impartial and dispassioned. Apportioning family goods, services, or energy among rivaling children might be an example. And certainly we sometimes do and should be allowed to respond affectively to strangers.

We feel what might be an empathetic sympathy and embarrassment when we witness, for example, someone else's public humilation or a parent pleading on television for the return of a missing child.

Marti Kheel (chapter 1, this volume) has said that the argument Singer and Regan make from "marginal cases" relies on an emotional appeal. The argument holds that we either revoke the moral standing of "defective" human beings or else grant standing to those animals that are intellectually and emotionally on par with these humans. Since we have some very strong feelings or intuitions about the humans the argument is persuasive: we are willing to accord moral status to animals rather than deny it to the humans.

What Kheel advocates, along with Mary Midgley, Sara Ruddick, and Robin Morgan, is what Morgan calls a *"unified sensibility,"* or a recognition of the "fusion of feeling and thought" as characteristic of moral life (chapter 1, this volume:48). Karen Warren (1990) is advocating something similar when she says that an ecofeminist ethic will emerge out of individuals' concrete relationships and experiences and will recognize a variety of affective responses along with formal and abstract principles, all in their appropriate contexts.

Kheel and Warren suggest that whenever possible we must "experience directly the full impact of our moral decisions," especially of those decisions that we make daily and so casually and that have such an enormous impact on the rest of sentient life (chapter 1, this volume:49). This implies that those individuals who believe that flesh eating is morally permissible or even morally neutral should visit chickens who are confined along with three to six other chickens in a cage the size of a record album cover in a battery shed that holds up to 10,000 other chickens. They should see bobby calves tethered in veal sheds and cows on the killing floor and witness a sow's confinement in the "iron maiden."[14] Those who condone animal research and testing should request a tour of laboratories at the nearest research university. They should see the equipment—the surgical tables, restraining chairs, "rape racks," and "guillotines"—and experience the smells and the sounds.[15]

Will these individuals still think and feel the same about such practices? I am not saying that moral disagreement will disappear when we expand the range of experiences or responses that enrich our moral lives. But I do agree with those who emphasize the importance of direct experience for making responsible choices *and* for articulating desperately needed new moral visions, particularly in animal and environmental ethics.

III

In this section I begin to give the research issue the kind of contextual attention that Singer and Regan fail to give it. This needs to be done before we can assess the role of abstract principles, including Singer's and Regan's principles, and of the affections in resolving the issue. In the course of recontextualizing the issue, I examine it holistically and explore several related ecofeminist themes.

I limit the focus of my discussion to the use of animals in biomedical research. I do *not* attempt to justify the use of animals in any such studies. In fact, I am sympathetic with Singer's and Regan's repugnance over using animals as research tools, even though I disagree with their arguments. What I have to say here has some special bearing on feminist critiques of androcentric science and on recent attempts to articulate "feminine" and especially feminist alternatives. If, as ecofeminists say, naturism is something that feminists should condemn and always avoid in their own work, then the use of 20 million research animals annually in this country deserves more attention in this feminist literature than it has received.[16]

The few ecofeminists who have written in any depth about animal research (Kheel, chapter 1, this volume; Collard 1988; Adams 1990) insist that we examine the issues contextually and holistically. Only then can we make knowledgeable and responsible decisions, in the rich sense of weighing facts, theoretical knowledge, and our affections. In this spirit, then, we should consider the many well-documented studies that demonstrate: (1) how animals are grossly overused and misused in research that is trivial, duplicative to the point of redundancy, badly designed, or that fails to use existing nonanimal alternatives or to develop them;[17] (2) how many researchers use species with more demanding psycho-social needs when those with less demanding needs will do; (3) how animals often do not serve as reliable models for human beings and how it can be very dangerous to extrapolate from results obtained from one species to another;[18] and (4) how federal and in-house regulations that are supposed to protect laboratory animals are grossly inadequate and how regulatory agencies are extremely lax in enforcing the few regulations that do exist.

In addition, as a variety of activists and ecofeminists have said, our society, including the medical establishment, needs to insist on such *proactive measures* as cleaning our air, water, soil, and the poisons from our grocery shelves if we are serious about our physical and psychological well-being. Americans see precious little of that from the National Institutes of Health, the world's largest funder of *reactive* animal research, or from the American Medical Association. And of course we are unlikely to see a preventative emphasis from these institutions, as feminists writing about science (e.g., Harding 1986), women's health care (e.g., Corea 1988), and technology (e.g., Merchant 1980; Collard 1988) have pointed out. As Collard puts it, these institutions use a strategy "typical of patriarchal control . . . whereby the integrity of matter (living and nonliving) is broken, artificially restored/recombined, and marketed in such a way (cure, improvement, etc.) as to elicit gratitude" (Collard 1988:79). Animal research is a part of the strategy, and animals are among its subjects, along with women, whose natural lives have been "enhanced" by these "helping" institutions in everything from our pregnancies to our breast size.

These mostly methodological considerations certainly are not lost on Singer and Regan, but they are superfluous to what Regan calls the "moral heart of the matter" (Regan 1983:384): the conflict between human and animal interests and our unjustified willingness to sacrifice the latter for the former. But for many thoughtful people the question of *whether* animals should be used in research is more pertinently one of *when* they should be used and *how* they will be treated, just as, to make some very imperfect comparisons, for many people the question of whether euthanasia is morally permissible is also a question of how and when it is performed, and for some, the question of "just" war is not so much a question of whether it is justifiable but of how and when. I am not claiming here that these three practices—euthanasia, "just" war, and animal research—are analogous; they are, in fact, significantly disanalogous. Instead, my point is that many people will consider any characterization of these issues that leaves out information about methodology and other contextual features to be decontextualized to the point of being misleading, even irrelevant.

How, exactly, do Singer and Regan themselves resolve this "moral heart of the matter"? In his chapter on research Regan advocates the total abolition of the use of animals in research, even granting, as he puts it, "that we face greater prima facie harm than laboratory animals presently endure if future harmful research on these animals is stopped, and even granting that the number of humans and other animals who stand to benefit from allowing this practice to continue exceeds the number of animals used in it" (Regan 1983:389).

But in his discussion of biomedical research, Regan also makes a distinction between "exceptional" sacrifice and "routine" or "institutionalized" sacrifice of animal life. And he says that any judgments we make about the former (lifeboat cases, for example) are not transferable to the latter (the routine and prevalent use of animals in research, for example); but he does *not* condemn the former, nonroutine sacrifice. This is a suggestive but much underdeveloped point. If Regan is saying that the nonroutine use of some animals might be justified in desperate times in extreme situations, then we will most certainly have to muck around in the contextual particulars to sort these cases out. Most of all, we will want to know what constitutes "nonroutine" use, that is, how many animals may be used with what frequency and for what. And I expect that there will be no pat formula for deciding this, that we will have to sort this out on a case-by-case basis.

Singer resorts to an argument that appears frequently in the literature. I call it the onus argument. His version of it follows:

> So whenever an experimenter claims that his experiment is important enough to justify the use of an animal, we should ask him whether he would be prepared to use a retarded human at a similar mental level to the animal he is planning to use. (Singer 1977:67)

Singer does *not* advocate using human beings as research subjects. He is making a point about consistency: an experimenter cannot consistently condone the use of an animal while condemning the use of a human being when each will suffer roughly the same. Singer is basically correct when he says that the research community bears the onus of justifying its use of animals, even when it is clear that some significant benefits could come of it. But there is also an onus on the rights community to justify their abolitionist stance, to justify *not* using animals, especially when we stand to lose some significant future benefits. Singer's response to that onus is to lead us into a utilitarian impasse. Arguing that there are no defensible grounds on which to base a choice does not make the problem go away. Oddly, Singer considers this impasse a kind of victory. I think that he has reached something more like a dead end, that this impasse is an indication that utilitarianism, at least in itself, is unable to resolve this problem. Utilitarianism might even *be* the problem; an impartial or misleading characterization of an issue can make it seem obdurate, unresolvable.

Recently, ecofeminist Ynestra King (1987) took to task a certain "Malthusian wing" of deep ecologists for their shallow analyses of the political and social causes of such environmental problems as global over-population and for the impracticality and bureaucratic heartlessness of their proposed solutions. I feel a similar frustration with the shallow utilitarian analysis of the research issue that leads to Singer's impasse, with the impracticality of the impasse itself as some sort of proposed resolution, and with Singer's and Regan's assumptions that our allegiance to principled demands will and should cut cleanly through any preexisting emotional or other bonds we might have to members of our own species, community, friends, family, or lovers who may suffer as a result of Singer's and Regan's recommendations.[19] My point is *not* to justify any and all of these bonds as automatic trumps against animals' sufferings. Rather than say that these bonds should count for nothing (as the animal rights literature suggests) or that they count for everything (as the research community suggests), I have been trying to show all along that there are numerous relevant issues that are neglected by both sides, including this one, and there may well be more than just two sides.

The following are among some of the more significant issues neglected by mainstream writers on animal research. I only gesture at them here and hope that they receive more attention in the future. First, can we justify sacrificing beings who are extremely vulnerable to the whims and powers of human beings? How do we justify sacrificing beings who are "innocent," that is, who are neither actually nor potentially culpable or even capable of any wrongdoing? We all seem to recognize some fairly stringent moral prohibitions against taking advantage of the innocent and the vulnerable, *even* in cases of self-defense, even in lifeboat cases. In fact, taking such advantage is often seen as especially malign. Do animals fall outside the scope of this prohibition completely, and if so, why? If not, why not? And if sometimes, then when and why?

Andrée Collard (1988) suggests that along with the self-serving appropriation of animals for the ostensive purpose of advancing human health, there is also a familiar attitude that "might makes right" with regard to the capture, breeding, genetic engineering, use and disposal of research animals. Every feminist knows that women have been and are affected by this form of arrogance in science, in the streets, in our own bedrooms and elsewhere. To condone such an attitude and practice in any context is to perpetuate it in all. Ynestra King puts this basic ecofeminist thesis forcefully when she says that "the hatred of women and the hatred of nature are intimately connected and mutually reinforcing" (King 1989:18).

Furthermore, one popular nineteenth-century antivivisectionist argument, advanced by George Bernard Shaw, among others, held that the appropriation of unwilling and unwitting subjects for research that is painful and deadly erodes any aspirations or pretensions we might have about living in a "civilized" society, about possessing a "civilized" character. Ecofeminists have made similar points with regard to the arrogant and violent appropriation of non-human nature and women, particularly by American and Anglo-European cultures. Collard says that we live in a society "dominated by the 'ideology of cultural sadism,'" one in which "violent acts are neutralized by virtue of being so common. In the case of animal experimentation, these acts are admired (published and replicated) and the actors honored (tenured and funded)" (Collard 1988:68). The same culture that at best is apathetic about and at worst valorizes the deaths of 20 million research animals in U.S. laboratories annually also allowed the country's 750,000 *reported* rapes during the 1980s, the murder of 50,000 women by their male partners, and the hospitalization of more women from beatings by their male partners than from auto accidents during that decade.[20] All this seems at least prima facie evidence that acts of violence against women have been similarly neutralized.

As a final consideration, we might also examine the affective schizophrenia of a country that spends more money than any other in the world on its "pets," while spending more than any other on animal research, much of it involving the use of cats and dogs, hamsters and bunnies. How and why do we circumscribe our collective and individual imaginations in this manner? Certainly whatever is going on here is complicated and beyond the scope of this paper. But our reasons for such seemingly arbitrary circumscription must include such obvious things as consumer convenience and the research and testing industry's secrecy about and, more recently, outright denial of the violence of so-called routine testing and research. Do we want to condone whatever sophisticated emotional bracketing is at work here? I should hope not. To do so is to give up any significant account of collective and individual moral responsibility regarding, as I have said before, the impact on the rest of sentient life of some of our most routine and intimate practices (e.g., what we eat) and consumer purchases (e.g., the dish soap we buy).

Surely we will not and probably cannot have the same affections or degrees of affection for the cat or dog in the laboratory that we have for the animals in our households, nor can we have the same feeling for a stranger's lost or abused child that we would have for our own child in a similar situation. These special ties *do* bind, and I am not recommending that we bracket them for the sake of blind impartiality, at least not always. While we cannot feel or care the *same* for every human being or animal, the feeling or caring that we do have for our immediate companions should extend some, via imagination and empathy, to our feeling for, our caring about, the plight of more extended others. And for those who have a rich enough moral imagination, this regard will cross species boundaries. Someone who has cared about a rock or a tree or a dog or a cat may well care about what happens to, and particularly about the destruction of, other rocks, trees, cats, and dogs. Such particular relationships can and should enhance one's capacity to empathize, "feel with," and act on behalf of others.

I am not saying that everyone who cares about laboratory animals will condemn experimentation. I am saying that we will at least cease to condone the practice so cavalierly. We will find that there are certain elements of moral tragedy in having to make some choices despite the daunting complexity of these situations, despite having few, if any, principles or precedents to guide us, despite having little or no assurance that we have chosen rightly. And regardless of how we choose, we may have to live with, as some have recently put it, irresolute, nagging "moral remainders."[21]

IV

I am convinced that as feminist theorists and practitioners we must address the interconnecting dominations of women, animals, and non-sentient nature, as ecofeminists insist, along with other social dominations, in order to understand sufficiently and correct any one and all of them. Ecofeminist analyses include those facets of patriarchal domination that are often neglected by other feminists, by environmental ethicists, *and* by animal rights proponents. I realize that I have made very few recommendations about when, if ever, we may use animals in research, although I have made my general antipathy toward such use clear. Nonetheless, and this may be obvious, I still feel some ambivalence over this issue, a gut sense that my antipathy is appropriate but that its grounds are not yet well enough articulated. I hope to inspire other feminist voices to help articulate these grounds and to do so in a way that avoids simplistic characterizations in terms of daughters and dogs.

ACKNOWLEDGMENTS

Many thanks to the *Hypatia* referees, Tony Crunk, and especially Karen Warren for their comments on an earlier version of this paper. I also gratefully acknowledge Cora Diamond's influence on my thinking about these issues.

NOTES

1. Regan (1983:400) cites this passage from Mill.

2. Diamond (1978) also uses the term "Singer–Regan approach." My characterization of the approach shares certain features with hers, but our characterizations are not the same.

3. I use the popular term "animal rights" to refer to political and philosophical debates over the moral status of mostly domestic, agricultural, and laboratory animals. I do not argue anywhere that animals have moral or legal rights.

4. Regan includes mammalian animals, one year and older, who are not psychologically impaired under the jurisdiction of this principle because, he says, we can be assured that these animals have preference interests. He also says that his is a "minimal" case, which means that he does not rule out the possibility of nonmammals and of mammals younger than one year having preference interests.

5. See, especially, Kittay and Meyers (1987).

6. For example, Singer (1979) says that we may eat "humanely" raised and slaughtered chickens and ducks because, he claims, they probably have no interests in their future; in fact, they probably have no notion of a "future" whatsoever, he says. Regan (1983), who wants to give ducks and chickens and other nonmammals, as well as mammals younger than one year, the "benefit of the doubt," does say that it is permissible to sacrifice fetal mammals and nonmammals in their early stages of development because they do not possess interests.

7. Deep ecologists eschew "shallow" ecologists' anthropocentric philosophies. A major tenet of the deep ecology movement is, as Arne Naess puts it, "the well-being of nonhuman life on Earth has a value in itself. This value is independent of any instrumental usefulness for limited human purposes" (Naess 1984:266; see also Naess 1973).

8. "The problem is not simply *that* value-hierarchical thinking and value dualisms are used, but *the way* each has been used *in oppressive conceptual frameworks* to establish inferiority and to justify subordination" (Warren 1990:128–29).

9. Both Singer (1977:21–22) and Regan (1983:324) make a distinction between the value of a "normal" human life and that of an animal, and each say the human life is the more valuable.

10. See Griffin (1978) and Adams (1990).

11. See Cheney (1987, 1989) and Warren (1990).

12. See, especially, Murdoch (1970), Gilligan (1982), Noddings (1984), and Ruddick (1980).

13. See Gilligan (1982) and Noddings (1984).

14. The "iron maiden" is used to confine a sow's movements after she delivers her litter. This is manufacturers' and breeders' slang for this device.

15. A "rape rack" immobilizes primates as they are impregnated (Benney 1983).

16. The U.S. Department of Agriculture and researchers currently say that 20 million animals are used annually for research in the United States. This figure may well be low because institutions are not required to report the use of mice and rats (80% of the animals used in research), and farm animals. Animal rights groups put the annual figure at 40 to 60 million.

17. Standards in the Animal Welfare Act that are supposed to define and control "trivial" experimentation and minimize redundancy are enforced by an institution's Animal Care and Use Committee, an in-house committee which generally consists of researchers and individuals friendly to animal research. Decisions about the numbers and types of animals used in an experiment and about whether to withhold pain medication are also left to the discretion of this in-house committee. I highly recommend the studies by the United Action for Animals, 205 East Forty-second Street, New York, N.Y. 10017, on duplication and redundancy.

18. Thalidomide was tested on several nonhuman animal species before being given to human beings. Insulin deforms mice and rabbits. Penicillin is toxic to guinea pigs.

19. Midgley (1983) has made a very similar point.

20. These figures are cited in "Hate Crimes Bill Excludes Women," *off our backs* 20, no. 6 (1990).

21. "'Moral remainders' refers to some genuine moral demands which, because their fulfillment conflicted with other genuine moral demands, are 'left over' in episodes of moral choice, and yet are not nullified" (Walker 1989:21).

References

Adams, Carol J. 1990. *The Sexual Politics of Meat: A Feminist Vegetarian Critical Theory*. New York: Continuum.

Benney, Norma. 1983. "All of One Flesh: The Rights of Animals." In *Reclaim the Earth: Women Speak Out for Life on Earth*, ed. Léonie Caldecott and Stephanie Leland, 141–50. London: Women's Press.

Cheney, Jim. 1987. "Ecofeminism and Deep Ecology." *Environmental Ethics* 9, no. 2:115–45.

——. 1989. "Postmodern Environmental Ethics: Ethics as Bioregional Narrative." *Environmental Ethics* 11, no. 2:117–34.

Collard, Andrée, with Joyce Contrucci. 1988. *Rape of the Wild: Man's Violence Against Animals and the Earth*. Bloomington: Indiana University Press.

Corea, Gena. 1988. *The Mother Machine: Reproductive Technologies from Artificial Insemination to Artificial Wombs*. London: Women's Press.

Diamond, Cora. 1978. "Eating Meat and Eating People." *Philosophy* 53:465–79.

Francis, Leslie Pickering, and Richard Norman. 1978. "Some Animals Are More Equal than Others." *Philosophy* 53:507–27.

Frey, R. G. 1980. *Interests and Rights*. Oxford: Clarendon Press.

Frye, Marilyn. 1983. "Arrogance and Love." In *The Politics of Reality*. Freedom, Calif.: Crossing Press.

Gilligan, Carol. 1982. *In a Different Voice: Psychological Theory and Women's Development*. Cambridge, Mass.: Harvard University Press.

Goodall, Jane. 1971. *In the Shadow of Man*. Boston: Houghton Mifflin.

Griffin, Susan. 1978. *Woman and Nature: The Roaring Inside Her*. New York: Harper & Row.

Harding, Sandra. 1986. *The Science Question in Feminism*. Ithaca, N.Y.: Cornell University Press.

Keller, Evelyn Fox. 1983. *A Feeling for the Organism: The Life and Work of Barbara McClintock*. New York: Freeman.

King, Ynestra. 1987. "What Is Ecofeminism?" *The Nation*, 12 December.

——. 1989. "The Ecology of Feminism and the Feminism of Ecology." In *Healing the Wounds: The Promise of Ecofeminism*, ed. Judith Plant, 18–28. Santa Cruz: New Society.

Kittay, Eva Feder, and Diana T. Meyers, eds. 1987. *Introduction to Women and Moral Theory*. Totowa, N.J.: Rowman & Littlefield.

Merchant, Carolyn. 1980. *The Death of Nature: Women, Ecology and the Scientific Revolution*. San Francisco: Harper & Row.

Midgley, Mary. 1983. *Animals and Why They Matter*. Athens: University of Georgia Press.

Murdoch, Iris. 1970. *The Sovereignty of Good*. London: Routledge and Kegan Paul.

Naess, Arne. 1973. "The Shallow and the Deep, Long-range Ecology Movement: A Summary." *Inquiry* 16:95–100.

——. 1984. "A Defense of the Deep Ecology Movement." *Environmental Ethics* 6, no. 3:265–70.

Noddings, Nel. 1984. *Caring: A Feminine Approach to Ethics and Moral Education.* Berkeley: University of California Press.

Regan, Tom. 1983. *The Case for Animal Rights.* Berkeley: University of California Press.

Ruddick, Sara. 1980. "Maternal Thinking." *Feminist Studies* 6, no. 2:342–67.

Singer, Peter. 1977. *Animal Liberation.* New York: Avon Books.

——. 1979. *Practical Ethics.* Cambridge: Cambridge University Press.

Walker, Margaret. 1989. "Moral Understandings: Alternative 'Epistemology' for a Feminist Ethics." *Hypatia: A Journal of Feminist Philosophy* 4, no. 2:15–28.

Warren, Karen. 1990. "The Power and Promise of Ecological Feminism." *Environmental Ethics* 12, no. 1:125–46.

☙

CHAPTER 5

Justice, Caring, and Animal Liberation

BRIAN LUKE

Carol Gilligan has described justice and caring as two distinct moral frameworks or orientations to ethical concerns.[1] The *justice* framework is characterized by abstraction, the application of general rules of conduct, an emphasis on restraining aggression, and a concern for consistency and the fair resolution of conflicting claims and interests. The *caring* framework, on the other hand, is characterized by its focus on the concrete and particular, its emphasis on the maintenance and extension of connection, and by its concern for responsiveness and the satisfaction of needs. Animal liberation is often framed as a justice issue, though, I will suggest, it may more appropriately be understood in terms of caring.

By *animal liberation* I mean opposition to institutions of animal exploitation such as vivisection, hunting, and animal farming. Two prominent philosophical defenders of animal liberation are Tom Regan and Peter Singer. Both work exclusively within the justice framework, presenting animal liberation as a matter of consistency and fair treatment, rather than

This chapter was first published in *Between the Species* 1992, vol. 8, no. 2. © 1992 John Stockwell. Expanded for Josephine Donovan and Carol J. Adams, eds., *Beyond Animal Rights* (New York: Continuum, 1996). Published by permission of the author.

in terms of responsiveness and the satisfaction of needs. We can start to see how the justice approach is ill-suited for animal liberation by considering the arguments of Regan and Singer.

Regan attempts to move the reader from a commitment to the respectful treatment of humans to a like commitment to the respectful treatment of normal adult mammals.[2] Regan points out that we do not in general think it is justifiable to harm one human to benefit others—we would object, for example, to killing a healthy man against his will in order to use his organs to save three sick persons. We do, however, think it appropriate to harm one animal to benefit other animals, human or otherwise; at least this is the way that vivisection, hunting, and animal farming are usually justified.

Regan argues that we are being inconsistent in treating humans and other mammals differently in this respect. The notion of inconsistency here is not self-contradiction but contradiction with the formal principles of justice, according to which like individuals should be treated alike. Now we protect humans against being vivisected, farmed, or hunted, presumably because such treatment would harm them through the infliction of pain and death. But Regan has shown in the first three chapters of his book that pain and death are also harms to normal adult mammals. So these animals are just as deserving of protection from vivisection, farming, and hunting as are humans. Because both humans and other mammals are harmed by pain and death, the two groups are relevantly similar, and we are inconsistent to treat them so differently.

The flaw in this argument I wish to emphasize is the move from same kinds of harms to relevant similarity. Most of us would admit that pain and death are harms for both humans and other animals. But this by itself does not show that humans and other animals are relevantly similar with respect to assessing the moral status of these common harms. Regan allows that certain capacities may be unique to humans, and it is conceivable that the presence of uniquely human capacities in an individual is relevant to the justifiability of harming that individual, even when the type of harm in question is one that can be imposed on nonhumans. In fact, according to Kantian theories, only rational individuals can be directly wronged. A Kantian could hold that killing is a harm both to humans and other animals, but that the wrongness of the harm arises only from its impingement upon the victim's rationality. Thus, killing a rational human would require special justification not needed for killing a nonrational animal, even though both are harmed by being killed.

I am not saying that I agree with Kantianism or with the idea that there are uniquely human capacities. I am only saying that as long as Regan's readers are willing to embrace these theories, they can without inconsistency reject Regan's move from "death and pain are harms for both humans and other animals" to "killing and inflicting pain require the same justification for both humans and other animals." Since this move is crucial to his argument as a whole, they can consistently reject Regan's case for animals' rights.[3]

Essentially the same type of maneuver allows rejection of Singer's argument for animal liberation. Like Regan, Singer attempts to move the reader, through considerations of consistency, from commitments concerning the appropriate treatment of humans to similar commitments concerning the appropriate treatment of animals.[4] Singer starts not with respect for humans but with opposition to racism and sexism. Singer argues that anyone who opposes racism and sexism does so on the basis of a principle of equal consideration, according to which we must give equal consideration to the interests of all people, regardless of their race or sex. But animals, at least all those capable of feeling pleasure or pain, have interests, so there is no reason, according to Singer, why they should be excluded from the scope of this principle of equal consideration. But animal farming and vivisection, Singer maintains, are considered acceptable practices only because we tend to give the interests of nonhumans much less consideration than the similar interests of humans. This devaluation of interests solely on the basis of species Singer calls *speciesism*, and he thinks his argument shows that we are inconsistent to oppose sexism and racism but not speciesism.

As with Regan, however, anyone willing to accept a Kantian view can reject Singer's entire argument without inconsistency. Singer presumes that opposition to sexism and racism must be based on the principle of equal consideration of interests. One could maintain, however, that sexism and racism are objectionable because they are disrespectful of the rationality of members of the oppressed races and sex. One could then consistently exclude nonhumans from moral consideration by holding that they lack the rational capacities of humans.

Again I emphasize that I am not endorsing Kantianism here. I am just showing that Regan's and Singer's arguments fail on their own terms. Both writers insist that they are relying on reason alone, and not emotion, to establish their animal liberationist conclusions. But the crucial step in their arguments, that humans and other animals are relevantly similar, cannot be established by reason alone.

Regan and Singer have the following response for Kantian rebuttals of their arguments.[5] Taking rationality as a necessary condition for moral considerability does give one permission to harm animals (if rationality is defined narrowly enough). But it also gives permission to harm many nonrational humans, such as infants, mentally retarded individuals, and people with brain damage or in comas. Thus, a commitment to protect these so-called marginal cases of humanity entails the rejection of Kantianism and the adoption of some more inclusive criterion of considerability. But any criterion broad enough to include marginal humans (for example, sentience or subjectivity) will also include nonhuman animals and thus support animal liberation.

This line of thought, called *the argument from marginal cases*, is no more successful than Regan's and Singer's main arguments in proving that animals have rights. On the one hand, the argument may be circumvented simply by giving up the commitment to protect marginal humans. R. G. Frey does this. He takes the marginal cases argument to present a dilemma: either oppose animal vivisection or condone the vivisection of marginal humans.[6] He then reasons:

> Very few people indeed would look in the face the benefits which medical research in particular has conferred upon us, benefits which on the whole have most certainly involved vivisection. . . . Therefore, we may find ourselves unable to make the choice in favour of antivivisectionism. . . . Accordingly, we are left with human experiments. I think this is how I would choose, not with great glee and rejoicing, and with great reluctance; but if this is the price we must pay to hold the appeal to benefit and to enjoy the benefits which that appeal licenses, then we must, I think, pay it.[7]

Frey forgets that "we" academics, presumably (hopefully?) escaping classification as marginal, would not be the ones to pay the real price for a choice in favor of vivisection.

Even those of us not quite able to match Frey's noble sacrifice of other humans to vivisection can still consistently evade the marginal cases argument, if we are so inclined. Suppose we "justify" the vivisection of animals by reference to their supposed lack of rationality. And suppose we allow that some humans also lack this rationality. This does not imply that we *must* vivisect marginal humans, only that we *may*. Thus, the protection of marginal humans could be made consistent with the vivisection of animals possessing comparable degrees of rationality by interpreting that protection as supererogatory. According to this line of thought we may vivisect marginal humans, because, like nonhuman animals, they lack a right to protection, but for nonbinding reasons we decide only to vivisect the nonhuman animals. This stratagem is employed by Bonnie Steinbock:

> I am willing to admit that my horror at the thought of experiments being performed on severely mentally incapacitated human beings in cases in which I would find it justifiable and preferable to perform the same experiments on nonhuman animals (capable of similar suffering) may not be a moral emotion. But it is certainly not wrong of us to extend special care to members of our own species.[8]

So like their main arguments, Regan's and Singer's backup argument from marginal cases fails to show any unavoidable inconsistency in supporting the exploitation of animals in vivisection, hunting, and farming, while rejecting any similar exploitation of human. Animal liberation is not a matter of consistency.

As arguments, justice-based approaches to animal liberation fail. The justice orientation also fails to capture the moral outlooks of many in the animal liberation movement. Justice-oriented writers cast the issue as, fundamentally, a comparison between the treatment of humans and the treatment of other animals. According to Regan, we harm animals to benefit others, we do not do this to humans (generally speaking), but there is no relevant difference between humans and animals to justify the dissimilar treatment. Thus animals are treated unfairly by comparison to the treatment of humans. For Singer, the comparative unfairness is in opposing sexism and racism but not opposing speciesism, when again there is no relevant difference between humans and other animals to support the distinction. For both Regan and Singer, and other writers within the justice framework, the basic moral judgment concerns the discrepancy between the treatment of humans and the treatment of other similar animals. What is called into question is the fairness, or what they more often refer to as the consistency, of a society that treats two relevantly similar groups of individuals in such totally different ways.

The emphasis on the consistency of the agent and the focus on comparing the treatment of humans and the treatment of other animals are quite distant from my motivations and those of others in the animal liberation movement. My opposition to the institutionalized exploitation of animals is not based on a *comparison* between human and animal treatment, but on a consideration of the abuse of the animals *in and of itself.* I respond directly to the needs and the plight of the animals used in hunting, farming, and vivisection. In objecting to these practices I am not comparing the treatment of humans and animals, and thinking "this is unfair because humans are protected from such usage." I am appalled by the abuses themselves—shooting, trapping, and poisoning; branding, castrating, forcibly impregnating, separating mother and young, tail docking, debeaking, confining, transporting in cattle cars, and slaughtering; burning, cutting, gassing, starving, asphyxiating, decapitating, decompressing, irradiating, electrocuting, freezing, crushing, paralyzing, amputating, excising organs, removing parts of the brain, socially isolating, inducing addiction, and imposing disease—these acts are repellant because of what they do to the animals. My moral condemnation of the acts arises directly from my sympathy for the animals, and is independent of the question of whether humans are protected from such abuse. To the extent that humans are also treated in these ways I object to that, too, but again, out of sympathy, and not considerations of fairness.

Let me give some examples of discourse that clearly show the sort of direct responsiveness I am talking about. A 1983 study on the psychology of slaughter contains quotes from college students who worked on a farm as part of their curriculum. One 19-year-old woman wrote:

> The first time I went into the slaughter room I had just haltered and pulled a steer into the waiting line. I could tell that the steer sensed what was going to happen to him. He was doing anything to get away. Then when I walked to the slaughter room I was amazed at the amount of blood. It was an awful feeling to look at that steer with its eyes open and his feet pointing up, so I had to look at the ceiling. Mr. —— told me to cut off the head with a saw. I couldn't do it so I left. I guess slaughtering affects me more than the usual person because I raised calves for 4-H at home and became quite attached to them—but I *don't* butcher them.[9]

A 19-year-old man wrote:

> It's pretty gross. I don't like having the dry heaves all day. Plus, I feel really bad for the cow. It's bad seeing a big animal turned into hamburger.[10]

The reactions described here are not comparative judgments of justice, such as "cutting off this steer's head is wrong because we don't do that to humans," but rather revulsion at bloodshed, pity for an animal struggling for his life, memories of animal friends, a sense of the loss and the waste of "a big animal turned into hamburger"—all elements of caring. Now these students do not identify themselves as animal liberationists, but the reactions they describe do not differ essentially from the reactions on which animal liberation is often based. Consider the following statements by people who do support animal liberation, either partially or completely:

> The production-line maintenance of animals . . . is without a doubt one of the darkest and most shameful chapters in human culture. If you have ever stood before a stable where animals are being fattened and have heard hundreds of calves bleating, if you can understand the calf's cry for help, then you will have had enough of those people who derive profit from it.
>
> I eat meat but rarely veal. . . . I could never bring myself to slaughter a cow. This is very difficult to do to any animal that one has taken care of for a long time.[11]

> Ninety percent of all pigs are now raised in indoor, near-dark, windowless confinement sheds. . . . I respond on an emotional level with horror at what each individual pig is subjected to and sympathize with each pig, whose extreme sociability is evidenced by these animals' increased popularity as pets. . . . As a lactating mother, I empathize with the sow whose reproductive freedoms have been denied and whose nursing experience seems so wretched. As a consumer and a vegetarian, I visualize this information when I witness people buying or eating "ham," "bacon," or "sausage."[12]

> I was one morning, while studying alone in the Natural History Museum, suddenly disturbed by a frightful burst of screams, of a character more distressing than words can convey, proceeding from some chamber on another side of the building. I called the porter in charge of the museum, and asked him what it meant. He replied with a grin, "It is only the dogs being vivisected in Monsieur Beclard's laboratory." . . . Therewith he left me, and I sat down alone and listened. Much as I had heard and said, and even written, before that day about vivisection, I found myself then for the first

time in its actual presence, and there swept over me a wave of such extreme mental anguish that my heart stood still under it. . . . And then and there, burying my face in my hands, with tears of agony I prayed for strength and courage to labour effectually for the abolition of so vile a wrong, and to do at least what one heart and voice might to root this course of torture from the land.[13]

No comparisons of human and animal treatment, or fixation on one's own consistency—upon seeing or hearing how animals are abused, there is an immediate reaction directed against that treatment, and based on that reaction, a moral judgment and decision to act.

In response to the criticism that their justice approach misses the fundamental importance of direct sympathetic responsiveness in the actual motivations of activists, Regan and Singer could point out that their work is not descriptive but normative—that is, that they are not trying to describe animal rights activists and their psyches[14] but, rather, to set out the best reasons we have for accepting the animal rights position. Such a response would be inadequate in two ways. First, it is doubtful that justice-based arguments do present the best reasons for animal liberation, given that those arguments are unsound, as I have shown above. More importantly, this response would incompletely characterize the projects Singer and Regan take for themselves, since, besides attempting to construct sound arguments, both writers explicitly indicate that they also want to further the animal liberation movement. This second part of their project, I would suggest, makes it incumbent upon them to attend to the actual motivations of activists. Arguments with little relation to the ethics of those who already affirm animal liberation are unlikely to bring new members into the movement or to help present activists maintain their commitment. Those of us who write or speak to move others should make presentations consonant with the real processes by which individuals come to reject animal farming, vivisection, and hunting.

In fact, Regan and Singer believe that they *are* taking these processes sufficiently into account in constructing their justice-based arguments. Each believes that sympathetic responsiveness to animals is an insufficient basis for the development of an animal rights perspective in most individuals. They feel that justice-based argumentation, or what they call *reason*, is necessary to augment people's sympathies. I will now describe why they believe this and why I think they are mistaken.

Regan questions whether an ethic of care can "go far enough."[15] He asks:

What are the resources within the ethic of care that can move people to consider the ethics of their dealings with individuals who
stand outside the existing circle of their valued interpersonal relationships? . . . Unless we supplement the ethic of care with some
other motivating force—some other grounding of our moral judgment—we run the grave risk that our ethic will be excessively conservative and will blind us to those obligations we have to people for
whom we are indifferent.

Nowhere, perhaps, is this possibility more evident than in the
case of our moral dealings with nonhuman animals. The plain
fact is, most people do not care very much about what happens to
them. . . .

And thus it is that a feminist ethic that is *limited to an ethic of
care* will, I think, be unable to illuminate the moral significance
of the idea that we (human) animals are not superior to all other
animals.[16]

To remedy this supposed limitation of the caring approach, Regan suggests the marshaling of *consistency* arguments such as those I have already
discussed.

Singer does "not think that an appeal to sympathy and goodheartedness
alone will convince most people of the wrongness of speciesism."[17] He
places his distrust of the caring approach within a sociobiological framework. In *The Expanding Circle* he argues that humans are disposed toward
kin altruism, reciprocal altruism, and group altruism, and that these dispositions can be explained in evolutionary terms. Singer sees the capacity
to reason and the practice of reason-giving as evolving independently of
the evolution of our sympathetic dispositions. Reason, however, can act
to override narrow sympathies, to expand our consideration beyond that
yielded by kin, reciprocal, and group altruism. Singer argues:

Altruistic impulses once limited to one's kin and one's own group
might be extended to a wider circle by reasoning creatures who can
see that they and their kin are one group among others, and from
an impartial point of view no more important than others.[18]

So, for Singer, humans have evolved instinctive capacities to respond
sympathetically only to a few individuals closely similar to or associated
with themselves. Therefore reason, in the form of the principle of equal

consideration of interests, must be applied for consideration to be extended to other clans, races, and species.

Given their low estimation of the human capacity to sympathize with nonhumans, we can understand why Regan and Singer might feel that their justice-oriented approaches to animal liberation are essential. If people do not care for animals, the supporters of animal liberation cannot presume that such affections are present in those they are trying to persuade. At best, they can assume the presence of some concern for humans and use this concern as a fulcrum, trying to impel their interlocutors to animal liberation through charges of inconsistency. This is precisely Regan's and Singer's justice-based strategy.

Now, I can understand how one might conclude that people do not care about animals, given the existence of such horrendous institutions as vivisection, factory farming, and sport hunting. Regan's and Singer's accounts, however, involve an oversimplistic understanding of the limitations of people's sympathies. For Regan it is a "plain fact" that people do not care about animals, while for Singer it is a genetic fact. On the contrary, I contend that this state of affairs is not "plain" but rather elaborate, and it is not genetic but socially constructed. Animal exploitation thrives not because people fail to care, but in spite of the fact that they do care.

The disposition to care for animals is not the unreliable quirk of a few, but is rather the normal state of humans generally. As Andrée Collard puts it: "Our common bond with animals is *natural* (of nature), *normal* (of the norm), and healthy (*wholesome*)."[19] If we shift our attention away from animal exploitation to other cultural phenomena, we can see the strength and depth of the human-animal bond. I will mention just four examples:

1. *Animal companions.* The practice of befriending animals, in its cross-cultural prevalence and its frequently avid pursuit, demonstrates the strength and depth of human interest in and affection for nonhuman animals. Approximately half of all contemporary Americans and Europeans live with nonhuman animals, or "pets," at any given time. Many Westerners do keep animals merely as status symbols, objects of domination, emblems of masculinity, or even as pieces of furniture. More commonly, however, the animals we live with are seen as companions and family members. In one survey, for example, companionship, love and affection, and pleasure ranked respectively as the top three self-reported "advantages of owning a pet."[20] Indigenous people also commonly befriend nonhuman

animals. And as in the industrialized West, when they do so their animal companions receive great attention and affection, and are viewed as family and community members.[21]

2. *Therapy.* Many people either socially withdrawn or in depressed states have been helped through the companionship of animals. These people were unable to interact positively with other humans, but could establish a connection with a friendly animal, often a dog or a cat.[22] This reinforces what most of us already recognize, that bonds with animals are sometimes *easier* to establish and maintain than bonds with humans.

3. *Rescue.* You may recall from 1988 the plight of three California gray whales off the coast of Point Barrow, Alaska. The iceholes through which the whales were surfacing to breathe were in the process of freezing over, which would result in the whales drowning. A rescue attempt was mounted, which ultimately cost $5.8 million and directly involved local subsistence whalers, professional biologists, environmental activists, 150 journalists, the oil industry, U.S. National Guard, and the U.S. and Soviet federal governments.[23] If we ask why the rescue was pursued at such great lengths, a cynical answer in terms of the self-interest of the participants would be to some extent correct. But to leave it at that would give a very superficial and distorted understanding of the final cause of the rescue. The participation of these groups in the whales' rescue served their interests only by virtue of a deep and widespread concern for the whales' well-being among people generally. The media, for example, cannot play to emotions people do not have: whale rescues boost ratings because people care about whales, especially whales who have become individualized through their special circumstances.

4. *Expiation.* James Serpell describes the almost universal presence, in cultures that hunt or slaughter animals, of mechanisms for mediating the guilt that such exploitation engenders.[24] Mechanisms that soothe the consciences of those who harm animals take many forms. Consider the following: many African tribes perform elaborate cleansing and purification ceremonies after killing an animal, others apologize to the slain. Ancient Babylonian priests, as part of the rite of animal sacrifice, would whisper in the slaughtered victim's ear: "This deed was done by all the gods; I did not do it." The Nuer people of the Sudan justify their consumption of cattle blood by claiming that periodic bleeding is beneficial to the animals' health. The Ainu of Japan also claim to benefit the bears they eat by maintaining that bears want to return to the spirit realm from which they came.[25] Western civilization has its own expiatory myths, most outstandingly the biblical

fable of divinely granted dominion over animals, and the scientific denial of animal subjectivity (originally expressed as *Cartesian animal automatism*, now more circumspectly maintained as *operational behaviorism*).

All these rituals and myths serve in some way to reduce the guilt feelings of those who harm animals. The general occurrence of guilt-mediating mechanisms around systems of animal exploitation contradicts the notion that humans are naturally indifferent toward animal welfare. People are generally inclined *against* harming animals: otherwise, there would be no need for social mechanisms that make killing somewhat more bearable— the exploitation of animals would be as straightforward as, say, drinking water or breathing air.

Attention to social phenomena such as befriending animals, therapeutic human-animal relationships, animal rescues and the ubiquity of expiatory mechanisms around animal exploitation brings a realization of the depth of the human-animal connection. This realization shifts the question, from Regan's and Singer's "How can we get people to oppose animal exploitation, given that they don't care?" to "How does animal exploitation continue, given that people do care?" The answer I would give to this latter question is that animal exploitation continues with great difficulty. Enormous amounts of social energy are expended to forestall, undermine, and override our sympathies for animals, so that vivisection, animal farming, and hunting can continue.

It is worth examining the mechanisms developed for subverting opposition to animal exploitation—the vast scope of these mechanisms underscores the continual threat human sympathies pose to the animal exploitation industries. Moreover, knowledge of the strategies used to block sympathetic opposition to animal exploitation focuses activism. Rather than constructing justice-based arguments with a view toward charging animal exploiters with inconsistency, we might better resist those corporate and personal manipulations deployed to forestall the expression of our sympathies for animals in animal liberationist politics.

Perhaps the most significant mechanism for forestalling opposition to animal exploitation in our society is reference to supposed divine permission. The idea of a biblical mandate to dominate animals can be applied in defense of any of the animal exploitation industries. Of course, this attempt to pass responsibility to God begs the question of our responsibility for choosing to affirm a nominally anthropocentric religion rather than an explicitly vegetarian religion such as Jainism. Also, Christians or Jews who might attempt to defer responsibility for animal exploitation to God are acting in bad faith, insofar as they are denying their responsibility for choosing to emphasize one biblical passage over another—for instance, Genesis 2:4–25 (in which animals are created after man, to be his helpers) rather than Genesis 1:1–2:3 (in which animals are created before humans, and are recognized as good independently of their relations with humans).

The deferral of responsibility for human exploitation of animals to God is naggingly incomplete without some suggestion as to why God would give "dominion" to humans. Men in the West have filled in this lacuna through the meticulous elaboration of a theory of nonhuman inferiority based on their supposedly deficient rationality. I argued above that if people are determined to maintain a notion of nonhuman inferiority, we cannot prove them to be inconsistent. In that sense we cannot prove that humans and other animals are moral equals. It is crucial to recognize the converse, however—namely, that neither can human superiority be objectively proven. Even if one could show that normal adult humans are more rational than nonhuman animals, there is still the insuperable problem of proving that beings of greater rationality have a right to exploit beings of lesser rationality.[26] The doctrine of human supremacy may be consistent, but so is its denial—justice-based arguments fail on *both* sides of the animal rights debate.

Regarding other animals as subhuman is thus more a choice than a recognition of some objective fact. In this context James Serpell's work is extremely significant.[27] He points out that regarding others as subhuman is a very potent mechanism for emotionally distancing ourselves from them. Moreover, he argues that only in cultures that have domesticated animals do people regard animals as subhuman. From these two observations he infers that we denigrate animals *because* we domesticate them—without this denigration, our sympathies would more seriously interfere with the work of slaughtering an animal who has come to trust us through a previously established relationship of feeding and protection. If he is correct here, then the notion of nonhuman inferiority is a thoroughly political doctrine propagated to facilitate animal exploitation. I noticed in my own case that once I became vegan, the idea of nonhuman animals as inferiors seemed not so much false as *meaningless*—since I no longer have a personal interest in the continuation of animal exploitation, the question of whether other animals are our inferiors is moot.

Divine permission and nonhuman inferiority are the most generally applied techniques for forestalling sympathetic opposition to animal exploitation. Each of the major animal exploitation industries—animal farming, hunting, and vivisection—also develops its own particular protective devices. Though these devices differ in their specific content, the various industries tend to follow a common set of strategies, such as: promulgating a cover story, denying the harm done to the animals, denying the animals' subjectivity, and derogating human sympathies for animals. Each of these strategies works through one of two processes: either by blocking some part of our awareness of what is happening so that sympathetic connection with the suffering animals cannot arise, or by providing strong disincentives for acting on any sympathetic feelings we may still have. The extensive network of academics, scientists, marketing experts, and popular writers who set themselves the task of easing the public mind shows that those in the business of exploiting animals have no doubts about the human tendency to sympathize with animals.

Cover Stories

Industry cover stories work to disincline us from sympathetic intervention. They all say in effect, "Well, there may be animals being harmed here, but what we're doing is so important, you better let us continue." The cover story for the animal farming industry, of course, is that they are providing food for people. Human consumption of animal flesh is portrayed as an unremarkable given, leading to a consumer "demand" for meat that simply must be met. For example: "[slaughtering] work is honest and necessary in a society which consumes beef"[28] and "the most commonly reported justification for slaughtering . . . was that people eat meat, so that slaughtering must be done by someone."[29] This story obscures the crucial facts that the taste for meat is culturally variable, not innate, that animal flesh is not a nutritional necessity for humans (indeed, the standard North American flesh-based diet is unhealthy), and that the animal farming industries do not passively respond to some mass insistence for meat, but rather actively construct markets for their products in order to accumulate profits.[30]

Animal vivisectionists similarly claim to be providing for significant human needs, in this case, our health needs. This story has successfully preempted sympathetic opposition to their routine confinement, injury, and killing of animals, inasmuch as most people who have awareness or concern about animal vivisection at all tend to oppose only the most egregiously cruel and useless experiments, but support the continuation of all the medical experimentation we have been told is so "necessary."

Vivisectionists respond to any challenges to animal experimentation by publicly pronouncing that we would all be dying earlier if not for their work, as in the following public service announcement made by former U.S. Surgeon General C. Everett Koop for the National Association for Biomedical Research:

> When I was born there was no vaccine for polio, no antibiotics, no way to treat diabetes or heart disease. As a result our life expectancy was just 52 years. Today, thanks to animal-based research, that figure is more than 72 years, which means that even those against animal research live to protest at least 20 years longer.[31]

Such fear-mongering, though invaluable for maintaining funding and public support, is scientifically invalid insofar as crediting increased life expectancy to "animal-based research" ignores contributions from public health improvements and from non-vivisectionist research.[32] Koop's analysis also completely passes over the iatrogenic effects of vivisection—the many ways people have been harmed by medicines developed through animal experimentation. We really do not know whether the animal vivisection paradigm has been more beneficial than harmful to society as a whole. Modern medicine, including animal vivisection, is a hierarchically organized male-dominated practice oriented around the control and invasive manipulation of bodies. This practice has developed at the expense of and in opposition to the previously existing woman-centered healing practices that were holistic, noninvasive, and community-based.[33] We simply cannot say what the overall health of our society would be if the enormous resources poured into modern medicine over the last century had instead been used to support women's ways of healing.

Defenders of the hunting system have faced an even greater challenge than vivisectionists and animal farmers. How do you explain the social necessity of men killing animals for the sheer joy of it? So far, they have come up with two cover stories: hunters kill animals for meat, and we need the hunting system to control population levels. Both these stories are exact reversals of reality. In many U.S. states we are told that deer population levels are so high that we must have a hunting system. Apart from sliding over the fact that in the U.S. deer are only two percent of the animals killed by hunters (most of the animals killed are doves, rabbits, squirrels, quail, pheasant, and ducks,[34] and it is never claimed that they are overpopulated), this statement disingenuously obscures that deer population levels are high *because* men like to kill bucks. Wildlife managers manipulate flora, exterminate natural predators, regulate hunting permits, and even at times breed and release deer, all in order to maintain herd sizes large enough to insure what they call a "harvestable surplus" of the animals men most like to kill.[35]

Most Americans support hunting for meat, but oppose hunting for trophies.[36] This is understandable: since most Americans eat the flesh of slaughtered animals, to oppose those who purportedly hunt for meat would put them in the awkward position of opposing fellow meat-eaters who at least do their own killing. Hunters are well aware of this fact and use it to deflect criticism of their sport. One hunting defender supports a growing practice among wildlife managers by advocating the self-conscious control of terminology to shift the connotation of hunting from pleasure to food-procurement:

> *Consider dropping the word "sport" to refer to hunting.* Fish and game departments are quietly changing the vocabulary of hunting; for instance they are replacing an emotional word such as *kill* with *harvest*. The word *sport* has many negative connotations when it is used to describe hunting. I have heard that the California Department of Fish and Game is phasing out the term *sport hunting*.[37]

This hunter's concern with "emotional" vocabulary shows his awareness of what motivates animal liberationism.

It is not that hunters simply talk about eating their "harvest," as often as possible they in fact do eat the flesh of killed animals in order to excuse their blood sport to the public (and to themselves):

> Using venison as a basic source of food gives the sport of deer hunting a sound, utilitarian foundation. We must remember that the non-hunting public does not accept deer hunting for either recreational purposes or antler collecting; the non-hunting public, however, accepts hunting when it is done to put deer meat on the table. As an old buck hunter once exclaimed: "If you don't eat it, don't shoot it."[38]

A glance at any of the innumerable hunting magazines on the stands clearly reveals the primary reasons men hunt—for the thrill of a challenging conquest, for the male bonding derived through cooperative killing, and for the male status gained through "antler collecting." It is not that men hunt to get meat, just the reverse, they eat the meat in order to hunt—that is, in order to gain ex post facto legitimation for the hunt itself. Hunters admit this most often when talking to each other, as in the following statement from Ted Nugent's *World Bowhunters Magazine:*

> Nobody hunts just to put meat on the table because it's too expensive, time consuming and extremely inconsistent. Everybody bowhunts because it's FUN![39]

Denying the Harms

Representatives of all the animal exploitation industries attempt to deny the harms done to animals. Toward this end there is routine and self-conscious use of euphemisms:

> A recent edition of the British *Meat Trades Journal* recommended a change in terminology designed to "conjure up an image of meat divorced from the act of slaughter." Suggestions included getting rid of the words "butcher" and "slaughterhouse" and replacing them with the American euphemisms "meat plant" and "meat factory."[40]

Similarly, vivisectors do not kill their animal subjects, they "dispatch," "terminate," or "sacrifice" them; while hunters are only "harvesting," "bagging," or "taking" the animals they shoot to death. This manipulation of language becomes manifestly deceitful, as when a fur industry spokeswoman recently spoke of animals trapped or anally electrocuted in order to sell their fur for profit as being *euthanized*, a word that actually means "killed painlessly to relieve suffering."[41]

Vivisectors routinely hide their injurious work, by restricting tours of research laboratories to the holding facilities, by attempting to block media portrayals of animal vivisection[42] and, notoriously, by the process known as *debarking*:

> Recently I visited the compound where animals are "conditioned" for the ordeal of experimentation at the University of California laboratories at La Jolla. There were well over a hundred dogs, all large: collies, German shepherds, huskies, and others. But there was not a sound from the four rows of crowded kennels: the

helpless victims had their vocal chords severed, which rendered them truly voiceless.[43]

If we cannot see them or hear them, we cannot sympathize with them, a point well appreciated by the founder of professional vivisection, Claude Bernard. He remarked that "laboratories are no less valuable to us for sheltering overly impressionable people."[44]

Hunters often attempt to minimize the harm they inflict by suggesting that death by bullet or arrow is less traumatic than the deaths these targeted animals would otherwise experience. This ignores the fact that human hunters specifically target large, healthy animals, exactly those least likely to die from disease, starvation, or nonhuman predation. One hunter, attempting to deflect sympathetic opposition to his sport, goes so far as to call deaths from bowhunting *peaceful*:

> if a bullet or broadhead [arrow] damages a vital organ, hemorrhagic shock will send a deer to a swift, painless, and peaceful demise. If the general public was aware of this knowledge, their minds could be set at ease and a major argument against hunting would fall by the wayside.[45]

The general public should also be aware that for every deer killed and retrieved by a bowhunter, one is hit and wounded but not retrieved.[46]

Especially by the animal farming industry, for whom every person is a potential customer, there is an ongoing effort to deny the harms done to animals. In recognition of the potential business loss threatened by a growing movement that explicitly advocates vegetarianism based on compassion for animals, meat industry representatives are attempting to frame animal farmers as the true animal welfarists:

> Our research shows that we can prevent long-term erosion of public support for the livestock industry. . . . We've got to do a better job of communicating with consumers, and letting them know that we, not the animal rights groups, are the animal welfare experts.[47]

The above quote is from the videotape "Animal Welfare," produced by the National Pork Producers Council and distributed to pig farmers. The narrator of this videotape mentions that newspaper, radio, and television ads are being produced and placed to communicate a message:

Livestock producers have always been dedicated to the humane treatment of the livestock in their care; first of all, it's good business. But more importantly, producers know it's the right thing to do.

The usual argument is that farmers have a business interest in maintaining the well-being of their "stock" since sick or unhappy animals do not grow as well or cannot be sold and therefore are not as profitable. In fact, today's factory farming systems (that is, farming systems in which animals are kept confined and immobilized for long periods of time) do turn a profit from animals generally unhealthy and in pain, since economies of scale allow the absorption of the early deaths of a small but not insignificant percentage of the animals. Pharmaceuticals are used to keep animals crowded in noxious conditions growing long enough to turn a profit.[48] Even in the most oppressive animal farming industries, such as egg laying by hens in battery cages, animal agriculturalists attempt to deny the harms to the animals: "Generally we try to provide exactly the environment which is most suitable for the bird."[49] One farmer, who keeps calves tethered for the entirety of their brief lives (so their unexercised flesh has the distinctive veal taste of a newborn), struggles to deny the cruelty:

> Some feel that it's rather cruel to the animals to keep them tied in there, but I point out that they're in a controlled environment, they, uh, the weather is, they never get real hot, or in the winter time it's never zero weather, there's no fly problem. And as a result, really, they've got a pretty good life in there . . . although they are chained.[50]

This description evokes the old halcyon picture of the farming family living in harmony and mutual affection with their animals. Even for traditional, less intensive animal farming, this picture erases the realty that farmers profit from the slaughter and commodification of farmed animals. The image persists, nonetheless, particularly in children's books. Animals, including farmed animals, are a favorite subject of children's books, but farmed animals are never shown being branded, castrated, debeaked, or slaughtered, they are always portrayed as protected friends.

For instance the book *The Midnight Farm* (described on its jacket as "a loving vision . . . of nature and humanity in harmony"), after visiting the peacefully sleeping farmed animals, concludes with the poem: "Here in the dark of the midnight farm/Safe and still and full and warm/Deep in the dark and free from harm/In the dark of the midnight farm."[51] Who are such images protecting from consciousness of the violent reality intrinsic to animal farming—children, or the parents who buy these books for them?

Denying Animal Subjectivity

In the second Genesis creation story, God created the animals as helpers for the lone first man, then brought them to the man, "to see what he would call them; and whatever the man called every living creature, that was its name" (2:19). Today some people call other living creatures "livestock," "game," "pets," "laboratory animals," "meat," and so forth, and in so doing they deny the animals' own subjectivity. Projecting human uses for these animals into their definitional essences forestalls sympathy by blocking our awareness that other animals have interests of their own that are systematically overridden by the animal exploitation industries.

Those who take an active role in exploiting animals—vivisectors, hunters, farmers, purchasers of meat—are particularly likely to apply the notion that the purpose of an animal's life comes from human interests. As one animal vivisector puts it:

> I grew up in the city, but we were very close to a farm community, and my values are farm values. I grew up thinking of animals as *for* something: some were for food, others were pets . . . each type of animal had its purpose. I think of laboratory animals in the same way: they were bred for research; that's what they're for.[52]

The hunter and writer Archibald Rutledge expressed a similar "that's what they're for" philosophy: "certain game birds and animals are apparently made to be hunted, because of their peculiar food value and because their character lends zest to the pursuit of them."[53]

It can certainly smooth the exploitation process to heed the counsel of agricultural scientists: "Forget the pig is an animal. Treat him just like a machine in a factory." And "the modern [egg] layer is, after all, only a very efficient converting machine."[54] Animals come to be seen as voids, beings whose inherently empty lives are redeemed only through the imposition of human purposes. A veterinarian giving me a tour of a vivisection facility pointed to a group of beagle puppies in a cage and said, "Beautiful, aren't they? At least this way they have a purpose." One vivisection textbook defines "experimental animal" as "part instrument, part reagent, a complicated and incidentally sentient system."[55] The breeders who supply vivisectors further this view of animals as tools with advertisement headlines such as "Now available in standard and stripped down model" (referring to guinea pigs with and without hair), "Building a Better Beagle," and "Specific Disease Model Available."[56]

Apparently the mere erasure of animal subjectivity is not sufficient to allow us to accept the harms done to animals—in each of the exploitation industries we see a definite construction of the animals as *willing* victims. The day after the 1990 March on Washington for the Animals, I heard a National Public Radio reporter discuss a slaughterhouse tour she had taken to see for herself whether the animal liberationist call for vegetarianism had any merit. She declared that she could see in the terrified animals' eyes that they would willingly go to slaughter if they understood the human purpose being served. This fantasy of animals longing to end up dead on our plates is promulgated through industry advertisements, such as the long-running Charlie the Tuna campaign (in which the fish repeatedly tries to get hooked), and more recently, a Domino's Pizza billboard displaying winged bison stampeding toward the viewer over the caption: "Buffalo Wings—They Come When You Call."[57] Just for kids, the meat industry provides schools with coloring books that show steers grinning all the way to the "meat packing company."[58]

A study of the advertisements placed by breeders who supply vivisectors found that the animals are often portrayed as "team-players" who facilitate the researchers' work in much the same ways as colleagues or other employees.[59] Advertisement copy describes the animals as research collaborators (mice are said to be "stalking cancer," a guinea pig is called the "unsung hero of bronchial research"). Animals are posed so as to appear to like laboratory equipment such as cages and jars of chemicals. Sexist stereotypes are used to portray animals as wanting to please the vivisector: "Female animals are shown as subordinate and desiring to please. 'Real anxious to please you' reads the text of an ad that has a drawing of a pregnant hamster in a maternity dress."[60]

A portrayal of the hunted animal as willing victim is apparently fairly common historically. In his book *In Defense of Hunting*, James Swan attempts to revive this myth, pointedly asking animal liberationists "How do you know that the animals really support you?" and sympathetically citing the beliefs of several indigenous cultures that "the success of the hunter is not just a reflection of skill but the choice of the animal."[61] Significantly, Swan also notes that the modern hunter "is challenged not so

much by fear as by overcoming guilt," echoing Ortega y Gasset's contention that "every good hunter is uneasy in the depths of his conscience when
faced with the death he is about to inflict."[62] The ascription of uneasiness
about inflicting harm makes sense, for how else can we understand the
recurring image of the willing animal victim—an image in such blatant
contradiction to the coercive intent of the cattle prod, the vivisectors' cages,
the hunters' bullets, arrows, lures, and camouflage—except as a salve to
the troubled conscience?

Derogating Sympathies for Animals

When harms to animals are effectively concealed or animals are convinc-
ingly portrayed as tools or willing victims, our sympathies cannot become
engaged. But these strategies are not always successful.[63] When people
do sympathize with exploited animals, the animal exploitation industries
protect themselves by belittlement, intending that such sympathies never
be taken seriously as the basis of individual action or public policy. An
example of this is the characterization of antihunters as "Bambilovers."
Many people have been emotionally affected by the movie *Bambi*, and it
is true that the movie is biologically inaccurate (deer do not really speak).
But the suggestion that opposition to hunting stems solely from exposure
to anthropomorphic depictions of animals derides sympathies for targeted
animals by implying that they are always irrationally based.[64]

The derogation of sympathies is typically done in gender-specific ways.
Women's expressions of sympathetic concern are expected and tolerated,
but they are not respected; rather, they are dismissed as female hysteria.[65]
Men, on the other hand, are typically not allowed to express such feelings.
For example, on one occasion at the annual live pigeon shoot in Hegins,
Pennsylvania, a boy, about eight years old or so, was crying at the sight of
pigeons being blown out of the air and then having their heads pulled off by
"trapper boys." As this boy turned away in tears, his dad grabbed and twisted
his head, forcing him to face the shooting, saying "you *will* watch."[66]

In the vivisection industry, founded by men and still male-dominated,
compassion for animals has been simultaneously feminized and derogated:

> As a young graduate student, he was running an experiment with
> rats. The experiment was over, and he was faced with the problem
> of what to do with the animals. He approached his advisor, who
> replied, "Sacrifice them." . . . "How?" asked my friend. . . . "Like

this," replied the instructor, dashing the head of the rat on the side of the workbench, breaking its neck. . . . My friend, a kind man, was horrified and said so. The professor fixed him in a cold gaze and said, "What's the matter, Smith, are you soft? Maybe you're not cut out to be a psychologist!"[67]

In this environment "softness" is not allowed, so men who would be scientists must establish their hard callousness, and women who would be scientists must be like the men. Susan Sperling tells of her graduate work in the early seventies under the supervision of a "great man" and "famous scientist." Her severe emotional turmoil after dissecting eight guinea pigs led her to conclude that she "would disappoint the famous man."[68]

This traditional association of scientific capacity with masculine callousness can become a liability, however, when vivisectors, like hunters and animal farmers, choose to deflect outside criticism by depicting themselves as compassionate animal welfarists. In an article published by the trade journal *Lab Animal*, Arnold Arluke reports that of the 130 vivisectors he interviewed, only 10 percent immediately admitted to any guilt feelings about their work, but after being given ample space to examine their feelings, fully 90 percent expressed what most people would consider "guilty" feelings.[69] Rather than continue the traditional suppression of such sympathetic hesitations, however, Arluke recommends that vivisection facilities support the expression of these feelings and help to manage and "redefine" them through stress management workshops and individual counseling. Apparently, many vivisectors somehow believe that feeling guilty about their work means they may be doing something wrong. But Arluke suggests that institutions remedy this moral naivety by teaching vivisectors that "guilt is really an indicator that the lab workers' consciences are alive and well."[70] Arluke makes clear that improving vivisection's public image is the ultimate point of bringing vivisectors' uneasiness out of the closet:

> If [institutions] acknowledge and attend to the types of uneasiness that I discussed earlier, it is possible that scientists and technicians may become more human in the public's eye.[71]

Insofar as deep and recurring hesitations are not recognized as the basis for compassionate social change, they are degraded. Thus Arluke's strategy continues to degrade the human disinclination to harm animals, no longer as a feminine vice, but now as a commendable stress to be therapeutically managed in the course of animal exploitation business as usual.

To sum up: justice-based arguments for animal liberation fail. But my own experience and the reports of others lead me to believe that direct responsiveness to need is more central to animal liberationism than concerns about consistency anyway. And contrary to the suppositions of the justice-oriented writers, the capacity to respond to animals is a deep and recurring feature of human life. That is precisely why societies that institutionalize animal exploitation must and do find ways to override and to undercut our sympathetic capacities.

The lesson I draw from this analysis is twofold, part heartening and part sobering. Heartening is the realization that the ethical basis of animal liberation is very simple and generally moving. A straightforward presentation of what the animals are like and what is done to them by hunters, vivisectors, and farmers can stir people, especially if the ideologies that block sympathy are simultaneously debunked.

But sobering is a grasp of the nature of the social forces allied against a true perception of animals, against an understanding of what is done to them, against the possibility of acting from compassion. The substantial power of institutionalized animal exploitation sustains ignorance, promotes fear, rewards cruelty, and punishes kindness. So, though the ethics of animal liberation are inherently appealing, the obstacles placed in the way of radical social change based on sympathy are daunting. This is not to say that those obstacles are insurmountable. Moving away from unsound and irrelevant justice-based arguments, taking instead a caring perspective that expects a human-animal bond, and that challenges any hindrances to this natural, normal, and healthy bond, allows us to continue moving toward a society in which animals have been liberated from human tyranny.

NOTES

1. Carol Gilligan, *In a Different Voice: Psychological Theory and Women's Development* (Cambridge, Mass.: Harvard University Press, 1982).

2. Tom Regan, *The Case for Animal Rights* (Berkeley: University of California Press, 1983).

3. I should note that Regan does not neglect this response to his argument: section 5.5 of his book is a rejection of Kantianism. Close examination, however, reveals that his argument against Kantianism is question begging. See Brian Luke, "From Animal Rights to Animal Liberation: An Anarchistic Approach to Inter-Species Morality" (Ph.D. diss., University of Pittsburgh, 1992), 15–16.

4. Peter Singer, *Animal Liberation* (New York: Avon Books, 1975), chap. 1.

5. Singer, *Animal Liberation*, and "The Significance of Animal Suffering," *Behavioral and Brain Sciences* 13 (1990): 9–12; Tom Regan, "An Examination and Defense of One Argument Concerning Animal Rights," *Inquiry* 22 (1979): 189–220.

6. R. G. Frey, "Vivisection, Morals and Medicine," *Journal of Medical Ethics* 9 (1983): 94–97.

7. Ibid., 97.

8. Bonnie Steinbock, "Speciesism and the Idea of Equality," *Philosophy* 53 (1978): 256.

9. Harold Herzog, Jr., and Sandy McGee, "Psychological Aspects of Slaughter: Reactions of College Students to Killing and Butchering Cattle and Hogs," *International Journal for the Study of Animal Problems* 4 (1983): 129–30.

10. Ibid., 130.

11. Konrad Lorenz, *On Life and Living* (New York: St. Martin's, 1988), 113.

12. Carol J. Adams, "Ecofeminism and the Eating of Animals," *Hypatia*: A Journal of Feminist Philosophy 6, no. 1 (1991): 134.

13. Anna Kingsford, quoted in John Vyvyan, *In Pity and in Anger: A Study of the Use of Animals in Science* (Marblehead, Mass.: Micah, 1988), 122–23.

14. À la Susan Sperling, *Animal Liberators: Research and Morality* (Berkeley: University of California Press, 1988), or Keith Tester, *Animals and Society: The Humanity of Animal Rights* (London: Routledge, 1991).

15. Tom Regan, *The Thee Generation: Reflections on the Coming Revolution* (Philadelphia: Temple University Press, 1991), 95.

16. Ibid., 95–96.

17. Singer, *Animal Liberation*, 255.

18. Peter Singer, *The Expanding Circle: Ethics and Sociobiology* (New York: Farrar, Straus and Giroux, 1981), 134.

19. Andrée Collard, with Joyce Contrucci, *Rape of the Wild: Man's Violence Against Animals and the Earth* (Bloomington: Indiana University Press, 1989), 70.

20. Joseph Quigley, Lyle Vogel, and Robert Anderson, "A Study of Perceptions and Attitudes Toward Pet Ownership," in *New Perspectives on Our Lives with Companion Animals*, ed. Aaron Katcher and Alan Beck (Philadelphia: University of Pennsylvania Press, 1983), 271.

21. James Serpell, *In the Company of Animals: A Study of Human–Animal Relationships* (New York: Blackwell, 1986), chap. 4.

22. Alan Beck and Aaron Katcher, *Between Pets and People: The Importance of Animal Companionship* (New York: Putnam, 1983), chap. 8.

23. Tom Rose, *Freeing the Whales: How the Media Created the World's Greatest Non-Event* (New York: Birch Lane, 1989).

24. Serpell, *In the Company of Animals*, chaps. 10 and 11.

25. Ibid., 145, 168, 153, 148.

26. Elizabeth Dodson Gray, *Green Paradise Lost* (Wellesley, Mass.: Roundtable, 1979), chaps. 1 and 2.

27. Serpell, *In the Company of Animals*, pt. 4.

28. William Thompson, "Hanging Tongues: A Sociological Encounter with the Assembly Line," *Qualitative Sociology* 6 (1983): 215.

29. Herzog and McGee, "Psychological Aspects of Slaughter," 130.

30. See, for example, John Robbins, *Diet for a New America* (Walpole, N.H.: Stillpoint, 1987); Jeremy Rifkin, *Beyond Beef: The Rise and Fall of the Cattle Culture* (New York: Dutton, 1992); and Carol Adams, *The Sexual Politics of Meat: A Feminist-Vegetarian Critical Theory* (New York: Continuum, 1990).

31. *Animal Welfare* (videotape, produced by the National Pork Producers Council, 1991).

32. Robert Sharpe, *The Cruel Deception: The Use of Animals in Medical Research* (Wellingborough, Eng.: Thorsons, 1988).

33. Barbara Ehrenreich and Deirdre English, *For Her Own Good: 150 Years of the Experts' Advice to Women* (Garden City, N.Y.: Anchor, 1978); Marti Kheel, "From Healing Herbs to Deadly Drugs: Western Medicine's War Against the Natural World," in *Healing the Wounds: The Promise of Ecofeminism*, ed. Judith Plant (Philadelphia: New Society, 1989), 96–111.

34. James Swan, *In Defense of Hunting* (New York: Harper, 1995), 8.

35. Ron Baker, *The American Hunting Myth* (New York: Vantage, 1985).

36. Swan, *In Defense of Hunting*, 9.

37. Ibid., 274.

38. Robert Wegner, *Deer and Deer Hunting: Book 3* (Harrisburg, Pa: Stackpole, 1990), 165.

39. Ted Nugent, "Fun. Good, Clean, Fun!" *Ted Nugent's World Bowhunters Magazine* 1, no. 3 (1990): 7.

40. Serpell, *In the Company of Animals*, 158–59.

41. *NBC Dateline*, 20 December 1994.

42. Vivisectors are not unanimously in favor of this tactic. See Deborah Blum, *The Monkey Wars* (New York: Oxford University Press, 1994), 160–62.

43. From a 1968 letter quoted in Vyvyan, *In Pity and in Anger*, 133.

44. Ibid.

45. *Quoted in Deer & Deer Hunting*, October 1991, 51.

46. Glenn A. Boydston and Horace G. Gore, "Archery Wounding Loss in Texas" (report, Texas Parks & Wildlife Department, 1986).

47. Norm Montague, chairman of the Animal Welfare Committee, National Pork Producers Council, on the videotape *Animal Welfare*.

48. Jim Mason and Peter Singer, *Animal Factories* (New York: Harmony, 1990).

49. *The Animals' Film*, section on factory farming, available from People for the Ethical Treatment of Animals.

50. Ibid.

51. Reeve Lindbergh, *The Midnight Farm* (New York: Dial, 1987).

52. Quoted in Mary Phillips, "Proper Names and the Social Construction of Biography: The Negative Case of Laboratory Animals," *Qualitative Sociology* 17 (1994): 134.

53. Jim Casada, ed., *Hunting and Home in the Southern Heartland: The Best of Archibald Rutledge* (Columbia: University of South Carolina Press, 1992), 30.

54. From *Farmer and Stockbreeder* and *Hog Farm Management*, quoted in Mason and Singer, *Animal Factories*, 1.

55. Quoted in Collard, *Rape of the Wild*, 59.

56. Arnold Arluke, "'We Build a Better Beagle': Fantastic Creatures in Lab Animal Ads," *Qualitative Sociology* 17 (1994): 143–58. The last example is from *Lab Animals* magazine.

57. "Buffalo wings" is an American locution for cooked chickens' wings served spicy as "appetizers."

58. Robbins, *Diet for a New America*, 128.

59. Arluke, "'We Build a Better Beagle.'"

60. Ibid., 154.

61. Swan, *In Defense of Hunting*, 121, 37.

62. Ibid., 29; José Ortega y Gasset, *Meditations on Hunting* (New York: Scribner, 1972), 88.

63. For example, D. Lawrence Wieder, "Behavioristic Operationalism and the Life-World: Chimpanzees and Chimpanzee Researchers in Face-to-Face Interaction," *Sociological Inquiry* 50 (1980): 75–103, points out that vivisectors must and do at times recognize animals as subjects, for without an awareness of the animals' subjective states they could not effectively manage them throughout the course of the experiment.

64. Matt Cartmill's book *A View to a Death in the Morning: Hunting and Nature Through History* (Cambridge, Mass.: Harvard University Press, 1993) contains a chapter on "The Bambi Syndrome," in which he concludes that "many hunting writers seem to think that if *Bambi* and other Disney products could somehow be suppressed, opposition to hunting would evaporate" (180).

65. I discuss these sexist dismissals and how animal liberationists might respond to them in "Taming Ourselves or Going Feral? Toward a Non-Patriarchal Metaethic of Animal Liberation," in *Animals and Women: Feminist Theoretical Explorations*, ed. Carol J. Adams and Josephine Donovan (Durham, N.C.: Duke University Press, 1995), 290–319.

66. Ingrid Newkirk, personal communication.

67. Bernard Rollin, *Animal Rights and Human Morality* (Buffalo, N.Y.: Prometheus, 1981), 109–10.

68. Sperling, *Animal Liberators*, 5–8.

69. Arnold Arluke, "Uneasiness Among Laboratory Technicians," *Lab Animal* 19 (1990): 33.

70. Ibid., 34.

71. Ibid., 38.

CHAPTER 6

The Caring Sleuth

Portrait of an Animal Rights Activist

KENNETH SHAPIRO

Manny Bernstein recalls the German shepherd who licked his toddler face when he fell off his tricycle, and the sadness he felt looking at a gorilla confined in a barren cage at the local zoo. Shortly after, at the age of six, Bernstein donned a Batman cape inscribed with the letters AP (for "animal pals") and liberated Goldie, his goldfish, into a nearby drainage ditch. Ingrid Newkirk, as a girl of fourteen in India, watched in horror through a window as an ox cart driver prodded his beast by thrusting his driving stick deep into the animal's rectum.

As adults, Bernstein and Newkirk are both animal rights activists. When he is not treating patients suffering from multiple personality disorder, clinical psychologist Bernstein edits and produces a journal on alternatives to animal-based research. In various arenas, he pressures research psychologists to alleviate animal suffering and, eventually, liberate their own Goldies. As founding director of People for the Ethical Treatment of Animals, Newkirk's window now opens onto the interior of a busy office complex, but she is still drawn to suffering. She oversees a sophisticated investigatory

This chapter was first published in *Society and Animals* 1994, vol. 2, no. 2. © 1994 by White Horse Press. Published by permission of the author.

apparatus that can reach into the locked files of the posh headquarters of a Paris-based cosmetic firm to find and follow an intricate trail: from the sales records of a shampoo, to one of its ingredients, to a laboratory that tested it on the shaved skin or eyes of rabbits locked in stockades.

Who are the animal rights activists, both national leaders and grass-roots workers? How do they live? What is their daily round? How did they get to be that way? This study attempts to answer these questions through the application of a method of qualitative analysis.

Neither Bernstein nor Newkirk is a "terrorist in a stocking mask," nor a "little old lady in tennis shoes." The latter discriminatory stereotype trivialized an earlier animal protection movement by portraying its adherents as ineffectual. More recently, the press's conferral of the terrorist image on contemporary animal advocates has threatened to discredit the current movement by marginalizing it as extremist.

Recent literature in the social sciences attempts to provide a more veridical understanding than does at least the sensational press. In his study of the activists who attended a major demonstration in Washington, D.C., Scott Plous found a diversity of viewpoints, lifestyles, and objectives that do not fit neatly into any one image or stereotype.[1] Susan Sperling found parallels between the contemporary movement and an earlier Victorian antivivisectionist movement.[2] Both arose in response to new scientific and technological developments viewed as dangerous or undesirable. In both movements, the concern with animal suffering is a convenient symbol for a broader evangelical and millenarian agenda. While distinguishing between welfarists, pragmatists, and fundamentalists, James M. Jasper and Dorothy Nelkin described the movement as a moral crusade.[3] Its members have genuine moral concerns and are on a well-intentioned quest. However, they also, particularly the fundamentalist subgroup, are quixotic and uncompromising. While not necessarily antiscience, their views of animals are not based on scientific understanding. Harold Herzog likened activists to religious converts, noting that they experience changes in fundamental belief and lifestyle, have a missionary zeal, and are often dogmatic in their positions.[4]

Other studies do not support the association of animal rights activism with fundamentalism. R. T. Richards and R. S. Krannich found that activists typically belong to several other socially progressive or liberal movements, notably civil rights, environmentalism, and feminism.[5] Robert Kimball found that liberal members of Congress vote for proanimal legislation more often than do conservative members.[6]

In his review of Sperling's work, Charles Magel identifies a pitfall of some of the social scientific literature:

> My last and most important criticism is that Sperling ignores the essential nature of the animal rights movement. In her analysis, animals [and animal experiments] are symbols of something else. Very much to the contrary, the animal rights movement is concerned about the *animals themselves.*[7]

Of course, these are not mutually exclusive possibilities—the animal as a symbol *and* as an object of concern in his or her own right.

However, in the present study, I try to stay close to the immediate experience, activities, and personal development of activists. While my approach may miss some of the historical backdrops, cultural contexts, and symbolic meanings of the movement, it hopefully provides a portrait of animal rights activists that captures how they manifestly relate to animals, the movement, and its opposition.

Method

The data consist of two sets of materials. First, a set of fourteen autobiographies of leaders of the movement, all save one published between 1986 and 1991 in *Between the Species: A Journal of Ethics.* As the distribution of this publication is largely within the movement, the personal accounts are probably more confessional than promotional or tactical in intent. All but three are U.S.-based.

The second set consists of twenty-one survey protocols of grassroots activists solicited at an animal rights conference in 1991. The survey consisted of two semistructured questions: (1) Describe the situation in which you first realized that you had a special interest in nonhuman animals. Estimate your age at the time. (2) What is it like to be an animal rights activist? Respond by describing a recent situation in which you clearly were being an animal rights activist. What was going on, what were you experiencing?

Consistent with other studies reporting on the gender constitution of the animal rights movement, the sample was predominantly female (23 of 35).[8] However, again consistent with other findings, the leadership was predominantly male (9 of 14). Most of the grassroots activists had at least a college education, and most spent at least thirty hours per week in their movement activities.

The analysis of data employed a modified version of a method developed in phenomenological psychology.[9] As described by Fred J. Wertz, in this qualitative method the investigator "demarcates meaning units" in each individual protocol to arrive at a description from a "first-person perspective, more or less in the subject's own language."[10] The investigator then performs a "psychological reflection" to describe each individual account "*as experienced, as behaved,* or more generally *as meant* by the subject."

Finally, through a second psychological reflection, the investigator arrives at a more generalized account of the structures of experience exemplified in the individual accounts. The primary finding of the study is a statement of this "general psychological structure." This description consists of the psychological meanings of the structure, and is not necessarily in the subjects' own language.

This method and form of results keys on the similar or common structures in the phenomenon under investigation. Of course, this does not exclude the existence of variations within the common constitutive or defining features.

Phenomenological psychology is an interpretive approach that accepts the necessity of investigator participation and denies the objectivistic ideal of detachment (compare participant observation in anthropology and ethnomethodology in sociology). It is, then, appropriate for the investigator to explicitly identify his or her point of view in approaching the study. In addition to being trained as a phenomenological psychologist and a clinical psychologist, for the past twelve years I have been involved in the animal rights movement at both the national and grassroots levels.

Results

Here I present a summary account of the experience of being an animal rights activist. The materials examined suggested organization into five themes. Following this description of the general psychological structure of this experience, the balance of the paper provides further exposition, discusses selected issues raised by the theme, and speculates about connections to other general psychological literature: an animal rights activist is an individual (1) whose primary concern is caring about animals; (2) who is primed to see suffering in animals; (3) who aggressively seeks out and skillfully investigates situations in which animals are suffering; and (4) for whom such caring, seeing, and seeking become pervasive aspects of daily life, embodied in his or her lifestyle. (5) Tensions created by the apparent contradiction between an attitude of caring and the aggressive exposure of human-originated animal suffering are resolved in one of several ways: embracing, suppressing, or losing touch with the caring.

CARING

Animal rights activists have a caring attitude toward nonhuman animals. Consider *attitude* here not as a specific belief about something—the earth is flat—but as something like the adolescent behavior of "copping an attitude." We are all familiar with the infuriating tone, disdainful gesture, slouching posture, and "cool" response to even the most serious situations that characterize teenagers. While limited to a particular developmental stage and most often transparently defensive, such an attitude is a pervasive personal style—a habitual way of experiencing and expressing the world through the body.

Caring about nonhuman animals is such an attitude. It means being attentive to them in a watchful and concerned way. More than just curiosity or interest, it is a positive inclining or leaning toward them, a sympathy for them and their needs. A caring attitude is one of continuous sensitivity and responsiveness, not a transitory awareness or a momentary concern.

Most activists report having some inkling of the attitude of caring in childhood, often between the ages of five and ten years old. Although not consciously adopted, for some it immediately becomes a habitual style, pervasively coloring most aspects of life. Others report a recrudescence, a more conscious adoption of the attitude in early adulthood, perhaps an intellectual awakening occasioned by reading Peter Singer's *Animal Liberation*.[11]

For other activists the moment of discovery is decidedly less cerebral. Like Newkirk's, the awakening of Helen Jones, founder of the International Society for Animal Rights, took place in an atmosphere of trauma:

> My first awareness of animal suffering was at the age of four or five. My mother took me to a zoo. As we entered we saw a large white rabbit, transfixed with fear, in a cage with a snake. Within a second or two the snake began swallowing the rabbit. . . . My mother never again entered a zoo. I did, many years later, only to collect evidence for a legal case.[12]

Michael Fox, senior staff member of the Humane Society of the United States, describes a very different experience:

> My first encounter with the miraculous and the mystical was as a child. I had a playground full of miracles. . . . Like the child in Walt Whitman's poem who went out into the world and became all that he perceived, I entered the mystical world of nature that my miraculous playground embraced, and became a part of everything . . . to play with a pond . . . to "mind" everything that I perceived in it, on it, and around it.[13]

Such first moments of absorption in other beings are an emotional and intuitive grasp of a relation rather than an intellectual justification of it. They are moments of the heart, not of the brain. The caring attitude is not itself a philosophical position, although it is the experiential bedrock for any philosophy that is more than sterile intellectual discourse.

For most people, however, the initial recognition is likely to involve a dog or a cat rather than a zoo animal or the amphibian denizens of Fox's boyhood Derbyshire pond. Adopting and living with a companion animal promotes a poignant awareness of the caring connection, one that is sometimes only fully realized in grief at the death of the animal. Tom Regan, author of the seminal work on animal rights philosophy, writes that although he entered the movement through Gandhi's views on nonviolence to animals, it was "the death of our dog that awakened my heart."[14]

A few activists report having what can be described as a conversion experience, a moment of sudden awareness that the path they have been following is strikingly uncaring. After years of research testing the toxic effects of radiation on primates, Don Barnes, now of the National Anti-Vivisection Society, dramatically discovered and adopted a view that made continuing this work utterly unthinkable.

However they occur, these are wrenching moments. There is shock in recognizing that it is possible, perhaps morally obligatory, to care about these others. It is as if one suddenly realizes that sitting in the next room is a family member whom one has somehow forgotten—or, at least, forgotten to love. Such moments are powerful. They bring about change at the level of basic attitudes—a person's consciousness is raised. He or she becomes, in the movement's term, an "animal person." Typically, he or she adopts a lifestyle that carefully avoids at least the grosser forms of animal exploitation.

Does an "animal person" only care about nonhuman animals? For many activists the caring connection extends beyond animals to various classes of oppressed humans and to ecosystems that include animals, humans, trees, and even rocks. A poll of subscribers to *Animals' Agenda*, a leading magazine of the movement, showing that the great majority are or have been active in other progressive social movements, supports this generality of the caring attitude.[15] John Broida, Leanne Tingley, Robert Kimball, and Joseph Miele found that undergraduates who take a position critical of animal research are more likely than uncritical students to have a personality profile associated with counseling, teaching, and other helping (caring) professions.[16]

In the other direction, Adelman M. Hills found that people who like people (people-oriented) also like animals, more than do thing-oriented people.[17] Historically, Henry Bergh, founder of the American Society for the Protection of Animals, also helped form the New York Society for the Prevention of Cruelty to Children. Frances Power Cobbe, a leader of antivivisectionism in late nineteenth-century England, was also a leading feminist.[18]

What is the developmental origin of this caring attitude? Our speculations here must take into account the fact that, according to the *Agenda* survey and other studies, roughly 75 percent of movement activists are women. We will consider three lines of argument.

The first has to do with social conditioning. Although child-rearing practices and cultural expectations are changing, girls' socialization still tends to foster nurturing, responsiveness, and caring behavior. Carol Gilligan has demonstrated that this difference in gender training affects not only behavior but the acquisition of a different moral framework.[19] Girls develop an ethic built on responsiveness to the needs of others in a personal setting, while boys forge a justice ethic based on abstract rules and universal principles.

A related explanation of individuals' participation in the movement is the nature of caring, which is itself based on an even more fundamental attribute, an empathic style of understanding the world. As a sympathetic response, caring is a judgment about someone else's neediness. Empathy, by contrast, is a feeling but not yet a judgment of need or an attempt to alleviate another's pain. It is a way of relating to the world that focuses on and directly apprehends the feelings, motives, and interests of other beings. Fox's boyhood play "minding" a pond, becoming part of the creatures that inhabit it, is an example of the empathic style in action, as are those exhilarating moments of self-forgetfulness induced by the performance of a great actor, dancer, or musician.

As a style of understanding, empathy is readily distinguishable from objective understanding, in which we try to stay outside an experience and our personal responses to it. The paradigm of objective understanding is experimental science.

A child's understanding of the world begins with something closer to empathy than to objective knowledge. After an early stage in which the child feels the mother's love or anxiety by a kind of immediate contagion— as if mother and child were one—he or she enters a stage Jean Piaget calls *animism*.[20] All objects—falling leaves, the toast popping up, as well as the meowing cat—are invested with intention. The toast wants to be eaten, just as the cat wants to be fed.

The first task of education is to "advance" the child, from this ensoulment of everything in the world that moves, to the more direct understanding provided by empathy. Later he or she is initiated into the task of constructing, primarily through inference rather than empathy, a world of impersonal objects related causally rather than intersubjectively.

This objective understanding is not gained without casualties. One cannot simultaneously infer and empathize, keep outside and go inside. Earlier empathic capabilities are subordinated and can grow rusty from disuse. Moreover, we are taught *not* to empathize with certain classes of objects. The deer we hunt, the chicken we eat, the mink we wear, and the frog we dissect are no longer individual subjects of a world we can empathically enter. They are objects, members of an abstract aggregate (the deer population), commodities for our consumption (meat or fur), or instruments for our learning (organism or laboratory preparation).[21]

Objective understanding, therefore, actively devalues emotional responsiveness and intersubjectivity—which threaten to create personal involvements and so violate the ideal of neutrality. In science's adoption of this ideal, these contaminate objective understanding by giving rise to bias. If, as we have described it, the caring attitude is a leaning toward, objective understanding cannot be caring. By contrast, empathy, although it is not yet a judgment or leaning, readily lends itself to caring. When I empathize with you, I experience, directly and intimately, what you need. We are close, if only for a moment and only imperfectly, for I have cohabited your world. If the paradigm of objective understanding is science, that of empathic understanding is care-taking.

The respective converses are also possible. I can exploit you more effectively by knowing your needs at the close hand provided by empathy; and I can care for you more effectively when I have coolly and objectively determined your needs. Nonetheless, it is clear, on psychological grounds, that empathy facilitates caring and, from the historical record, that objectification is the handmaiden of instrumental use—that is, of exploitation.

During childhood, both sexes learn to abandon the bald egocentrism of infancy. In general, girls are socialized to leave the self through immediate empathic involvement in another person, while boys are encouraged to assimilate the self to an objectified understanding of the wider world. It therefore follows that women in the animal rights movement outnumber men because they have been socialized to retain an empathic style of understanding and a personal style of relatedness—subject to subject rather than subject to object.

A third explanation of the origin of the caring attitude suggests that it is based on identification with the oppressed. According to this analysis, because women in Western culture are themselves oppressed, they are more likely than men to identify with other oppressed groups and so to predominate in numbers (though not in leadership roles) in progressive social movements. Moreover, women's identification with nonhuman animals may occur because their oppression shares certain structural and linguistic terms.[22] Both women and animals require "husbanding" (husband, husbandry); both can be a good piece of meat ("Are you a breast or a leg man?"—advertisement for Purdue chicken); and both are fair game (objects of the hunt).

SEEING SUFFERING

In the sketch of his childhood, Bernstein relates that even at the age of four or five, he saw the suffering of nonhuman animals. The ability to see suffering is characteristic of animal rights activists; their solicitous leaning toward animals positions them to notice their suffering.

But how does this distinguish them from anyone else? Surely everyone can see suffering? On the contrary, many, if not most people, do not see it. To understand how this is possible, we need to clarify what it means to see, exploring two different perspectives—one dealing with human perception and the second with its object, in this case nonhuman animals.

As there are different styles of understanding, so there are different styles of seeing. Two people look at a person wearing a fur coat. One sees elegance and beauty, the second sees dead animals, and the suffering and exploitation they underwent when alive. In spite of the movement's public exposés of the fur business, some people remain genuinely ignorant of the living and dying conditions of trapped and ranch animals; and, of course, individuals have different interests and values. Other people, however, literally do not perceive the suffering, because of a particular style of seeing akin to denial, an unwitting disavowal of certain emotionally laden themes or issues. Questioned directly, such individuals may indicate knowledge of these subjects, even though they are able to block full awareness of its emotional implications.

Another style of seeing, both subtler and more common, involves a distinction between *registering* and *reporting*, and leads to the claim that animal rights activists are people who consistently register suffering.[23] Consider, for example, a visit to the museum. It is crowded; you have not allowed enough time, and you rush through the exhibition. Do you see the Rembrandt? Yes, you see it, but you do not really take it in, fully take stock of it, appropriate it. You look at it, but, while aware that this is a Rembrandt and that a Rembrandt has certain striking and inimitable features, you are too hurried to grasp them fully or let them sink in. Your style of seeing in that moment is more like receiving a report of a Rembrandt than being fully present to one.

As a group, animal rights activists see suffering in a more robust and appropriative way: they register suffering. While not radically or grossly disavowing it, most other people are conscious of it somewhat vaguely, as they were aware of the nightly body count of famine victims in a far-off land, as reports of events remaining always at a distance. Even people interested in animals—the casual horseback rider, the owner of a purebred dog, the birdwatcher—are usually cognizant only of the problems of animals that are objects of their special interest.

Kim Bartlett, editor of *Animal People*, describes a moment in her life when a shift occurred in how she saw suffering: "Shortly after [going dove hunting], I went to a bullfight across the [South Texas] border. Nothing registered but the music. The blood didn't seem real."[24] But only a few years later:

> I received a piece of mail. . . . It was about fur and contained . . .
> pictures of a fox and rabbit caught in leghold traps. The look in their
> eyes pierced my soul. . . . I sat down and cried.[25]

A combination of institutional arrangements, linguistic sleights of hand, and defensive operations sustain this style of seeing as reportage. Animals in factory farms, fur ranches, and laboratories are located at remote distances and physically hidden from us. They are maintained in aggregates that make it difficult to relate to their individual suffering. As consumers, we see them packaged in ways that conceal their animal origins and any provenance of suffering. Animals are also concealed through language—"fruits of the sea." Cognitively, many people exaggerate the categorical distinctions between human and nonhuman species of animals. Such overdrawn distinctions then allow "outgroup biases" to come into play.[26] These further distance "us" from "them," and support the failure to register their suffering. A final style of seeing—abstract seeing or seeing past the suffering—is found both in the movement and among its detractors. It allows us to pass over the real animal or animals before us and move to a symbolic plane. We see injustice, speciesism, or the "death of nature," not the suffering animal. Of course, no one can stay constantly in the existential moment. The fully engaged seeing, registering, leaves us vulnerable to the suffering and injustices of the world, while abstract seeing deflects and softens their impact. Eventually, we must abstract, contextualize, integrate, make sense of things.

However, these modes can also function as blocks to perception. When we adopt them as a habitual style of seeing, we lose touch with the experiential foundations of our value systems. The hunter who sees past the death throes of the buck he or she has shot to the abstraction "the deer," a "population" that needs "culling," never sees the pain. Nor, occasionally, does the animal rights activist who sees past the frustration and boredom of hens in tiers of cages the size of this page. The caged animals become a symbol for something else—perhaps the transformation of traditional agriculture to factory farming.

In addition to styles of seeing that deflect us from directly registering suffering, a prior block may occur in the nature of animals. After all, we can only see suffering if it exists; and many people, in both laboratory and slaughterhouse, have long maintained that animals do not suffer—or, at least, that we cannot know whether they do.[27]

Some argue, for example, that suffering—a distinct emotional response characterized by fear and anxiety—while usually associated with physical pain, is not inseparable from it. The runner who painfully but elatedly extends him or herself to cross the finish line first is not suffering. According to this reasoning, animals could experience pain without suffering. Some researchers, in fact, suggest that suffering implies an awareness that pain or distress represents a threat to one's integrity or well-being. The questioning of nonhuman animals' capacity to experience such awareness further fosters styles of seeing that fail to register animal suffering.

In addition to these considerations of the nature of nonhuman animal experience, another backdrop to seeing their suffering is the human proclivity to take nonhuman animals as metaphors of ourselves. Although some deny animals the capacity to manipulate symbols, no one denies their ability to bear them. From Aesop's fables to Kipling's *Just So Stories* to Disney's animations, folk and modern cultures have required animals to bear a rich load of meanings to help us understand (or just stand) ourselves. As symbols they have served as repositories of both our valorized (wise as an owl) and our denigrated (animal or bestial) human characteristics. The symbols come to function as opaque layers, masking our perception of the real animals' true nature and immediate plight. If our perception of animals is so laden with metaphors of ourselves, how can we be sure that their suffering is not our own, projected? This symbolic density also allows us to limit our experience of their suffering to reportage rather than registration.

Caring *can* be sentimentalized, and sensitivity to suffering can be a projection of human characteristics onto nonhuman animals. There is a minority in the movement on whom childhood exposure to the early Disney has left a certain proclivity to the maudlin. As a group, however, the caring of animal rights activists is informed by a sophisticated understanding of animals, both their suffering and the institutional and ideological origins of that suffering.[28]

Armed with this knowledge, their empathy and caring, animal rights activists register the suffering of nonhuman animals. However, while a necessary condition, the registration of suffering is not a sufficient one, for it does not yet imply a commitment to action. Animal rights activists not only know that animals suffer, they live to do something about it.

Seeking Suffering

But pain and suffering are often the hidden ingredients . . . [so] we have to go behind the closed doors, behind the sanitized wrap.[29]

In an earlier era, a carter beat a horse until the welts were bloody and, exhausted and overheated from the burden of pulling a heavily laden carriage, the animal collapsed on the street. Today, a research assistant takes a baboon away from her or his protesting mother, and places the infant in a cage that will serve as experimental home and school in the ensuing (de)formative months of emotional and intellectual development. The first was a highly visible public event, while the second occurs behind layers of sanitized, justificatory, and obscuring wrap—federal regulations, institutional animal care and use committees, specialized scientific journal articles, high security lab facilities.

Even to the eye desensitized in the various ways I have described, public display of human-induced suffering in animals is still available, and there is still individual abuse—acts defined by their aberration from norms of acceptable behavior. However, the modern era has brought its own forms of institutionalized exploitation (factory farms, "animal models" of every form of physiological and psychological disorder) and with them new norms of the acceptable and the aberrant. To some extent a difference between the contemporary animal rights movement and its late nineteenth-century predecessor is a shift in focus from policing individual abuse to the development of a radical critique of institutional practices. Indeed, part of the current debate within the movement (rights versus welfare) hinges on the philosophical and strategic merits of that shift. Yet even beneath the surveillance of individual abuse by traditional humane society officers and the desire of some to focus on improving animal welfare within present institutions, lies a common impulse to effect still more fundamental structural changes.

What has shifted is less the locus of critique than the visibility of its object. The contemporary animal rights worker must actively seek suffering. To find it typically requires an investigatory posture combining classic Holmesian analysis of direct physical evidence with the use of sophisticated technological tools.

Today's activist is a skillful sleuth who has learned to follow trails through the labyrinths of democratic and bureaucratic political processes, to hear hints in diplomatic pronouncements, to defog regulatory smoke screens, to "search" online abstracts of biomedical research proposals. Holmes's magnifying glass is of little use here, for the animals are nowhere in sight. Investigative work begins with reading texts rather than with deductions from physical evidence. Even the texts, however, do not refer to animals and certainly not to their suffering. In a trade report on agricultural production, in place of animals there are numbers of pounds of meat and their market value. The animals are an absent referent, not even present by allusion. The relation between meat and living animals is unspoken as the animals who suffered and died within this productive enterprise were from the outset meat on the hoof.

Suffering is also hidden in time: in a past traced from the eggs in the cake back to the factory farm. Or it is a future event presaged by a notice of a proposed marine park and the consequent capture of dolphins to reside there to entertain us.

To the animal rights activist, these are all bloody trails—as bloody as that literal trail left by the blood and sweat of the exhausted cart-horse. To discover and follow them, our latter-day Sherlock Holmes is trained in politics, diplomacy, science, economics, high-tech information retrieval; she possesses a skill in textual interpretation worthy of a postmodernist scholar. Primed by caring and sensitivity to suffering and equipped with a range of approaches, committed activists dedicate themselves to seeking and exposing suffering behind closed doors—suffering implicitly present between the lines of a bowdlerized text, beneath the red tape of a Byzantine political process, in a future only adumbrated or a past reconstructed like a revisionist history, from fragments and clues disregarded by others.

PERVASIVENESS OF THE SEEKING

People who have an affinity to nonhuman beings are drawn like magnets to places where these individuals are suffering. It's a horrible thing—your car steering wheel turns to the right and off you go because down that lane there is a slaughterhouse or something.[30]

Moreover, sleuth work is insidious, for it is difficult to stop seeking. What begins as a certain sensibility to suffering crystallizes into an avocation—volunteering at the local shelter—then becomes a vocation and, finally, turns into a way of life. Without intending it, animal rights activists find that they are increasingly and, eventually, perpetually on call:

To devise a political strategy is one thing. To live everyday life is another. . . . It means to walk in the streets and see butcher shops, pharmacies, furrier shops, perfumeries, or to sit in restaurants not far from people eating animal flesh. Or to love and cherish persons who help to perpetuate the exploitation. Or to enjoy the beauty of spots and the enchantment of towns that conceal the exploitation behind the serene facades.[31]

The workday of research, inquiry, and confrontation does not end neatly at the office door. Whether seeking them or not, the activist senses traces of animal suffering and exploitation all around. The street in which she walks is no longer an open road, a horizon of stimulating possibility and chance encounter, but a set of potential clues, hints, suspect provenances. All roads become part of a network of bloody trails. Paradoxically, what is everywhere hidden, forgotten, denied, erased, transmuted, manufactured is yet everywhere present. The shopping mall, the restaurant, the city, but not less the woods and the sea—each has its own network of bloody trails. For animal rights activists, there is meat in their soup, animal-based research in their medicine. . . . They can't stop seeing or seeking the suffering.

TENSIONS AND CONFLICT

> It is just so very troublesome to be sensitive to the suffering of others. . . . It takes so much out of a person and sometimes I believe it takes too much happiness away.[32]

The preoccupation with seeking suffering colors the physical landscape of the world. When Fox returned to the hillsides of his childhood, he saw them differently. He could no longer glory in the "mystical world of nature" and the "sense of renewal" gained through "emotional connectedness" to it. Beyond the real changes in that environment (now overstocked with sheep) and the inevitable sobriety of maturity, his loss is an occupational hazard, which perhaps has comparable forms in every social movement committed to basic change.

This (dis)coloration of the natural and animal scene also extends to the human landscape. Being a careful sleuth involves looking for trouble. Whether in the conventional style of a probe of the political process, an inquiry under the Freedom of Information Act, or in the more activist style of surveillance and infiltration, investigators are viewed by the targets of the investigation as troublemakers. Information gained exposes and pressures those targeted to change.

On a more interpersonal level, seeing and seeking what others do not notice and do not want to notice promotes certain forms of social interaction, attempts to convince others of the presence of exploitative practices. Particularly at the grassroots level, activists often present themselves as witnesses to animal suffering, testifying to strangers, acquaintances, and intimates alike. Activists' styles vary from a cool, controlled presentation of factually and philosophically grounded arguments to an impassioned striving to find the one compelling image to cut through the rationalizations that justify suffering.

Whatever the style, these are emotionally loaded moments, and they can arouse strong feelings in even the most seasoned campaigner. Beneath the concern for the well-being of animals and the inevitable measuring of one's own effectiveness lies another set of emotional dynamics: seeking and finding suffering induce anger and indignation—at both suspected perpetrators and consumers who collaborate in exploitation. At times, the impulse to blame and treat people with scorn, or even vengeance, is difficult to resist.

Some activists throw blood on fur-wearers not so much to educate and induce change—or to tactically stigmatize a symbol of high fashion—as to transform them literally into dripping bloody trails. The desire to make the bloody trail visible merges with a wish to smear others with guilt. Moreover, the dynamics of this dramatic example can generalize to even casual encounters if chronic anger gives vent to an intolerance that is almost always counterproductive for the activist. Can these feelings be those of a caring person?

Caring and anger are not, of course, inherently contradictory. I have no doubt that I still love my son even in that moment when we are both taken aback at the strength of my outburst at the end of a long rainy Saturday afternoon. An anger laced with intolerance and entitlement, however, corrodes caring; sensibility and intolerance of others' insensibility cannot be bedfellows for long. Aggressive investigation, confrontation, protest, and demonstration often met by stonewalling and, more recently (as a result of the movement's effectiveness), by counteroffensives, can suppress caring.

These occupational tensions between caring and anger can even threaten the activist's motivation. The fact that most people go about their business as if the activist's agenda were irrelevant to the world's "real" problems—while others argue that it is wrong-headed, misguided, even dangerous and unethical—induces self-doubt. Uncertainties arise about one's competence and motives, about being peripheral or weird, about missing the pleasures of a conventional life in which work is left at the office. Doubts can undermine confidence in one's account of the world and the positions taken. Perhaps, after all, the suffering is necessary; perhaps exploitation is part of the natural order of things. Perhaps caring and aggressively exposing suffering are contradictory, and the caring is counterfeit or, on balance, hurtful.

One further twist is that the activist, in seeking out suffering, offends her own caring sensibility, incites her own pain and distress, disappointment and disillusionment. The activist is looking for trouble in the further sense that what is sought is suffering. Its discovery is itself troubling, particularly to a caring person who habitually registers that suffering. She is searching for something; she wants to find it and is committed to finding it *and* does not want to find it. The sense of accomplishment, even of exhilaration at finding it, is, at best, bittersweet and, at worst, heart-rending. In exposing the bloody trail, the animal rights activist creates her own bloody trail; human pain commingles with the animals' suffering.

In the last few years I have become increasingly aware of losing touch with something precious to me. I am standing on a cliff at the head of Linekin Bay on the coast of Maine, idly watching the sea. The tide is coming in, the breezes play on the water, fish jump at the surface, gulls careen above, an occasional osprey hovers. Idyllic, yes, but I no longer fully find it so. Something in the periphery of my awareness nags at me. I notice hundreds of parti-colored buoys polka-dotting the bay, and now I recognize what distracts me. These buoys mark the death-row cells of countless lobsters and crabs who have found their way into but not out of the sunken traps. I remember a more innocent and fully engaged participant in such panoramas, myself as I wandered through the fields and gardens of my childhood and discovered nature and animals for the first time. My first sighting of a bluebird was stunning in a way irretrievably lost to me, for bluebirds now appear in an ecology of insecticides, introduced species, habitat destruction, and managed bluebird trails.

Between the sadness and the self-questioning, an impulse to remain uninvolved, to tend one's own garden, can gain momentum.

RESOLUTIONS

How do activists deal with the melancholy, the self-doubts, and the potential alienation from the wider society? How do they choose, among the coping styles available, one that will be most constructive for the individual and for the animals?

The most common resolution, in this and other social movements, is the constitution of a community of like-minded individuals brought together through investigations, exposés, demonstrations, and conversations. As individuals and as a community, animal rights activists are privileged to live fulfilling lives in which dedication to the well-being of others extends beyond the traditional pales of family, ethnic group, or even nation. As members of the animal rights community, activists have a sense of belonging, of sharing common values and purpose. They are "at home"—with themselves, in their relations with other people and animals, in a world that they both belong in and help to form. After the rugged natural beauty of Maine with its white-water canoeing and hiking was transformed for me into a landscape booby-trapped—as my neighbor's effort to rid his garden of "nuisance" animals one day resulted in the trapping of my own beloved dog—I helped found a new home in Maine. A small group of us formed a more neighborly group who would work together to lobby against trapping, to expose mistreatment in unmarked warehouse poultry "farms," and to provide students the right to alternatives to dissection.

Ours was a community in the fullest sense of the word. Activists share not simply a workplace or a job or even a set of values but a concrete way of life embodied in daily activities. Just as nonhuman animal suffering pervades society, so every aspect of activists' lives—diet, dress, diversions—is designed to expunge the taint of animals exploited for human ends. They embrace caring for animals by bearing witness at every mundane turn to the possibility of living their caring within a mutually supportive community.

Yet, if this sense of community can offset the disaffection often felt with respect to the larger society, it also has its pitfalls. It may result in a heightening of insularity and, consequently, in diminished effectiveness through a pattern of preaching to the converted. It may even reduce one's usefulness to animals by the phobic constriction of one's life (for example, to avoid driving because insects are killed against the windshield) or to become obsessively preoccupied with one's own purity. (Is it acceptable to eat honey from free-ranging bees?)

A second resolution involves suppressing the caring. Paola Cavalieri states: "The extent and pervasiveness of animal exploitation are such that only by closing your eyes a little can we keep the hope of affecting reality, and the grit to do it."[33] Newkirk expresses the temporary suspension of caring through a metaphor of building a "protective wall." Only by "steeling" herself, showing no emotions, is she able to do her work as a "conscientious investigator" of animal cruelty. Others suppress caring more systematically—distancing themselves from direct contact with suffering by conducting a campaign at some remove from the actual scene of the exploitation, developing and administering an animal rights organization, or writing on the issues.

A third resolution or style of coping occurs when self-righteous indignation creates an attitude more hateful than caring. More than suppressing or suspending caring, here the activist actually loses touch with it. Such a person can be a liability to the cause, playing into the efforts of vested interests in animal exploitation to polarize the movement into revolutionist and reformist camps. Often this posture of indignation involves a rigid adherence and preoccupation with principle. In place of caring and the registration of suffering, the knee-jerk application of a philosophy reduced to slogans can support an unforgiving bearing. Unwittingly, the activist collaborates with the press's readiness to oversimplify issues. The public is asked to choose between such extreme alternatives as whether or not to sacrifice a single mouse to save a million human lives, or to accept as reform a measure that allows a veal calf enough space to turn around in his crate.

To some extent, these three styles of dealing with the particular tensions inherent in this movement appear at different stages in the career of an activist. In an early stage, an individual often experiences an extended period of enthusiastic embracing of the community of caring. At a later stage, the activist realizes the depth of resistance to change and may move to a more self-protective position by suppressing the caring or by burying it beneath a rigid application of right and wrong.

Caring remains the foundation of the animal rights movement. The most accurate image of the animal rights advocate is that of a caring individual who persists in assertively and, when necessary, aggressively exposing animal suffering. A grassroots activist writes:

> I often look at things and situations in a very animal aware way. I see the degradation of animals in a lot of things. Being an animal rights activist, I feel a great urgency to change the world and I always have to deal with the fact that my ideas are not very popular. . . . Usually people are very defensive and annoyed when I talk about animal rights . . . they feel it's an attack on them and their lifestyle and they don't see the bigger picture.[34]

Notes

1. Scott Plous, "An Attitude Survey of Animal Rights Activists," *Psychological Sciences* 2 (1991): 194–96.

2. Susan Sperling, *Animal Liberators: Research and Morality* (Berkeley: University of California Press, 1988).

3. James M. Jasper and Dorothy Nelkin, *The Animal Rights Crusade: The Growth of a Moral Protest* (New York: Free Press, 1992).

4. Harold Herzog, "The Movement Is My Life: The Psychology of Animal Rights Activism," *Journal of Social Issues* 49 (1993): 103–21; Shelley L. Galvin and Harold A. Herzog, "The Ethical Judgment of Animal Research," *Ethics and Behavior* 2 (1992): 263–87.

5. Rebecca T. Richards and Richard S. Krannich, "The Ideology of the Animal Rights Movement and Activists' Attitudes Toward Wildlife," in *Transactions of the Fifty-sixth North American Wildlife and Natural Resources Conference* (Washington, D.C.: Wildlife Management Institute, 1991), 363–71.

6. Robert Kimball, "Liberal/Conservative Voting Records Compared to Interest in Animal Protection Bills," *PSYeta Bulletin* 9 (1989): 7–9.

7. Charles Magel, "Animal Liberators Are Not Anti-Science," *Between the Species* 6 (1990): 204–13.

8. Jasper and Nelkin, *Animal Rights Crusade*; Plous, "Attitude Survey."

9. Amedio Giorgi, *Psychology as a Human Science: A Phenomenologically Based Approach* (New York: Harper & Row, 1970).

10. Fred J. Wertz, "Method and Findings in a Phenomenological Psychological Study of a Complex Life-Event: Being Criminally Victimized," in *Phenomenology and Psychological Research*, ed. Amedio Giorgi (Pittsburgh: Duquesne University Press, 1985), 168.

11. Peter Singer, *Animal Liberation* (New York: Avon, 1975).

12. Helen Jones, "Autographical Notes," *Between the Species* 4 (1988): 70.

13. Michael W. Fox, "Autobiographical Notes," *Between the Species* 3 (1987): 98–99.

14. Tom Regan, "The Bird in the Cage: A Glimpse of My Life," *Between the Species* 2 (1986): 93.

15. Richards and Krannich, "Ideology."

16. John Broida, Leanne Tingley, Robert Kimball, and Joseph Miele, "Personality Differences Between Pro- and Anti-Vivisectionists," *Society and Animals* 1 (1993): 129–45.

17. Adelman M. Hills, "The Relationship Between Thing–Person Orientation and the Perception of Animals," *Anthrozoös* 3 (1989): 100–111.

18. Richard Ryder, *Animal Revolution: Changing Attitudes Toward Speciesism* (Oxford: Blackwell, 1989), 107, 174.

19. Carol Gilligan, *In a Different Voice: Psychological Theory and Women's Development* (Cambridge, Mass.: Harvard University Press, 1982).

20. Jean Piaget, *The Child's Conception of the World* (1930), as cited in John Phillips, *The Origins of Intellect: Piaget's Theory* (San Francisco: Freeman, 1969), 109.

21. Kenneth J. Shapiro, "The Death of the Animal: Ontological Vulnerability," *Between the Species* 5 (1989): n.p.

22. Carol J. Adams, *The Sexual Politics of Meat: A Feminist-Vegetarian Critical Theory* (New York: Continuum, 1990).

23. Robert Sokolowski, *Husserlian Meditations: How Words Present Things* (Evanston, Ill.: Northwestern University Press, 1974).

24. Kim Bartlett, "Blinded by the Light: Or How Nature Triumphed over Nurturance," *Between the Species* 6 (1990): 95.

25. Ibid.

26. Scott Plous, "Psychological Mechanisms in the Human Use of Animals," *Journal of Social Issues* 49 (1993): 11–53.

27. Ibid., 26–27.

28. Stephen Kellert, "Perceptions of Animals in America," in *Perceptions of Animals in American Culture*, ed. R. J. Hoage (Washington, D.C.: Smithsonian Institution Press, 1989), 5–24.

29. Theresa C. Corrigan, "A Woman Is a Horse Is a God Is a Rat: An Interview with Ingrid Newkirk," in *And a Deer's Ear, Eagle's Song, and Bear's Grace: Animals and Women*, ed. Theresa Corrigan and Stephanie Hoppe (Pittsburgh: Cleis, 1990), 164.

30. Ibid., 163.

31. Paola Cavalieri, "Reflections," *Between the Species* 6 (1990): 156.

32. Emmanuel Bernstein, "Empathy Toward Animals and Other Sentient Beings: A Very Personal Account," *Between the Species* 3 (1987): 152.

33. Cavalieri, "Reflections," 157.

34. From one of the survey protocols collected at the National Alliance for Animals Conference in 1991, Washington, D.C.

CHAPTER 7

Attention to Suffering

Sympathy as a Basis
for Ethical Treatment of Animals

JOSEPHINE DONOVAN

Many feminists, including myself, have criticized contemporary animal advocacy theory for its reliance upon natural rights doctrine, on the one hand, and utilitarianism, on the other. The main exponent of the former approach has been Tom Regan, and of the latter, Peter Singer. However different the two theories may be, they nevertheless unite in their rationalist rejection of emotion or sympathy as a legitimate base for ethical theory about animal treatment. Many feminists have urged just the opposite, claiming that sympathy, compassion, and caring are the ground upon which theory about human treatment of animals should be constructed. Here I would like to further deepen this assertion.

To do so I will argue that the terms of what constitutes the ethical must be shifted. Like many other feminists I contend that the dominant strain in contemporary ethics reflects a male bias toward rationality, defined as the construction of abstract universals that elide not just the personal, the contextual, and the emotional, but also the political components of an ethi-

This chapter was first published in *Journal of Social Philosophy* 27, no. 1 (1996) and in Josephine Donovan and Carol J. Adams, eds., *Beyond Animal Rights* (New York : Coninuum, 1996). © 1996 by Josephine Donovan. Published by permission of the author.

cal issue. Like other feminists, particularly those in the "caring" tradition, I believe that an alternative epistemology and ontology may be derived from women's historical, social, economic, and political practice. I will develop this point further below.

In addition to recent feminist theorizing, however, there is a long and important strain in Western (male) philosophy that does not express the rationalist bias of contemporary ethical theory, that in fact seeks to root ethics in emotion—in the feelings of sympathy and compassion. Why this tradition has been overshadowed by rationalist theory is a question beyond my scope. What I would like to do here is, first, summarize the main components of this sympathy tradition; second, extend recent feminist theorizing on the subject; and third, conclude with the idea that what we need is a refocus in our moral vision—a shift in the cultural ethical episteme—so that people will begin to see and attend to the suffering of animals, which is happening all about them. Here I will rely on theorizing about "attentive love" developed principally by Iris Murdoch (under the influence of Simone Weil), but anticipated by over a century of sympathy theory expounded by such major Western philosophers as David Hume, Arthur Schopenhauer, Martin Buber, Edmund Husserl and other phenomenologists, such as Max Scheler and Edith Stein. Murdoch indeed exhibits a thorough awareness of this tradition—especially of the contribution of Hume and Schopenhauer—in her latest book, *Metaphysics as a Guide to Morals* (1993).

It was Immanuel Kant who formulated the rationalist rights-based ethic that has dominated the contemporary field. In his Preface to the *Fundamental Principles of the Metaphysics of Morals* (1785) Kant rejects feeling or inclination as a morally worthy motive for ethical action. Rather, he stipulates, for an action to be ethically significant it must be performed out of a sense of duty. Indeed, "an action done from duty must wholly exclude the influence of inclination."[1] Kant's rejection of sentiment or sympathy as a base for moral decision-making or action seems to reflect three concerns: one, emotions are volatile (what one feels today one may not feel tomorrow) (276); two, the capacity for sentiment is not evenly distributed (and thus those who exhibit sympathy may act more morally by inclination than those who do not) (277); three, for these reasons a sentimental ethic is not universalizable—one cannot establish thereby universal ethical laws (281). The second and the third point suggest that an ethic based on sentiment or sympathy or care is incompatible with the claims of justice—that everyone be treated equally and fairly. Most defenses of and attacks on a sympathy-based ethic revolve around these points.

Kant also formulated what has become the dominant Western view of animals: that they are instrumental to human interests—are means to human ends but not ends in themselves worthy of moral consideration. Because Kant's views have been extensively criticized by animal rights theorists, notably Tom Regan in his *Case for Animal Rights*, I will not further treat them here. Schopenhauer, however, sounded the keynote of this critique when he exclaimed: "genuine morality [is] outraged by the proposition . . . that beings devoid of reason (hence animals) are *things* and therefore should be treated merely as means":[2]

> I regard such propositions as revolting and abominable. . . . Thus, because Christian morality leaves animals out of account . . . they are at once outlawed in philosophical morals; they are mere "things." . . . They can therefore be used for vivisection, hunting, coursing, bullfights, and horse racing, and can be whipped to death as they struggle along with heavy carts of stone. Shame on such a morality . . . that fails to realize the eternal essence that exists in every living thing, and shines forth with inscrutable significance from all eyes. (96)

Kant's objection to an ethic rooted in emotional response, or sympathy, betrays a conception of emotion that construes it as irrational, uncontrollable, and erratic. Like other rationalists, Kant seems to imagine that emotional experience necessarily obliterates rational thinking. Kantian theorist Tom Regan follows in this vein when he accuses "ethic-of-care feminism" of "abjur[ing] the use of reason."[3]

But a considered and sophisticated response to such charges has been developed by sympathy theorists. They argue that experiencing sympathy is a complex intellectual as well as emotional exercise. Philip Mercer, for example, in his very useful study *Sympathy and Ethics* (1972), claims that in fact sympathy includes "a *cognitive* element."[4] Like Max Scheler (see below), Mercer is careful to distinguish between empathy and sympathy. Where the former may involve "losing oneself" in another's feelings, the latter requires keeping a certain distance so as to imaginatively construct the other's situation accurately and thereby to understand it intellectually as well as emotionally (9).

H. B. Acton in "The Ethical Importance of Sympathy" (1955) similarly argues that sympathy is a "form" of rationality.[5] It is not "as partial and impulsive" as critics have claimed (65); it is "not a primitive animal feeling but an exercise of the imagination requiring self-consciousness and comparison" (66).

In his phenomenological exploration of empathy, Husserl identifies it as an imaginative exercise that requires judgment and evaluation:

> I try to picture to myself, standing *here*, how I would look, how I would feel, and how the world would appear if I were *there*—in the place of that body which resembles mine and acts as I might. My imaginative projection into the place of another, conjoined with the two types of data given by the senses [appearance and behavior] makes empathy possible.[6]

Mercer describes a similar imaginative construction but specifies that as a basis for ethical judgment and action, sympathy (again not empathy) should involve not projecting oneself into another's situation but rather figuring out how the other is feeling: "it is not enough that I should imagine how *I* should feel if *I* were in the other person's place; I have to imagine how [the other] feels" (9).

The most developed analysis of sympathy remains phenomenologist Max Scheler's *The Nature of Sympathy* (1913, 1926). Scheler elevates sympathy into a form of knowledge (*Verstehen*, or understanding) that he proposes as an epistemological alternative to the objectification of the Cartesian scientific mode. Scheler indeed was a founder of the phenomenological school in the social sciences, which relies upon a method of "psychological sympathy" where the researcher attempts to imaginatively construct the reality of the subject, rather than objectifying him or her as data to fit mathematical paradigms.[7] Scheler proposed his method not just for the social sciences, however, and not just for humans. Rather, he contends, "understanding and fellow-feeling [*Mitgefühl*] are able to range throughout the *entire* animal universe. . . . The mortal terror of a bird, its sprightly or dispirited moods, are intelligible to us and awaken our fellow-feeling."[8]

Scheler argues that humans need to develop (or redevelop) their sympathetic intellectual capacities in order to decode the symbolic language of nature. Humans need to learn to read this language in order to truly understand natural life, including animals. "We can understand the experience of animals," he notes, by attending to their behavioral and expressive signs: these have as their referent the animal's emotional and psychological state. "For instance when a dog expresses its joy by barking and wagging its tail . . . we have here . . . a *universal grammar* valid for all languages of expression" (11).

Similarly, other forms of natural life have a "grammar of expression" that humans can learn to understand; this understanding is both intellectual and emotional:

> The fullness of Nature in its phenomenological aspect still presents a vast number of fields in which the life of the cosmos may find expression; fields wherein all appearances have an *intelligible coherence* which is other and more than mechanical, and which, once disclosed by means of the universal mime, pantomime and grammar of expression is found to mirror the stirrings of universal life within. (104)

Thus, Scheler is proposing that animals and other natural forms have a "language" that is accessible if humans attend to it, one that is elided by the mathematizing pretensions of modern science:

> We must rid ourselves henceforward of our one-sided conception of Nature as a mere instrument of human domination. . . . We must learn once more "to look upon Nature as into the heart of a friend" [*Faust* I.3220]. . . . Hence the first task of our educational practice must be to revive the capacity for identification with the life of the universe, and awaken it anew from its condition of dormancy in the capitalist social outlook of Western man (with its characteristic picture of the world as an aggregation of movable quantities). (105)[9]

Thus, Scheler proposes an epistemological mode of sympathetic understanding as a valid tool of knowledge, which will reveal realities that are not seen or understood by the Cartesian mathematizing mode of science. St. Francis of Assisi is presented as exemplary; in his "emotional relationship to Nature . . . natural objects and processes take on an expressive significance of *their* own, without any parabolic reference to . . . human relationships" (87). Humans must develop this kind of sympathetic understanding (*Verstehen*) as a cognitive mode to decipher nature's *own* language, to see organic life *as it is*, not as translated into manipulable objects for human use. Scheler does not, therefore, see sympathy as a whimsical, erratic, and irrational response, but rather as a systematic investigatory tool, a form of knowledge.

An interesting recent exploration of how such an approach might work in practice is to be found in Kenneth Shapiro's "Understanding Dogs Through Kinesthetic Empathy, Social Construction, and History" (1989). Shapiro (following Paul Ricoeur as well as Scheler) suggests that we need a new "interpretive science in which the object of study is an autonomous subject, more textlike than thinglike, and, hence, to be understood rather than explained."[10] By use of what he calls "kinesthetic empathy" Shapiro attempts to understand his dog Sabaka. He does this by imaginatively entering into the dog's bodily movements and reactions, thus deciphering the realities of the dog's "life-world" (to borrow a term from Husserl).

Edith Stein, who studied with Husserl, developed a similar concept, which she called "sensual empathy" (a "sensing-in" of the body of another).[11] Such an effort yields knowledge of another's suffering. "Should I perhaps consider a dog's paw in comparison with my hand. I do not have a mere physical body . . . but a physical limb of a living body. . . . I may sense-in pain when the animal is injured" (55).

A somewhat similar approach is proposed by John A. Fisher in "Taking Sympathy Seriously: A Defense of Our Moral Psychology Toward Animals" (1987). Fisher notes that "the sympathetic experience of . . . animals entails some understanding of what it is like to be them—for example, of what it is like to be huge and to walk on four legs, to have a large trunk, and so forth."[12] (Here the terms *empathy* and *sympathy* are used somewhat interchangeably, and Stein and Shapiro tend to see the experience as a kind of visceral emotion, as opposed to Fisher; but what is important is that they all maintain that a sympathetic imaginative construction of another's reality is what is required for an appropriate moral response.)

Environmental ethicist Paul Taylor argues that such knowledge must be the basis of any environmental ethic. It is only by close study and observation of organisms that one can come to understand their reality, their telos, their needs:

> As one becomes more and more familiar with the organism and its behavior, one becomes fully sensitive to the particular way it is living out its life cycle. . . . The final culmination of this process is the achievement of a genuine understanding of its point of view and . . . an ability to "take" that point of view.[13]

Such a process is not anthropomorphic, nor need it deny the separate and different reality of the other organism. Rather it is a process of learning—through careful attention and observation—what the other's reality really is, respecting that different reality, and developing an ethical response that is appropriate to that creature's reality (110).

All of these theorists are saying in answer to Kantian charges that sympathy is irrational that, on the contrary, it involves an exercise of the moral imagination, an intense attentiveness to another's reality, which requires strong powers of observation and concentration, as well as faculties of evaluation and judgment. It is a matter of trying to fairly see another's world, to understand what another's experience is. It is a cognitive as well as emotional exercise.

The ability to extend the moral imagination in this way is not, they argue, necessarily a natural gift (though some, notably Scheler and Schopenhauer assert that women are more able to exercise sympathetic understanding than men); rather, it is an intellectual and emotional practice that can be learned. As we have seen, Scheler contends that "the first task of our educational practice must be to revive the capacity for identification with the life of the universe" (105). Mercer, too, believes that people can and should be trained in emotional knowledge (105). Feminist theorist Rosemarie Tong even suggests that a Kantian mechanistic rules-based ethic may lead to a deadening of the moral imagination.[14] Perhaps the most extensive recent plea for a reinstatement of sympathy education into the school system comes from Nel Noddings, who believes that "the maintenance and enhancement of caring [should be] the primary aim of education." She advocates instituting such practices as "caring apprenticeships," for example.[15]

Sympathy theorists argue, moreover, that one can in fact have no morality, no justice even, without first having sympathy. Acton, for example, observes that "a certain amount of sympathy is required if anyone is even to *notice* that someone else is in need of help" (62). And without such attention, there would be no morality, "for without [sympathy] there would be no helping, and hence no beneficence, and help and beneficence are necessary for morality" (66).[16]

In arguing therefore that sympathy is the sine qua non of ethical decision-making and action, sympathy theorists contend that sympathy precedes justice. Such precedence obtains ontogenetically, some claim; logically, others claim; and metaphysically, yet others contend.

Scheler maintains that one's feelings of sympathy are rooted in earliest childhood, or in what Freudians call the preoedipal phase. One's first feelings are "the instinctive identification of mother-love" (98). Only gradually is this "replaced, in the later stages of childhood, by merely vicarious feeling," which remains as the undergirding of "fellow-feeling [*Mitgefühl*]" (98). In his introduction to Scheler's work, W. Stark amplifies this idea: "originally, the experience of self and the experience of others is in no way differentiated: the child feels the feelings and thinks the thoughts of those who form [her or his] social environment. It takes a long time before [perceptions are sorted out] as 'mine' and 'others'" (xxxix). Others, thus, "live in *us*" (xl), which forms the basis of sympathetic identification, preceding the emergence of egocentricity.

Brian Luke in "Justice, Caring, and Animal Liberation" (chapter 5, this volume) claims that sympathy for animals is indeed a deep, primary disposition that is only obscured and repressed by a process of intense social conditioning. Noting the extensive guilt expiation ceremonies that attend animal killing in traditional cultures, Luke suggests that the existence of such guilt (along with other social practices) is testimony to "the depth of the human–animal bond" (134). The fact that laboratory experiments and slaughterhouse practices are kept hidden from the public suggests, once again, shame or guilt over the violation of the human–animal bond. "Enormous amounts of social energy are expended to forestall, undermine, and override our sympathies for animals, so that vivisection, animal farming, and hunting can continue" (136).

A number of eighteenth-century theorists—including Shaftesbury, Hutcheson, Hume, and Adam Smith—claimed that humans have an innate sense of sympathy and that this is the basis for moral awareness. The Third Earl of Shaftesbury maintained that there is an innate "moral sense" that is rooted in one's sense of kinship with others.[17] Francis Hutcheson extended Shaftesbury's idea that there is an innate moral faculty, contributing further to what Keith Thomas has labeled the "new sensibilities" that developed during the century, including sensitivities to animal cruelty (many of the humane societies originated as the result of this new emphasis on the feelings as a guide to moral action).[18]

David Hume, picking up on his predecessors, insists that there is a "natural sympathy" "implanted in our nature."[19] "Would any man, who is walking along, tread as willingly on another's gouty toes, whom he has no quarrel with, as on the hard flint and pavement?" (61). From such examples, Hume maintains:

> we must, a priori, conclude it impossible for such a creature as man to be totally indifferent to the well or ill-being of his fellow-creatures, and not readily . . . to pronounce, where nothing gives him any particular bias, that what promotes their happiness is good, what tends to their misery is evil, without any further regard or consideration. (65)

"Morality," he concludes, "is determined by sentiment. It defines virtue to be *whatever mental action or quality gives to a spectator the pleasing sentiment of*

approbation; and vice the contrary" (129). Moreover, "the approbation or blame
. . . cannot be the work of our judgment, but of the heart; and is not a specula-
tive proposition or affirmation, but an active feeling or sentiment" (131).

Scientific credibility has been added to eighteenth-century theorists'
claims for innate, natural sympathy by Charles Darwin and, more recently,
the sociobiologists. They argue that natural selection has resulted in the
phenomenon of "kin altruism," which is an innate concern about the survival of one's kin (and thus one's genes) found in most animals. Darwin
in fact claimed in *The Descent of Man* (1871) that in higher mammals such
altruism was extended to nonkin.[20]

In a recent and interesting extension of this view, "Animal Liberation
and Environmental Ethics" (1988), J. Baird Callicott suggests that since
domestic animals have historically been part of the immediate human
community (and thus in a sense "kin"), *kin altruism* establishes a natural
base for human concern and emotional attachment. There is, he claims,
a kind of "evolved and unspoken social contract" between these animals
and humans.[21]

Writing in direct confutation of Kant's ethical theory, Schopenhauer,
like Hume, also contends that morality is rooted in sympathy: "only insofar as an action has sprung from compassion does it have moral value"
(144). And compassion, he maintains, requires a kind of empathetic
identification so that one can understand the other's situation. "I suffer
directly with him, I feel his woe just as I ordinarily feel only my own. . . .
But this requires that I am in some way *identified with him,* in other words
that this *difference* between me and everyone else, which is the very basis
of my egoism, is eliminated" (144). (It should be noted that later sympathy theorists, such as Scheler and Mercer, criticized Schopenhauer and
Hume, respectively, for relying on empathy rather than sympathy, and
thus sanctioning a loss of self in the identificatory process, which Scheler
and Mercer reject.)

Schopenhauer, however, emphasizes the emotional component of
compassion. One understands another's pain through "the everyday phenomenon of *compassion,* of the immediate *participation* . . . in the *suffering*
of another. . . . It is simply and solely this compassion that is the real basis
of all *voluntary* justice and *genuine* loving-kindness" (144).

"Boundless compassion for all living things is the firmest and sur-
est guarantee of pure moral conduct" (172). Schopenhauer specifically
includes animals in this moral community. In a compassion-based ethic
"the *animals* are also taken under its protection. In the European systems

of morality they are badly provided for, which is most inexcusable. They are said to have no rights . . . [and be] without moral significance. All of this is revoltingly crude, a barbarism of the West" (175).

Schopenhauer's ethical theory is rooted in his metaphysics, which entails the Indian distinction between what he called (in his magnum opus) the "Will" and the "Idea." The Will is a kind of undifferentiated pool of Being to which all living creatures belong. It underlies the screen of appearances, of separate individuals, the *Māyā* or the Idea. It is through the pool of Being that we are linked to all other creatures, and it is through compassion that we know that connection; it breaks through the barriers of individuation and egoism (210).

Like Schopenhauer and Hume, succeeding sympathy theorists claim that sympathy logically precedes justice; that is, there must first be the experience of sympathy before there can be any justice claims. Indeed, it is sympathy that determines who is to be included under the umbrella of justice. As environmentalist Fisher notes, "sympathy is fundamental to moral theory in that it determines the range of individuals to which moral principles apply" (245, n.5). And it is "our sympathetic response to animals [that] makes them a part of our moral community" (228).

Mercer also explains: if we take as the fundamental maxim of justice that one "treat everyone alike," then it becomes a question of who counts as "everyone." That decision is determined by the extent to which one can sympathize with the entity (132). In elaborating, Mercer specifies that sympathy only occurs between creatures who can feel. "'Sympathy' has regard for 'the other' solely in respect of his [or her] capacity to feel and to suffer" (4). The sympathetic agent must be "a thinking and feeling being" and the object of sympathy must be "at least a feeling being" (5). The awareness that the other has feelings, or is a subject of feelings, means that one can no longer see that creature as an object. "If we actively sympathize with someone then we cannot treat him as an object, as an instrument for our own self-satisfaction; on the contrary we see him as a being possessing individual worth and existing in his own right" (124). In other words, sympathy engenders moral respect, and thus determines who deserves to be treated on equal terms. The concept of justice, therefore, according to Mercer, is relevant only to sentient beings (133).

Acton also maintains that sympathy establishes claims for equal treatment or justice. This is because sympathy requires treating another's needs as comparable with one's own. It leads one to realize that "the other['s] distress is at least *comparable* with [one's own], and the road has been opened up . . . to the demand for equal treatment of equal needs. Sympathy requires that every sentient being shall *count*" (66). Scheler, like Schopenhauer, agrees that sympathy frees us from the "illusion" of "'ego-centricity' . . . the illusion of taking one's own environment to be the world itself" (58). "The dissipation of this illusion . . . [enables] us to grasp how a [person], or living creature . . . is our *equal in worth*" (60). Thus, again, sympathy is seen as opening up and determining notions of justice.

Scheler also maintains that an individual encounter with suffering should make us aware of suffering in general. Thus "the pure sentiment of fellow-feeling is released as a permanent disposition, spreading far beyond the occasion which first inspired it, towards *everybody and every good thing*" (60). This brings us to the third issue Kantian theorists hold against sympathy-based ethics, that it is nonuniversalizable.

In his recent book *The Thee Generation* (1991) Tom Regan criticizes "ethic-of-care" feminism for its failure to provide a means of universalizing the individual experience of caring and sympathy. "What are the resources within the ethic of care that can move people to consider the ethics of their dealings with individuals who *stand outside* the existing circle of their valued interpersonal relationships?" (95). In fact, he argues, "most people do not care very much about what happens to [nonhuman animals] . . . their care seems to be . . . limited to 'pet' animals, or to cuddly or rare specimens of wildlife. What, then, becomes of the animals toward whom people are indifferent, given the ethic of care?" (96). In short, how does one generalize beyond the individual particular instance of caring or compassion to include all creatures within an ethic of care?

Regan argues that such extension can only come through logic. One extends one's care for one's own children to one's neighbors' children because it is illogical and inconsistent not to do so. "Whether I care or not [emotionally for the neighbors' children], I ought to and it is logic that leads me to the realization of this 'ought'" (140). Regan's characteristic rejection of emotion or sympathy as a base for moral decision-making is apparent here. Isn't it also likely that if one's neighbors' children were in harm, one would sympathize with them and care enough to help them? And isn't it unlikely that one would stop to figure out principles of logic and consistency to determine an appropriate moral action, if say, those children were crying in pain? (Of course, one can conjure up qualifying circumstances that will affect one's decision whether to help the children or not, but that is irrelevant to the question at hand—which is whether one responds on a rational or emotional basis to the suffering of nonkin.)

It is clear in fact that one can and often does feel sympathy for complete strangers. If I watch on television children starving in Somalia or hear about the brutal rape of women in Bosnia, people I know little about and certainly do not know personally, I nevertheless *feel* sympathy; I care about their plight and am moved to try to help them. Thus, I contend—along with Hume and other sympathy theorists—that sympathy is easily universalized.

Virginia Held argues in a recent critique of rationalist ethics that in its reliance on theory based on universal, abstract "persons," it neglects the experience of the "particular other," the personal emotional relationship one has with a real person. But, she contends, "particular others" need not be individual people one knows personally; rather, they can be "actual starving children in Africa with whom one feels empathy . . . not just those we are close to in any traditional context of family, neighbors, or friends. But particular others are still not 'all rational beings' or 'the greatest number'"—the latter allusions to Kantian and utilitarian abstractions, respectively.[22] It is a particular qualitative experience that is missing in contemporary rationalist theory, the emotional sympathetic understanding of another creature. It is this "personalist" dimension that sympathy theorists would restore to ethical theory.

We see now that sympathy theorists refute Kant by arguing that sympathy is in fact a form of knowledge that includes a cognitive dimension. It is not, therefore, whimsical and erratic, nor does it entail obliteration of the thinking or feeling self. It is easily universalized, although, as Luke points out, such extensions are often muted by powerful social and political institutions.

A number of feminists, including myself, have asserted that ethical theory about animal treatment should be grounded in what these earlier theorists called sympathy. In her important 1985 article "The Liberation of Nature" (chapter 1, this volume), Marti Kheel called for "a recognition of the importance of feeling and emotion and personal experience in moral decision-making" (52) about animals. Noting that much evil is obfuscated through abstract rationalization, which serves to distance one from its actuality, Kheel suggests that personal experience of evil might bring its reality home. For example, those who "*think* . . . that there is nothing morally wrong with eating meat . . . ought, perhaps, to visit a factory farm or slaughterhouse to see if [they] still *feel* the same way" (49).[23]

Some feminists have developed Carol Gilligan's "ethic of care" as a base for animal defense theory. See especially Deane Curtin's "Toward an Ecological Ethic of Care" (chapter 3, this volume).[24] Though it has received much criticism and amplification (see, especially, Larrabee 1993; Kittay and Meyers 1987), Gilligan's *In a Different Voice* (1982) remains the classic statement of the care ethic. In this framework:

> The moral problem arises from conflicting responsibilities rather than competing rights and requires for its resolution a mode of thinking that is contextual and narrative rather than formal and abstract. The conception of morality as concerned with the activity of care centers moral development around the understanding of responsibility and relationships, just as the conception of morality as fairness ties moral development to the understanding of rights and rules.[25]

Thus, Gilligan identifies an ethic that is rooted in the kind of sympathetic understanding proposed by the sympathy theorists introduced above.

Such an ethic, historically, has been confined largely to the domestic sphere and to women. Leaving aside the question of whether as mothers women are biologically predisposed toward caring for their young (I leave it aside because biological determinism is simply an inadequate explanation of human [and indeed much nonhuman animal] behavior), it is apparent that women's historical social and economic practice has been of a caring nature. In addition to maternal practice (on this, see Sara Ruddick 1989), women have nearly universally engaged in use-value production as their primary economic experience. Use-value production means the creation of products for immediate use or consumption by members of the household (clothes, food, and the like). It is a "caring labor," to use Hilary Rose's term.[26]

A number of theorists (particularly Nancy Hartsock, Linda Nicholson, and Eli Zaretsky) have shown how in the West a division of moral labor accompanied the historical division between the public and private spheres with their divergent economic practices.[27] In an interesting recent exploration of the subject, "Eco-Feminism and Deep Ecology" (1987), Jim Cheney ties Gilligan's caring ethic to the gift-exchange economy characteristic of preindustrial societies:

> If we were to describe the ethical voices characteristic of people living within the two economies, they would be the two ethical voices described by Carol Gilligan, the (gendered) male voice associated with the market economy and the very different (gendered) female voices associated with the gift economy.[28]

Cheney proceeds to argue that the Gilligan caring ethic should form the basis of environmental ethical theory.

Several theorists (in addition to Cheney, especially Virginia Held and Annette Baier) have pointed out that rights theory is rooted in the contractual relationships of a market economy. Baier in fact notes that rights theory and the Kantian rationalist ethic were developed for an elite of white property-holding males. Kant himself excluded women from the moral community of "rights-holders" (along with animals). Women, in fact, formed a kind of "moral proletariat" who carried on the necessary caring labor in the home, while men enjoyed the privileges and rights of public citizenship.[29] This is not to say that the notion of equal rights should be abolished or that ideas of justice are automatically specious; it *is* to say that, historically, Western women came out of a different ethical tradition than men, one that has been identified by Gilligan as the "caring ethic." It makes sense then that because there is much that is valuable in this ethic, feminists who are concerned about animal welfare would seek to locate an animal treatment ethic within this tradition.

To do so, however, feminists must insist that it be framed within a political perspective. Caring is an important ethical point of departure, but to be effective it must be informed by an accurate political view. A number of theorists (including especially Sara Ruddick and Deane Curtin)[30] have made this point. As a good example of how the caring perspective is enriched by a political framework, consider Marilyn Friedman's discussion of the famous Heinz hypothetical (that Gilligan among others discusses). Here the issue concerns a man, Heinz, whose dying wife can only be saved by a particular drug. The druggist's prices are unfairly high, so that Heinz cannot afford the drug. The ethical question posed in the hypothetical is what is the proper moral course for Heinz? Should he obey the law (and presumably let his wife die) or steal the drug and save his wife? Friedman points out that the real answer to this question lies in a political analysis of a system that denies health care to people who cannot afford it and that "allows most health care resources to be privately owned, privately sold for profit in the market place, and privately withheld from people who cannot afford the market price."[31] While the traditional Kantian response to the Heinz dilemma is that he should not steal (Kant: "I am never to act otherwise than *so that I could also will that my maxim should become a universal law*" [281]), and the ethic-of-care response is that he should steal, because in this particular context his responsibility is to his wife and because stealing is a lesser evil than death, a political ethic-of-care response would include the larger dimension of looking to the political and economic context within which people must make moral decisions. Thus, the corporate-controlled health-care system becomes the primary villain in the piece, and the incident should serve to motivate action to change the system. This is the real ethical act that should emerge from the Heinz dilemma. On the other hand, a political ethic-of-care would not abandon Heinz in the abstractions of a political critique; it would also support him in obtaining the drug (by stealing, if indeed that is the only way to secure it, and if indeed the drug is as miraculous as it is supposed to be—ecofeminists are also skeptical of drug industry claims of efficacity; see Kheel's "From Healing Herbs to Deadly Drugs" [1989]).[32]

Carol Adams's *Sexual Politics of Meat* (1990) is a good example of a work that lays out the political (in this case, patriarchal) context of meat-eating. So, while a caring ethic focuses on the suffering of the animal, it is enlarged by an understanding of the symbolic cultural significances of meat-eating, which Adams explains (see also Jeremy Rifkin, *Beyond Beef* [1992]).[33] Such awareness of cultural ideologies enable the formation of appropriate ethical actions because they help to explain who profits from certain practices, such as meat-eating, and who therefore continues to promulgate propaganda on their behalf. It is important to understand the role of the meat lobby or the National Rifle Association (in promoting hunting, for example) in furthering institutionalized sanctions of these practices. Indeed, as Luke points out, massive institutional strategies have been mobilized on a national level to obscure the reality of animal suffering. Part of any ethical response must therefore be to counter these lies, to lift the veil on animal agony.

In addition to assessing power relations, a political perspective also involves a consideration of needs. On the individual level, the caring response must include a determination of a person's or animal's needs. As Rita Manning notes, caring requires "a willingness to give . . . lucid attention to the needs of others."[34] This attitude, which some have labeled "attentive love" (see below), goes beyond just respecting the rights of another.

Within a political perspective, needs assessment has a wider scope. While relatively undeveloped in liberal political theory, some Marxist theorists have focused on this issue. Agnes Heller has analyzed the social construction of the artificial consumer needs that fuel a capitalist society in her *Theory of Need in Marx* (1974).[35] She proposes the concept of *radical needs* as a revolutionary force whereby people become aware of their qualitative, spiritual needs beyond reified manufactured needs, and demand their satisfaction.

In her analysis of the Gilligan ethic, Seyla Benhabib proposes (following Jürgen Habermas) a "communicative ethic of need interpretations."[36] This means an ethic where the oppressed have an opportunity to voice their needs and where ethical decision-making is conducted in a dialogic process. Unlike universalistic rights-based theories, such an ethic would not elide the reality of the "concrete other," which remains "the *unthought*, the *unseen*, and the *unheard* in such theories" (168).

"One consequence of this ethic . . . is that . . . moral theory is enlarged so that not only rights but needs" are addressed (169). An assessment of animal needs must therefore be a part of any caring ethic for the treatment of animals. Indeed, further extension of needs theory into the area of animal welfare should be developed.

No ethic, therefore, exists in a political vacuum, and thus while it is important to ground ethics in a personal sympathetic response, it is also important to take a larger view, placing the individual instance within a political understanding of the cause and an assessment of the needs of the sufferer. The individual response is thus generalized not in a Kantian sense but within the framework of political analysis.

No ethic can therefore be apolitical; nor can any epistemology. The way we see the world—what in fact we see—is shaped by our understanding of its power relations and by our values. Much of this is taught, passed on through the mechanisms that reproduce cultural ideology, such as the schools, the churches, the media. It therefore often reflects uncritically the viewpoint and interests of the dominant powers in society.

Some feminists, notably Alison Jaggar and Nancy Hartsock, have argued that marginalized people may have an alternative perspective or standpoint that is more valid than the dominant view because it sees realities—pain and need—that are elided by controlling ideologies, which are motivated to distort the truth to perpetuate the status quo.[37] Women may be seen therefore as providing an alternative perspective—that codified in the "caring ethic," which is rooted, as we have seen, in women's historical social and economic practices.

In a recent article entitled "Moral Understandings: Alternative 'Epistemology' for a Feminist Ethics" (1992), Margaret Urban Walker calls for "a profound and original rebellion against the regnant [ethical] paradigm,"[38] which she labels the "*universalist/impersonalist tradition*" (168)—in short, the Kantian rationalist/rights tradition noted here. In its stead she proposes "an *alternative moral epistemology*, a very different way of identifying and appreciating the forms of intelligence which define moral consideration" (166). Components of this alternative epistemology include those elements of feminist ethics identified here, such as paying "attention to the particular," constructing moral issues in "contextual and narrative" (Gilligan 1982:19) frames, and using a conversational or dialogical mode in moral decision-making (166). In an earlier article, "Animal Rights and Feminist Theory" (chapter 2, this volume), I argued that an ethic for the treatment of animals must be grounded "in an emotional and spiritual conversation with nonhuman life-forms" (76). Such a conversation can emerge only when attentive love is directed at the other.

Attentive love is an exercise of the moral imagination, as urged by the numerous sympathy theorists cited above. The term derives, however, specifically from Simone Weil, who in 1942 stated:

> The love of our neighbor in all its fullness simply means being able to say to him [or her]: "What are you going through?" It is a recognition that the sufferer exists, not only as a unit in a collection, or a specimen from the social category labeled "unfortunate," but as [an individual], exactly like us, who was one day stamped with a special mark by affliction. For this reason it is enough, but it is indispensable, to know how to look at him [or her] in a certain way.
> This way of looking is first of all attentive.[39]

But it is Iris Murdoch who elaborated Weil's insight into a central moral idea, one that numerous feminists have seized upon as establishing the necessary epistemology for a caring ethic.[40] Murdoch developed the idea in several articles and in her book *The Sovereignty of Good* (1971). "Attentive love" is a moral reorientation that requires developing one's powers of attention. It is a discipline similar to that exercised by great artists or scholars (Weil used the idea originally in an essay on the discipline of scholarly study). As other sympathy theorists remarked, this reorientation breaks down solipsistic barriers; it forces attention without, to others and to what they are experiencing. Murdoch notes, "The direction of attention is, contrary to nature, outward, away from self which reduces all to a false unity, toward the great surprising variety of the world, and the ability to so direct attention is love" (66). In acknowledging Weil's coinage of the term, Murdoch says she meant by it "the idea of a just and loving gaze directed upon an individual reality" (34). Such attention, Murdoch urges, is "the characteristic and proper mark of the active moral agent" (34).

Like Mercer, Murdoch recognizes that actually seeing another's reality means constituting him or her as a subject with separate needs from one's own: "The more . . . [it is] seen that another . . . has needs and wishes as demanding as one's own, the harder it becomes to treat a person as a thing" (66).

Recognizing the other as a subject means constituting the other as a *Thou*, not an *It*, to use Martin Buber's celebrated distinction. While Buber's moral epistemology (which is rooted in the phenomenological existentialism of some of the sympathy theorists noted above), is usually assumed to apply only to humans, promoting a kind of moral humanism, in fact Buber himself applies it to animals and other living beings.

In a moving meditation on a tree Buber writes:

> I contemplate a tree.
> I can accept it as a picture. . . .
> I can feel it as a movement. . . .
> I can assign it to a species. . . .
> But it can also happen, if grace and will are joined, that as I contemplate the tree I am drawn into a relation, and the tree ceases to be an It. . . .
> Does the tree have consciousness, similar to our own? I have no experience of that. . . . What I encounter is neither the soul of a tree nor a dryad, but the tree itself.[41]

In his theory of environmental ethics, Paul Taylor calls for a similar attentiveness to the particular reality of individual organisms as the basis for a human relationship to nonhuman life-forms:

> As one becomes more and more familiar with the organism being observed, one acquires a sharpened awareness of the particular way it is living its life. One may become fascinated by it and even get to be involved in its good and bad fortunes. The organism comes to mean something to one as a unique, irreplaceable individual. . . . This progressive development from objective, detached knowledge to the recognition of individuality . . . to a full awareness of an organism's standpoint, is a process of heightening our consciousness of what it means to be an individual living thing.[42]

Taylor further maintains that we must be "'open' to the full existence and nature of the organism . . . let the individuality of the organism come before us, undistorted by our likes and dislikes, our hopes and fears, our interests, wants, and needs. As far as it is humanly possible to do so, we comprehend the organism as it is in itself, not as we want it to be" (120).

A feminist moral epistemology calls for the just and loving attention seen in these examples.[43] Rooting ethics in right seeing is nothing new. As Rosemarie Tong remarks, "even Aristotle said that ethical decisions rest in perception—in perceiving, in *seeing through one's experiences* to the moral truth beneath appearances" (228). But in the past, she argues, the great philosophers of the Western tradition "failed in their abstract moral vision because they failed in their daily moral vision. Not seeing the oppression that surrounded them, they shaped an abstract ethics that may have served to protect the interests of those in power" (229).

Sympathy theory of the past, long eclipsed, is now reinforced by a powerful new wave of ethical theory proposed by "ethic-of-care" feminists, who derive their ethic from the experience of the oppressed, urging that ethics be rooted in caring practice and an epistemology of attentive love. Such a focus need not—indeed must not—lose sight of the political context in which our moral awareness develops and our moral actions take place. But it also does not lose sight of the individual case. Contrary to Kantian rationalism, it envisages *both* the personal *and* the political.

Like Buber, people exercising attentive love *see* the tree; but they also see the logging industry. They see the downed cow in the slaughterhouse pen; but they also see the farming and dairy industry. They see the Silver Spring monkey; but they also see the drug corporations and university collaboration.

A political analysis is thus essential—particularly for formulating an effective and appropriate ethical response. But the motivation for that response remains the primary experience of sympathy. By redirecting the national focus to the suffering reality of individual animals, I believe we can reawaken the sympathetic response and reactivate the moral imagination, as outlined in this article. The animal defense movement need no longer rely solely on abstract utilitarian and rights-based claims of equal justice for animals. Rather it should recognize that a viable ethic for the treatment of animals can be rooted in sympathy, a passionate caring about their well-being.

NOTES

1. Immanuel Kant, *Kant Selections*, ed. Theodore Meyer Green (New York: Scribner, 1957), 279. Further references follow in the text.

2. Arthur Schopenhauer, *On the Basis of Morality* (1841; reprint, Indianapolis: Bobbs-Merrill, 1965), 95. Further references follow in the text.

3. Tom Regan, *The Thee Generation: Reflections on the Coming Revolution* (Philadelphia: Temple University Press, 1991), 142. Further references follow in the text.

4. Philip Mercer, *Sympathy and Ethics: A Study of the Relationship Between Sympathy and Morality with Special Reference to Hume's Treatise* (Oxford: Oxford University Press, 1972), 8. Further references follow in the text.

5. H. B. Acton, "The Ethical Importance of Sympathy," *Philosophy* 30 (1955): 66. Further references follow in the text.

6. Frederick A. Elliston, "Husserl's Phenomenology of Empathy," in *Husserl: Expositions and Appraisals*, ed. Frederick A. Elliston and Peter McCormick (Notre Dame, Ind.: University of Notre Dame Press, 1977), 223.

7. Floyd Matson, *The Broken Image: Man, Science, and Society* (Garden City, N.Y.: Anchor, 1966), 240; H. Stuart Hughes, *Consciousness and Society: The Reconstruction of European Social Thought, 1890–1930* (New York: Vintage, 1961), 187–88, 311.

8. Max Scheler, *The Nature of Sympathy*, trans. Peter Heath (1913, 1926; reprint, Hamden, Conn.: Archon, 1970), 48. Further references follow in the text.

9. Scheler erroneously sees the Western dominative attitude toward nature as "a legacy of Judaism" (*Nature of Sympathy*, 105). While the Hebrew Bible does sanction human domination, the Christian tradition heavily reinforced this thesis, and the Cartesian epistemological basis for modern science can hardly be seen as Judaic in origin. (Scheler also, of course, strongly criticizes Christianity.) Schopenhauer also—in even more offensive terms—attributed the Western derogation of animals to Judaism (the "*foetor Judaicus*") (*On the Basis of Morality*, 175, 177, 187). Schopenhauer's anti-Semitism, as well as his sexism, is, of course, abominable.

10. Kenneth J. Shapiro, "Understanding Dogs Through Kinesthetic Empathy, Social Construction, and History," *Anthrozoös* 3, no. 3 (1989): 184.

11. Edith Stein, *On the Problem of Empathy* (1916; reprint, The Hague: Martinus Nijhoff, 1966), 54–55. Further references follow in the text.

12. John A. Fisher, "Taking Sympathy Seriously: A Defense of Our Moral Psychology Toward Animals," in *The Animal Rights/Environmental Ethics Debate: The Environmental Perspective*, ed. Eugene C. Hargrove (Albany: State University of New York Press, 1992), 233.

13. Paul W. Taylor, "The Ethics of Respect for Nature," in *Animal Rights/ Environmental Ethics Debate*, ed. Hargrove, 109–10. A further reference follows in the text.

14. Rosemarie Tong, *Feminine and Feminist Ethics* (Belmont, Calif.: Wadsworth, 1993), 64. Further references follow in the text.

15. Nel Noddings, *Caring: A Feminine Approach to Ethics and Moral Education* (Berkeley: University of California Press, 1984), 174. Noddings seems ambivalent, however, on whether or to what extent human caring should be extended to animals. See *Caring*, chap. 7, and her "Comment" on my "Animal Rights and Feminist Theory" (chapter 2, this volume), *Signs: Journal of Women in Culture and Society* 16, no. 2 (1991): 418–22. See also my "Reply to Noddings," *Signs: Journal of Women in Culture and Society* 16, no. 2 (1991): 423–25.

16. See also John Kekes, "Moral Sensitivity," *Philosophy* 59 (1984): 3–19.

17. See Joseph Duke Filanowicz, "Ethical Sentimentalism Revisited," *History of Philosophy Quarterly* 6, no. 2 (1989): 189–206, for a recent reassertion of Shaftesbury's system as "a genuine and live option for contemporary ethical theory" (189).

18. Keith Thomas, *Man and the Natural World: A History of the Modern Sensibility* (New York: Pantheon, 1983), 175–76.

19. David Hume, *An Enquiry Concerning the Principles of Morals* (1777; reprint, La Salle, Ill.: Open Court, 1960), 146, 67. Further references follow in the text.

20. James Rachels, *Created from Animals: The Moral Implications of Darwinism* (Oxford: Oxford University Press, 1990), 77, 147–57. Further references follow in the text. See also Helena Cronin, *The Ant and the Peacock: Altruism and Sexual Selection from Darwin to Today* (Cambridge: Cambridge University Press, 1991).

21. J. Baird Callicott, "Animal Liberation and Environmental Ethics: Back Together Again," in *Animal Rights/Environmental Ethics Debate*, ed. Hargrove, 156. Callicott offers a two-communities theory here, claiming that human treatment of domestic animals should operate according to one ethic, and of wild animals, to the other. Less successfully, he attempts to argue that a Humean sympathy ethic also undergirds deep ecology theory, in particular the "land ethic" of Aldo Leopold—a thesis he develops in "The Conceptual Foundation of the Land Ethic," in *Companion to "A Sand County Almanac": Interpretive and Critical Essays* (Madison: University of Wisconsin Press, 1987), 186–217—but such an abstract use of the term *sympathy* would seem to rob it of meaning. Sympathy must be rooted in feelings for the particular, the concrete other.

22. Virginia Held, "Feminism and Moral Theory," in *Women and Moral Theory*, ed. Eva Feder Kittay and Diana T. Meyers (Totowa, N.J.: Rowman & Littlefield, 1987), 118.

23. See also Linda Vance, "Ecofeminism and the Politics of Reality," in *Ecofeminism: Women, Animals, Nature,* ed. Greta Gaard (Philadelphia: Temple University Press, 1993), 136.

24. Karen Warren extends the idea of care to mean intense appreciation of nature. In a celebrated passage she explains how in rock climbing she developed an emotional, respectful—indeed caring—attitude for the rock: "At that moment I was bathed in serenity. I began to talk to the rock in an almost inaudible, child-like way, as if the rock were my friend. . . . Gone was the determination to conquer the rock. I wanted simply to work respectfully with the rock as I climbed. . . . I felt myself caring for this rock" ("The Power and the Promise of Ecological Feminism," *Environmental Ethics* 12 [1990]: 134–35). Greta Gaard points out, however, that later in the same article Warren blithely sanctions the killing of a deer, to which she does not seem to extend the same caring attitude ("Ecofeminism and Native American Cultures: Pushing the Limits of Cultural Imperialism," in *Ecofeminism,* ed. Gaard, 296–97). The reason for Warren's inconsistency, I suggest, is that she is coming out of deep ecology theory, which notoriously elides the suffering of individual animals in its rush to embrace "ecoholism." Feminists Marti Kheel ("Ecofeminism and Deep Ecology: Reflections on Identity and Difference," in *Reweaving the World: The Emergence of Ecofeminism,* ed. Irene Diamond and Gloria Feman Orenstein [San Francisco: Sierra Club, 1990], 128–37) and Ariel Kay Salleh ("Deeper than Deep Ecology: The Eco-Feminist Connection," *Environmental Ethics* 6 [1984]: 339–45) have criticized deep ecology theory. I will not review these critiques here except to reaffirm that a feminist caring ethic for the treatment of animals must be rooted in appreciation, understanding, and sympathy for the animals as individuals. Following Mercer (see p. 183) I contend that sympathy or caring obtains between *feeling* beings: "'Sympathy' has regard for 'the other' solely in respect of his [or her] capacity to feel and to suffer" (*Sympathy and Ethics,* 4). Thus, Warren's use of the term *caring* is inappropriate. One can appreciate or respect a rock but one cannot feel sympathetic concern for it: such compassion is appropriate only for sentient or at least living creatures.

25. Carol Gilligan, *In a Different Voice: Psychological Theory and Women's Development* (Cambridge, Mass.: Harvard University Press, 1982), 19.

26. Hilary Rose, "Hand, Brain, and Heart: A Feminist Epistemology for the Natural Sciences," *Signs: Journal of Women in Culture and Society* 9, no. 1 (1983): 83.

27. Nancy C. M. Hartsock, *Money, Sex, and Power: Toward a Feminist Historical Materialism* (New York: Longman, 1983); Linda Nicholson, "Women, Morality, and History," in *An Ethic of Care: Feminist and Interdisciplinary Perspectives,* ed. Mary Jeanne Larrabee (New York: Routledge, 1993), 87–101; Eli Zaretsky, *Capitalism, the Family and Personal Life* (New York: Harper & Row, 1976).

28. Jim Cheney, "Eco-Feminism and Deep Ecology," *Environmental Ethics* 9 (1987): 115–45.

29. Annette Baier, "The Need for More than Justice," in *Science, Morality, and Feminist Theory*, ed. Marsha Hanan and Kai Nielsen (Calgary: University of Calgary Press, 1987), 50.

30. Sara Ruddick, "From Maternal Thinking to Peace Politics," in *Explorations in Feminist Ethics: Theory and Practice*, ed. Eve Browning Cole and Susan Coultrap-McQuin (Bloomington: Indiana University Press, 1992), 141–56; Deane Curtin, "Toward an Ecological Ethic of Care" (chapter 3, this volume). See also my own discussion in *Feminist Theory: The Intellectual Traditions of American Feminism*, rev. ed. (New York: Continuum, 1992), 199–200.

31. Marilyn Friedman, "Care and Context in Moral Reasoning," in *Women and Moral Theory*, ed. Kittay and Meyers, 202. Further references follow in the text.

32. Marti Kheel, "From Healing Herbs to Deadly Drugs: Western Medicine's War Against the Natural World," in *Healing the Wounds: The Promise of Ecofeminism*, ed. Judith Plant (Philadelphia: New Society, 1989), 96–111.

33. Carol J. Adams, *The Sexual Politics of Meat: A Feminist-Vegetarian Critical Theory* (New York: Continuum, 1990); Jeremy Rifkin, *Beyond Beef: The Rise and Fall of the Cattle Industry* (New York: Dutton, 1992).

34. Rita Manning, "Just Caring," in *Explorations in Feminist Ethics*, ed. Cole and Coultrap-McQuin, 45.

35. Agnes Heller, *The Theory of Need in Marx* (London: Allison & Busby, 1978).

36. Seyla Benhabib, "The Generalized and the Concrete Other: The Kohlberg–Gilligan Controversy and Moral Theory," in *Women and Moral Theory*, ed. Kittay and Meyers, 168. Further references follow in the text.

37. Alison M. Jaggar, *Feminist Politics and Human Nature* (Totowa, N.J.: Rowman & Littlefield, 1983), and "Love and Knowledge," in *Gender/Body/Knowledge*, ed. Alison M. Jaggar and Susan R. Bordo (New Brunswick, N.J.: Rutgers University Press, 1989), 145–71; Donovan, *Feminist Theory*, 89–90, 198–200.

38. Margaret Urban Walker, "Moral Understandings: Alternative 'Epistemology' for a Feminist Ethics," in *Explorations in Feminist Ethics*, ed. Cole and Coultrap-McQuin, 165–75. Further references follow in the text.

39. Simone Weil, "Reflections on the Right Use of School Studies with a View to the Love of God" (1942), in *The Simone Weil Reader*, ed. George A. Panichas (New York: McKay, 1977), 51.

40. See, especially, Walker, "Moral Understandings"; Ellen L. Fox, "Seeing Through Women's Eyes: The Role of Vision in Women's Moral Theory," in *Explorations in Feminist Ethics*, ed. Cole and Coultrap-McQuin, 111–16; Ruddick, *Maternal Thinking: Toward a Politics of Peace* (Boston: Beacon, 1989); Robin S. Dillon, "Care and Respect," in *Explorations in Feminist Ethics*, ed.

Cole and Coultrap-McQuin, 69–81; Meredith W. Michaels, "Morality Without Distinction," *Philosophical Forum* 17, no. 3 (1986): 175–87; and Iris Murdoch, *The Sovereignty of Good* (New York: Schocken, 1971). I elaborated these ideas earlier in "Beyond the Net: Feminist Criticism as a Moral Criticism," *Denver Quarterly* 17, no. 4 (1983): 40–57.

41. Martin Buber, *I and Thou* (1923; reprint, New York: Scribner, 1970), 57–59. See also Buber's discussion of his exchange of glances with a cat (144–46) and his treatment of a horse as thou in *Between Man and Man*, rev ed. (1947; New York: Macmillan, 1965), 23. Another important work that argues for the "Thouness" of animals is Gary A. Kowalski, *The Souls of Animals* (Walpole, N.H.: Stillpoint, 1991).

42. Paul W. Taylor, *Respect for Nature: A Theory of Environmental Ethics* (Princeton, N.J.: Princeton University Press, 1986), 120–21. A further reference follows in the text.

43. Taylor, a rationalist, would probably resist the term *loving* here, even though his description comes very close to the Murdoch/Weil notion of attentive love, applied to natural life. In *Respect for Nature*, Taylor insists on the Kantian distinction between acting out of rational duty and acting out of emotional inclination. He rejects the latter on familiar Kantian grounds (85, 90–91, 126–27).

CHAPTER 8

Caring About Suffering

A Feminist Exploration

CAROL J. ADAMS

> Those in power typically advocate rules and rationality, others,
> relatedness and caring.
>
> —Ellyn Kaschak

In the wake of the appearance of *The Sexual Politics of Meat*, attempts were made to determine my feminist stance on animal rights as a philosophy. *The Sexual Politics of Meat* did not offer any helpful clues on this subject. It was not my goal to approach the oppression of animals in the manner of Peter Singer or Tom Regan. Not only had this been done, but my work had a different source, and in the early years, I was working without the benefit of their major texts. My goal was to expose the roots of animal exploitation in the construction of the patriarchal subject. I needed to make visible the invisible—the lives of women and the experience of animals used by humans—while identifying the theoretical structures that maintained this invisibility. Neither the philosophical language of rights nor that of interest seemed to intersect with this goal—nor could they since their analysis of animals' status ignored the issue of human male domination.

An earlier version of this chapter was presented as a keynote at Ecofeminist Perspectives: The Twenty-Second Annual Richard R. Baker Philosophy Colloquium, University of Dayton, April 1, 1995. First published in Josephine Donovan and Carol J. Adams, eds., *Beyond Animal Rights* (New York: Continuum, 1996). © 1996 by Carol J. Adams. Published by permission of the author.

Although the theoretical debates about claims on behalf of animals' rights and interests did not personally appeal to me, what, I wondered, was the appropriate theoretical approach to establish animals as having other than instrumental value? Rights, it seemed to me, at least said, minimally, "do not touch." And there are many times when that is exactly what I feel about the exploitation of animals. I want to intervene and proclaim this. But then I began more closely to study both the issue and myself. My own evolution toward animal defense was because of the sudden loss of a Welsh pony, and the feelings that I experienced when I tried to eat a hamburger the night of that pony's death. Certainly I knew firsthand how relationships can catalyze one into refusing to view animals instrumentally. Moreover, it seemed that it is because animal advocates *care* that many gravitate to the language of rights.

While writing *The Sexual Politics of Meat*, I was unaware of the "rights-care" debate. When I learned of the debate, I was worried because ethics of care discussions seemed to reinforce certain assumptions about women and our caregiving role in Western patriarchal culture.

Was caring a survival skill developed under oppression? If caring was necessitated by women's lack of power, and a negotiation from this position of powerlessness, then to reclaim it as the source for transforming people's relationship with animals would only further women's oppression. But jettisoning the ethic of care because caring was an aspect of our oppression seemed to be the wrong approach. My own evolution had occurred precisely because I cared about animals. Were the day to come when women's oppression was eradicated, would we also wish to eradicate caring for others? Would not some form of caring survive the transformation of women's status?

Then I came to realize—thanks to feminist analyses of care—that the male ideal of the autonomous individual, on which rights theory is based, is fraudulent. As feminist psychotherapist Ellyn Kaschak points out,

> It would seem that men have just as much difficulty separating and individuating as do women, and that the ideal of separation and individuality is a somewhat unnatural act which must be accomplished largely by illusion. If men define women, children, and even physical aspects of the environment as extensions of themselves, then their own difficulties with separation are made invisible. Men so often report experiencing women's reactions to their behaviors as an extension of their own that we must consider that men lack a good sense of where their boundaries end and women's

begin. . . . The construction of a separate and individual self directly reflects the masculinist predilection to make invisible the context and interconnections between people and all living things. This is the same perspective that leads to perceiving concepts as universal rather than as contextually bound.[1]

Kaschak thus reorients the rights-care debate by pointing out that the notion of the autonomous individual (the ontology that accompanies rights) is dependent on the relational ontology of care, but it renders invisible the whole network of relationships that are sustaining the solitary individual. Given this insight, we have to recognize that the idea of the independent rights-bearer depends, without acknowledgment, on the ontology of care.

The articulation of animal rights philosophy presumes an autonomous individual, traditionally a "man of reason," the Enlightenment idea of the autonomous seeker in an agonistic and lone quest for knowledge. But, as noted, the idea of autonomy is an illusion, because it depends on the invisibility of women's caring activities.

If we define being relational as feeling responsible for, and defining, one's self-worth by the success or failure of one's relationships and by being sensitive to the expressed and unexpressed emotional needs of others, then it would appear that women, in general, are more relational than are men, in general. However, if we consider that men's independence and separateness viewed contextually emerge as emotional and physical dependence upon women— wives, lovers, secretaries, graduate assistants, nurses, and so on— then men are certainly as relational as women, if not more so.[2]

In short, the unacknowledged context for animal rights philosophy is the fact that we live in a patriarchal culture. An entire cadre of female support allows for the illusion of the autonomous rights-holder.

Consider, for instance, when Tom Regan writes "of a new generation, *The Thee Generation*." He describes it as,

a generation of service: of giving, not taking, of commitment to principles not material possessions, of communal compassion not conspicuous consumption. If the defining question of the present generation is What can I get for me? the central question of this new generation is What can I do for thee?[3]

It may now be "the thee generation" for men but it has always been "the thee generation"—of sacrificial service to others—for women. Thus, Regan's construction fails to acknowledge women's care-giving—the exact problem that rights discourse has at the theoretical level.

I value nurturing and caring because it is good, not because it constitutes women's "difference." Similarly, I do not value animals because women are somehow "closer" to them, but because we experience interdependent oppressions. I support animals because they are oppressed and because I care about their experiences of harm, pain, and suffering: I wish to intervene to end their oppression.[4] Clearly, the animal advocacy movement is committed to ending animal suffering, as well. But, it has failed to engage a central question: What are the implications that animal suffering occurs within the context of a patriarchal culture?

Caring, Emotions, and Theory

Sexual inequality influences our attitudes toward and responses to suffering in numerous ways. To begin with, suffering itself, as an experience, is socially constructed as feminine. Furthermore, emotions are denigrated as untrustworthy and unreliable. They have long been viewed as invalid sources of knowledge. Moreover, they are equated with women, with being "womanish." Given the patriarchal mind/body dualism, the working assumption appears to be that caring about and emotionally responding to suffering are not trustworthy as the foundation of theory.

In accepting as two primary texts, Singer's *Animal Liberation* and Regan's *The Case for Animal Rights*—texts that valorize rationality—the animal defense movement reiterates a patriarchal disavowal of emotions as having a legitimate role in theory making. The problem is that while on the one hand it articulates positions against animal suffering, on the other hand animal rights theory dispenses with the idea that caring about and emotionally responding to this suffering can be appropriate sources of knowledge.[5]

Emotions and theory are related. One does not have to eviscerate theory of emotional content and reflection to present legitimate theory. Nor does the presence of emotional content and reflection eradicate or militate against thinking theoretically. By disavowing emotional responses, two major texts of animal defense close off the intellectual space for recognizing the role of emotions in knowledge and therefore theory making.

As the issue of caring about suffering is problematized, difficulties with animal rights per se become apparent. Without a gender analysis, several important issues that accompany a focus on suffering are neglected, to the detriment of the movement.

Animal rights theory offers a legitimating language for animal defense without acknowledging the indebtedness of the rights-holder to caring relationships. Nor does it provide models for theoretically engaging with our own emotional responses, since emotions are seen as untrustworthy.

Because the animal advocacy movement has failed to incorporate an understanding of caring as a motivation for so many animal defense activists, and because it has not addressed the gendered nature of caring—that it is woman's duty to provide service to others, while it is men's choice—it has not addressed adequately the implications that a disproportionate number of activists are women motivated because they care about animal suffering.

Animal rights theory that disowns or ignores emotions mirrors on the theoretical level the gendered emotional responses inherent in a patriarchal society. In this culture, women are supposed to do the emotional work for heterosexual intimate relationships: "a man will come to expect that a woman's role in his life is to take care of his feelings and alleviate the discomfort involved in feeling."[6] At the cultural level, this may mean that women are doing the emotional work for the animal defense movement. And this emotional work takes place in the context of our own oppression.

The Sex-Species System

Before we can explore the gendered nature of various responses to suffering, we must establish the social and political environment in which suffering and caring about suffering take place.

Feminism identifies this environment as sexist. Animal defenders see it as speciesist. Clearly, as I have argued in *The Sexual Politics of Meat* and *Neither Man nor Beast*, sexism and speciesism are interconnected, mutually reinforcing systems of oppression and ways of organizing the world. The species barrier has always been gendered and racialized; patriarchy has been inscribed through species inequality as well as human inequality. The emphasis on differences between humans and animals not only reinforces fierce boundaries about what constitutes humanness, but particularly about what constitutes manhood. That which traditionally has been seen to distinguish humans from animals—qualities such as reason and rationality—has been used as well to differentiate men from women, whites from people of color. Species categorization is one aspect of a racist patriarchy. "Man" (read: white man) exists as a concept and a sexual identity through negation ("not woman, not beast, not colored"—that is, "not the other").[7]

The best way to convey this analysis of the overlapping, interdependent relationship of sexual inequality and species inequality is by referring to our current racist patriarchy as instituting a *sex-species system*.[8] An ecofeminist analysis of racist patriarchal dualisms identifies dyads that organize our world. These dyads include:

man	woman
human	animal
white	"colored"
mind	body
reason	emotion

It is not simply that the Western dualistic worldview has divided us from each other, from animals, from a sense of self that thinks and feels in a continuous, related way, so that it could be said that we think through our feelings, feel through our thinking. Nor is it only that the dominated side of the dualism is in service to the dominant side.[9] It is also—and very specifically—that the inequality attributed to the colored-female-body-animal side is *sexualized*. That is, the colored, female, animal is the body that is constructed as available for sex. Kaschak explains:

> Several decades ago, Karen Horney noted that "the prerogative of gender [is] the socially sanctioned right of all males to sexualize all females, regardless of age or status"—to observe, evaluate, and use the female body for their own purposes. . . . Although not all men may choose to exercise this right actively, no woman can choose to opt out of this system.[10]

As Kathy Barry cogently argues in *The Prostitution of Sexuality*:

> When society becomes sexually saturated, sex is equated with the female body—where it is gotten, had, taken. . . . Sexual saturation of society is a political accomplishment of male domination. . . .

When sex is objectified and human beings are reduced to vehicles for acquiring it, sexual domination enters into and is anchored in the body.[11]

The sex-species system insures that white, "rational" men have access to female animal bodies. In *The Sexual Politics of Meat*, I explain how it is that nonhuman animal bodies of either sex are rendered female. "Prey"—from whales to foxes—are called "shes" whether they are male or female.[12] Similarly, women's bodies, especially the bodies of women of color, are seen as animal.

Racism is clearly a part of the sex-species system. Not only does it use an animalizing discourse about oppressed, disenfranchised, and marginalized people (imputing that they *are* animals, that they are *like* animals, or that they are *closer* to animals—that is, using a species hierarchy), but it sexualizes these now-animalized bodies, insisting on the availability of "colored" female animal bodies, and claiming that these sexed bodies sexually desire being violated as well as sexually desiring animals as partners.[13] Bestiality is often the pornographic focus characteristic of a speciesist racist patriarchy. Fixated on women of color having sex with animals, such pornography actually reverses the agent: most acts of forced sex with animals involve men as agents. Yet, in pornography, the agent is frequently cast as a woman of color.[14] Here is the sex-species system at work: men taking/making sex with colored "female" animal bodies. This is racialized sexual oppression.[15] As Patricia Hill Collins argues:

> African-American women's experiences suggest that Black women were not added into a preexisting pornography, but rather that pornography itself must be reconceptualized as an example of the interlocking nature of race, gender, and class oppression. At the heart of both racism and sexism are notions of biological determinism claiming that people of African descent and women possess immutable biological characteristics marking their inferiority to elite white men. In pornography these racist and sexist beliefs are sexualized.[16]

Building on an analysis of Alice Walker's, Collins explains how it is that pornography depicts white women as objects and black women as animals:

> As objects white women become creations of culture—in this case, the mind of white men—using the materials of nature—in this

case, uncontrolled female sexuality. In contrast, as animals Black women receive no such redeeming dose of culture and remain open to the type of exploitation visited on nature overall. Race becomes the distinguishing feature in determining the type of objectification women will encounter. . . . Publicly exhibiting Black women may have been central to objectifying Black women as animals and to creating the icon of Black women as animals. . . . The treatment of all women in contemporary pornography has strong ties to the portrayal of Black women as animals.[17]

To support her claim that "in pornography women become nonpeople and are often represented as the sum of their fragmented body parts," Collins draws on the analysis of Scott McNall, who observes:

This fragmentation of women relates to the predominance of rear-entry position photographs. . . . All of these kinds of photographs reduce the woman to her reproductive system, and furthermore, make her open, willing, and available—not in control. . . . The other thing rear-entry position photographs tell us about women is that they are animals. They are animals because they are the same as dogs—bitches in heat who can't control themselves.[18]

Because of the sexualizing of the nondominant side of the dyad (the colored-woman-body-animal), and because whiteness, on its own, does not intervene in the sex-species system solely as privilege, women of all races are seen as woman-body-animal. As a result, women's orifices are a part of the accessible environment available to men. As Catharine MacKinnon points out, we live "in a society of sex inequality—where sex is what women *have* to sell, sex is what we are, sex is what we are valued for, we are born sex, we die sex."[19]

The sex-species system appears to be deceptively divisible, seeming to be two different systems (women's issues on the one hand, animal issues on the other). This keeps us from making connections. Insisting that we recognize the sex-species system does not insinuate that this is *all* that we must recognize, it is simply insisting that without recognizing the interdependence of the sex-species system, our actions and analyses are fragmented and fractured.

This schema contributes the ecofeminist insight into the devaluation of the body to the radical feminist understanding of the specific sexual use of women's bodies. The sexualized female animal body is consumable when alive through sex acts and pornography,[20] and consumable, if non-human, when dead, as food or clothing or scientific material. The mobility of women in the sex-species system means that sometimes we may be unmarked humans in relationship to animals (especially as we benefit from their exploitation) and if we are white in relationship to people of color, while in relationship to those who are the generic humans (men), we are animalized.

A sense of entitlement accompanies men's status in the sex-species system. Psychotherapist Kaschak proposes that male entitlement means that men have extensive boundaries that subsume others. This is male privilege. For women and marginalized men, the boundaries we believed we established for ourselves and our bodies are not acknowledged or respected. Animals often are not seen as individuals and thus remain undifferentiated from each other. Thus, the concept of boundaries for animals—self-imposed or otherwise—rarely arises.

The suffering of women, the other animals, and disenfranchised, colonized peoples occurs within this sex-species system, which remains as well the unacknowledged context for animal rights philosophy and activism.

Is Suffering Generic?

We conventionally talk about human suffering and animal suffering as different phenomena. Elaine Scarry, in an otherwise cogently argued book, *The Body in Pain*, believes:

> a dividing line can be drawn between human hurt and animal hurt; for the displacement of human sacrifice with animal sacrifice (and its implicit designation of the human body as a privileged space that cannot be used in the important process of substantiation [the process by which we establish meaning]) has always been recognized as a special moment in the infancy of civilization.[21]

Most people agree with her, it seems, as we have a rather persistent hierarchy regarding pain and suffering: that it is different for human animals than for nonhuman animals.[22] However, many of the qualities of suffering are in fact nonspecies specific. As Bernard Rollin pointed out years ago, "the most eloquent signs of pain, human *or* animal, are non-linguistic."[23] Scarry confirms that the most prominent qualities of pain are its unsharability, its resistance to language, its active destruction of language. Indeed, pain brings "about an immediate reversion to a state anterior to language, to the sounds and cries a human being makes before language is learned."[24]

Pain, Scarry might have observed, thus eradicates one of the most firmly held demarcating points between humans and other animals: language use. Indeed, pain's "resistance to language is not simply one of its incidental or accidental attributes, but is essential to what it is."[25] It shatters language. In doing so, it transposes humans to an animal status. Does Scarry avoid stating the obvious—that it renders humans "animal-like"—because she has so much conceptually invested (all of civilization!) in keeping human and animal pain separate?

James Rachels points out that

> we have virtually the same evidence for animal pain that we have for human pain. When humans are tortured, they cry out; so do animals. When humans are faced with painful stimuli, they draw back and try to escape; so do animals. Pain in humans is associated with the operation of a complex nervous system; so it is with animals. . . . Darwin stressed that, in an important sense, their nervous systems, their behaviours, their cries, *are* our nervous systems, our behaviours, and our cries, with only a little modification.[26]

But animals also express pain differently. This, too, is important to acknowledge. Feminist scientist Lynda Birke explains that "some species, particularly ungulates (hoofed mammals) do not usually whimper and squeal."[27] Bernard Rollin insists, "Animals do show unique pain behaviour. It just doesn't happen to be human pain behaviour. But, then why should it be?"[28]

The animal defense movement often ends up saying, "animals suffer like humans," thus gesturing toward a generic human suffering model. This is problematic in two ways: first, because it maintains anthropocentricity (animals suffer like human beings [rather than unpacking the idea and saying, "all animal bodies—ours included—suffer in many similar ways"]). Second, because it maintains androcentricity, male-centeredness. It does so because human suffering is much more likely to be conceptualized according to men's experiences rather than women's. In fact, because of the sex-species system, women's suffering and the harms we experience are different from men's.

MEN'S SUFFERING

Men's suffering (as men) is often construed to be purposeful. It is suffering for a good. Men's suffering has meaning and is attended to (consider the attention in past years to prostate cancer as opposed to breast cancer, or molested boys over molested girls). Suffering and dying in war is a primary example of suffering for a good. Also, men's suffering is often episodic, not chronic; it occurs in a situation that one is accidentally in, such as being injured or killed by random gunfire ("being in the wrong place at the wrong time"). On the other hand, men's suffering that is neither purposeful nor episodic is usually caused by a political ideological context, such as racism or homophobia. African-American men, Native men, and other men of color suffer for their biological markedness, their race, which makes their maleness conditional. Gay men suffer from homophobia, from being seen as an abomination of "nature's" intent for men, which is to have sex with female bodies.

WOMEN'S SUFFERING

Women's suffering similarly can be the result of our ideological context, that is, sexism. Women *as women* suffer from a chronic violence that is ongoing, not episodic.[29] It is violence against women *un*modified (woman *qua* woman). This does not mean that women are "victims," but that we must anticipate that we will be victimized because we are women, because of the sex-species system that renders us sexed female animal bodies.[30] The sex-species system also renders other bodies, including at times certain men's bodies, as sexed female animal bodies. Catharine MacKinnon explains how "gender is a substantive process of inequality":

> To be victimized in certain ways may mean to be feminized, to partake of the low social status of the female, to be made into the girl regardless of biological sex. This does not mean that men experience or share the meaning of being a woman, because part of that meaning is that inferiority is indelible and total until it is changed for all women. It does mean that gender is an outcome of a social process of subordination that is only ascriptively tied to body and doesn't lose its particularity of meaning when it shifts embodied form. Femininity is a lowering that is imposed; it can be done to

anybody and still be what feminine means. It is just women to whom it is considered natural.[31]

Not only is violence against women our context, rather than an episode, but our suffering from this violence is for no good reason. Unlike militarism, which offers ready explanations for men's suffering in times of military engagements, women's ongoing suffering from violence has no inherent redemptive qualities to it. Nor is it socially constructed as meaningful. Consequently it is not attended to; it is ignored. We women may and do spend many hours trying to figure out why sexual violence happened to us, but sexual violence is both ongoing and incomprehensible. Women's suffering could be stopped if our culture made a commitment to stopping sexually abusive and possessive behavior, mainly on the part of men. Unfortunately, our society has not done so.

The violence we suffer from is agential—that is, it is done by an agent. I refer to this, therefore, as *agential suffering*. But that agency—usually a particular man—is denied by language deriving from the sex-species system.[32] Our suffering is thereby mystified. Not wanting to acknowledge that deliberate violence is done by men, people use racist language and label acts of violence "dark,"[33] or they use speciesist language and label violence "animal." Such language suggests that violence is uncontrollably part of men's nature, the side one can't fathom (the dark side), the part one can't control (the beast within). But in reality men have not lost control when they act violently toward women; their violence is deliberate. Nowhere is this more apparent than when animals are harmed by woman-batterers. Men batter to gain control. Batterers can obfuscate why they batter when it is physical violence (claiming "I 'lost' control and punched her"—the "dark" side explanation). They can confuse the issue of sexual assault (asserting "she was teasing me and said she wanted it"—the "it-brought-out-the-animal-in-me" explanation). But loss of control is harder to defend when an animal is the victim because the deliberateness of the violence is exposed in the description ("I 'lost' control and then cut the dog's head off and then nailed it to the porch"). There is not much leeway for a man to say he tortured animals and it was out of his control. It is clearly willful and deliberate.[34] But our culture does not want to recognize this willfulness, this deliberateness, or so far has failed to, and thus sexually abusive and possessive behavior is not stopped.

Why does our culture continue to sanction sexual violence? One explanation is offered by Robin West, who, in a feminist law review article, explains:

One reason that women suffer more than men is that women often find painful the same objective event or condition that men find pleasurable. . . . For the man, the office pass was sex (and pleasurable), for the woman, it was harassment (and painful); for the man the evening was a date—perhaps not pleasant, but certainly not frightening—for the woman, it was a rape and very scary indeed. Similarly, a man may experience as at worst offensive, and at best stimulating, that which a woman finds debilitating, dehumanizing, or even life-threatening. Pornographic depictions of women which facilitate by legitimating the violent brutalization of our bodies are obvious examples.[35]

In other words, *our* harm is *their* pleasure.

Thus, suffering for men and for women is in certain respects different, because men and women are differently inscribed in the sex-species system.

Animal Suffering

Animal suffering is something else again. Sometimes it is said to be for a good reason; sometimes it is denied to be suffering; sometimes we do everything possible to avoid confronting reminders of animal suffering. Often their suffering is considered irrelevant, because one way or another it benefits humans. As their bodies are dematerialized as whole bodies to service our pleasures from fragmented body parts (leather, fur, meat, objects of scientific study), their suffering is rendered immaterial to assuage our conscience. To abet this instrumental use of animals' bodies, they are deliberately kept anonymous (don't name anyone you wish to consume). As opposed to efforts at memorializing slain anonymous humans, we are specifically not to remind people of slain anonymous animals. Nevertheless, despite all these obfuscations, it is clear that much animal pain is produced for human pleasure.

People often get upset when they are reminded of animal suffering and deaths, but a speciesist culture generally keeps people from being exposed to this upsetting information (see Luke in this volume). Thus, individuals are insulated from exposure to animal suffering, though their consequent emotional upset would be both valid and a valid foundation for theorizing. When I complained to an animal advocacy group that the graffiti-applied fur coats they were using in an advertising campaign might encourage the street harassment of furwearing women, I was informed that the city's bus system had refused to carry images that featured trapped furbearing animals. Steve Baker reports similar problems for British animal defense groups: "In 1990 the RSPCA found itself requested by the Advertising Standards Authority [ASA] to withdraw a press advertisement featuring a photograph of a dead horse suspended from a meat hook in an abattoir, as the ASA thought it likely to cause 'distress and revulsion' to the public." Antibullfighting posters were seen as too disturbing, so they were not allowed in British airports.[36]

The responses to individual cases of animal suffering that receive media attention, the outpouring of offers of assistance, the ongoing concern, the anger at perpetrators—reveal how intense awareness and action on behalf of an individual animal's suffering can be. Bernard Rollin observes, "to be morally responsive to pain in animals, one must ideally know animals in their individuality."[37] Of course, the cultural construction of animals is such that this is precisely what we are usually denied: knowledge of the individual animal being consumed for supper, knowledge of the individual animal being worn. Often, animals are never even seen as possessing individual identities.

It may be argued that even if we know the individual animal who is suffering, we cannot know the animal's experience of pain. But this is precisely the claim Elaine Scarry makes about human pain, that we cannot know another's pain. She explains:

> A person whose pain it is, knows it effortlessly, the person whose pain it is not, cannot know it even with effort.
>
> For the person whose pain it is, it is "effortlessly" grasped (that is, even with the most heroic effort it cannot *not* be grasped); while for the person outside the sufferer's body, what is "effortless" is *not* grasping it.

Scarry expands upon this insight in a way specifically relevant to this discussion of animals' suffering:

> It is easy to remain wholly unaware of its existence; even with effort, one may remain in doubt about its existence or may retain the astonishing freedom of denying its existence; and finally, if with the best effort of sustained attention one successfully apprehends it, the aversiveness of the "it" one apprehends will only be a shadowy fraction of the actual "it."[38]

212 of FOUNDATIONAL ARTICLES

The person in pain encounters pain that cannot be denied; the person outside of pain encounters pain that cannot be confirmed. This is true whether we are speaking of human or nonhuman animal pain.

SHOULD SUFFERING BE APPROPRIATED?

In *The Sexual Politics of Meat* I raised a concern about the way that the experience of animals under human oppression becomes a metaphor for peoples' experience—that is, the absent referent enables animals' experience of suffering to be appropriated.[39] We lose sight of the animal and focus on the violence, for instance, when we use metaphors about meat and butchering to protest the treatment of human beings, but do not see the terms as inherently troubling. Just so with using the Holocaust and other experiences of incomprehensibly immense suffering as metaphors. These metaphors attempt to make others' experience "borrowable."

It is not for us to compare suffering. We should *acknowledge* suffering, but not compare it. Acknowledging grants the *integrity* of the suffering, while comparing assumes the *reducibility*, the objectification of suffering. When the issue is animal suffering, the choice appears to be between asserting the basic unknowability of all pain (including that of animals') versus articulating anthropocentric examples of pain to convey animals' suffering. Clearly, when factory farms and slaughterhouses are compared to concentration camps, there is little question which choice is made. The standard is still human.

Just as the fact of women's suffering—and the suffering of marginalized men who are made to suffer as females—disappears when a heroic notion of men's suffering prevails, so animal suffering is ignored unless appropriated to human suffering to make it expressible. But this is anthropocentric. Why not talk about the way animals—including us—suffer? Instead of saying, "animals' suffering is like human's," relying on metaphors, why not say animal suffering in their body is *theirs*? Since the experience of suffering is individual, a recognition of the individual is necessary before suffering can be acknowledged. But, once we do recognize the specific character of suffering, we must learn to cope with this sensitivity because such knowledge is wrenching. It interferes with human pleasure.

Our Own Suffering

How one has dealt with one's own pain influences one's ability to care about and respond to another's suffering.

GENDERED RESPONSES: STOICISM VERSUS SACRIFICE

The very idea of long-suffering or ongoing suffering is that it is a female experience—that it is unmanly. It is manly not to succumb to suffering or even to admit its existence. To deny its existence is seen as admirably manly personal stoicism. But denial creates an inability to sympathize with others' suffering, blocking empathy, and it also often prevents men from acknowledging their own suffering.

On the other hand, as noted above, women are socialized as the primary caretakers and nurturers of the family.[40] Women are therefore socialized to the role of being sensitive to others' needs and suffering.

CONSTRICTION AND DISSOCIATION

Traumatic dissociation or "constriction" may characterize a victim's response to ongoing violence:

> when a person is completely powerless, and any form of resistance is futile, she may go into a state of surrender. The system of self-defense shuts down entirely. The helpless person escapes from her situation not by action in the real world but rather by altering her state of consciousness. Analogous states are observed in animals, who sometimes "freeze" when they are attacked.[41]

For instance, survivors report how, during an attack—especially if it was part of a chronic situation of violence in which they lived with or knew their abuser well—they left their body and watched what happened to them from the ceiling. The developed ability to dissociate may mean that cues regarding impending danger may be neglected. It separates us from our bodies, and our time/space. We may literally lose hours that cannot be accounted for. Can we connect to others' bodies if to survive we must actively disconnect from our own?

SURVIVORS AND VICTIMS

Kaschak explains that boundaries say "this is where I end and you begin."[42] Boundaries involve "knowing who one is and who one is not."[43] Being a survivor means that one has integrated one's own suffering and restored one's ability to maintain boundaries. But to fully recover more needs to be done. Judith Herman observes that "where there is no way to compensate for an atrocity, there is a way to transcend it, by making it a gift to others."[44] A survivor's mission involves recognizing that she has been a victim, understanding the effects of her victimization, and then transforming the meaning of this victimization "by making it the basis for social action."[45] Herman comments that "although giving to others is the essence of the survivor mission, those who practice it recognize that they do so for their own healing."[46] Some animal defense activists are engaging in their own survivor's mission; some, however, are still being victimized themselves. Some activists, especially those who are women, may be participating in victims' missions, where self-sacrifice is confused with the ethic of care. The self needs to be taken care of too.

A victim is someone currently still undergoing abuse or who has not successfully integrated past abuse. Past abuse needs to be rendered conditional, rather than determinative, in nature. But if our violation occurs when we are young, we are often deprived of the ability to create boundaries for ourselves. The result, especially for survivors of child sexual abuse, is that "many survivors have such profound deficiencies in self-protection that they can barely imagine themselves in a position of agency or choice. The idea of saying no to the emotional demands of a parent, spouse, lover, or authority figure may be practically inconceivable."[47] In a movement, such as the animal defense movement, where the majority of the grass-roots activists are women and the majority of national leaders are men, this problem of saying no to authority figures may militate against some activists setting protective boundaries for themselves.

For women who have not integrated the experience of their own victimization, their intervention on behalf of animals can be fraught with problems. They have not restored or perhaps have not been allowed to establish adequate boundaries for saying to another "you stop here." While not saving themselves (and perhaps being unable to do so given the cultural structures that protect abusers), they nevertheless still try to save others.

How do we respond effectively to the numbingly uncalculable numbers and intensity of animal suffering while protecting our own selves? If I feel so deeply the suffering of animals, where does the "I-that-is-I" stop? In the face of failure to respond to animals' suffering by the vast majority of people, the question often seems to be, "If I don't care for this animal, who will?"

Animal defense activists often insist to other activists "the animals need you." When this happens, suffering *for* the animals is valorized. Because caring is so marginalized theoretically, there is little attention to equiping activists to be self-protective in response to immense suffering. A singular focus that gives attention to only one part of the sex-species system (in this case, the experience of the other species), will reinforce women's sacrificial way of saving others rather than working against our own oppressions. We put our oppression aside to address someone else's.

The challenge for women is to define our own boundaries, so that we are simultaneously saying "I will care for myself" as we care about and respond to the suffering of others. We must do all this while also learning to recognize men's definitions, sexuality, and needs not as part of ourselves but as part of the sex-species system, which is the context of our lives.[48]

SUPPRESSION

With suppression, all of one's emotional energy is given over to dealing—or in fact, not dealing—with one's own pain. To protect oneself from feeling one's own pain, one cannot feel anyone else's pain either. It may be that no one else's pain compares to what these individuals are experiencing or have experienced. They cannot experience suffering in ways that are redemptive, because they have made themselves incapable of recognizing (their own) suffering. They use all available energy to suppress recognition of their own suffering. It is a refusal to identify, by those who suffered or continue to suffer, with others who suffer.

IDENTIFICATION WITH THE AGGRESSOR

To avoid caring about suffering, an individual may identify with those causing the suffering, with those in power.[49] Consequently, one identifies with the consumer, not the consumed. Additionally, since dominance is eroticized, the harm/pleasure dialectic pertains (our harm is their pleasure, others' harm is our pleasure). In other words, identifying with the aggressor may offer certain hedonic rewards.

DEPRIVATION

We may be confused about what our suffering constitutes. Sometimes, loss of a privilege feels like suffering. I call this *subjective suffering*[50] because to the person experiencing it, it is unpleasant, even though it may not seem significant to others. Unable to recognize that this privilege had been gained through the sex-species system, for instance, the privilege of using pornography or eating meat, men may conclude that this loss constitutes significant suffering. Losing access to what one feels entitled to may indeed cause pain, but this is not comparable to agential suffering (suffering deliberately caused by another). Loss of pleasure may subjectively feel unpleasant. As a result, challenges to privilege and entitlement are often received hostilely (being against pornography is cast as antisex, puritanical; being against the consumption of animals is ascetic, self-denying). In this accusation, the loss of pleasure is acknowledged. But what remains invisible is the sex-species system. It is this that establishes the privileged to take pleasure in harm to others' bodies.

Why Do We Fail to Care About and Respond to the Suffering of Others?

We may not respond to the suffering of others because of denial, in order to avoid our own pain. However, societal forces also discourage responding.

DENIAL OF OUR OWN EMOTIONS

In a radically dualistic patriarchy such as ours, minds are not supposed to feel. Hyperationality rationalizes the suffering of others by denying it, disengaging from it, refusing to acknowledge it. As we have seen, part of the training to manhood is that men are not supposed to feel, are not supposed to acknowledge that others' suffering matters. Because emotions are felt to be untrustworthy, many men feel all negative emotions as anger.[51] Because men are socialized in this way, the complex feelings of sadness, depression, horror, and other emotions, including anger, that arise in response to caring about animals' suffering and exploitation, all become funneled into the feeling of anger alone.

Several animal advocacy men have told me that they spent years insisting they did not care for animals, because they did not feel caring was an appropriate response. They needed to appear rational, "in control," distanced from animals. With the appearance of ecofeminist writings on animals, they felt such relief because they now had a language that legitimated the idea that one might care for animals and that this was an appropriate motivation for activism.

Besides the constraint on men *qua* men caring about another's suffering, gay men may feel a constraint on expressing their emotions out of a fear that that might reveal them to be gay. They may fear that acknowledging to others that they care about animals will "out" them or, if out, that people will respond to some stereotype of gayness and emotionality rather than to themselves as individuals.

I have been aware as I rear two vegetarian sons how our emphasis on caring about animals demarcates them from the boys who are their friends. They are encouraged to explore a range of emotions in response to their awareness of animals' experience under human oppression.

We May Not Respond to Others' Suffering, Because the Harm to an Individual Is Not Seen

Why is the harm to an individual not seen? First, *the individual may not be seen, because the victim has been dematerialized.* In other words, no individuality remains to identify with. For instance, animals' bodies are literally dematerialized as a whole, complete body. Similarly, the victim of pornography may be dematerialized, both literally—because of shots that focus on certain body parts—and by the argument that pornography is about "ideas," not about women and our bodies.

Second, *the harm to an individual is not seen, because of ideological construction.* The victims (because of the way that species, race, sex, and sexual identity are constructed in the sex-species system) are viewed as too inconsequential to matter. Because the victims have been trivialized, the issue can be trivialized as well. We can see this operating in queries about animals that pose the question, "Why else are they here?"

Third, *the individual is so devalued that the harm is not seen.* This occurs when a group of persons is chronically harmed, and thus constructed precisely as violable, as victims. Speaking of Linda Marchiano ("Linda Lovelace"), Catharine MacKinnon observes:

> It is apparently difficult to carry on about the ultimate inviolability of the person in the face of a person who has been so ultimately violated. . . . If it happened and it hurt her, she deserved it. If she didn't deserve it, either it didn't happen or it didn't hurt her. If she says it hurt her, she's oversensitive or unliberated.[52]

What results is a double standard of harm: "the degradation of women stigmatizes women to the point where that degradation is taken as evidence that there was nothing of value to which harm could be done; a raped or pornographed person is damaged goods hardly worth the respect a recognition of her harm would bring."[53] As a result of such circular reasoning, harm to a now-degraded individual does not require our attention.

We May Not Respond to Others' Suffering, Because the Harm Is Invisible

Harm may not be acknowledged as harm. For example, Catharine MacKinnon observes that pornography "makes harm to women invisible by making it sex."[54] If the harm is acknowledged, it is seen as simply a part of the structures of society, acceptable in part because it benefits those with privilege. We need to remember that "an aspect of the power of privilege is to ignore."[55] Sarah Hoagland points out, "much ignorance is the result of ignoring."[56] Elsewhere I have argued that as a rule vegetarians know a great deal more about the process of producing "meat" to be eaten, than do those who eat animals.[57] Similarly, when pornography is thought to be about "sex," then the sexual inequality that pornography promotes and benefits from simply disappears.

Rationalizations: Animals Exist to Be Eaten and Women Choose to Be Porn Objects

Various rationalizations may confuse an attempt to recognize harm. For instance, many meat eaters hold to a comforting notion that it is only because of their meat eating that certain animals exist. They believe that animals are luckier to have been born than never to have existed at all, and credit the existence of the animals to their demands for the bodies of dead animals to consume. Of course, one who is not born cannot actually regret one's nonexistence.[58] If confused ideas of existence palliate the fact of harm, notions of free will provide permission to ignore the oppressive nature of pornography and prostitution: "Those women chose to do this, didn't they?" Such ideas presume that the equality feminists seek has already been achieved.

If one knows one is being inconsistent—that is, that someone is being harmed for one's own pleasure—the response may be to defend oneself against one's inconsistencies rather than to acknowledge that one is being inconsistent. Awareness of harm is displaced by the desire to protect one's pleasure. Joel Kovel summarizes this thought process, "Since this set of ideas is inconsistent and will stand neither the test of reason nor of my better values, I am going to distort it, split it up, and otherwise defend myself against the realization."[59] The structure of the absent referent, which I introduced to explain the interdependent oppressions of women and animals in *The Sexual Politics of Meat*, functions in part to relieve one of dealing with one's own inconsistencies. Through the functioning of the absent referent, the individual may be recognized but the harm is absent, or the harm is acknowledged but the individual being harmed is invisible. In either case, pleasure is protected.

Saving Animals Is Not Enough

The context for animal suffering is a sex-species system that establishes interdependent oppressions. Further, gender construction influences our experience of and responses to this suffering. These two interrelated insights raise basic questions about the current assumptions of the animal rights movement.

Because men in our society are programmed to perceive all negative emotions as anger, those who feel only anger in response to animal suffering, rather than the complex of emotions that accompany anger, may experience animal defense as a battle rather than as a process. Of course, if animal defense is seen as a war, men's feelings of suffering about the other animals are rendered comprehensible. But the referent is no longer the animals, it is the battle. This maintains the hyperrationality that disengages from feelings. And it provides a heroic, male-identified framework for one's work to "save the animals."

Animal defense activism emphasizes "saving the animals." Activists, whether they allow themselves to experience emotional responses to the suffering of animals or not, and whether or not they then feel these emotions solely as anger, may see themselves as the "saviors" of animals. This language encourages a determined single-mindedness for both women and men in response to very complex sex-species structural inequalities leaving men's roles and privileges intact. For instance, when feminists raise concern about various animal defense activities aligning with pornography (see example below), a predominant response is "We are too busy saving the animals. You can discuss this all you want, but we need to spend our energy saving the animals."

This approach privileges animal suffering as the sole criterion for activism. We cannot save all the animals from suffering. Animals literally die by the millions every day. What this appeal to animal suffering does, however, is to keep the notion of human suffering unproblematized. This means that women's suffering is not stipulated as being different from men's suffering. The comment "You can discuss this all you want, but we need to spend our energy saving the animals" de facto includes another: "other humans' suffering is not important enough for us to consider compared to what animals suffer." It also implies the justification: "To save animals, I can cause other humans' suffering." What results is that animal defenders may violate women's boundaries to protest the use of animals by our culture. An example is in order.

What began initially as an advertisement campaign in which naked supermodels proclaimed "I would rather go naked than wear fur" expanded into joint receptions hosted by People for the Ethical Treatment of Animals and *Playboy* magazine. Many animal defense activists were pleased by the media attention this alignment with pornography produced, including interviews in *Penthouse* magazine. But to its critics this media campaign announced precisely the problem with the current state of animal rights activism and theory that leaves gender unproblematized.

The animal defense movement may end up using sexualized images of women and aligning with pornographers such as *Playboy* and *Penthouse* because of people's responses to the representation of animal suffering. Recall that people's reactions to stark images of animal suffering resulted in the banning of these images. Precisely because emotions are both feared and seen as untrustworthy, and precisely because animal suffering prompts emotional reactions, the animal rights movement is prevented from using images of animal suffering. What remains to be used?

Recall, as well, that harm to women through pornography is invisible, because it is constructed as sex. Representations of harm to animals are de facto made invisible through lack of access to outlets for billboards and advertisements. As a result, harm to women through a pornographic "I'd-rather-go-naked-than-wear-fur" ad becomes the acceptable way to raise the issue of harm to animals. Ironically, this compromise results in a focus on naked women's bodies rather than harmed animals, and thus actually upholds, rather than disturbing, the sex-species system.[60]

In the sex-species system, speech that harms and silences women—pornography—is protected speech. In fact, pornography is now the most prosperous media category in the United States. But the *representation* of harm to animals that documents suffering and is framed politically ("this should not be") is *not* protected speech.[61] Images that remind people of animals' suffering are banished; animals in traps or being tortured cannot be shown. Yet pornography documents women in traps, women being tortured, and this is protected speech. Harm to women through pornography gives great pleasure. Representations of harm to animals give little pleasure.

When naked female supermodels appear in advertisements that challenge furwearing, male entitlement is undisturbed. Our concern should not be that women can be sexy and attractive without wearing fur, but that women's status as sexy, attractive objects for men needs to be challenged. The message to men appears to be: you can still have objectified bodies in your life—they simply cannot be the bodies of nonhuman animals. Thus, a humanocentric focus continues: the issue of fur is presented as being about sexy women instead of the oppression of furbearing animals. The individuality of animals, and thus the individuality of their suffering, is never acknowledged. Instead, men's definitions, sexuality, and needs are identified as of primary concern to the animal defense movement. Meanwhile, the task for women remains for us to recognize men's definitions, sexuality, and needs *not* as part of ourselves but as part of the sex-species system, which is the context of our lives. Our caring about animals occurs in this context.

Caring for Bodies

Attention to suffering makes us ethically responsible. Only oppressors can deny the importance of suffering to the individuals who suffer or who respond to that suffering. However, as we have seen, gender construction influences our experience of suffering and our responses to this suffering. This remains unacknowledged within animal rights theory and activism. The failure to incorporate a gender analysis exposes the limitations of animal rights. When we incorporate a gender analysis, we move beyond animal rights.

Elaine Scarry observes that power "is always based on distance from the body."[62] A relationship exists between reclaiming the body and its full range of feeling, and reclaiming animals' bodies, including women's. A feminist care ethic for the treatment of animals offers the possibility of such reclamation.

ACKNOWLEDGMENTS

Thanks to Chris Cuomo, Marie Fortune, Greta Gaard, Lori Gruen, Susanne Kappeler, Irena Klaver, Brian Luke, Barbara Noske, Kim Stallwood, John Stoltenberg, and Noel Sturgeon for their insights and conversations. In thinking about rights and care, I have been deeply influenced by conversations over the years with Marti Kheel, Batya Bauman, Susanne Kappeler, Tom Regan, Linda Vance, Karen Warren, and especially by Josephine Donovan, whose careful reading of earlier drafts of this essay was invaluable to my thought process.

NOTES

1. Ellyn Kaschak, *Engendered Lives: A New Psychology of Women's Experience* (New York: Basic Books, 1992), 136, 150. The epigraph to this chapter is from 125.

2. Ibid., 115.

3. Tom Regan, *The Thee Generation: Reflections on the Coming Revolution* (Philadelphia: Temple University Press, 1991), 3.

4. Thanks to Susanne Kappeler for her help in articulating this position.

5. For a discussion of emotions as legitimate sources for theory, see Carol J. Adams, *Neither Man nor Beast: Feminism and the Defense of Animals* (New York: Continuum, 1994), 185–88.

6. Dick Bathrick, Kathleen Carlin, Gus Kaufman, Jr., and Rich Vodde, *Men Stopping Violence: A Program for Change* (Atlanta: Men Stopping Violence, 1987), 39.

7. On this, see Adams, *Neither Man nor Beast*, esp. 9–13.

8. Thanks to a conversation with John Stoltenberg for provoking this insight. I am not subsuming race here but arguing that race becomes a mobile discourse under this system.

9. See Val Plumwood's excellent analysis in *Feminism and the Mastery of Nature* (New York: Routledge, 1993).

10. Kaschak, *Engendered Lives*, 68.

11. Kathleen Barry, *The Prostitution of Sexuality* (New York: New York University Press, 1995), 26.

12. On this, see Carol J. Adams, *The Sexual Politics of Meat: A Feminist-Vegetarian Critical Theory* (New York: Continuum, 1990), 72–74. The cultural feminizing of prey animals does not preclude the possibility that certain works of fiction may focus on the maleness of some animals (*Moby-Dick, The Bear*) as an essential aspect of its plot.

13. See my analysis in *Neither Man nor Beast*, chap. 4, "On Beastliness and a Politics of Solidarity."

14. It is hard to determine percentages for any specific form of pornography over against any other kind simply because one cannot survey all the pornography now available, especially because of the proliferation of computer-mediated pornography. See Carol J. Adams, "'This Is Not Our Fathers' Pornography': Sex, Lies, and Computers," in *Philosophical Perspectives on Computer-Mediated Communication*, ed. Charles Ess (Albany: State University of New York Press, 1996), 147–70.

15. I am indebted to the analysis of Kimberlé Crenshaw on the racializing of sexual harassment for my understanding of this. See Kimberlé Crenshaw, "Whose Story Is It Anyway? Feminist and Antiracist Appropriations of Anita Hill," in *Race-ing Justice, Engendering Power: Essays on Anita Hill, Clarence Thomas, and the Construction of Social Reality*, ed. Toni Morrison (New York: Pantheon, 1992), 412.

16. Patricia Hill Collins, *Black Feminist Thought: Knowledge, Consciousness, and the Politics of Empowerment* (Boston: Unwin Hyman, 1990), 170.

17. Ibid., 170, 171, 172.

18. Ibid., 172, quoting Scott G. McNall, "Pornography: The Structure of Domination and the Mode of Reproduction," in *Current Perspectives in Social Theory*, ed. Scott McNall (Greenwich, Conn.: JAI Press, 1983), 4:197–98.

19. Catharine A. MacKinnon, "Liberalism and the Death of Feminism," in *The Sexual Liberals and the Attack on Feminism*, ed. Dorchen Leidholdt and Janice G. Raymond (Elmsford, N.Y.: Pergamon, 1990), 10.

20. On this, and the harm of pornography generally, see Catharine MacKinnon, *Feminism Unmodified* (Cambridge, Mass.: Harvard University Press, 1987), and *Toward a Feminist Theory of the State* (Cambridge, Mass.: Harvard University Press, 1989); Catherine Itzin, ed., *Pornography: Women, Violence, and Civil Liberties* (Oxford: Oxford University Press, 1993); Susanne Kappeler, *The Pornography of Representation* (Minneapolis: University of Minnesota Press, 1986); Andrea Dworkin, *Pornography: Men Possessing Women* (New York: Perigee, 1981); and Laura Lederer, ed., *Take Back the Night: Women on Pornography* (New York: Morrow, 1980).

21. Elaine Scarry, *The Body in Pain: The Making and Unmaking of the World* (New York: Oxford University Press, 1985), 148.

22. Pain, harm, and suffering are not precisely interchangeable concepts, yet they are often used interchangeably. In the context in which I am placing pain—that is, pain caused by an outside agent—pain announces that harm has been done. But pain is not necessarily experienced for harm to have occurred. Because of dissociative states, one may no longer feel the pain caused by harm. Tom Regan unpacks what he sees as the implications of Bentham's posing the question about animals as being preeminently a question about suffering: "The question is, Can we cause them pain so intense and long-lasting as to make them suffer? That is a more central moral question since, if

we can cause animals to suffer, then what we do to them not only can hurt them, it can harm them; and if it can harm them, then it can detract from the experiential quality of their life, considered over time; and if it can do that, then we must view these animals as retaining their identity over time and as having a good or ill of their own. For Bentham to put the question in terms of suffering rather than pain suggests that he recognizes a deeper and . . . a truer resemblance between us and them than that we both may be hurt. It is that we both may be harmed" (*The Case for Animal Rights* [Berkeley: University of California Press, 1984], 96).

23. Bernard Rollin, *Animal Rights and Human Morality* (Buffalo, N.Y.: Prometheus, 1981), 32.

24. Scarry, *Body in Pain*, 4.

25. Ibid., 5.

26. James Rachels, *Created from Animals: The Moral Implications of Darwinism* (Oxford: Oxford University Press, 1990), 131.

27. Lynda Birke, *Feminism, Animals, and Science: The Naming of the Shrew* (Buckingham, Eng.: Open University Press, 1994), 91.

28. Bernard E. Rollin, *The Unheeded Cry: Animal Consciousness, Animal Pain, and Science* (Oxford: Oxford University Press, 1990), 146.

29. The idea that suffering for men is episodic and suffering for women is contextual is the insight of feminist theologian Mary E. Hunt.

30. For statistics on violence against women, please consult Carol J. Adams, "Toward a Feminist Theology of Church and State," in *Violence Against Women and Children: A Christian Theological Sourcebook*, ed. Carol J. Adams and Marie M. Fortune (New York: Continuum, 1995), 15–16.

31. MacKinnon, *Feminism Unmodified*, 234, n. 26.

32. See my discussion of the words *battered woman* and *meat* as examples of this nonagential language in *Neither Man nor Beast*, 101–2.

33. See, for example, David Finkelhor, Richard J. Gelles, Gerald T. Hotaling, and Murray A. Straus, eds., *The Dark Side of Families: Current Family Violence Research* (Beverly Hills, Calif.: Sage, 1983).

34. Michael Jackson's reflections enriched my understanding of this phenomenon. This paragraph draws on my article "Woman-Battering and Harm to Animals," in *Animals and Women: Feminist Theoretical Explorations*, ed. Carol J. Adams and Josephine Donovan (Durham, N.C.: Duke University Press, 1996), 55–84.

35. Robin L. West, "The Difference in Women's Hedonic Lives: A Phenomenological Critique of Feminist Legal Theory," *Wisconsin Women's Law Journal* 3 (1987): 81.

36. Steve Baker, *Picturing the Beast: Animals, Identity, and Representation* (Manchester, Eng.: Manchester University Press, 1993), 234.

37. Rollin, *Unheeded Cry*, 152.

38. Scarry, *Body in Pain*, 4.

39. For a discussion of the absent referent, see Adams, *Sexual Politics of Meat*, 40–44.

40. Carol S. Pearson, *The Hero Within: Six Archetypes We Live By* (New York: Harper & Row, 1989), 99.

41. Judith Herman, *Trauma and Recovery* (New York: Basic Books, 1992), 42.

42. Kaschak, *Engendered Lives*, 131.

43. Ibid.

44. Herman, *Trauma and Recovery*, 207.

45. Ibid.

46. Ibid., 209.

47. Ibid., 112.

48. I am drawing on Kaschak, *Engendered Lives*, 87, in this sentence.

49. Thanks to Gus Kaufman, Jr., for suggesting this as a response to suffering.

50. Lori Gruen suggested this term to acknowledge that people losing privilege are indeed suffering, though it may not be socially constructed as such.

51. See John Stoltenberg for a discussion of "Why Can I Feel Nothing When Someone I Love Feels Pain?" in *The End of Manhood: A Book for Men of Conscience* (New York: Penguin, 1993), 182–88.

52. MacKinnon, *Feminism Unmodified*, 13.

53. Katharine T. Bartlett, "MacKinnon's Feminism: Power on Whose Terms?" *California Law Review* 75 (1987): 1562.

54. MacKinnon, "Liberalism and the Death of Feminism," 11.

55. Sarah Lucia Hoagland, *Lesbian Ethics: Toward New Values* (Palo Alto, Calif.: Institute for Lesbian Studies, 1988), 207.

56. Ibid.

57. Adams, *Neither Man nor Beast*, 25–36.

58. See my discussion of this issue in ibid., 69–70.

59. Joel Kovel, *White Racism: A Psychohistory* (New York: Vintage, 1971), 19.

60. Despite the fact that it is the radical feminist analysis that establishes how the sex-species system oppresses animals, to defend the use of pornography and the association with pornographers to further animal rights, animal defenders must resort to a liberal feminist argument. Liberal feminism is the feminist analysis least amenable to arguments regarding the necessity of intervening to stop animal suffering (or nature's exploitation). Within the context of liberal feminism, efforts for vegetarianism and against harm to women in pornography and prostitution are greeted as puritan, legislative, controlling.

This is because, as I argue above, a radical political analysis is missing: one that establishes that a preexisting privilege permits "apolitical" pleasure.

61. For an insightful discussion of free speech protection for pornography, but not for hunt protesters, see Maria Comninou, "Speech, Pornography, and Hunting," in *Animals and Women*, ed. Adams and Donovan, 126–48.

62. Scarry, *Body in Pain*, 46.

PART II

Responses, 1998–2006

CHAPTER 9

Toward a Non-Property Status
for Animals

THOMAS G. KELCH

> In his thoughts, Herman spoke a eulogy for the mouse who had
> shared a portion of her life with him and who, because of him, had
> left this earth.
>
> "What do they know—all these scholars, all these philoso-
> phers, all the leaders of the world—about such as you? They have
> convinced themselves that man, the worst transgressor of all the
> species, is the crown of creation. All other creatures were created
> merely to provide him with food, pelts, to be tormented, extermi-
> nated. In relation to them, all people are Nazis; for the animals it is
> an eternal Treblinka."
>
> —*Isaac Bashevis Singer*[1]

The magnitude of exploitation of animals is astonishing. Scientists use millions of animals in experiments each year in the United States, most, if not
all, of which are unnecessary and of no real scientific value. Humans farm
millions of tons of meat each year. In animal experiments and farming,
the conditions and treatment of animals is often appalling. It is doubtful that
many people would personally subject animals to such treatment. Nonetheless, behind the curtain of laboratory and barn doors, the carnage continues.

This article originally appeared in a longer version as "Toward a Non-Property Status
for Animals," *New York University Environmental Law Journal* 6, no. 3 (1998): 531–85.
© 1998 by *New York University Environmental Law Journal*. Reprinted by permission of
the journal and the author.

Legally these practices are ultimately supported in this country by the notion that animals are property and do not have any rights protecting them from this type of exploitation.[2] The law of property acts as a justification for practices that are, insofar as the law is concerned, just economically efficient uses of resources.

That animals are property and, thus, do not have rights is a concept of ancient lineage that is expressed in our common law. But the common law is not an impotent steed fenced by history; it has the liberty and, in fact, the duty to migrate to higher ground when facts and moral awareness dictate. Although some have argued that the common law is not a ripe mechanism for change as it relates to the protection of the interests of animals,[3] a fresh judicial view of the status of animals is, perhaps, the best means presently available to change the legal view of animals as property, given that legislative efforts to protect interests of animals have been largely ineffective. This article proposes that the common law is a ripe mechanism for changing the view of animals as property. Under the principles and methodology of the common law, the concept of animals as property can and should be jettisoned.[4] It is an appropriate time for the judiciary to take an evolutionary step in the development of the common law and remove animals from their status as mere property.

It is evident that animals are in fact not like inanimate objects, the things we ordinarily identify with the idea of property. Animals feel pain, have emotions, give and return love, and some even have characteristics of reason and language. This article makes a proposal for the direction of this evolutionary stride, arguing that animals should be viewed not as property but as the holders of fundamental rights—rights conceived more broadly than in the liberal natural rights tradition as those granted a rational citizen,[5] but rather as conceived in the feminist ethic-of-care tradition (see below), where it is held that rights are owed those creatures who have moral status as living subjects, who have feelings and emotions, a telos of their own, and with whom one can communicate reciprocally.

In Anglo-American jurisprudence, the law of property has developed largely as common law.[6] In this common law tradition, animals are considered pieces of property. This idea is made clear in explicit statements of the courts.[7] The tradition of animals as property is also evident from other aspects of the law; for example, the measurement of damages for the tortious injury or killing of an animal. Here we find that, as a general rule, the measure of damages for such acts is the market value of the animal, as is the case when inanimate property has been damaged.[8] This kind of damage remedy results in what many claim to be extraordinarily low damage awards for the injury or killing of animals, especially in the case of pets.

The status of animals as property impacts many areas of the law, including standing in animal rights cases. Since animals are property and have no rights, representatives of animals cannot assert the interests of animals in the judicial system. Only persons have interests protected by the law. As a result, the only way that an issue relating to the welfare of an animal can come before a court is if some human can assert a personal interest at stake relating to the animal sufficient to result in standing.[9] One such interest would be property rights in the animal. Without such a right, however, standing becomes problematic for one asserting the interests of an animal.

Standing is typically described as requiring the following three factors:[10] (1) an injury in fact; (2) a causal connection between the alleged injury and the conduct in question; (3) the alleged injury must be able to be redressed by a judicial remedy.[11]

For those desiring to assert the interests of animals in the context of laboratory experiments, the major impediment to representing these interests is establishing an injury in fact. The injury in fact to the plaintiff need not be economic; it can be aesthetic, ecological, conservational, or recreational.[12] Nonetheless, those who have attempted to assert the interests of animals have found it difficult to establish an injury. For instance, in *Animal Legal Defense Fund (ALDF) v. Espy*,[13] it was held that the ALDF did not have standing to challenge the United States Department of Agriculture's (USDA) failure to include mice and rats within the Animal Welfare Act's definition of "animal," as was seemingly intended by Congress.[14] ALDF's inability to obtain information regarding the numbers of mice and rats used in experiments was not a sufficient injury to confer standing.[15] It is, indeed, often said that a "mere interest" in an issue is not enough to constitute standing.[16] The injury alleged must be distinct and palpable, rather than a nebulous injury to a concerned bystander.[17]

That animals used in experiments and food production are the property of persons other than those asserting the interests of the animals makes it particularly difficult to assert an injury and obtain judicial review. It is similar to trying to obtain judicial relief against a neighbor to prevent her from destroying her car by drilling holes in it.

Due to these problems, some scholars are trumpeting fundamental change in the law of standing. For example, Professor Christopher Stone has asserted that both animals and the environment itself should have standing to assert injuries.[18] He argues that the environment and natural entities generally should be seen as having rights that can be asserted through human representatives. This may be viewed as the next logical step in a natural extension of the concept of "rights," just as we have seen this concept expand to include women and previously excluded races. While Justice William O. Douglas supported providing standing to "environmental objects,"[19] the idea has not yet found wide backing.

While animals are still generally regarded as property, the law in this area has not been entirely stagnant. There has been at least torpid movement away from the view of animals as property, in both judicial decisions and legislative enactments. In the area of judicial common law development, some courts have moved away from always using a market value measure of damages for injuries to and killing of animals. Claims for emotional distress for tortious injury or killing of an animal have found their way into the law. Other cases have allowed the "special value" of the animal to the owner to be the measure of damages, rather than just market value.[20]

Some cases have gone so far as to challenge the ordinary notion of animals as property. For example, in *Corso v. Crawford Dog and Cat Hosp., Inc.*, a case involving the question of the proper measure of damages for mishandling the body of a dog that was euthanized, the court stated that companion animals should be seen as occupying a status above that of ordinary property:

> This court now overrules prior precedent and holds that a pet is not just a thing but occupies a special place somewhere in between a person and a piece of personal property. . . . [A] pet is not an inanimate thing that just receives affection; it also returns it. . . .
>
> This decision is not to be construed to include an award for the loss of a family heirloom which would also cause great mental anguish. An heirloom while it might be the source of good feelings is merely an inanimate object and is not capable of returning love and affection. It does not respond to human stimulation; it has no brain capable of displaying emotion which in turn causes a human response. Losing the right to memorialize [*sic*] a pet rock, or a pet tree or losing a family picture album is not actionable. But a dog—that is

something else. To say it is a piece of personal property and no more is a repudiation of our humaneness. This I cannot accept.[21]

The court held that the plaintiff was entitled to more than market value damages for the conduct of the defendant in losing the body of the dog and replacing it with a dead cat. The court was careful to note that it was not ruling on the basis of heirloom cases that allow special damages for the loss of an heirloom. Rather, the court recognized that pets are something more than property, due to the fact that animals are living creatures with feelings, emotions, and affection, and are more than just objects. The court also relied on the fact that humans feel differently about animals than they do about inanimate things. Animals have a place in our emotional lives that is unique. They are felt to be in many ways like us—something that cannot be said of inanimate objects.

A similar view was expressed in a concurring opinion in *Bueckner v. Hamel*, where the issue concerned the amount of damages to be awarded when the defendant shot two of the plaintiff's dogs. The court affirmed an award of both compensatory and punitive damages, and the concurring opinion of Justice Andell stated:

> The majority cites *Arrington v. Arrington*, 613 S.W.2d 565, 569 for the proposition that animals are treated as property in the eyes of the law. I agree that this is an established principle of law. But animals are not merely property. . . .
>
> This language [from the *Arrington* case] is strikingly different from that used in disposing of inanimate property. This could only have been because animals are so different from other types of property. . . . Because of the characteristics of animals in general and of domestic pets in particular, I consider them to belong to a unique category of "property" that neither statutory law nor case law has yet recognized.
>
> Many people who love and admire dogs as family members do so because of the traits that dogs often embody. These represent some of the best of human traits, including loyalty, trust, courage, playfulness, and love. This cannot be said of inanimate property. At the same time, dogs typically lack the worst human traits, including avarice, apathy, pettiness and hatred.
>
> Scientific research has provided a wealth of understanding to us that we cannot rightly ignore. We now know that mammals share

with us a great many emotive and cognitive characteristics, and that the higher primates are very similar to humans neurologically and genetically. It is not simplistic, ill-informed sentiment that has led our society to observe with compassion the occasionally televised plights of stranded whales and dolphins. It is, on the contrary, a recognition of a kinship that reaches across species boundaries.

The law must be informed by evolving knowledge and attitudes. Otherwise, it risks becoming irrelevant as a means of resolving conflicts. Society has long since moved beyond the untenable Cartesian view that animals are unfeeling automatons and, hence, mere property. The law should reflect society's recognition that animals are sentient and emotive beings that are capable of providing companionship to the humans with whom they live. . . .

Losing a beloved pet is not the same as losing an inanimate object, however cherished it may be. Even an heirloom of great sentimental value, if lost, does not constitute a loss comparable to that of a living being.[22]

Justice Andell's opinion states even more clearly the appreciation that animals are unlike objects and at the very least occupy a special status somewhere above ordinary property. It is the special characteristics of animals that elevate them to a status above mere objects. This, Justice Andell recognizes, has been proven by science; it is now for the law to evolve to acknowledge this fact.

Current legislation and common law doctrines have been relatively ineffective, however, in protecting animals from improper treatment. State anti-cruelty laws, for example—most of which were enacted in the 1800s—typically do not provide real protection for animals, because they focus on the effect cruelty has on the human perpetrator, require evidence of intent, and largely exclude farm animals.[23] Moreover, penalties are fairly minor and enforcement is lax.

Federal laws—including the Animal Welfare Act—have been similarly impotent. The major flaw in the Animal Welfare Act (and amendments) is that it does nothing to regulate farming and it fails to provide for ethical review of the use of animals in experiments.[24] Similarly, the Human Slaughter Act, which defines as "humane" grisly methods,[25] has done little to improve the treatment of animals. While many laws, therefore, cite animal protection as their goal and/or purpose, these statutes have nonetheless had little impact on the major areas of animal exploitations in animal experimentation and farming. This statutory law is largely just another mechanism protecting the property interests of owners in their animals. The sanctity of the owner's property interest ultimately prevails over any perceived interests of animals.

On the bright side, however, there have been some recent developments, both in judicial decisions and statutes, that indicate an ongoing evolution of views toward taking the interests of animals into consideration in decision-making. The remainder of this article now focuses on the implications of these and other changes in society and its mores for the common law of animals as property.

The common law operates largely through stare decisis, the following of precedent. This can appear to be the blind worship of legal history but, as will be shown, the common law is and has been a mechanism for change. In certain circumstances it veers away from precedent, and can be the seed for change in the law.

If the common law is to be an effective vehicle for change in the law of property so that animals are no longer considered mere property, there must be a means for change of the common law so that such a transformation may occur. The common law is, in fact, well suited to such change, particularly, as will be shown, given known facts and societal evolution.

The common law is not meant to be rigid; rather it is intended to be flexible so that it may evolve over time.[26] This evolutionary capacity has been used to liken the common law to a living being:

> The common law is not rigid and inflexible, a thing dead to all surrounding and changing conditions, it does expand with reason. The common law is not a compendium of mechanical rules, written in fixed and indelible characters, but a living organism which grows and moves in response to the larger and fuller development of the nation.[27]

Given this evolutionary character, the court in *Oppenheim v. Kridel*, from which this quote is taken, took the stride of allowing a wife to make a claim for criminal conversation, an action previously denied a woman under the common law. The Supreme Court has agreed with this evolutionary principle, stating that "capacity for growth and adaptation is the peculiar boast and excellence of the common law."[28]

Given that the ability to adapt is built into the common law, what is the appropriate basis for such adaptation? Professors P. S. Atiyah and Robert

Summers have identified three major bases for change in common law rules: (1) changes in circumstances occur such that precedent becomes substantively obsolete; (2) growing moral and social enlightenment shows that the substantive values underlying the law are no longer acceptable; or (3) the precedent was substantively erroneous or badly conceived from the beginning.[29] These bases for change in the common law will be used as a foundation for analysis of whether there is a need for change in the common law of animals as property.

The changes in circumstances that can ground a change in a common law rule are of many varieties. In *Funk v. United States*, the court found that changes in similar common law rules over the years was a consideration in concluding that the rule prohibiting a wife from testifying in her husband's criminal trial should be changed. The court noted that the relation of husband and wife had changed since the original rule was adopted, giving a reason for change in the rule. In discussing cases involving water and property laws, the *Funk* court clarified that these concepts apply far more broadly than just in criminal matters. According to *Funk*, "[W]here the reason of a rule ceased, the rule also ceased, and it logically followed that when it occurred to the courts that a particular rule had never been founded upon reason, and that no reason existed in support thereof, that rule likewise ceased."[30] Thus, where there are changes in society such that the reason for a rule no longer exists, the rule should be changed.

In general, there are three major strands of change compelling courts to modify common law rules. The first is change in the empirical facts or understanding of the world. These changes may be modifications in general knowledge or scientific knowledge. For example, fourteen-year-olds may be competent witnesses because society has determined that children of this age are more mature now than they were in the past.[31] The second strand of change is maturation of society. The foremost example of this in recent history may be the changing role of women in society and the many transformations in the common law that have been wrought by this change in society. The third strand of change is change in the law itself. When the rules that surround and relate to a particular doctrine have changed, it is usually time to change the doctrine as well.

Progress of moral and social doctrines can also be the impetus for modification of common law doctrines. The many cases dealing with the changing role of women in society can also be observed as instances where there has been a change in the mores of society such that there is need for change in long-standing doctrines of the common law.[32] These changes result from the gradual moral and societal changes extending rights to women.[33]

The general theory underlying the concept that changes in moral and social sensibilities are reasons for change in the common law is that once the reason for a rule ceases, so must the rule.[34] The court in *Ketelson v. Stilz* explained:

> The common law by its own principles adapted itself to varying conditions and modified its own rules so as to serve the ends of justice as prompted by a course of reasoning which was guided by these generally accepted truths. One of its oldest maxims was that where the reason of a rule ceased the rule also ceased, and it logically followed that when it occurred to the courts that no reason existed in support thereof, that the rule likewise ceased, and perhaps another sprang up in its place which was based upon reason and justice as then conceived. No rule of common law could survive the reason on which it was founded.[35]

Thus, when the moral and social reasons for a rule have been rejected by society, so should the rule.

It is also the case that rules that are determined to have been erroneous from the beginning should be modified under the mechanics of the common law. Cases like *Brown v. Board of Education* and common law cases that recognize rights in women that were previously unrecognized fall into this category.

In addition to the three mechanisms for change of the common law noted by Atiyah and Summers, there is another reason for change that is useful to identify separately. Modifications in legislation relating to women, for example, have been influential in changes in the common law relating to women.[36]

It is therefore possible to identify four main determinants of change in common law doctrines:

1. Changes in circumstances causing precedent to become substantively obsolete.
2. Growing moral and social enlightenment.
3. Originally erroneous doctrine.
4. Trends in legislation.

These determinants often overlap; and the boundaries are not always distinct. Nonetheless, they provide a shorthand of utility in analyzing the appropriateness of changing a common law rule.

There have obviously been many changes in the world since the law holding animals to be property first arose thousands of years ago. As it turns out, a number of these changes are relevant to the status of animals as property today.

Science has fundamentally altered our view of animals and the place of humans in the universe, particularly in the last 200 years. As has been discussed, present legal doctrine is founded on a view of animals as fundamentally different from humans and subject to domination by humans. This hierarchic view of the relation of humans and animals had its most influential proponent in Descartes who insisted that animals were just soulless machines without pain, feelings, or emotions.[37] This "machine" view of animals pervaded science for centuries, leading to probably the most gruesome acts against animals in history.

Descartes's view still has a substantial impact in scientific circles. The hold that this view exerts on the scientific community can be illustrated by considering animal experiments relating to pain. Under a Cartesian view, however, animals do not experience pain. Their cries are just like the squealing of a drill press. There is, nevertheless, substantial scientific and common sense evidence that animals do feel pain.[38] Responsible science has in fact concluded that animals do experience pain and suffering.

It is the Cartesian view of the world, however, that grounds the common law doctrine of animals as property. The hold the Cartesian view has on the law is obvious from previous exposition. Under this view, animals are just "things," like machines of bolts and sheet metal, and may be treated as such.

The human-centered view of nature—with machine-like animals and humans with souls, real experiences, and reason—is one that has been gradually replaced since the Renaissance.[39] What has been established by science is that humans are just another animal in the evolutionary chain and humans are much like other animals—there are no clear distinguishing characteristics, only differences in the degree to which animals and humans have certain characteristics.

The theory of evolution tells of the kinship of all animals. The gulf between humans and other animals evaporated in the Darwinian revolution. Humans, as one animal in the evolutionary chain, have no claim to a special position. That humans and other animals share similar mental capacities was recognized by Darwin.[40] He contended that the differences in respective mental capacities were a matter of degree, not kind. Darwin argued that some animals feel pleasure and pain, have most of the complex emotions that humans have, possess imagination and reason to some extent, and may even have memory and reflection on that memory.

The traditional view of the relation of humans and other animals finds little factual support in evolutionary theory. Two of the main implications of evolution are that the gulf between humans and other animals is not as large as many contend, and that the similarities between the two outweigh the differences. Thus, evolutionary theory shows that the special place of humans in the world that grounds our present common law is fictional.

It appears also that there are strong reasons under modern science and moral theory to suppose that rationality is not a characteristic justifying a morally relevant distinction between humans and non-human animals. Again, the supposed gulf between humans and non-human animals on which the common law idea of animals as property is based is non-existent.

Advances in our knowledge about animals, in short, through evolution and other scientific discoveries, strongly question, if not dispel, the myth of special status or characteristics that justify a human-centered view of the universe. In the end, both science and the implications of science upon moral theory show that the traditional view of humans as clearly distinguishable from other animals, upon which the common law is based, is fundamentally flawed and not consistent with modern science.

Changes in our moral perceptions of the world are occurring such that one can seriously question the substantive values which underlie the traditional common law view of animals. The history of moral development has been a continual expansion of the objects of moral concern. This is born out in modern moral theory. In the last thirty years there has been considerable movement in moral theory toward seriously considering the interests of non-humans.

There are two main traditional strands of thought which are used to justify the moral consideration of animal interests. The first is what one might refer to as "natural rights" theory. The primary proponent of this view is Tom Regan. Regan rejects the idea that there is something special about humans, like rationality, that makes humans morally superior to animals. Rather than use a rationality test to determine what entities are subject to moral consideration, Regan proposes the "subject-of-a-life" criteria as the basis for an entity being entitled to moral consideration.[41] Under Regan's theory, subjects-of-a-life have special inherent value, merit moral concern, and are entitled to respectful treatment. Subjects-of-a-life have rights.

The second strand of ethical thought on these issues is the utilitarian view, primarily put forth by Peter Singer.[42] Singer argues that the preferences of all entities are entitled to equal consideration. There are no privileged entities whose preferences are entitled to special consideration. In this way the preferences or interests of all entities, including animals, are taken into consideration in the calculation of overall utility.

The natural rights and utilitarian theories have dominated the philosophical debate on the moral status of animals. There is, however, a developing alternate view proposed by feminist theorists.[43] The feminist perspective challenges both traditional strands of moral thought. With respect to the natural rights view, feminist theory is concerned about the subject-of-a-life criteria that is used to found rights. "Rationality" was historically used as a distinguishing feature to lump women and animals together as not having rights. While Regan does not use "rationality" as a criterion, the subject-of-a-life criterion is not far from rationality as it requires complex consciousness and cognitive abilities.[44] This criterion is seen as underinclusive in that it may exclude from consideration many entities that one would want to protect.

The utilitarian perspective is closer to the view of feminists since it considers preferences and suffering. Indeed, the feminist perspective has as its foundation sensibility to the feelings of other creatures, as Josephine Donovan illustrates by quoting from Rousseau: "[animals] partake in some measure of our nature in virtue of that sensibility with which they are endowed . . . if I am obliged not to injure any being like myself, it is not so much because he is a reasonable being, as because he is a sensible being."[45] It is because animals have feelings and stones do not that we distinguish between the two.

Though utilitarianism may be more sympathetic to these concerns, the feminist perspective criticizes it as well. Utilitarianism has a weakness in that it does not provide a precise standard for measuring the interests to be weighed. This weakness can allow for the intrusion of traditional prejudices into the utility calculation. In addition, the utilitarian calculation mathematizes morality, thus miring it in a rationalistic calculative mode of moral reasoning that distances moral entities from the decision-maker and the situations to which moral concepts apply.[46]

Feminists believe that the ensnaring of morality by the western philosophical tradition is the major problem with the two dominant strands of moral thought on animals. The subjective, feeling elements of humans are erased or subdued by the Newtonian/Cartesian epistemology which is used in science and western moral thought. Everything is reduced to mechanical, manipulable, and repeatable processes. Emotions toward irrational animals are not permitted in this world view; this is left to the female. The natural rights and utilitarian theories participate in this Newtonian/Cartesian objectivist stance. They distance themselves from both feelings and emotions, and present themselves in the guise of the objective rational argument demanded in the western tradition. They try to attack science from the perspective of the scientists.[47]

Feminists argue from outside of this perspective. They propose an alternative epistemology, one divorced from the credo of domination of nature by humans. Instead, feminists propose different sorts of relations of humans to the world. Donovan points to several of these elements of feminist thought. Rather than see the role of humanity as one of conquest, our relation to the world can be viewed as one of reciprocity and exchange. Feminists reject the subject-object mode of interaction with the universe. Our intellect is not at odds with that of other creatures, but is viewed as continuous with that of other forms of life. From a perspective concentrating on feelings and emotions, we can see all creatures as sacred and entitled to respect. Rather than a hierarchy of being in the world, there is a seamless web of relations between animals and humans. Moreover, from a maternal perspective, one can feel a reverence for all forms of life.[48]

The feminist viewpoint, then, spotlights the subjective and the emotive over the objective and the scientific. From this position one can proclaim the moral value of animals, based on compassion, sympathy, and other emotions that lie deep inside of us. The same cannot be accomplished from a stance of detached objectivism which, after all, is the perspective that has resulted in the present legal status of animals.

These threads of moral thought have not taken hold in academic circles, although they have invaded popular culture and our social fabric. Many animal protection organizations such as People for the Ethical Treatment of Animals (PETA) have been formed in response to injustices the farm industry and animal experiments do to animals. The use of fur has been substantially reduced. Many manufacturers have stopped using animal experiments for the purpose of testing cosmetics. There has been a shift over the past several hundred years from a view of animals as tools to a more neutral approach that allows animals to be viewed as having rights.[49]

Popular attitudes toward animals seem to be moving away from the traditional one of human dominance over "dumb animals." For example, animal cruelty is part of the violence on television about which people are concerned.[50] A substantial part of the populace believes that animals are relevantly similar to humans. There is evidence to suggest that most Americans believe that animals have emotions like humans.[51]

That popular attitudes toward animals are changing is also evident in American case law reviewed earlier. In the *Bueckner* and *Corso*[52] cases we see that there is some change in judicial views of animals such that animals are no longer seen as mindless objects that are merely property to be used by humans.

The ethical debate and social attitudes are moving away from the traditional view of "animal as machine" and toward recognition of the scientific reality that animals are different from humans only in degree, not in kind. Thus, moral and social enlightenment points toward a critical review of the position of animals as property.

One need not linger on the issue of whether the idea of animals as property was originally erroneous. As has been shown, the common law view of animals as property is founded on concepts that modern science has disproved. As a result, relegation of animals to the status of property was substantively flawed at the outset since it was based on faulty factual premises about the nature of humans and animals.

There has been a significant amount of legislation that attempts to address, though generally unsuccessfully, issues relating to the interests of animals. At the state level there have been some attempts to strengthen the protection of animals, like the Pasado law, which puts the teeth of possible conviction for a felony in animal cruelty law.[53]

Even though these legislative exertions have been primarily ineffective, they demonstrate a trend toward addressing animal interests. This trend then supports the assertion that the time is appropriate for a change in the common law relating to animal interests and, in particular, the status of animals as property.

From all of the foregoing, one can see that circumstances have changed since our common law notions of animals as property were created; that moral and social theory have advanced to take into consideration animal interests; that the original grounding of the concept of animals as property was erroneous; and that legislative trends show increasing concern with protecting animal interests. Since each of these factors favors alteration of present common law doctrine, it is now time for the judiciary to take that step.

Given the strong reasons for changing present doctrines concerning the property status of animals, the next question one must address is precisely what change should be made. It is evident that animals are not like inanimate objects, the things that we ordinarily identify with the idea of "property." Animals feel pain, have emotions, give and return love, and some even have characteristics of reason and language. Feminist writers teach us that there is something different about our relations with animals from our relations with inanimate things. We have feelings and sympathy toward animals that we do not have toward inanimate property. We may feel badly about a broken vase, but not in the same way that we do about the death of a pet. Animals are fundamentally different from the inanimate objects that we consider property because they are, in Regan's words, "subjects-of-a-life," having a telos that can be affected for good or ill by our actions.

Since animals are quite distinct from other things that we ordinarily consider to be property, and since all of the factors suggesting a need for change in the common law favor a change in the concept of animals as property, I submit that this doctrine should be eliminated from our law. Thus, the first proposal for change in the common law is the following:

Proposition 1: Animals are not property.

Our law expresses a dualism here. There is property and there are persons—entities with rights. But if animals are not property, then what is their status? If animals are not property then they must migrate to the realm of entities with rights. In line with both natural rights theory and feminist theory, I propose that animals should be determined to be the holders of legal rights.

Proposition 2: Animals are holders of legal rights.

These rights would be based on the fact that animals have interests; that their lives can fare well or badly based upon how they are treated. If the rights that should be accorded to animals are based on these interests, what rights would these interests create? I propose use of the elements of an animal's telos or nature, rather than the elements that make an animal the subject-of-a-life in Regan's terminology, as the measure of the rights of a creature. The reason for this is, in line with Donovan's arguments, that the subject-of-a-life concept may be too restrictive. It may, in the end, include only a fraction of creatures that have the characteristics giving them interests entitled to protection.

If the interests of an animal are based on the elements that constitute its telos, then the rights of animals should be centered on this telos and the fulfillment of it. Therefore, we have Proposition 2.1:

Proposition 2.1: Animals have the right to fulfill their telos.

The elements of being able to live in accord with this telos has been expressed by Roger Galvin as the ability to live in accord with one's nature, instincts, and intellect.[54] This might include the right to have habitat conditions which allow normal expression of the telos. It would surely require that the animal be free from exploitation by humans which, by definition, is an interference with the fulfillment of an animal's telos. Note that the telos of different sorts of animals is distinct; thus, it is likely that the rights of different animals will vary accordingly. The more complex the animal, the more complex are its interests and, thus, its rights.

While precisely cataloging the rights of animals is impossible due to the inherent flexibility of the telos standard, there are some fundamental overarching rights that would seem to apply generally to all sorts of animals:

Proposition 2.1.a: Animals are to be free from human-inflicted pain except where such pain is inflicted for the benefit of the animal.
Proposition 2.1.b: Animals are to be free from restraint, except where restraint is for the protection of the animal.
Proposition 2.1.c: Animals are to be free from human interference with the physical conditions, including habitat conditions, required for the fulfillment of the animal's telos.

The first two of the above propositions are self-explanatory. Note, however, that exceptions are made for restraint and pain such as is necessary for the protection of the animal, such as where medical attention is necessary. The last proposition is aimed, in part, at broad ecological conditions, but is really broader than this in that it protects "physical conditions," which may include more than ecological conditions. It would include such conditions as those necessary to maintain domestic animals that do not exist in the broader ecological setting.

Many also frequently complain that if animals had rights, there would be no way to determine exactly what these rights are and there would be no one able to assert these rights in the legal system. These problems are easily solvable. Given the relatively simple lives and interests of animals, it seems that we really need not be perplexed by the defining of animals' interests. We can easily identify their needs. We know from their behavior, for example, that they wish to be free of pain and to pursue certain goals that are within their natures.

With respect to a legal mechanism for assertion of animal interests, we can allow animal groups or concerned individuals to be the "guardians" of the interests of animals. This is hardly foreign to the law, as guardians are routinely appointed for children and those not competent to assert their own claims. There is even a ready test that can be borrowed from the standing case law to see if an organization or individual should be allowed to act as the guardian of the interests of an animal or animals. This is the test proposed in *Animal Lovers Volunteer Association v. Weinberger*,[55] which dealt with the standing of an animal organization to assert claims relating to animal interests. The court appeared to suggest that an organization can have standing when there is a longevity of commitment in the organization to preventing inhumane treatment of animals. This test can be used to determine if an entity or individual is an appropriate person to assert the rights of animals.

A move from the traditional view of animals as property to one recognizing the rights of animals is monumental. To recognize rights in animals as described above would be to fundamentally change the way we live, as it would ultimately end farming of animals and animal experimentation. But as has been shown, under traditional analysis of what is necessary to require a change in the common law, the elements necessary for such change presently exist. Thus, the proposal, while appearing to be radical, actually fits within traditional views of appropriate change to the common law.

It is perhaps too much to suppose that the changes proposed above will occur in one decisive gesture, but movement in this direction is called for and has even found some support in the judiciary. While some scholars despair at the slow and halting movement of the law in this area, this is the way most change occurs. Of the proposals made here, there is no reason why a gradual change in the common law cannot occur. Proposition one is the foundation of such a progression and, as has been noted, there is movement in the common law in this direction. Once this proposition is accepted, the content of animals' rights can be developed as society progresses toward recognizing the interests of animals. Ultimately we will have what might be termed an Animals' Bill of Rights. We now require only the courage of our jurists to press in the direction required under our inherited notions of the common law.

NOTES

1. Isaac Bashevis Singer, *The Letter Writer from The Seance and Other Stories*, in Jon Wynne-Tyson, *The Extended Circle: A Commonplace Book of Animal Rights* 335 (1989).

2. Gary L. Francione, "Animal Rights and Animal Welfare," 48 *Rutgers L. Rev.* 397, 434–45 (1996); Gary L. Francione, "Animals, Property, and Legal Welfarism: 'Unnecessary' Suffering and the 'Humane' Treatment of Animals," 46 *Rutgers L. Rev.* 721, 731–37, 770 (1994).

3. Gary Francione, "Animals as Property," 2 *Animal L.* i, iv–v (1996).

4. This is a view that has been argued previously. See Roger W. Galvin, "What Rights for Animals? A Modest Proposal," 2 *Pace Envtl. L. Rev.* 245 (1985).

5. Tom Regan, *The Case for Animal Rights* (1983).

6. This can be seen in the writings of Blackstone, Holmes, and Pound. William Blackstone, *Commentaries on the Law of England*, II, 15–19, 20–21, 384–87, 401–5 (1969); Oliver Wendell Holmes, Jr., *The Common Law* 206–46 (1881); Roscoe Pound, *The Spirit of the Common Law* 185–87, 197–200 (1921).

7. *Bueckner v. Hamel*, 886 S.W.2d 368, 370 (Tex. Ct. App. 1994) (holding that dogs are personal property); *Hawaii v. LeVasseur*, 613 P.2d 1328, 1330 (Haw. Ct. App. 1980) (stating that dolphins do not have the status of "another" under the Marine Mammal Protection Act, as they are just property).

8. Peter Barton and Frances Hill, "How Much Will You Receive in Damages from the Negligent or Intentional Killing of Your Pet Dog or Cat?" 34 *N.Y. L. Sch. L. Rev.* 411, 412 (1989); Joseph H. King, Jr., "The Standard of Care for Veterinarians in Medical Malpractice Claims," 58 *Tenn. L. Rev.* 1 (1990); Debra Squires-Lee, "In Defense of Floyd: Appropriately Valuing Companion Animals in Tort," 70 *N.Y.U.L. Rev.* 1059 (1995); "Measure, Elements, and Amount of Damages for Killing or Injuring Cat," 8 *A.L.R.4th* 1287 (1981); "Measure and Elements of Damages for Killing or Injuring Dog," 1 *A.L.R.3d* 997 (1965).

9. *Fund for Animals v. Lujan*, 962 F.2d 1391, 1395 (9th Cir. 1992).

10. *Int'l Primate Protection League v. Adm'rs of Tulane Educ. Fund*, 895 F.2d 1056, 1058 (5th Cir. 1990); Barbara O'Brien, "Animal Welfare and the Magic Bullet: The Use and Abuse of Subtherapeutic Doses of Antibiotics in Livestock," 67 *U. Colo. L. Rev.* 407, 428–29 (1996).

11. *Animal Welfare Inst. v. Kreps*, 561 F.2d 1002 (D.C. Cir. 1977) (listing and discussing the factors required for standing in an animals rights case). A court may deny standing if the plaintiff bases the claim on the rights of third parties or does not state a claim that "falls within the zone of interests to be protected or regulated by the statute in question." Bridget Klauber, "See No Evil, Hear

No Evil: The Federal Courts and the Silver Spring Monkeys," 63 *U. Colo. L. Rev.* 501, 508 (1992).

12. *Sierra Club v. Morton*, 405 U.S. 727, 734–35, 738 (1972).

13. *Animal Legal Defense Fund (ALDF) v. Espy*, 23 F.3d 496 (D.C. Cir. 1994).

14. 7 U.S.C. § 2132. See also *Hawaii v. LeVasseur*, 613 P.2d at 1330 (stating that the protection of the Animal Welfare Act extends to all warm-blooded animals, and that regulations manifested a policy to protect the well-being of laboratory animals).

15. *ALDF v. Espy*, 23 F.3d at 501–3 (indicating that although this inability did constitute an informational injury, it did not fall within the "zone of interests" protected or regulated by the Animal Welfare Act).

16. See, for example, *Int'l Primate Protection League v. Inst. for Behavioral Research, Inc.*, 799 F.2d 934, 938 (4th Cir. 1986) (denying standing to the International Primate Protection League based on a mere interest in the issue of animal rights for primates).

17. *Animal Lovers Volunteer Ass'n., Inc. v. Weinberger*, 765 F.2d 937, 939 (9th Cir. 1985).

18. Christopher D. Stone, "Should Trees Have Standing—Toward Legal Rights for Natural Objects," 45 *S. Cal. L. Rev.* 450, 453–55, 464–66, 488–89 (1972); see also Cass R. Sunstein, *After the Rights Revolution: Reconceiving the Regulatory State* 210–17 (1990) (arguing that traditional notions of standing should not be applied to rights under certain modern regulatory schemes).

19. See, for example, *Sierra Club v. Morton*, 405 U.S. at 741–55 (Douglas, J., dissenting).

20. Barton and Hill, "How Much Will You Receive in Damages?" at 422; King, "Standard of Care for Veterinarians," at 24–26.

21. *Corso v. Crawford Dog and Cat Hosp., Inc.*, 415 N.Y.S.2d 182, 183 (N.Y. Civ. Ct. 1979).

22. *Bueckner v. Hamel*, 886 S.W.2d at 368.

23. Laura G. Kniaz, "Animal Liberation and the Law: Animals Board the Underground Railroad," 43 *Buff. L. Rev.* 765, 790 (1995). See also Daniel S. Moretti, *Animal Rights and the Law* 1 (1984); Bernard E. Rollin, *Animal Rights and Human Morality* 120–23 (1992); Francione, "Animals, Property, and Legal Welfarism," at 768–69; Thomas R. Malia, "Annotation, Applicability of State Animal Cruelty Statutes to Medical or Scientific Experimentation Employing Animals," 42 A.L.R.4th 860, 861 (1985); David J. Wolfson, "Beyond the Law: Agribusiness and the Systemic Abuse of Animals Raised for Food or Food Production," 2 *Animal L.* 123, 135–38 (1996)

24. 7 U.S.C. §§ 2131–59 (1994). See also Henry Cohen, "Federal Animal Protection Statues," 1 *Animal L.* 143 (1995) (cataloguing and summarizing over

forty federal statutes that include animal protection); Rollin, *Animal Rights and Human Morality*, at 124–25.

25. 7 U.S.C. §§ 1901–6 (1994), at § 1902 (1994) (stating that treatment is "humane" as long as all animals are rendered insensitive to pain by a single blow or gunshot, or an electrical, chemical, or other means that is rapid and effective before being shackled, hoisted, cast, or cut; alternatively the animal must suffer a loss of consciousness by the simultaneous and instantaneous severance of the carotid arteries with a sharp instrument).

26. *Lutwak v. United States*, 344 U.S. 604, 615 (1953) (stating that the common law is not immutable, but is flexible); *Funk v. United States*, 290 U.S. 371, 383 (1933) (allowing wife of defendant to testify in criminal trial contrary to prior common law rule); *Hurtado v. California*, 110 U.S. 516, 530 (1883) (allowing prosecution for murder in state court by information rather than grand jury indictment); *United States v. Schoefield*, 465 F.2d 560, 561 (D.C. Cir. 1972), cert. denied, 409 U.S. 881 (1972) (stating that the common law is not "frozen"); *Larsen v. General Motors Corp.*, 391 F.2d 495, 506 (8th Cir. 1968) (stating that the common law is not sterile and rigid, and serves the best interests of society by adapting to emerging and developing needs of our time); *Ketelson v. Stilz*, 111 N.E. 423, 425 (Ind. 1916) (stating that the common law is flexible and expandable); *Rozell v. Rozell*, 22 N.E.2d 254, 257 (N.Y. 1939) (quoting *Oppenheim v. Kridel*, 140 N.E. 227, 230 (N.Y. 1930) (stating that common law is flexible and like a living organism).

27. *Oppenheim*, 140 N.E. at 230.

28. *Hurtado*, 110 U.S. at 530. See also *Funk*, 290 U.S. at 381–83.

29. P. S. Atiyah and Robert Summers, *Form and Substance in Anglo-American Law* 134 (1987).

30. *Funk*, 290 U.S. at 381–82, 385–86, 384 (quoting *Ketelsen*, 111 N.E. at 425).

31. *Schoefield*, 465 F.2d at 561.

32. *Funk*, 290 U.S. at 381–82; see also *Schoefield*, 465 F.2d at 561.

33. *Oppenheim*, 140 N.E. at 228–30.

34. *Rozell*, 22 N.E.2d at 255–57.

35. *Ketelson*, 111 N.E. at 425.

36. *Funk*, 290 U.S. at 381–82; see also *Schoefield*, 465 F.2d at 560.

37. René Descartes, "Animals Are Machines," in *Animal Rights and Human Obligations* 60 (Tom Regan and Peter Singer, eds., 1976); Gerald Carson, *Men, Beasts, and Gods: A History of Cruelty and Kindness to Animals* 36–42 (1972).

38. Tom Regan, *All that Dwell Therein* 6–27 (1982); Bernard E. Rollin, *The Unheeded Cry: Animal Consciousness, Animal Pain, and Science* 107–201 (1989); Peter Singer, *Animal Liberation* 7 (1990).

39. Steven M. Wise, "How Nonhuman Animals Were Trapped in a Nonexistent Universe," 1 *Animal L.* 15, 34–41 (1995).

40. Charles Darwin, "Comparison of the Mental Powers of Man and the Lower Animals," in Regan and Singer, *Animal Rights and Human Obligations*, at 72–81.

41. Regan, *Case for Animal Rights*, at 243–48.

42. Singer, *Animal Liberation*; Peter Singer, *Practical Ethics* 56–57, 62–64, 67 (1993).

43. Josephine Donovan, "Animal Rights and Feminist Theory" (chapter 2, this volume).

44. Id. at 62.

45. Id. at 63 (quoting Jean-Jacques Rousseau, *The Social Contract and Discourse on the Origin and Foundation of Inequality Among Mankind* 172 [Lester G. Crocker, ed., 1967]).

46. Donovan, "Animal Rights," at 64.

47. Id., at 65, 69, 72. This is not meant to be and is not a definitive catalog of feminist thought on these issues, but rather is a sampling of the sorts of ideas that can constitute a feminist epistemology as it relates to animal issues.

48. Id. at 72–73.

49. See, for example, Lilly-Marlene Russow, "Changing Perceptions of Animals: A Philosophic View," in *Perceptions of Animals in American Culture* 25–39 (R. J. Hoage, ed., 1989).

50. Broadcasting Standards Council, "A 'Snapshot' of Television in 1995," M2 Presswire, June 12, 1996, available in 1996 WL 10345028.

51. Gordon M. Burghardt and Harold A. Herzog, Jr., "Animals, Evolution and Ethics," in Hoage, *Perceptions of Animals in American Culture*, at 136.

52. *Bueckner*, 886 S.W.2d at 371; *Corso*, 415 N.Y.S.2d at 183.

53. Steve Anne Chambers, "Animal Cruelty Legislation: The Pasado Law and Its Legacy," 2 *Animal L.* 193, 193–95 (1996).

54. Galvin, "What Rights for Animals?" at 253.

55. *Animal Lovers Volunteer Ass'n. v. Weinberger*, 765 F.2d at 937.

CHAPTER 10

ॐ

Protecting Children and Animals from Abuse

A Trans-Species Concept of Caring

JAMES GARBARINO

Introduction

Although my professional career has been spent seeking to improve the quality of life for children, I come from a family of avowed and unabashed animal lovers. From my childhood, I recall clearly that the greatest outrage arose in my parents and siblings from stories of cruelty to animals. When the cowboys and Indians battled on television or in the movies, it was for the wounded *horses* that the greatest sympathy was reserved. In fact, in the household of my childhood it was accepted practice to root for the animals whenever they were in conflict with humans.

I have found many expressions of this heritage in my own life as an adult. For many years my first social interactions each day have been with the animals who have lived as part of my household. The tone of these interactions sets the stage for the rest of my day. Rising before other humans in the household, I encountered the canine. For a decade this

This chapter was first published in Frank R. Ascione and Phil Arkow, eds., *Child Abuse, Domestic Violence, and Animal Abuse: Linking the Circle of Compassion for Prevention and Intervention* (West Lafayette, Ind.: Purdue University Press, 1999). Published by permission of Purdue University Press and the author..

meant Abby—her head resting patiently on the side of the bed, with tail wagging, generally assuming the attitude of adoration for which dogs in general and Labs in particular are known and regarded. Indeed, among the many social relationships in which I have been involved as an adult human, my relationship with Abby was clearly the most simply positive. Abby died several years ago, and now it Dharma—a Lab/Dalmation mix—who greets me each morning. Here in this essay I bring the historical and contemporary nature of my relationships with animals to my understanding of what we can and should mean when we speak of "humane treatment"—of children and animals.

In this I am not alone. Josephine Donovan dedicated her analysis of "Animal Rights and Feminist Theory" (chapter 2, this volume) "to my great dog Rooney . . . whose life led me to appreciate the nobility and dignity of animals." This is particularly interesting and important in the present context, because in her article Donovan recounts the fact that one of the contributions of feminist theory to the formulation of animal rights is the assertion that it is from their capacity to *feel* that the rights of animals derive. As outlined by psychologist Carol Gilligan (1982), this orientation to feelings stands in sharp contrast to conventional and traditional masculine thinking which sees the origins of rights either in the ability to think or in the use they serve in the human community. I begin my analysis on precisely this issue: that any genuine understanding of the rights of children *and* animals must arise out of empathy. *We (and they) feel. Therefore we are entitled.*

Trans-Species Kinship

When Desmond Morris (1967) referred to the human race as "the naked ape," he acknowledged an important though clearly controversial thread in our civilization, namely the recognition of kinship between people and animals. The theological implications of acknowledging this kinship has long been a battleground. In the nineteenth century it pitted evolutionists and creationists in a knock-down-drag-out fight that continues today in the backwaters of academic discourse as well as in the town halls and boards of education in some of our more "fundamentalist" communities. What are the boundaries of our identity as humans versus that of "other" animals? To be "we" or not to be "we." That is the question.

In the latter part of the twentieth century the arena for this debate is found in the more radical propositions of the "animal rights" movement. Listen to Carl Sagan (1977) ask *the* fundamental question of research on the social and psychological competence, the emotional, mental, and linguistic processes of the apes: "If they are 'only' animals, if they are beasts which abstract not, then my comparison is a piece of sentimental foolishness . . . but I think it is certainly worthwhile to raise the question: Why, exactly, all over the civilized world, in virtually every major city, are apes in prison?" Anyone who wishes to explore this question in dramatic visual depth need only view the film *Greystoke: The Legend of Tarzan and the Apes.* Having done so, simply visit a zoo and sit before the apes with open eyes, open mind, and open heart. Or, have breakfast some morning with me and Dharma-dog.

But how far can we take this kinship? And what does it imply for the cooperation of child welfare and animal welfare programs and policies? There are scientific, philosophical and logistical dimensions to this question. Modern science tells us that the linguistic and intellectual abilities of some animals are quite impressive—reaching the operational level of young children in some cases. Clearly, there are some animals who are functionally "superior" to some humans—at least in some respects. As Sagan put it: "How far will chimpanzees have to go in demonstrating their abilities to reason, feel, and communicate before we define killing one as murder, before missionaries will seek to convert them." I do not want to walk the well-documented path of those over the centuries who have sought to establish the ability of dolphins to analyze or gorillas to learn to use language. Others have done a good job of that. Rather, I want to consider briefly a series of issues that arise in my mind as I contemplate efforts to link child protection and the protection of animals.

Child welfare and animal welfare ought to be natural collaborators, even if in practice there have been historical wedges driven between these two caring communities. Certainly the more we postulate the need for a general ethic of caring the more we can see a natural collaboration. What is more, the repeatedly documented correlation between child maltreatment and the abuse and neglect of animals (Ascione 1993) warrants a synchronicity of effort. The fact is that professionals who uncover one sort of abuse in a household should be on special alert for the other. Thus, child protection investigators should be trained to be on the lookout for animal abuse—both as a condition bolstering their concern for the children and as a step in the direction of cost effectiveness by forwarding their observations to animal protection professionals. The reverse is true for animal protection officers, as well, that is using the occasion of investigating animal abuse as an opportunity to do an assessment of the quality of care for any children co-habiting with the animals in question. This sort of coordination ought to be a matter of elementary human policy at the highest community and state levels. Rather than closing ourselves off to the suffering of beings beyond our professional or institutional mission, we should at the very least conceptualize a generic empathy for the victimized as part of our core missions.

Is a Unitary Approach to Children and Animals Wise?

Despite the obvious need for a generic approach to protecting the vulnerable, we should consider the possible limits of this approach. Perhaps we can restate this question in the following way: Is it wise to have unbounded empathy? Can our circle of caring extend outward without limitation, to include all beings? Certainly empathy is one of the foundations upon which to build morality in general, and a morality of child and animal protection in particular. *When we open ourselves to the feelings of abuse we create a prima facie case for protection.* Conceptual discussions of "aggression" or "punishment" may result in an abstract conclusion that children need discipline, that punishment is an acceptable strategy, that under stress parents may engage in aggression. But look at a child who has been beaten or burned and the feelings create a powerful moral mandate. We reserve a special brand of judgment for those who inflict or profit from such violence to children. And we see a practical basis for this moral concern when we look at the links between child abuse and subsequent violent criminality—as I have done in my book *Lost Boys* (1999).

But can we say the same when the topic is animals? Who can bear to look at a fox mutilated in a trap. Obviously the fox hunter can. Is he just an insensitive clod or a sadistic maniac? How is he different from the person who can tolerate or even enjoy being witness to or perpetrator of the suffering of an abused child? It is easy enough to see the similarities—unless you have known a hunter who cares for his children with gentleness and compassion.

Popular culture sometimes struggles with this issue. One recent example was to be found in the film *Powder*, in which a rather odd young man possesses the capacity for *imposing* empathy on others. At one point in the film he confronts a deer hunter by transmitting a wounded deer's feelings to the hunter. The hunter—regretfully and against his will—disposes of his rifle collection and abandons hunting immediately. Who (other than a masochist who actually enjoys pain) could do otherwise? This, of course, is behind the oft-repeated insight that if fish could scream there would be far fewer among us who could bear to cast a baited hook into the water. If we could hear their scream—and we now know they feel pain—would it take a psychopath or sadist to blithely hook them and then let them asphyxiate at the bottom of a boat? I know that as I have expanded the boundaries of my own empathy there came a point where I could imagine the screaming of fish—and then ceased to be able to cast that baited hook. And this comes from a person who as a boy "loved" to go fishing!

Can We Accommodate "Human Rights" and "An Ethic of Caring"?

In practice, this issue of unlimited empathy is not a matter of much concern in most situations, most of the time. The more common problem, it would seem, is not too much empathy, but too little. Dealing with the most obvious cases of both child and animal abuse and neglect already strains our response capacities to, and beyond, the breaking point. However, some of us recognize that the foundation for *child* protection is *childhood* protection, because child maltreatment is at least in part a social indicator, that is, an indicator of deficiencies in the supportive quality of the social environment. Thus, by examining the values and policies that either support or undermine quality of care for children (childhood protection) we understand better the factors that generate the need for child protection among vulnerable families. This analysis leads to a focus on "social toxicity" in the community and the larger society (Garbarino 1995). Similarly, we can make progress in animal protection by focusing on the foundation for animal protection in the larger issue of the very concept of an ethic of caring for non-human life forms. This is where the animal rights movement intersects with animal protection.

Indeed, according to those who have worked with the most victimized among the human population (i.e., the most horribly abused who become perpetrators of heinous violence and end up in prison), the loss of human dignity is the principal precipitator of "bestial" violence. They were the focus of my own work for 15 years as both a researcher and an expert witness in murder trials. Psychiatrist James Gilligan (1996) worked with these individuals in the Massachusetts prison system for a long period and from his experience learned that shame based upon denial of basic human rights is the engine that drives the violence machine. A rights-based culture is a culture that has a chance of establishing the reservoirs of self-worth and positive identity that promote high standards of care for children—and animals. An ethic of caring is the goal if we are to build the foundation for both child and animal welfare and protection. But how do we sort out the difficult issues we face as human beings who rely upon non-human species of various types for our livelihoods and how do we reconcile our fundamental moral loyalty to our own species in our dealings (from a position of power) with other species?

Perhaps Albert Schweitzer offered some clues decades ago when he propounded the view that the farmer plowing his field to raise food who thereby kills thousands of flowers is doing God's work, while if that same man gratuitously kills even one flower along the road on his way home that evening he has committed a sin. This focus on necessity and instrumentality is a clue, but only that. Human wants create gratuitous suffering and destruction for animals when animals are valued solely on the basis of instrumentality. To wit, the following cases, which to my mind represent stark differences in their moral foundations.

> When my son was six years old he was bitten by a raccoon in the forest of northern New York State. There was a chance that the raccoon was rabid. To rule out rabies, it was necessary to submit the animal's brain to analysis, which meant that the raccoon had to die.

> It has been reported that in order to test the toxicity of new cosmetics before they are placed on the market for human use, they are applied to the eyelids of rabbits. By all accounts, the result is excruciating for the rabbits and effective as a pretest for human use.

In seeking an ethic of caring for non-human life forms I am looking for a system that consistently generates the "right" answers for these two situations that seem on the surface to bear a distinct similarity. Sacrificing the raccoon to save the life of my son was the right answer. Sacrificing the rabbits so that a new shade of eye makeup is available is the wrong answer. What moral framework generates the decision to sacrifice the raccoon but not the rabbits? That is what I seek, what we need.

I have no delusions that this search is easy or unambiguous. Many a vegetarian would quickly argue that the line should be drawn at the sacrifice of sentient beings for human consumption. And yet, there are very few among us—even among vegetarians—who would accept an absolute equivalence between human and animal lives. Put another way, who would dispute that is the moral distinction between killing and eating a child versus a beloved dog? Few would—at least in principle.

But, were a ship sinking at sea who would approve of saving a dog, a cat, or a chimp over *any* human being? (My mother, for one, if the person in question had shown him or herself to be morally inadequate.) And, who could approve of a policy that rationed food in favor of the pets of the rich in place of the children of the poor? Who indeed. A look at the economic realities of life for poor children around the world and rich pets in every country tells us that this policy exists *de facto*.

Is there no way out of this quandary? The answer, I think, is "not absolutely." There is only dialogue in social, cultural, and historical context. There is no absolute definition of child maltreatment, only a series of tentative negotiated settlements in which science and society reach an accommodation about how much risk is acceptable, how much pain is necessary, and how far to push the limits of essential empathy (Garbarino, Guttmann, and Seeley 1986). Is the circumcision of baby boys physical abuse? Is the use of nude children in artistic photographs sexual abuse? Is the teasing of children psychological abuse? Is abortion child abuse? It depends. It depends. It depends.

It depends upon how and to whom we apply the concept of rights, how far we extend the ethic of caring, and what we learn about the consequences of these actions for development. Is abortion the killing of a child or a discretionary medical procedure? Is the slaughter of cows to make hamburgers murder or business? Most of us struggle to negotiate a path through this maze of contradictions and compromises.

The same is true of the lines between the standards applied in protecting children and animals. We seek an expansion of caring, the progressive application of an ethic of caring that conveys respect within the terms available to us in our culture—both our local culture, and what the cultures of the larger world have to offer.

I believe we would do well to seek an ever-expanding ethic of caring, in part because dignity, respect, and caring knit together a social fabric that clothes all who are dependent upon the powerful. Desmond Morris (1967) observed that "the viciousness with which children are subjected to persecution is a measure of the weight of dominant pressures imposed on their persecutors." This seems true when we examine the socioeconomic and demographic correlates of child maltreatment.

But by the same token, the cruelty with which animals are treated seems a measure of the cultural foundations for cruelty in general. We know there is some empirical connection developmentally—cruelty to animals bears some correlation with subsequent cruelty to children (Ascione 1993).

In principle and in fact, when we say that someone is treating a child "like a dog" we tell a great deal about the person and the culture from which they come. Linking our animal protection efforts to a general ethic of caring for non-human life forms is, I think, a powerful strategy for elevating the quality of care for both animals and children.

Opening our eyes and hearts to the rights of animals to dignity and caring (even when we accept their use as instrumentalities under carefully controlled and evaluated conditions to meet the needs and improve the welfare of human beings) is one foundation for establishing the minimum standards of care for children. Animal protection and child welfare are natural partners.

References

Ascione, F. 1993. "Children Who Are Cruel to Animals: A Review of Research and Implications for Developmental Psychopathology." *Anthozoös* 6:226–47.

Garbarino, J. 1995. *Raising Children in a Socially Toxic Environment*. San Francisco: Jossey-Bass.

——. 1999. *Lost Boys: Why Our Sons Turn Violent and How We Can Save Them*. New York: Free Press.

Garbarino, J., E. Guttmann, and J. W. Seeley. 1986. *The Psychologically Battered Child*. San Francisco: Jossey-Bass.

Gilligan, C. 1982. *In a Different Voice: Psychological Theory and Women's Development*. Cambridge, Mass.: Harvard University Press.

Gilligan, J. 1996. *Violence: Our Deadly Epidemic and Its Causes*. New York: Putnam.

Morris, D. 1967. *The Naked Ape: A Zoologist's Study of the Human Animal*. New York: McGraw-Hill.

Sagan, C. 1977. *The Dragons of Eden: Speculations on the Evolution of Human Intelligence*. New York: Ballantine.

CHAPTER 11

୫୬

The Role of the Rational and the Emotive in a Theory of Animal Rights

THOMAS G. KELCH

Introduction

Since its genesis,[1] the concept of legal rights has so dilated that some lament it has been pushed beyond its appropriate boundaries and no longer has meaning.[2] On the other hand, others recognize the expansion of legal rights as a natural evolution of social, political, and legal structures.[3] The possible extension of rights to animals is an example of this evolution. To many, however, the idea of "rights" for animals seems odd because our ordinary understanding of animals as "things" is incommensurable with their having legal rights.[4]

The purpose of this article is to review and analyze the conceptually fragmented law and literature concerning the foundations of legal rights, and to propose a way of looking at rights that is favorable to the extension of rights to animals. It is not my purpose here to present an argument for the existence of animal rights, although I believe this result is correct; rather, my purpose is to present a conceptual mechanism for analyzing the application

This chapter was first published in *Boston College Environmental Affairs Law Review* 27 (1999). Published by permission of Boston College Law School and the author..

of rights to animals. In accomplishing this task it is imperative to review not only the animal rights literature, but also law and literature relating to human rights, since human rights theories are often applied to animals.

The asserted conceptual foundations of legal rights are manifold. Many debate what grounds rights in both the human and animal rights arenas, and there are even those who contend that the concept of rights should be jettisoned altogether.[5] Review of this debate yields one obvious conclusion—there is no consensus on the appropriate grounding of rights either concerning humans or animals.

Such a review shows there are a number of theoretical camps concerning how rights are grounded.[6] There are several theories founded on Wesley Hohfeld's famous dichotomous concepts of rights/duties and powers/liabilities.[7] Others, particularly in the animal rights area, state that the foundation of rights is the existence of "interests" that need protection. Here, rights are granted to those who have interests. Rights may also be viewed as founded on a contract hypothetically arising from some "original position." They may be the expression of societal goals. They may just be concepts giving rise to certain remedies in our legal system. There are yet other views.

One common, although not necessarily universal, strand in these myriad theories is to assert that there is *one* foundation for the concept of rights. In other words, one specifiable sort of thing or set of things constitutes the ground on which the profusion of rights lies. This article contends that this obsessive search for one element or one clearly defined set of elements to buttress rights has caused our thought to go awry. Instead, properly speaking, legal "rights" have multifarious grounds and foundations, not one. Any right can appropriately be explained by any number of theories, all of which aid in our understanding of the right in question. As such, we may see the grounding of rights not as a single solid foundational block, but as interwoven webs of numerous conceptual strands.

This article further asserts that an essential strand in this web that is ignored in the law and literature is an emotive element composed of sympathy and caring, or more simply, "compassion." Our Western analytical, scientific culture abhors such assertions, but our concept of rights cannot be fully understood or explained without such an element. Emotion is an essential aspect of our nature and our thought, and it likewise enters our concept of rights. Moreover, due to, among other things, the fact that animals cannot formally assert rights or communicate their interests, this emotive aspect plays a more prominent role in considering animal rights issues than in human rights concerns.

I. The Need for Rights

Why be concerned with the notion of rights? Legal protection may be given to animals without cloaking it in the rhetoric of rights. Indeed, utilitarian theory eschews rights for utility calculations.[8]

Those enamored of critical legal theory and feminist theory frequently deride rights as tools of repression and the status quo. Those taking this tack may, for example, point out that to say one has a right does not mean that this right is either enforceable or exercisable.[9] To be meaningful, rights must be positive; there must be an obligation in others to respect them and they must be enforceable.[10]

Critical legal studies scholars deride rights by asserting that rights merely protect entrenched interests in society.[11] They choose to analyze the legal system from a position outside these entrenched views that include the concept of rights.[12]

Although there is controversy over the usefulness of rights in feminist literature,[13] some of this literature views rights as simply part of the male way of viewing the world.[14] In this view, rights are a means of male domination and exploitation of women, animals, and nature.[15] Rights are necessary only because of the competitive and antagonistic system that has been created by male-dominated culture.[16]

To socialists, rights are capitalist ploys; those who are disadvantaged in the system are accorded certain rights, but these rights are not meaningfully exercisable by them, given their position in society.[17] Rights may only be a pathology of capitalist society resulting from its underpinnings of competition and self-interest.[18] Rights are necessary to sort out the inevitable conflicts created by a capitalist system. In a more benevolent society, the need for the supposed protection of rights might be lessened or nonexistent.[19]

Closer to the animal rights issue, Mary Midgley has argued that the concept of rights is in conceptual trouble.[20] She claims that the concept is too ambiguous to be truly useful, and, for this reason, cannot be effectively utilized.[21]

> The ambiguity of terms like "right," then, does not just express a mistake, but a deep and imperfectly understood connection between law and morality. This is why eighteenth-century revolutionaries were able to exploit these ambiguities with such effect in their campaign for

the rights of man. Obscure concepts can often be used effectively for reform in this way, so long as they are employed only on issues where their practical bearing is clear. . . . The actual word "right," however, cannot, as far as I can see, be salvaged for any clear, unambiguous use in this discussion. It can be used in a wide sense to draw attention to problems, but not to solve them. In its moral sense, it oscillates uncontrollably between applications which are too wide to resolve conflicts ("the right to life, liberty and the pursuit of happiness") and ones which are too narrow to be plausible ("the basic human right to stay at home on Bank Holiday").[22]

Some of the problems with the concept of rights may be found in the Western world view.[23] Rights may just be an artifact of dualistic Western thought.[24] The world, in this view, is populated with innumerable dualities, including us/them, subject/object, and right/no-right.[25] This Western world view is also composed of various hierarchies that form the structures on which rights hang.[26] Without such hierarchical structures there might be no need for rights to protect one level of the hierarchy from another. Further, the striations of this hierarchy can be used to justify denying rights to those at low levels of the hierarchy, like animals.[27]

Notwithstanding these criticisms, there may be good reason not to jettison the concept of legal rights.[28] Rights are such an ingrained aspect of our legal system that it seems unlikely they could be purged without the demolition of the current structure of society. Rights are not only deeply set into our legal system, they are a central focus of our legal language. As legal structures, rights also serve the mundane but useful function of shifting the burden of proof to the entity potentially infringing a right to prove that such infringement is appropriate.[29] Moreover, it has been argued that rights are necessary facets in the functioning of any human community.[30] In such a community there are necessarily obligations and entitlements in members of the community; these obligations and entitlements are expressed as rights.

We have seen that no one can be a member of a community unless there are both things which are due from him to fellow members and things which are due to him from them. . . . His rights (what he is entitled to as a member) consist in all that is due to him; his obligations, of all that is due from him. A community consists of its members in the sense that, unless there are members there cannot be a community. Since to be a member of community is *inter alia* to have rights, without rights there cannot be a community. Having rights is a part of human social living in any form, so there have to be rights if there is to be any human social life at all.[31]

It is also difficult to see how some rights fit into the structure of oppression described by some critics. While such arguments may seem applicable to property rights, it is hard to see the right against self-incrimination, or of free speech, or to be free from unreasonable searches as tools of oppression. Such rights combat oppression.

II. The Myriad Theories of Rights

A. HOHFELDIAN THEORY

Perhaps the most popular way of speaking about legal rights was formulated by Wesley Hohfeld.[32] In the Western tradition, he described legal relations in terms of various opposites and correlatives.[33] The opposites he discussed are right/no-right, privilege/duty, power/disability, and immunity/liability.[34] The correlatives are right/duty, privilege/no-right, power/liability, and immunity/disability.[35] In analyzing these terms, Hohfeld found that in legal discourse the term right is typically used broadly to include any legal advantage.[36] He found this use of the term to be overbroad. Instead, he believed that the term "right" should be restricted in use to describe those things that correlate to duties.[37] "Right" in his theory is synonymous with "claim."[38] Rights are simple and atomic; rights are claims based on duties.[39]

Hohfeldian theory has been refined by later scholars including Carl Wellman.[40] Wellman does not base rights on single Hohfeldian elements, like *a* duty or *an* immunity. Rather, he claims that a legal right is "a system of Hohfeldian positions that, if respected, confers dominion on one party in the face of some second party in a potential confrontation over a specific domain *and* are implied by the legal norm or norms that constitute that system."[41] One difference between Wellman's view and that of Hohfeld is that Wellman views rights not as simple concepts composed of individual elements, but as complexes potentially composed of many Hohfeldian liberties, powers, duties, and immunities.[42] Nonetheless, these complexes of Hohfeldian elements have a core element or unifying constituent.[43] Thus, there is some duty or other element that stands at the core of a right acting as the cement that holds the other elements of the right together.

While Hohfeldian theory itself is primarily descriptive, Wellman's theory is normative. Wellman contends that there is an objective morality that grounds rights.[44] There are true moral propositions and these moral propositions can be utilized to construct Hohfeldian elements from which rights may be fabricated.[45] Legal rightholders then are those persons who have moral rights.[46]

Hohfeld, of course, did not focus on animal rights issues. Wellman's explication of Hohfeld's theory is not favorable to extending rights to animals. His theory requires that a rightholder be able to assert dominion; that is, a rightholder must be able to make claims against others.[47] To assert this dominion, Wellman requires a rightholder to have a "will" or the ability to act as an agent, and animals presumably do not have this capacity.[48] L. W. Sumner, using a Hohfeldian framework, has also concluded that animals cannot have rights since those who are rightholders must be able to comply with normative rules, which excludes animals.[49] On the other hand, Gary Francione has found Hohfeldian theory to support granting rights to animals, but not in any sense that is actually favorable to the interests of animals.[50]

One might raise a number of objections to Hohfeldian theory. Insofar as Hohfeld posits a "duty implies right" theory, it is not clear that all moral and legal duties imply rights. While a dispute over the rights of parties to a contractual dispute may fit conveniently into Hohfeld's structure, it is not evident that the theory can address more peculiar cases involving rights.

For instance, one can have a moral duty to do the dishes, but it is difficult to assert that anyone or anything has a right that you do so.[51] One might say I have the duty to do the dishes to those with whom I live. But even so, it is difficult to view them as rightholders. Further, if I live alone, to whom could the duty be owed? Surely not to the dishes. To myself then? It is not clear that a duty to oneself can exist.[52] Closer to the law, we say that we have duties to the dead through mechanisms like wills, though there is no extant entity having a right corresponding to this duty. Thus, there are instances of duties without corresponding rights.[53]

Similarly, we can see rights existing independently of duties.[54] We may, for instance, have a right to think or behave in a certain way without there being any perceptible duty corresponding to the right.[55] Seeing $20 on the sidewalk, two people may have the right to pick it up, but there is no duty on the part of either party to allow the other to do so.[56]

Some philosophers assert that those who correlate rights with duties

define "duty" much more broadly than is appropriate. Arthur Schopenhauer argues that "duties" are frequently referred to as any act that happens to be praiseworthy.[57] According to Schopenhauer, "duty" should be
limited to circumstances where the omission to act would be a wrong.[58]
Thus, duty exists only where there is an obligation to act, not where the
obligation is to refrain from acting. Where one's obligation is to abstain
from interfering, such an obligation is not a duty.[59] Duties then depend
on a party having an obligation to act; the paradigm case being where a
person has entered into an express agreement to perform an act.[60]

Further, since Hohfeld's theory is largely descriptive, it does not really
tell us what grounds our duties and, thus, what ultimately grounds rights.
While Hohfeld's theory may help us to identify and explicate legal issues,
it is not a method for determining social and legal philosophical issues.[61]
More underlies rights than bare duties; duties themselves have grounds.
Rights may have moral, policy, or emotive foundations, none of which are
explained in Hohfeldian theory. Wellman's adaptation of Hohfeld attempts
to address this question by providing an objective morality from which
are constructed the complexes of Hohfeldian elements that ground rights.
This theory, however, requires us to accept that there is an extant objective
morality and to agree upon that objective morality.[62] This is a project of
considerable magnitude.

Hohfeldian theory, even in Wellman's conception, is based on an
assumption of conflict underlying rights. There must be two protagonists
in confrontation before talk of rights arises.[63] It is not clear that such conflict must exist for there to be proper talk of rights. A person has a right
to free speech outside of confrontational situations where parties are pitted against one another. Conflicts involving rights raise questions of remedy—what mechanism do we use to resolve conflicts involving rights—not
questions of the content or existence of rights. To view rights as inherently
adversarial reflects a peculiar Western philosophical and political stance,
one in which human relations are necessarily adversarial. Conflict is not,
however, an essential element of the nature of rights.

As will be developed later,[64] there are aspects of rights that cannot be
captured in any complex of Hohfeldian elements. For this reason, some
commentators argue that the Hohfeldian elements, rights, powers, privileges, and immunities, are not sufficiently robust to cover all of the matters relevant to rights; other elements are of significance.[65] There are, for
example, emotive aspects to our concept of rights that are beyond the ken
of this theory. Thus, despite the contribution of Hohfeldian theory to our

understanding of rights in certain contexts, there are areas in which the theory lacks the fullness that the concept of rights deserves.

B. Interests as the Foundation of Rights

Perhaps the most often used theory to ground moral rights in animals is interest theory. The argument underlying this theory has been described as progressing in this fashion:

1. All and only beings with interests can have rights.
2. Animals can have interests.
3. Therefore, animals can have rights.[66]

Although the first premise may be disputed, arguments relating to this theory frequently focus on the second premise—whether animals can have interests.

Those who espouse this theory claim that animals have interests in that they have goods for themselves.[67] These goods include being free from pain, having physiological needs met, and fulfilling their *telos*, their role or nature. Tom Regan, for example, claims that those entities that are the "subject of a life" have interests worthy of protection.[68] Being the subject of a life entails having beliefs, desires, perceptions, a sense of the future, an emotional life, and a psychological identity over time.[69] Similarly, Joel Feinberg posits that to have interests there must be things that are good for the entity as a result of its nature and the entity must have a conative life.[70] Freedom from pain is probably the most often cited interest mentioned as a foundation for animal interests,[71] but as Regan and Feinberg describe, it is not the only one.

Feinberg conceives of interests as compounds of desires and aims.[72] In addition, Feinberg argues that to have desires and aims requires that an entity have beliefs.[73] To define "interests" in this sophisticated way may considerably narrow the entities that can have interests and, in fact, may preclude animals from having them.[74]

One obvious problem with interests as the basis for rights is that when we speak of "interests," we generally mean something that is asserted by an entity. To say that I have an interest in a piece of property or to be free from harassment includes the idea that I can assert this interest within some institutional structure. Animals, of course, are not capable of asserting interests in this way.[75]

This problem can be solved by recognizing that interests can, and often are, asserted by representatives. We allow persons who are incapable of asserting interests themselves, the deceased or incompetent, to be represented by executors, custodians, or guardians. There is little reason to believe that animals cannot be represented in a legal system in a similar way. In this regard, Feinberg distinguishes two types of legal representatives.[76] The first is a representative who acts as the mouthpiece of the principal, doing precisely as directed by the principal.[77] The second is a representative for a passive principal where the agent makes judgments on behalf of the principal.[78] This type of representative is used to represent incompetents and the interests of unknown future claimants in bankruptcy cases.[79] Animals cannot have representatives of the first kind for obvious reasons, but surely can have representatives of the second kind.

Interest theory, perhaps since it has been often used as a basis for animal rights, has been regularly criticized. It has, for example, been argued that to have interests one must have a will; one must be able to assert one's interests.[80] For this reason, it is said that animals cannot be rightholders. As we have observed, however, this is patently false even in our present legal structures. We say that incompetents have rights, though they cannot themselves assert them. We even say that unidentified future claimants, entities who are unknown or may not yet exist, have rights to representation.[81] Thus, this objection lacks merit within existing legal structures.

To say that interests are the basis for rights, however, may paint with too broad a brush. For example, it may be "in the interest" of a tree not to be cut down, but most people would not say that a tree has the right not to be cut down. Similarly, I may have an interest in having wine with dinner, but we would not say I have a right to wine with dinner. In the case of the tree we can solve the problem by requiring that an entity have consciousness or, in Regan's terminology, be the subject of a life to have rights. On the other hand, this may be seen as an arbitrary and unjustified dividing line. This line, however, does have some sense in that only conscious entities can perceive their interests and this must count for something in defining and measuring the strength of interests. One might also solve the problem by asserting that trees do have interests.[82]

My interest in wine with dinner presents a different problem. We use "interest" language to describe preferences that are in no sense essential or of great import. With respect to such things we do not use the language of rights. Thus, to define rights in terms of interests, the definition must refer to some subset of interests, not everything referred to in everyday parlance as interests. We are left then with the task of setting parameters on which interests ground rights and which do not. Interests that ground rights must be of some special purport essential to carrying out our *telos*.

Another criticism of interest theory has been explicated by R. G. Frey. According to Frey, to have an "interest" requires two things: that something be in the interest of the entity and that the entity ought to have concern about the thing.[83] The former requirement is illustrated by saying that "good health is in the interest of X."[84] Thus, animals can have interests in this way insofar as there are goods that are in their interest.[85] But, according to Frey, farm tractors can also have interests in this sense.[86]

Frey's second aspect of an interest is illustrated by saying "X has an interest in good health."[87] To have an interest in this prescriptive sense requires that an entity have beliefs and desires about the thing in question being good.[88] Interests in this sense, Frey argues, cannot be said to exist in animals.[89] This is based on the claim that animals cannot have beliefs and desires. This latter assertion is founded on the argument that in order to have beliefs and desires one must have language, and animals do not have linguistic capacity.[90] Similarly, Frey argues that animals do not have emotions which also might be a ground of interests.[91] According to Frey, emotions also require beliefs and desires.[92]

One objection to Frey's argument is that there are simple desires that do not require complex processes like beliefs or emotions, and therefore do not require language. Frey rejects this, stating that no such simple desires exist in those without linguistic capacity.[93] Frey asserts this position without clear support.

Frey's challenge to the idea that interests can exist in animals is a serious one. Nonetheless, it is founded on a number of controversial and possibly incorrect premises. It has been argued by Regan that the prescriptive element is really not necessary for there to be interests extant in animals that are not extant in tractors.[94] Further, it is not clear that at least some animals do not have desires and beliefs, or that desires and beliefs require language.[95] Animals exhibit desires and beliefs by their behavior. We frequently see them pursuing things that appear to be goals. Also, some animals may use language.[96]

At bottom, the interest theory of rights is the one most frequently asserted in support of animal rights. Interest theory, however, is not without difficulties that limit its usefulness as the sole ground for asserting rights in animals.

C. Dignity as the Foundation of Rights

Rights may be grounded in the characteristic or set of characteristics that constitute "dignity." Here it is argued, based on the philosophy of Immanuel Kant, that humans and perhaps other creatures have a characteristic or set of characteristics that we call dignity, that dignity is of value (presumably moral value) and that rights are necessary to protect the value of this dignity.[97] The sense of dignity involved here is not an "empirical" sense, that is, to act in a "dignified" way, but is dignity in the sense of being a creature having intrinsic value.[98]

Alan Geworth has found this inherent value to arise out of the value of purposive actions taken by entities.[99] He argues that purposive actions by agents have worth to those agents and from this worth agents regard themselves and others as having dignity.[100] Since all agents see other agents pursuing purposive actions as having dignity, we must commit to grant rights to all such agents so that they may pursue those actions that give them dignity.[101]

Steven Wise has stated that dignity may be a basis for granting rights to animals.[102] While it is ordinarily thought that dignity requires full Kantian autonomy, that is, the ability to be completely rational in making choices, Wise states that a lower threshold, what he calls "realistic autonomy," is actually used by courts to determine the existence of dignity-related rights.[103] This realistic autonomy is something less than the perfect ability to make choices.[104] Wise supports realistic autonomy as the foundation of dignity rights by noting that there is case law granting rights to humans who clearly do not have cognitive abilities necessary to make fully rational decisions.[105] Wise argues in *Rattling the Cage* that at least chimpanzees and bonobos can meet this formulation of autonomy.[106]

Whether this project will ultimately be successful in imbuing animals with meaningful rights will depend on how broadly the concept of realistic autonomy is interpreted. It may be that it will only bring within the concept of dignity a small number of animals. If the hope is to make rights widely applicable to animals, then dignity as a basis for animal rights may not be successful.

D. CONTRACTUAL AND OTHER THEORIES OF RIGHTS

Some theorists, including John Rawls, ground rights and other aspects of the legal system on a hypothetical contract basis.[107] In such a theory, we imagine ourselves in some original position, like the state of nature, and determine what sort of contractual arrangement we would arrive at if we were to create a society in which we are required to live with others. In this hypothetical original position, however, we are told in advance that we are rational entities, that is, humans; it is not possible that we ultimately be instantiated as some other species. The contractual view requires reciprocity—there can only be obligations between those capable of respecting the interests of others.[108] This makes sense if one is grounding one's theory in contract. A reciprocity requirement is obviously not favorable to animals since they are not rational beings able to engage in this kind of interplay. The theory is then conceptually loaded against animals.

One problem with assuming a requirement of rationality in our hypothetical contracting parties is that it leaves out of consideration some humans that nearly everyone believes have rights—infants, children, and the mentally handicapped—but do not have full rationality. Also, if we proceed from the hypothetical standpoint of some original position, it is hard to conceive why we must assume that we will not ultimately be instantiated as a species other than human. Indeed, Rawls's theory can be construed to protect the interests of animals.[109] Presumably, we would do this by assuming in our original position that we might come into the world as nonhuman animals.

It is also argued against this contractual theory that it assumes there are some grounding rules prior to the hypothetical contract.[110] In other words, there must be some foundational rule that requires that we go along with the result of the contract that arises out of the original position.[111] What is this rule and how is it grounded? Without this rule and its foundation, the theory is incomplete and rests on unexplained premises.

At its nadir, this theory does not address how we actually ground rights in our legal system, but rather how we might explain the genesis of a legal system that has rules like ours. It is, thus, an interesting conceptual exercise, but not one that explains the way we actually ground rights or the considerations and policies that actually go into rights.[112]

Except in the case of interest theories and Wise's dignity theory, one common strand runs through the theories reviewed: a focus on human, as opposed to animal or ecological, concerns. There has nevertheless been some movement by scholars to spotlight other problems. Laurence Tribe, for instance, outlines a view of ecological issues that is not anthropocentric. He proposes a new paradigm for thinking about ecological issues that looks beyond human needs and concerns.[113] The present anthropocentric paradigm, according to Tribe, defines the world as raw material to be manipulated for human demands.[114] This manipulation is performed within a structure of Western dichotomies, God/man, human/animal, etc.,[115] that manufactures boundaries between these concepts that cannot be bridged. Tribe calls this the "theory of transcendence" under which human needs transcend all other concerns, including ecology or animals.

A theory that moves diametrically away from such anthropocentricity is one of "imminence" that sees value and sacredness in all of nature and its constituents.[116] To Tribe, however, such a view proves too much; it may not be possible or appropriate for society to go this far in changing its fundamental principles.[117]

Instead, Tribe suggests a synthesis of the transcendence and immanence theories.[118] Such a view avoids the ecological pitfalls of anthropocentrism.[119] Tribe's view comprehends reverence for nature—nature is something more than just fodder for the satisfaction of human desires.[120] Accordingly, there are obligations to animal and plant life.[121] Tribe notes in this regard that rights have been given, in certain circumstances, to entities other than humans, like churches, corporations, and animals in animal welfare laws.[122]

It should be clear by now that there are many divergent and complex views regarding what rights are and what our reasons are for respecting them. The views range from those of critical legal studies scholars and some feminists who believe rights have little or no utility, to those who believe that rights can be used to solve myriad problems, including protection of animals. One typical and critically important characteristic of the many foundational concepts of rights is their attempt to ground rights in some single concept or a very restricted set of concepts. But before discussing this issue, a closer look at rights concepts and animals is required.

III. Rights Theory and Animal Rights

Whatever underlying theory of rights one chooses to accept, when the issue is whether animals have rights, discussion inevitably focuses on the issue of what characteristics an entity must have to be a rightholder. It is generally thought that possessors of rights all must share some one common attribute.[123]

In a prior article, I discussed the justifications for different treatment of humans and animals that ground views that animals cannot have rights.[124] I will not restate in detail these justifications, but will outline the arguments concerning the characteristics necessary to be a rightholder.

Some scholars ground rights in rationality. Contractarian theorists require rational agency in order to participate in contracting in the original position.[125] A diluted rationality theory, however, might be used to argue for placing animals in the domain of rightholders. For instance, if one said that sentience or consciousness, rather than rationality, was the key to rights, then at least some animals might be included among rightholders. For example, Tom Regan proposes that rightholders are entities that are "subjects-of-a-life."[126] This criterion requires that the animal be something more than just conscious; the animal must have, among other characteristics, beliefs, desires and perceptions, a sense of the future, an emotional life, and a psychological identity over time.[127] This criterion may spread rights very thinly, however, since it is not clear how many animals have all of the elements necessary to be subjects of a life.

Moral autonomy also has been asserted to be the characteristic necessary to have rights. To have rights under this theory, an entity must be one that can comply with normative constraints.[128] Such a theory excludes from the group of rightholders animals, incompetents, and children.[129]

It is also argued that in order to have rights one must be able to make claims—to assert one's rights.[130] Without modification, this requires that a rightholder have linguistic and other abilities that are characteristic of those who have considerable cognitive abilities. The idea can, however, be modified to allow for assertion of rights by animals through the use of representatives.[131]

Alan White proposes that those who possess rights are those who can be sensibly spoken about in "the full language of rights."[132] To be spoken about in the full language of rights requires that an entity be able to assert and exercise rights.[133] This, he contends, rules animals out as possessors of rights, since it requires rationality and linguistic ability.[134]

If we ground rights in interests, we broaden the group of entities to whom rights may be granted. If we view being free from pain as an interest that animals possess that is worthy of respect, then rights for animals can be constructed from this interest. Interests might, in addition, include things like physical liberty and freedom in such a way as to construct even more complex rights for animals.

It is not my intent to settle the issue of what characteristic or characteristics are necessary to be a rightholder. Rather, I merely point out that there is considerable impetus toward identifying some single property as the foundation for being a rightholder.

IV. Morality and Legal Rights

In discussing questions of legal rights, it is useful, if not crucial, to determine whether there is or should be a connection between legal rights and morality. Are legal rights just conventional legal remedies as a realist might contend or are they connected, at least ideally, to some system of moral principles?

Legal positivists, who have wielded considerable influence in this century, deny a connection between law and morality.[135] For legal positivists, there is no law apart from government and its institutions and, as a result, no rights apart from those ceded by the state.[136] Philosophically, this idea can be traced to Kant, who saw morality existing in the realm of reason, quite separate from the sensible world where the law and, thus, rights operate.[137] Similarly, Oliver Wendell Holmes stated that morality requires us to look at the internal state of mind of an actor, while the law concerns itself only with external signs.[138]

Nonetheless, there are those who continue to claim a connection between law and morality, and thus, between legal rights and morality. It has been stated that morality logically precedes the law.[139] In this vein, it is argued that while we can have morality without law, we cannot have law without morality.[140] Morality is necessary for the law, since without it there can be no basis for a general obligation to follow the law.[141] In other words, for law to be efficacious, there must be a transcending moral rule that directs compliance with the law.

Natural rights theorists, of course, base the law on moral theory.[142] Carl Wellman, for example, ultimately grounds rights in fundamental moral principles in his expansion of Hohfeldian theory.[143] In his theory, those who have legal rights are exactly those who have moral rights.[144]

There are, of course, a number of ways to connect law and morality. One might subscribe to the idea that there are ontologically extant moral principles finding their source in God or elsewhere that are the basis for the law. On the other hand, one might take a less metaphysically challenging position and claim that there are natural rights that issue from moral theory, but this moral theory does not require ontological entities to represent this morality.[145] Or one might say that moral rights are based on true moral propositions that bear on human conduct in a way that has practical consequences and relevance.[146] To say that there are moral rights, then, is to say that there are true moral reasons, the truth of which can be proven.[147] These moral rights can then be translated into legal rights.[148] The fundamental rights we view as extant in the context of international law are an example.[149]

Yet looser connections between law and morality might exist. H. L. A. Hart claims, for example, that while there may be no simple identification of moral with legal rights, there is some "intimate" connection.[150] For Hart, morality creates limits on one's freedom to interfere with others, thereby determining the content of legal rules and rights.[151]

Ronald Dworkin also believes that morality plays a role in legal rights. He distinguishes between "goals" that he sees as supported by policy arguments and "rights" that are supported by moral principles.[152] Thus, there is a qualitative distinction between matters supported by policy and matters supported by moral principle. The latter acquire the status of rights. Those who claim that rights are based on "interests" also ground the existence of these interests on moral arguments, thereby grounding rights in moral principles.[153] Even critics of rights, like Mary Midgley, recognize that if there are rights, they are in some way linked to morality.[154]

For the purposes of this article it will be assumed that there is or should be a connection between morality and law. There is good reason to take such a position. The divorce of law from morality can be seen as the foundation for systems, like Nazism, that base what is right on the wielding of power.[155] Such legal systems may be avoided by firmly grounding the law in accepted moral principles. It is not the purpose of this article to specify these moral principles or to propose a moral theory. Nor is it my goal to claim that there is some set of ontologically extant moral principles that can by one means or another be discovered.[156] Rather, all that need be said is that law and rights have, or should have, a connection to moral principles, whatever these may be—the collective moral precepts of society, true moral propositions, or natural law.

V. Analysis and Synthesis of Rights Theories

Western thought tends to attempt to reduce disparate concepts to a unified theory. We look for one explanation that resolves all of our questions about a subject. For example, the Holy Grail of physics is the search for a unified theory, resolving conflicts in quantum theory and general relativity theory.

While such a structure may fit hard sciences, in human affairs one must question its efficacy.

Similarly, we look at the issue of rights as one that requires *a single* explanation. Hohfeld sees rights as correlative with duties. Wellman refines this by founding rights on a set of Hohfeldian elements, revolving around a single central core. Regan and others see rights as founded in interests. Other theories see rights variously as remedies, reasons, goals, or rhetoric. The common theme is that there is *an* explanation.

Is there *an* explanation of the foundations or sources of rights? Might rights have diverse sources? The notion that a single conceptual foundation adequately describes legal rights appears dubitable.[157] It seems wrong as a matter of fact because it has been widely recognized in the law, at least since Hohfeld, that rights can be described in many ways.[158] As a matter of theory it appears wrong because "importantly different notions of a right, each of them proper, might profitably coexist in the law."[159]

When we ask about the foundation or source of a right we actually have many valid answers. For example, if one asked about the foundation of the right to own property, one might say that under the generally accepted moral principles of our society, private property is a fundamental good that we protect through the creation of a "right."[160] Wellman or others might subscribe to some natural inherent liberty right to own property exclusive of others; a person who appropriates property through her effort is protected by a right.[161] Or we might say that a person has rights in property because we grant a remedy to the person with title to property when there is some interference with the property. This allows the smooth functioning of society and its institutions. The goal of maximizing wealth in society may be a ground for promoting rights in private property. In one way or another each of these concepts grounds our idea of rights in property, and all of these ideas are in some sense correct.[162]

In an interest theory we can identify the interests of persons who should be free from unnecessary pain and suffering as a foundation for the right to be free from such cruel and unusual punishment. Societal goals supporting a ban on cruel and unusual punishment may include making society compassionate and feeling. In the rhetoric of liberal societies, we see this right as fundamental to the dignity of humans. Again, as in the case of property rights, we can ground the right to be free from cruel and unusual punishment in several ways, all of which appear well founded.

Looking at rights as grounded in a single concept or foundational idea is an oversimplification. Rights are complex concepts founded on moral, policy, societal, and cultural ideas.[163] Thus, we should not focus on finding some single basis for a right, but on discovering the sundry elements of a right. The more bases we find for a right the more firmly convinced we may be that it is a legitimate and well-founded right. Indeed, it might be appropriate to call rights "composites"—they are compounds of numerous interconnected ideas that mingle together in a loosely cohesive whole. Unlike Wellman's view of rights as complexes of Hohfeldian components, this "composite" view is not limited in the kinds of things that can serve as foundations for rights and is not committed to some core element as the ultimate foundation of each right. The core of a right may be molecular rather than atomic; it may be a composite of various ingredients.

Perhaps W. V. O. Quine's view of knowledge is an apt analogy.[164] Quine viewed knowledge as composed of interconnecting links (think of a spider web) joined at the core by certain fundamental principles.[165] These central principles are strongly held beliefs that are not easily swayed. As we move away from these central principles, new information may modify the structure of the web. The foundational principles at the center of the web, however, will generally be left unaffected by new information. With respect to rights, certain central ideas may ground rights, while various subsidiary ideas surround these central concepts. The general stability of rights concepts over time is attributable to the strength of the central principles founding rights. The capacity for change over time comes from the gradual reshaping of the perimeter of the web and ultimately, through this reshaping process, modification of the central principles through evolving morals, goals, and other principles.

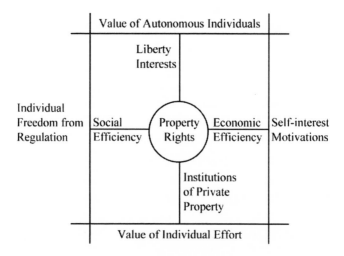

Consider the earlier example of property rights. In the figure, a number of central founding principles compose a property right, all of critical importance, surrounded by lesser subsidiary ideas. This schematic obviously oversimplifies the relations of these concepts. More connections could be made between the various principles and many other subsidiary principles could be mentioned.[166] Nonetheless, this schematic can be seen as "a family tree" for the conceptual foundation of a right to property. It is in this fashion that I believe rights are actually grounded.

VI. An Emotive Aspect of Animal Rights

A. The Unity of Emotion and Reason

1. Emotion and Moral Theory

Generally, emotions are thought to be unimportant to moral theory.[167] It is a maxim of Western thought that one is to avoid contamination of moral theory with compassion, sympathy, or caring.[168] This extension of a religion of science into moral theory[169] may ultimately be credited to Kant.[170] In Kant's moral theory, duty is the foundation of morality, and through the application of reason we discover our duties.[171] Reason is distinguished from emotion. This distinction assumes that emotion is irrational.

In Western thought, what is rational is good and what is not rational is bad.[172] Emotions, overwhelming feelings that cloud rationality and ultimately have deleterious effects, facilitate irrationality. There are certain "commonplaces" or prejudices that we have about emotion and rationality that lead to these views.[173] Cool rationality is believed to be the best state for inquiry and acquisition of knowledge, and emotions must always be in tight control lest we stray from the proper path to understanding.[174]

This gulf between morality (and, thus, law) on one side and emotion on the other is followed by most modern theorists on animal rights issues. Peter Singer, for example, makes a point of stating that his foundation for a new way of looking at the treatment of animals is devoid of emotive elements.[175] Tom Regan also does not allow for consideration of emotion in his interest theory.[176]

There are, nonetheless, those who espouse a role for the emotive in moral theory. For example, some feminist thinkers hold open a role for compassion in moral thought, though not for the purpose of finding a foundation for rights.[177] From this perspective emotion and compassion are a normal part of the human condition and can be utilized to ground and analyze moral positions.[178] One might say that morality, at bottom, requires that one care about or have certain feelings about an issue.[179] Without such feelings there is no morality.[180]

Though perhaps ordinarily foreign to our thought, the idea that emotion plays a role in morality can be extracted from major thinkers in our Western tradition. While most philosophers hold the view that reason must conquer passions, David Hume reversed this idea and claimed that reason should be the slave of passion.[181] Hume was of the view that the passions are the basis for all moral thought. His view was based on the idea that reason is inert; it is just the mechanism used for the discovery of truth or falsehood—it concerns the relation of ideas or the existence of facts.[182] Passions, volitions, and actions are not susceptible to being true or false and, thus, cannot be the subject of reason.[183] Morality is concerned with actions, and since actions have their basis in passions, passions are the foundation of morals.[184] To those who attempt to ground morals in reason, Hume states:

> There has been an opinion very industriously propagated by certain philosophers, that morality is susceptible of demonstration [through reason]; and tho' no one has ever been able to advance a single step in those demonstrations; yet 'tis taken for granted, that this science may be brought to an equal certainty with geometry or algebra.[185]

Morals are not matters of fact and therefore are not the subject of reason. Nor are morals demonstrable with use of reason:

> But can there be any difficulty in proving, that vice and virtue are not matters of fact, whose existence we can infer by reason? Take any action allow'd to be vicious: Wilful murder, for instance. Examine it in all lights, and see if you can find that matter of fact, or real existence, which you call *vice.* In which-ever way you take it, you find only certain passions, motives, volitions and thoughts. There is no other matter of fact in the case. The vice entirely escapes you, as long as you consider the object. You never can find it, till you turn your reflection into your own breast, and find a sentiment of disapprobation, which arises in you, towards this action.[186]

Hume states that there is an innate moral sense that grounds our moral awareness.[187] The vice and virtue that we see in the world are determined by certain impressions or sentiments (feelings) that are innate in humans.[188]

Moral evaluations are perception—kinds of pains and pleasures.[189] Morality is felt, not judged.[190]

These moral impressions are natural in the sense that all humans have them and all societies reflect them.[191] Moral feelings are rooted in our constitution and temper, and cannot be jettisoned except through disease or madness.[192] Marcia Lind argues that Hume viewed emotions as complexes of both feeling and cognitive elements that are inextricably connected and hard wired into our constitutions.[193] Hume can therefore avoid the charge of being a radical subjectivist concerning morality.[194] Since there is a natural method of connecting feelings with the objects of feelings, this method can be discovered without subjectivism.[195]

Schopenhauer held a similar view of the root of morality. He saw compassion as the foundation for morality and an undeniable fact of human consciousness. Compassion is original and immediate, and resides in human nature itself.[196] Even Western science admits of these ideas. Research concerning kin altruism suggests that there is an innate sense of sympathy in other animals, and through Darwinian theory we must recognize this as a part of our makeup.[197]

Plato too, though in a more subtle way, held that emotion has a role in morality. He thought that although reason is in control of the passions, they are allies in the search for moral truth.[198] Aristotle thought that to be a good person one must have the right emotional makeup.[199] Thus, there is considerable support, even in Western thought, for the view that emotion plays a role in moral theory.

As noted earlier, the exile of the emotive from moral theory is based on the idea that emotion is dangerous and must always be governed by reason. It is asserted, by focusing on certain extreme cases of emotional outbursts, that emotions are undesirable elements in inquiry and elsewhere.[200] We view emotion as causing utter subjectivity due to the lack of any element of reason.[201] It is thought that emotion is the antithesis of rationality.[202] To allow emotive aspects into moral theory is to descend into an abyss of irrationality and mysticism.

This dichotomy of emotion and reason is false. Reason is sometimes mistaken.[203] Reason can go astray through undue credulity or skepticism, or inappropriate acceptance of authority.[204] There are indeed times when it is appropriate to say "don't get rational about this," just as we sometimes admonish people not to get emotional.[205] Indeed, Justice William Brennan decried the cold harshness of our focus on reason as being a threat to the human dignity that is the basis of our constitution:

The framers [of the United States Constitution] operated within a political and moral universe that had experienced arbitrary passion as the greatest affront to the dignity of the citizen. . . . In our own time, attention to experience may signal that the greatest threat to due process principles is formal reason severed from the insight of passion.[206]

There are, in all acts of reason, emotive elements in the background.[207] The entry of emotion into consciousness does not empty the mind of reason.[208] Cognition and reason remain notwithstanding the surfacing of emotion into consciousness.[209] If emotions are complexes of both feeling and cognitive elements, then the commonplaces about emotions cannot be maintained.[210] For example, to have compassion, the main emotional element of relevance to animal issues, involves both intellectual and emotional understanding.[211] It is, thus, unlikely that we can ever separate emotion from reason. Our concern, then, in applying emotive elements to moral and legal issues should not be to avoid all emotion but to avoid emotion devoid of reason.

Emotion threatens reason only when it is uncontrolled,[212] not in the more typical cases of controlled emotion. Ordinarily emotions are unmomentous, long lasting, diffuse, and pervasive.[213] Examples are the affection we may have for a friend or the dull fear of going to the dentist. Emotions are not just the extreme occurrences that we often call "emotional" responses.[214] Instead, much of our emotional life is found "in the backgrounds, the tones and tastes of life."[215] The mundaneness of ordinary emotional life has been described in the following way:

[T]here is no action without affect, to be sure not always an intense, dramatic affect as in an action of impulsive rage, but more usually a total, sometimes quite marked, sometimes very subtle and hardly noticeable mood, which nevertheless constitutes an essential background of every action.[216] Thus, emotion is ordinarily a normal, unmomentous and not necessarily disruptive part of our experience.[217]

The employment of the emotive in moral and legal discussions will surely be met with criticism. One problem with adding an emotive element to moral theory is that emotions are not universal.[218] Each person's emotional response to a situation is different and thus will inevitably cause dispute concerning how these responses should be incorporated in moral and legal theory.

It is not, however, necessarily the case that such responses will be divergent. If Hume was correct that humans have some innate sense of compassion, then emotional responses of different individuals should be similar.[219] Moreover, even moral and legal theories presumably founded on utterly rational bases differ as to their efficacy and application. Thus, the possibility of dispute is hardly confined to a moral theory incorporating emotive aspects.

There is, then, considerable support for the view that emotion should play a part in moral theory. The precise role of emotion in such a theory is not within the scope of this article, but at least some explanation of the function of emotion in moral theory is in order.

2. The Role of the Emotive in Moral Theory

There are a number of uses to which emotions can be put in moral theory. Our emotional responses reveal what is of moral value to us.[220] For example, when we are angered at a slight against some person we know, our anger reveals that we value the person slighted.[221] Our emotion of anger contains not only the emotion itself but the moral value we attach to the object of the emotion.[222] Similarly, being emotionally upset at the outbreak of war reveals the value we place on human life and suffering.[223] Our emotions are important not only in that they reveal value, but also in what values they reveal—like the friendship shown by anger from the slight or the value of life revealed in feelings toward those suffering in war.[224]

In addition, emotions are morally relevant as motivators to action.[225] By pushing us to believe and desire certain things, emotions drive us to act.[226] Acting along with reasoned judgment, emotions give us grounds for action.[227] They act as instrumental aids in our reasoning process, motivating action on behalf of others.[228] Emotions move us to perform in the interests of those that we value, whether human or animal, and this performance can take the form of rescuing the afflicted, pushing for legislation to help those in need, or any other action in the interest of those we have feelings toward.

Similarly, emotions aid us in noticing and attending to things that are of value to us.[229] They guide us in obtaining the knowledge and information necessary to take ethical actions.

Contrary to ordinary thinking, emotions act as aids in rational inquiry.

Emotion provides the interest in a subject to which we apply rational thought.[230] This intellectual interest is required for rational inquiry to proceed.[231] Emotions also guide the course of inquiry[232] by directing us in certain intellectual directions. Because emotions focus our attention on certain issues, they help assure that our rational processes lead to determinate outcomes.[233] For this reason, emotions have been described as "determinate patterns of salience among objects of attention, lines of inquiry, and inferential strategies."[234] Emotion determines which elements of a problem we focus on and direct our attention to, thereby aiding the inquiry and discovery of solutions. Emotions also help us in predicting the behavior of others in response to actions.[235] Without emotion, rational inquiry would be hampered.[236]

Along the same lines, emotion is necessary for making evaluative judgments.[237] In this regard, it has been argued that those who lack emotion are epistemologically disadvantaged in making such judgments.[238] Since emotion is necessary to see the values inherent in a situation, a lack of emotion will cause a person to overlook and fail to apply moral values to a situation.[239] Thus, only those who are emotionally engaged can make informed and proper evaluative judgments.[240] This is shown by the fact that those who have emotional deficiencies have trouble making proper evaluative judgments.[241] Such persons fail because they are affectless or lack feelings appropriate to the circumstances.[242]

The connection between emotion and evaluative judgments is so strong that some philosophers have categorized emotions as being evaluative judgments.[243] This theory views emotions as kinds of factually based beliefs that are partly evaluative.[244] For example, fear is the belief that some danger looms.[245] This view, however, may oversimplify emotion as it fails to explain the diversity of emotional phenomena—for example, emotions that do not seem to be based on full-fledged beliefs.[246] For this reason, Patricia Greenspan has refined this evaluative judgment view of emotion. She claims that emotions are object-directed affects whose object is an evaluative proposition—a statement of value.[247] Emotions, then, turn out to be compounds of two elements: (1) affective states of comfort or discomfort and (2) evaluative propositions.[248] Fear would then be a feeling of discomfort and the fact (or imagined fact) that danger looms, the latter being the evaluative proposition that is the subject of the feeling of discomfort.[249] In this way, the evaluative proposition need not reach the level of being a belief, it need just be a structured evaluation.[250] Emotions thus can be seen as a broader set of phenomena than is the case if emotions always require a belief as their foundation.

From Greenspan's view we can more clearly see how emotion acts with reason in making practical reasoned judgments. To make judgments, one needs the evaluative aspect of emotions.[251] Emotions, by acting in part to evaluate the world around us, are used in reality testing by humans and are as valuable as rational thought in making these evaluations.[252] This is not to say that emotions control our processes of rational thought (the passions are properly in the control of reason), but emotions do, at least sometimes, perform the evaluative work in our reasoned decision making.[253] Due to this connection between emotion and rational decision making, Stocker takes the view that it is simply impossible to separate out the emotional from the rational.[254]

Emotion then serves morality in a number of ways. It reveals what is of moral portent. It is a moral stimulator. It is a necessary element in evaluation of moral issues. It may, in fact, not be separable from our rational thought processes at all.

3. The Role of Emotion in the Law

If emotion is an aspect of morality, and morality is relevant to the law, then the law can and should reflect emotive concerns. Indeed, there are many aspects of the law that derive largely from emotive concerns. Damages are awarded for emotional distress.[255] Such damages are founded on a sense of compassion for the suffering of others even though suffering cannot be as easily measured in commercial script as can other elements of damage.

The criminal law provides many emotive features. In providing remedies for the sake of victims and society at large we are evincing emotion in the law. When we refer to "victim's rights" we speak about our compassion for those who have been victimized.[256] When we speak of retribution we are venting emotions of anger, indignation, and remorse.[257] We explicitly recognize the significance of emotion in reducing penalties in crimes influenced by overheated emotions or mental disturbance.[258] In sentencing criminals we sometimes weigh compassion not only for the victims, but also for the criminal. We may even see emotion play a role in the doctrine of self-defense. The intentions of the other party to a conflict, her emotions, may play a role in whether a claim of self-defense is warranted.[259]

Property law, too, has elements of the emotive. Heirlooms, the value of which are largely emotional, are specially prized in the law, and emotional attachment to goods is an element in determining remedies for loss or damage to such goods.[260] Moreover, emotional value is taken into consideration in exemption laws.[261] Emotional value has also been imported to the area of damages for injury or death of companion animals.[262]

It is clearly false to contend that the law is or should be bereft of emotive considerations. Why, then, should our concept of rights be devoid of emotive considerations?

4. What Emotions Are Relevant to Morality, Law, and Animal Rights Issues?

If emotion plays a role in moral thought, and if there is a role for morality in concepts of legal rights, then it must be recognized that there is or should be an emotive aspect to our concepts of rights. Part of what we are doing in protecting rightholders is expressing compassion and respect.[263] As such, we are recognizing an element of compassion in our concept of rights.

But precisely what types of emotions are relevant to morality, law, and animal rights issues? Arthur Schopenhauer argued that the only actions that have moral worth are those done exclusively for the benefit of another.[264] For my action to have moral worth I must actually suffer the woe of another and be identified with her.[265] For Schopenhauer, compassion allows for this sacrifice and is the foundation of morality.[266]

> It is simply and solely this compassion that is the real basis for all *voluntary* justice and *genuine* loving-kindness.[267] Only insofar as an action has sprung from compassion does it have moral value; and every action resulting from any other motive has none. As soon as this compassion is aroused, the weal and woe of another are nearest to my heart in exactly the same way, although not always in the same degree, as otherwise only my own are. Hence the difference between him and me is no longer absolute.[268]

The primacy of compassion in morality is recognized by Rousseau:

> Mandeville well knew that, in spite of all their morality, men would never have been better than monsters, had not nature bestowed on them a sense of compassion, to aid their reason: but he did not see that from this quality alone flow all those social virtues, of which he denied man the possession. But what is generosity, clemency,

or humanity but compassion applied to the weak, to the guilty, or to mankind in general? Even benevolence and friendship are, if we judge rightly, only the effects of compassion, constantly set upon a particular object: for how is it different to wish that another person may not suffer pain and uneasiness and to wish him happy? . . . In a word, it is rather in this natural feeling than in any subtle arguments that we must look for the cause of that repugnance, which every man would experience in doing evil, even independently of the maxims of education.[269]

According to Schopenhauer, compassion makes another's suffering my motive for action in two ways. First, it prevents me from injuring others.[270] Second, it incites me to aid others.[271] This latter aspect is the highest level of compassion.[272] In having this proactive compassion, the barriers between oneself and others are broken down.[273]

While I do not subscribe to many of Schopenhuaer's views, I do believe that he correctly identifies compassion as the spring from which our moral sensibilities flow. And it is this emotion that I believe should play a central role in our discussion of the moral and legal issues relating to animal rights. Indeed, there is reason to think that compassion plays a special role in the area of animals rights—an even more pivotal role than it plays in human moral and human rights issues.

B. The Role of Emotion in a Theory of Animal Rights

If morality is connected to legal rights and emotion is appropriately considered in moral theory, then emotion must play a role in how we view rights issues. If emotive concerns are relevant to rights issues, they are of particular force in the case of animal rights. From Descartes's likening of animals' howls of pain to the screeching of machinery, to modern vivisection, our culture has trained us that feelings and emotions are not to be squandered on nonhuman animals. There is no need for concern for them since they do not feel pain or suffering, at least not in the way that we do. There is no reason to feel for them. Feelings are reserved for humans and specifically only those close to us—family and friends.

We know that the Cartesian view is myth. Animals do experience pain.[274] Animal pain physiology, though differing in certain ways from that of humans, operates in largely the same way as does human pain physiology.[275] Not just pain, but anxiety and other forms of suffering exist in animals.[276]

Contrary to the Cartesian world view, there is good reason to have compassion for animals since they have the kind of suffering and pain that are appropriately objects of this emotion. To break the hold of Cartesian theory, it is of particular importance in our consideration of animal rights issues to, as we naturally do with respect to humans, fittingly consider our emotions. That it is culturally accepted to do so with humans, but not necessarily so with animals, makes its import in the latter case greater than in the former.

To the extent that the interests of animals are considered in the composite view of rights that I have described, these interests will include animal pain, anxiety, and the like. To evaluate these matters is, at least in part, to have feelings of compassion. Thus, to the extent that interests are part of the reason that we grant rights to an entity, the only way that these interests may be properly gauged is through our own emotional experiences and evaluations.

Animals cannot speak for themselves. They cannot communicate to us through our familiar means of language. The only way that communication can occur is through observations of animal behavior. As a result, to determine the needs and interests of animals it is necessary to reason by use of analogy from our own experiences.

> If we assume that another being has interests, and ask whether this imposes duties upon us, we must resort to reasoning by analogy. We infer certain inner processes from physical manifestations, which we know to be associated with such processes in ourselves. Such reasoning by analogy may involve greater or lesser difficulties according to the nature of the given case, but this much is certain: either we cannot apply it at all or we must always apply it. Those who advance the argument in question [that we cannot know of an animal's interests] must, then, in order to be consistent, assert that men have no more rights than animals—neither would have any rights at all.[277]

As a part of this reasoning by analogy we must consider the inner processes of animals by analogy to our own. Moreover, since animals cannot communicate in our language, analysis by analogy to our feelings is even more crucial in the case of animals than in the case of humans. Thus, emotional responses are a necessary part of evaluation of the interests of animals and rights that may arise from these interests.

How might emotional considerations affect our analysis of animal rights issues? While it is not intended here to present in detail precisely what a theory of animal rights would look like if it appropriately considered emotional aspects of the issue, a few ways in which emotion might impact the analysis of animal rights issues can be outlined. On the issue of whether it is fitting to attribute rights to animals in order to protect them from ill treatment, we might ask whether we feel compassion for their suffering. We might ask whether we feel attachment to them, whether we feel a sense of kinship to them, whether we feel a sense of awe at their resilience, and whether these feelings give us a reason to grant them rights. These feelings, none of which put us across an impenetrable gulf from reason, can be seen as elements counting in the analysis of whether rights ought to be accorded to animals.

If we conclude that animals should be accorded rights, as I believe they should, what role might emotion play in determining what rights we grant to animals? Our primary emotional response to animals is to feel compassion for their suffering. As Jeremy Bentham stated, "the question is not, Can they reason? nor, Can they talk? but Can they suffer?"[278] Our emotional response to animal suffering must be considered in determining whether a practice violates an animal right. Given that most, if not all of us feel compassion for animals in laboratories or factory farms, this response is a strong reason supporting the abolition of such practices as a matter of right.

Similarly, our feeling of compassion toward those with restrictions on their liberty and freedom would count against practices engaged in by circuses, zoos, and other institutions that confine animals. These same feelings may lead us to broader environmental and ecological issues bearing on the liberty and freedom of not only wild animals, but ourselves.

To achieve the result of applying appropriate emotional responses to questions concerning animal rights requires unifying our rational and emotional natures. One way to do this is to actually experience the conditions that cause human compassion for animals.[279] To experience what is done in animal experiments, in the slaughterhouse, or on the factory farm will allow us both to feel and to apply our capacity of reason to real conditions. If we consider our rational nature and appropriate feelings about animal issues, our emotional reactions suggest according rights to animals. Such considerations will also help guide us in determining the content of those rights.

Conclusion

Western thought makes us skeptical about the application of emotion in morality and the law. As a result, emotional responses to the plight of animals and others is thought to play no role in animal or human rights issues.

Our theories of rights are modeled on Western scientific reductionism. They are examples of attempts to find a "unified theory" of rights; we seek in morality and law to find something that physics cannot. Rights are thought to be grounded in interests or in some core element of an overarching rational moral theory. Or rights are just remedies that can be empirically discovered in the pages of a law book and the institutions that enforce its precepts.

In reality, rights are not so simple or easily accessed. Rights are actually composites of many elements. When we say that "X has a right to Y" we are saying many things. We are saying that X has an interest in Y, that certain duties are owed to X with regard to Y, that there is a moral imperative behind X's right, and that X is to have a remedy if she is denied Y, and so on.

What we are also saying is that we have some emotional response to X in relation to Y, that we feel that it should morally and legally be the case that X is protected in regard to Y. But this emotive aspect is generally ignored in moral and legal theory. As has been shown, however, there is a role for emotion in moral theory, and if we believe that moral theory is relevant to legal theory, then emotion must play some role in the construction of rights.

I do not suggest that we abandon reason in considering issues of animal rights. Rather, we should consider emotion as a part of our analysis of animal rights issues. Indeed, because of our history of staunchly denying the relevance of feelings toward animals, and due to our inability to communicate with animals and determine their needs and interests, the emotional aspect of our relationships with animals is more important in determining appropriate treatment of them than in the case of humans. If we recognize the emotional aspects of our nature, and take a balanced and unified approach to applying our rational and emotive natures to issues of animal rights, we will have a more realistic and honest approach to animal rights issues.

NOTES

1. It is generally thought that the concept of legal rights arose in either the fourteenth or seventeenth century, but it has also been argued that this concept originated in the thirteenth century. See Charles J. Reid, "The Canonistic Contribution to the Western Rights Tradition: An Historical Inquiry," 33 *B.C. L. Rev.* 37, 37–41 (1991).

2. L. W. Sumner, *The Moral Foundation of Rights* 15–18 (1987). See also *Sowers v. Civil Rights Comm'n*, 252 N.E.2d 463, 474–75 (Ohio Ct. App. 1969) (stating that "rights" are often too broadly construed, and noting that liberties are not rights, but immunities).

3. Christopher D. Stone, "Should Trees Have Standing?—Toward Legal Rights for Natural Objects," 45 *S. Cal. L. Rev.* 450, 488 (1972).

4. Steven M. Wise, "Hardly a Revolution—The Eligibility of Nonhuman Animals for Dignity—Rights in a Liberal Democracy," 22 *Vt. L. Rev.* 793, 833 (1998).

5. See *infra* notes 10–26 and accompanying text.

6. See *infra* Section II.

7. See *infra* notes 40–65 and accompanying text.

8. Peter Singer, *Animal Liberation* 5–8 (2d ed., 1990).

9. Claims of this nature by socialists and feminists are discussed in Ted Benton, "Animal Rights: An Eco-Socialist View," in *Animal Rights: The Changing Debate* 19–41 (Robert Garner, ed., 1996).

10. Id. at 32.

11. Samuel J. M. Donnelly, *The Language and Uses of Rights: A Biopsy of American Jurisprudence in the Twentieth Century* 38–41 (1994).

12. Id. at 42.

13. Barbara Stark, "International Human Rights, Law, Feminist Jurisprudence and Nietzsche's 'Eternal Return': Turning the Wheel," 19 *Harv. Women's L.J.* 169, 169–75 (1996).

14. Josephine Donovan, "Animal Rights and Feminist Theory" (chapter 2, this volume), 58, 64–72.

15. Id.

16. Marti Kheel, "Nature and Feminist Sensitivity," in *Animal Rights and Human Obligations* 261 (Tom Regan and Peter Singer, eds., 1989).

17. Benton, "Animal Rights: An Eco-Socialist View," at 33.

18. Id. at 35.

19. Id. at 36–37.

20. Mary Midgley, *Animals and Why They Matter* 62 (1983).

21. Id. at 61–64.

22. Id. at 62–63.

23. Marti Kheel, "The Liberation of Nature: A Circular Affair" (chapter 1, this volume), 39.

24. Id. at 39–40.

25. Id. at 40.

26. Id. at 40–41.

27. Id. at 43–44.

28. Benton believes that rights would be necessary even in a society lacking the supposed scarcity and conflict of capitalist society. See Benton, "Animal Rights: An Eco-Socialist View," at 36.

29. Stone, "Should Trees Have Standing?" at 488.

30. A. J. M. Milne, *Human Rights and Human Diversity: An Essay in the Philosophy of Human Rights* 125 (1986).

31. Id. at 115.

32. Courts have utilized Hohfeld's structures for analysis of legal terms in case law. See *California v. Farmers Mkts., Inc.*, 792 F.2d 1400, 1403 (9th Cir. 1986) (describing property as a complex of rights, powers, privileges, and immunities, citing Hohfeld); *Lake Shore and M.S. Ry. Co. v. Kurtz*, 37 N.E. 303, 304 (Ind. App. 1894).

33. Wesley N. Hohfeld, *Fundamental Legal Conceptions* 36 (1923).

34. Id.

35. Id.

36. Id. at 36–38, 71.

37. Id. at 38, 71–72. Some case law has reflected this idea. For example, *Sowers v. Civil Rights Comm'n*, 252 N.E.2d 463, 474, holds that liberties are not properly considered rights, but rather are immunities.

38. Hohfeld, *Fundamental Legal Conceptions*, at 38.

39. Sumner, *Moral Foundation of Rights*, at 33.

40. Carl Wellman, *Real Rights* (1995); Carl Wellman, *A Theory of Rights: Persons Under Laws, Institutions, and Morals* (1985). A similar project of refining the Hohfeldian description of rights is pursued by Sumner, *Moral Foundation of Rights*, at 18–53. A Hohfeldian system has also been used to analyze environmental issues. See Peter Manus, "One Hundred Years of Green: A Legal Perspective on Three Twentieth Century Nature Philosophies," 59 *U. Pitt. L. Rev.* 557, 570 passim (1998).

41. Wellman, *Real Rights*, at 8.

42. Id. at 80–82. See also *California v. Farmers Mkts., Inc.*, 792 F.2d 1400, 1403 (9th Cir. 1986) (describing property as a complex of rights, powers, privileges, and immunities, citing Hohfeld).

43. Wellman, *Real Rights*, at 81–82.

44. Id. at 160–71.

45. Id.

46. Id. at 132.

47. Id. at 105–36.

48. Id. at 118–23. The concept of "will" is a philosophically loaded concept that is not clearly defined by Wellman.

49. Sumner, *Moral Foundation of Rights*, at 203.

50. Gary L. Francione, *Animals, Property and the Law* 95–97 (1995).

51. That duties may exist without corresponding rights is explained by Alan R. White, *Rights* 62–64 (1984).

52. Wellman, *Theory of Rights*, at 22. The problematic nature of duties to oneself is discussed in Leonard Nelson, *System of Ethics* 126–35 (Norbert Guterman, trans., 1956).

53. White, *Rights*, at 62–64.

54. Id. at 64. See also H. L. A. Hart, "Are There Any Natural Rights?" in *Theories of Rights* 81–82 (Jeremy Waldron, ed., 1984).

55. White, *Rights*, at 64.

56. Hart, "Are There Any Natural Rights?" at 80–81.

57. Arthur Schopenhauer, *Philosophical Writings* 215 (1996).

58. Id.

59. Id.

60. Id.

61. Arthur L. Corbin, Foreword to Wesley Newcomb Hohfeld, *Fundamental Legal Conceptions* xi (1964).

62. See *supra* notes 39–46 and accompanying text.

63. Wellman, *Real Rights*, at 8.

64. See *infra* Sections V–VI.

65. Albert Kocourek, "Tabulae Minores Jurisprudentiae," 30 *Yale L.J.* 215, 222–25 (1921). Some have also argued that Hohfeld's theory contains more elements than are necessary to describe rights. See Joseph William Singer, "The Legal Rights Debate in Analytical Jurisprudence from Bentham to Hohfeld," 1982 *Wisc. L. Rev.* 975, 992–93 (1982).

66. R. G. Frey, *Interests and Rights: The Case Against Animals* 5 (1980). See also Nelson, *System of Ethics*, at 136–44.

67. Joel Feinberg, "The Rights of Animals and Unborn Generations," in *Philosophy and Environmental Crisis* 43–68 (William T. Blackstone, ed., 1974).

68. Tom Regan, *The Case for Animal Rights* 243 (1983).

69. Id.

70. Feinberg, "Rights of Animals and Unborn Generations," at 43–68.

71. Frey, *Interests and Rights*, at 139–67.

72. Feinberg, "Rights of Animals and Unborn Generations," at 53.

73. Id. These issues are also discussed in Regan, *Case for Animal Rights*, at 34–35.

74. See *infra* notes 88–94 and accompanying text for discussion of issues relating to grounding interests in beliefs and desires.

75. One might, however, see animals as asserting interests when they protect themselves from others or assert dominion over territory. Thus in some ways animals can be seen as asserting interests. They just are not able to do so in the context of institutions requiring use of language.

76. Feinberg, "Rights of Animals and Unborn Generations," at 47–48.

77. Id.

78. Id.

79. *In re Johns Manville*, 36 B.R. 743, 757–58 (Bankr. S.D.N.Y. 1984).

80. Wellman, *Real Rights*, at 116, 119.

81. *In re Johns Manville*, 36 B.R. at 757–58.

82. Stone, "Should Trees Have Standing?" and accompanying text.

83. Frey, *Interests and Rights*, at 19.

84. Id. at 78.

85. Id. at 79.

86. Id. at 80–81.

87. Id. at 78.

88. Id. at 82–83.

89. Id. at 83.

90. Id. at 85.

91. Id. at 122.

92. Id. at 123, 127.

93. Id. at 107.

94. Id. at 19.

95. Jacques Vauclair, *Animal Cognition* 137–45 (1996); James Rachels, "Do Animals Have a Right to Liberty?" in Regan and Singer, *Animal Rights and Human Obligations*, at 214–18.

96. Vauclair, *Animal Cognition*, at 101–5.

97. Alan Geworth, "Human Dignity as the Basis of Rights," in *The Constitution of Rights* 10, 11, 24 (Michael J. Meyer and W. A. Parent, eds., 1992). See also Wise, "Hardly a Revolution," at 869–70.

98. Geworth, "Human Dignity as the Basis of Rights," at 12.

99. Id. at 21.

100. Id. at 23.

101. Id. at 24.

102. Wise, "Hardly a Revolution," at 900.

103. Id. at 874.

104. Id. at 873–74.

105. Id. at 877–78. See also *Care and Protection of Beth*, 587 N.E.2d 1377, 1381 (Mass. 1992).

106. Steven M. Wise, *Rattling the Cage: Toward Legal Rights for Animals* (2000).

107. John Rawls, *A Theory of Justice* 111 (1971). See also Rachels, "Do Animals Have a Right to Liberty?" at 221–22.

108. Rachels, "Do Animals Have a Right to Liberty?" at 222.

109. Rosemary Rodd, *Biology, Ethics, and Animals* 241–50 (1990).

110. Evelyn B. Pluhar, *Beyond Prejudice* 235 (1995).

111. Id.

112. Many other theories have been advanced to explain legal rights but typically have not been applied to animal rights issues. For example, legal realists regard rights as remedies such that having a right requires having the power to obtain a remedy. See Donnelly, *Language and Uses of Rights*, at 15; Wise, "Hardly a Revolution," at 816. Ronald Dworkin described several views of rights, including rights as trumps that override policies contrary to the right, and rights as reasons used to justify results of legal disputes. See Donnelly, *Language and Uses of Rights*, at 18, 20. H. L. A. Hart has also reasoned that to have a right is to have a reason to restrict the freedom of others. See Hart, "Are There Any Natural Rights?" at 83–84, 89. Rights have also been described as entitlements, resources, rhetoric, and a reflection of the goals of society. See Milne, *Human Rights and Human Diversity*, at 102; Donnelly, *Language and Uses of Rights*, at 25, 45. Rights have even been based on consequentialist moral theory and recognized as a means of enabling communication between groups. See Sumner, *Moral Foundation of Rights*, at 163, 188.

113. Laurence H. Tribe, "Ways Not to Think About Plastic Trees: New Foundations for Environmental Law," 83 *Yale L.J.* 1315, 1326–27 (1974).

114. Id. at 1330.

115. Id. at 1333.

116. Id. at 1336–37.

117. Id. at 1338.

118. Id.

119. Id. at 1340.

120. Id. at 1341.

121. Id. at 1341–42.

122. Id. I do not think the analogy between animals and corporations is a good one. To say that rights other than human rights are recognized when rights are given to corporations and churches is to ignore that the constituents of such organizations are humans. Thus, to the extent that these entities have rights, they are just a form of human rights.

Many people, including myself, dispute that animals have been given rights in the law. There are certain laws that protect animals from certain kinds of treatment, but these do not constitute grants of rights. These laws are little more than laws that prevent vandalism to private property and do not provide for redress on behalf of the animals. They may be seen as laws ultimately intended to protect certain human interests. Nonetheless, for an exposition of the view that some present laws create rights in animals, see Wise "Hardly a Revolution," at 910–13.

123. See *supra* notes 32–122 and accompanying text.

124. Thomas G. Kelch, "Toward a Non-Property Status for Animals" (chapter 9, this volume).

125. Rawls, *Theory of Justice*, at 111–12.

126. Regan, *Case for Animal Rights*, at 243.

127. Id.

128. Sumner, *Moral Foundation of Rights*, at 203.

129. Id.

130. Feinberg, "Rights of Animals and Unborn Generations," at 43–44.

131. Id. at 47.

132. White, *Rights*, at 89.

133. Id. at 90.

134. Id.

135. Donnelly, *Language and Uses of Rights*, at 15; Wise, "Hardly a Revolution," at 843; Richard Posner, *The Problems of Jurisprudence* 10–11 (1990).

136. Donnelly, *Language and Uses of Rights*, at 15; Wise, "Hardly a Revolution," at 843.

137. George P. Fletcher, "Law and Morality: A Kantian Perspective," 87 *Colum. L. Rev.* 533, 535 (1987).

138. Michele Moody-Adams, "On the Old Saw that Character Is Destiny," in *Identity, Character, and Morality* 111, 113 (Owen Flanagan and Amelie Oskenberg Rorty, eds., 1990).

139. Milne, *Human Rights and Human Diversity*, at 28.

140. Id. at 141–42.

141. Id.

142. See, for example, Wellman, *Theory of Rights*, at 107–70.

143. Id.; Wellman, *Real Rights*, at 132–35.

144. Wellman, *Real Rights*, at 132.

145. Id. at 169–70.

146. Id.

147. Id. at 132.

148. Id.

149. See, for example, Wise, "Hardly a Revolution," at 846–57.

150. Hart, "Are There Any Natural Rights?" at 77, 79.

151. Id.

152. Ronald Dworkin, *Taking Rights Seriously* 90 (1978).

153. Regan, *Case for Animal Rights*, at 87–88.

154. Midgley, *Animals and Why They Matter*, at 62–63.

155. Wise, "Hardly a Revolution," at 843.

156. Wellman, *Theory of Rights*, at 122–31 (stating that such ontological moral principals are not necessary to argue for connection between law and morality).

157. Sumner, *Moral Foundation of Rights*, at 19–20.

158. Id. at 19.

159. Id. at 19–20.

160. Robert H. Welson, "How to Reform Grazing Policy: Creating Forage Rights on Federal Rangelands," 8 *Fordham Envtl. L.J.* 645, 645–46 (1997).

161. John Locke saw labor as the foundation of ownership of property. See id. at 646.

162. Consider another example. We say that there is a right in criminals not to suffer cruel and unusual punishment. It is evident that our moral sense is offended by the rack and whip. Thus, a concept of rights grounded in any tenable moral theory supports a prohibition on cruel and unusual punishment.

163. This idea is in line with Donnelly's horizons theory. See Donnelly, *Language and Uses of Rights*, at 15.

164. W. V. O. Quine, "Truth by Convention," in *The Ways of Paradox* 77, 101–3 (1976).

165. Id.

166. To represent this schematically, however, would require more than the two dimensions provided by a sheet of paper.

167. Michael Stocker, *Valuing Emotions* 1 (1996).

168. A number of emotions may be relevant to moral thought. The ones that appear of relevance to animal issues are sympathy and empathy. Sympathy is a harmony of feelings between entities, while empathy is identification with or vicarious experiencing of the feelings of another. The most relevant emotion here may be empathy. Nonetheless, to capture both feelings of sympathy and empathy, I will generally refer to "compassion" as the emotion most relevant to moral issues as they relate to animals.

169. Stephen R. L. Clark, *The Moral Status of Animals* 154 (1977).

170. Josephine Donovan, "Attention to Suffering: Sympathy as a Basis for Ethical Treatment of Animals" (chapter 7, this volume), 175–76.

171. Marcia W. Baron, *Kantian Ethics Almost Without Apology* 112 (1995). Baron argues that perhaps Kant has been misinterpreted. She sees the typical view of Kant's moral theory as not ascribing importance to love, fellow feeling, and the like to be a defect in Kantian moral theory, but reads Kant as actually allowing a role for the emotive in morals. She argues that Kant encourages the development of sympathetic and other feelings as a part of morality (212–18). To Baron, Kant finds value in emotions in motivating us to do those things that are "imperfect duties," those things that we cannot be expected to do from duty alone (220). These emotions must, however, be controlled by reason (203).

172. Stocker, *Valuing Emotions*, at 91–92.

173. Id. at 92.

174. Id.

175. Singer, *Animal Liberation*, at ii–iii.

176. Regan, *Case for Animal Rights*, at 123–24.

177. See, generally, Karen J. Warren, "The Power and the Promise of Ecological Feminism," 12 *Envtl. Ethics* 125 (1990).

178. Brian Luke, "Justice, Caring, and Animal Liberation" (chapter 5, this volume), 130, 132–34.

179. Kheel, "Liberation of Nature," at 46–47; Kheel, "Nature and Feminist Sensitivity," at 259–60.

180. Id.

181. Ronald De Sousa, "The Rationality of Emotions," in *The Liberation of Nature* 127 (Amelie Oskenberg Rorty, ed., 1980).

182. David Hume, *A Treatise of Human Nature* 510 (1969).

183. Id. at 509–10.

184. Id.

185. Id. at 515.

186. Id. at 520.

187. Id. at 520–21. See also Donovan, "Attention to Suffering," at 181.

188. Hume, *Treatise of Human Nature*, at 520–21.

189. Id.

190. Id.

191. Id. at 526.

192. Id. See also Marcia Lind, "Hume and Moral Emotions," in Flanagan and Rorty, *Identity, Character, and Morality*, at 133, 142–43.

193. Lind, "Hume and Moral Emotions," at 142–43.

194. Id. at 144.

195. Id. at 144–45.

196. Schopenhauer, *Philosophical Writings*, at 208.

197. Donovan, "Attention to Suffering," at 182.

198. De Sousa, "Rationality of Emotions," at 127.

199. Stocker, *Valuing Emotions*, at 1.

200. Id. at 94–95.

201. Lind, "Hume and Moral Emotions," at 133.

202. Wise, "Hardly a Revolution," at 824. Wise describes the "subjective" as nonlogical and incapable of proof.

203. Stocker, *Valuing Emotions*, at 93.

204. Id. at 94.

205. Id. at 99–100.

206. William Brennan, "Reason, Passion and 'The Progress of the Law,'" 10 *Cardozo L. Rev.* 3, 17 (1988).

207. Stocker, *Valuing Emotions*, at 100.

208. Kheel, "Liberation of Nature," at 46–47; Kheel, "Nature and Feminist Sensitivity," at 259–60; Midgley, *Animals and Why They Matter*, at 33–35.

209. Kheel, "Liberation of Nature," at 46–47.

210. Lind, "Hume and Moral Emotions," at 142–43 (discussing emotions as complexes of feeling and cognitive elements).

211. Donovan, "Attention to Suffering," at 176.

212. Stocker, *Valuing Emotions*, at 92.

213. Id. at 8.

214. Id. at 84.

215. Id. at 85.

216. Id. at 8 (quoting Ernest Schachtel, *Metamorphosis* 20 [1984]).

217. Stocker, *Valuing Emotions*, at 8, 11.

218. Donovan, "Attention to Suffering," at 184. One response to the problem of a lack of universalizability is to say that this does not constitute a defect in a moral theory. See Stocker, *Valuing Emotions*, at 144–45. I will, nonetheless, assume that it is a defect and address it as such.

219. Donovan, "Attention to Suffering," at 185.

220. Stocker, *Valuing Emotions*, at 56–57.

221. Id. at 57.

222. Id.

223. Id. at 56–57.

224. Id. at 83.

225. Stocker, *Valuing Emotions*, at 83. See also Amelie Oskenberg Rorty, "Explaining Emotions," in *Explaining Emotions* 105 (Amelie Oskenberg Rorty, ed., 1980); Patricia S. Greenspan, *Emotions and Reason* 14 (1988).

226. Greenspan, *Emotions and Reason*, at 159.

227. Id. at 137.

228. Id. at 152–59, 173.

229. Stocker, *Valuing Emotions*, at 85.

230. Id. at 100–101

231. Id. at 101–2.

232. De Sousa, "Rationality of Emotions," at 138–39.

233. Id. at 141.

234. Id. at 137.

235. Id. at 137–38.

236. Stocker, *Valuing Emotions*, at 100–101.

237. Id. at 105–6.

238. Id.

239. Id.

240. Id. at 193.

241. Stocker, *Valuing Emotions*, at 108–12.

242. Id.

243. Greenspan, *Emotions and Reason*, at 3.

244. Id.

245. Id.

246. Id.

247. Id. at 3–4.

248. Id. at 4.

249. Id.

250. Id. at 54.

251. Id. at 175–76.

252. Id. at 121.

253. Stocker, *Valuing Emotions*, at 125.

254. Id.

255. David A. Cathcart and Richard K. Stavin, "Emerging Standards Defining Contract, Emotional Distress and Punitive Damages in Employment Cases," C108 ALI-ABA 493, 547 (1995) (stating that damages for violation of the Civil Rights Act include compensation for emotional distress); Ken Feagins, "Wanted—Diversity: White Heterosexual Males Need Not Apply," 4 *Widener J. Pub. L.* 1, 9 (1994) (noting that emotional distress is part of damage awards in discrimination cases); Risa B. Greene, "Federal Legislative Proposals for Medical Malpractice Reform: Treating the Symptoms or Effecting a Cure?" 4 *Cornell J.L. & Pub. Pol'y* 563, 584 (1995) (noting that part of the purpose of tort law is to compensate for emotional distress); Douglas T. Miracle, "Punitive Damages, Jury Discretion and the 'Outer Limits' of the Fourteenth Amendment in Civil Cases," 13 *Miss. C. L. Rev.* 221, 252 (1992) (arguing that the concept of compensatory damages has broadened to include damages for emotional trauma).

256. Jose Felipe Anderson, "Will the Punishment Fit the Victims? The Case for Pre-Trial Disclosure, and the Uncharted Future of Victim Impact Information in Capital Jury Sentencing," 28 *Rutgers L.J.* 367, 399 (1997); Patrick M. Fahey, "*Payne v. Tennessee*: An Eye for an Eye and Then Some," 25 *Conn. L. Rev.* 205, 261–62 (1992); Martha Minow, "Surviving Victim Talk," 40 *UCLA L. Rev.* 1411, 1416, 1428–29 (1993).

257. Stocker, *Valuing Emotions*, at 140. See also Ashley Paige Dugger, "Victim Impact Evidence in Capital Sentencing: A History of Incompatibility," 23 *Am. J. Crim. L.* 375, 399 (1996) (showing that retribution in criminal justice is based on venting of anger of the victim's loved ones); Benjamin E. Rosenberg, "Criminal Acts and Sentencing Facts: Two Constitutional Limits on Criminal Sentencing," 23 *Seton Hall L. Rev.* 459, 484 (1993) (claiming that retribution is "an expression of society's anger and moral outrage"); Thomas J. Walsh, "On the Abolition of Man: A Discussion of the Moral and Legal Issues Surround-

ing the Death Penalty," 44 *Clev. St. L. Rev.* 23, 38 (1996) (noting that retribution is not based on reason and logic, but on anger).

258. *State v. Thornton*, 730 S.W.2d 309, 312–15 (Tenn. 1987) (finding that killing done in passion is not murder in the first degree; it may be manslaughter or second-degree murder); Benjamin J. Lantz, "*Arave v. Creech*: A 'Cold-Blooded, Pitiless' Disregard for Constitutional Standards," 21 *New Eng. J. on Crim. & Civ. Confinement* 97, 124 (1995) (stating that manslaughter is killing done in the heat of passion); Richard E. Shugrue, "The Second Degree Murder Doctrine in Nebraska," 30 *Creighton L. Rev.* 29, 38–39 (1996) (citing New York and Nebraska law concerning reduction in charge of murder to manslaughter if the killing was done in the heat of passion); Carol S. Steiker and Jordan M. Steiker, "Let God Sort Them Out? Refining the Individualization Requirement in Capital Sentencing," 102 *Yale L.J.* 835, 856 (1992) (citing Model Penal Code provisions providing for reduction in first-degree murder to second-degree murder in the case of killing while impaired by emotional disturbance).

259. Stocker, *Valuing Emotions*, at 151.

260. See, generally, *Campins v. Capels*, 461 N.E.2d 712 (Ind. Ct. App. 1984) (stating that court may consider sentimental value of goods in determining damages for destruction of jewelry).

261. *In re Wilson*, 213 B.R. 413, 414 (Bankr. D.R.I. 1997); *In re Dillon*, 113 B.R. 46, 50 (Bankr. D. Utah 1990).

262. *Corso v. Crawford Dog and Cat Hosp. Inc.*, 415 N.Y.S.2d 182, 183 (N.Y. Civ. Ct. 1979); *La Porte v. Associated Indeps., Inc.*, 163 So.2d 267, 268–69 (Fla. 1964). See, generally, Debra Squires-Lee, "In Defense of Floyd: Appropriately Valuing Companion Animals in Tort," 70 *N.Y.U.L. Rev.* 1059 (1995).

263. Donnelly, *Language and Uses of Rights*, at 82.

264. Schopenhauer, *Philosophical Writings*, at 202–3.

265. Id. at 204.

266. Id.

267. Id.

268. Id.

269. Jean-Jacques Rousseau, *The Social Contract and Discourses* 74–76 (1993). Greenspan also notes the significance of what she calls identificatory love, a concept like compassion, in motivating and causing moral actions. See Greenspan, *Emotions and Reason*, at 62–63, 74.

270. Schopenhauer, *Philosophical Writings*, at 207–8.

271. Id.

272. Id.

273. Id. at 223–24.

274. Tom Regan, *All That Dwell Therein* 6–27 (1982); Bernard E. Rollin, *The Unheeded Cry: Animal Consciousness, Animal Pain and Science* 107–201 (1989); Singer, *Animal Liberation*, at 9–13, 15.

275. Rollin, *Unheeded Cry*, at 64–66. See also Andrew Rowan, *Of Mice, Models, and Men: A Critical Evaluation of Animal Research* 77–79 (1984).

276. Rowan, *Of Mice, Models, and Men*, at 82–83.

277. Nelson, *System of Ethics*, at 138.

278. Jeremy Bentham, *An Introduction to the Principles of Morals and Legislation* 381, n. 330 (1961).

279. Kheel, "Liberation of Nature," at 49; Kheel, "Nature and Feminist Sensitivity," at 262–63.

CHAPTER 12

The Ethic of Care and the Problem of Wild Animals

GRACE CLEMENT

Recently, a number of feminists concerned with the welfare of nonhuman animals have challenged the prevailing approaches to animal defense theory. A collection of essays, *Beyond Animal Rights: A Feminist Caring Ethic for the Treatment of Animals*, challenges the "rights" or "justice" approaches usually taken by animal defense theories, most notably those of Peter Singer (1992) and Tom Regan (1983), and argues in favor of an ethic of care for our relations to nonhuman animals. This work arises out of feminist discussions over the past fifteen years of the "feminine" ethic of care and its relationship to the "masculine" ethic of justice. Those writing in *Beyond Animal Rights* have extended this discussion by recognizing that the care-justice debate is important not only for relationships among humans but for human relationships to nonhumans as well. For what has been called the ethic of justice in this discussion is in fact the rationalistic and individualistic approach to morality that has long been taken to be *the* moral point of view in the Western tradition. According to its critics, this moral point of view has resulted in our culture's subordination and devaluation not only

This chapter was first published in *Between the Species*, no. 3 (August 2003). © 2003 by Grace Clement. Published by permission of the author.

of women, but of nonhuman animals and nature as well. If this is the case, then Singer's and Regan's extensions of the ethic of justice to include non-human animals, however well-intentioned, are doomed to failure because they are part of a larger paradigm contrary to these goals.

In this essay, I will examine the claim that an ethic of care is prefer-able to an ethic of justice for our relationships with nonhuman animals. To limit my discussion, I will focus on our obligations to animals, even though there are obviously important questions about our obligations to nonanimal members of the biotic community, and I will focus on the morality of eating animals, even though this is only one of many impor-tant moral questions about our treatment of nonhuman animals. While I regard the care proposal as promising, I will argue that the distinction between domestic and wild animals raises an important problem for it: while the ethic of care seems to fit our interactions with domestic animals well, it is at best unclear how it might guide our interactions with wild animals. I will consider three different alternative moral approaches to wild animals: a holistic environmentalist approach, an individualistic jus-tice approach, and a justice approach in interaction with and influenced by a care approach. By drawing on the lessons of the recent care/justice debate regarding human-to-human relations, I will show that the third of these alternatives works best. Because I do not regard care and justice as dichotomous, I see this not as a rejection of the thesis of *Beyond Animal Rights* but as a sympathetic extension of it.

The "Introduction" to *Beyond Animal Rights* provides four reasons for thinking that an ethic of care is more appropriate for our relationships to nonhuman animals than an ethic of justice (or, what is generally consid-ered the same thing, a rights theory).[1]

First, an ethic of justice "envisages a society of rational, autonomous, independent agents whose territory or property is entitled to protection from external agents" (Donovan and Adams 1996:14), and thus uses rationality as a test of moral considerability, a test which nonhumans are likely to fail. On the other hand, the ethic of care focuses on relationships *between* indi-viduals rather than on separate individual identities, and thus requires no such test of rationality for moral considerability. Second, an ethic of justice "presumes a society of equal autonomous agents, who require little support from others, who need only that their space be protected from others' intru-sions" (Donovan and Adams 1996:15). But humans and animals are in most ways *unequals*, and thus better fit into the care model which assumes an inherent inequality between carer and cared-for. Third, an ethic of justice is a rationalistic approach, prioritizing reason and suppressing emotion-based appeals for animal welfare. However, feelings play a central role in human relationships to animals, and the ethic of care regards feelings as morally relevant and informative. Finally, an ethic of justice tends to be abstract and formalistic, focusing on universal rules of morality, while our complex relationships with nonhuman animals seem better accounted for by the ethic of care's contextual approach focusing on the particulars of given situations.

These objections to exclusively justice-oriented approaches are valuable. The extent to which prevailing approaches to animal welfare are *exclusively* justice-oriented and thus problematic is evident in Singer's (1992) and Regan's (1983) insistence that moral arguments must not appeal to our feelings about animals. Singer begins his book *Animal Liberation* with an anecdote about a woman he met who described herself as an animal lover even as she offered Singer a ham sandwich. While acknowledging that many people have strong feelings for nonhuman animals that *may* move them to act in defense of animals, both Singer and Regan regard this woman's inconsistency as typical of a feeling-based approach to ethics. They hold that in general, our feelings lead us to be biased toward those close to us—toward pets, for instance, or, more generally, toward humans—instead of to recognize injustice however near or far from us it occurs. Instead of appealing to emotions, Singer's and Regan's arguments appeal to the purely rational demand for consistency. For instance, they appeal to so-called borderline cases—human beings of severely diminished capacities who we nonetheless count fully in our moral thinking. If these individuals are fully morally considerable, the argument goes, then consistency demands that we likewise count nonhumans of like capacities as fully morally considerable. This sort of argument uses the purely rational demand for consistency to extend the borders of moral considerability far beyond the starting point of human beings.

Yet the success of this attempt to banish appeals to feelings from moral argumentation comes into question when we ask how this starting point was justified in the first place: How are we sure that all human beings are entitled to full moral considerability? Are there purely rational grounds for this claim, or, more likely, does this claim depend on a basic feeling or conviction we share about the importance of human beings? In fact, it would be hard to find a moral argument that does not make a crucial appeal to emotion—it's just that sometimes emotions are so widely shared that they seem unquestionable, and thus somehow rational. Our feelings may not provide infallible moral guidance, but sometimes they are all we have to appeal to. Perhaps, then, we ought to proceed not by banishing feelings from our moral considerations on the grounds that they are unreliable, but by paying *more* attention both to our feelings *and* to the mechanisms by which they are and can be socially manipulated (Luke 1995, chapter 5, this volume). As the authors of *Beyond Animal Rights* point out, this is an approach that the ethic of care is much more attuned to than the ethic of justice.

While the ethic of care is certainly a promising approach to our relationships with nonhuman animals in this and other ways detailed in *Beyond Animal Rights*, there is a difficulty with this approach left largely unaddressed by these authors. That is, the arguments in this book make domestic animals the paradigm, and it seems at least possible that they work *only* for domestic animals. We can see this by returning to the four arguments offered in the book's "Introduction."

First, the ethic of justice is said to be inappropriate for our dealings with nonhuman animals because it "envisages a society of rational, autonomous, independent agents whose territory or property is entitled to protection from external agents" (Donovan and Adams 1996:14). Without addressing the difficult issue of the rationality of nonhuman animals, the autonomy and independence of at least wild animals can be and has been defended. In fact, environmental ethicists have long emphasized the difference between wild and domestic animals along these lines: Aldo Leopold wrote that the essence of environmental ethics was "reappraising things unnatural, tame, and confined in terms of things natural, wild, and free" (Callicott 1992:67). According to environmental ethicist J. Baird Callicott, wild animals are autonomous and independent, while domestic animals are human creations which are *metaphysically* unfree. By this Callicott means that domestic animals are nothing but what we have selectively bred them to be, such that it is as meaningless to speak of *setting free* domestic animals as it would be to speak of setting free a chair. Callicott and other environmental ethicists may be speaking of autonomy in a different sense than the rational autonomy used as a criterion by those defending an ethic of justice, but in any case it seems at least somewhat appropriate to think of human relationships with *wild* animals in terms of a society of independent agents whose territory is entitled to protection from others.

The second argument against the justice approach to nonhuman animals likewise seems to apply to domestic rather than to wild animals. Again, the ethic of justice "presumes a society of equal autonomous agents, who require little support from others, who need only that their space be protected from others' intrusions." The editors of *Beyond Animal Rights* continue: "But domestic animals, in particular, are dependent for survival upon humans. We therefore have a situation of unequals, and need to develop an ethic that recognizes this fact" (Donovan and Adams 1996:15). Clearly, in this argument domestic animals are taken as paradigmatic, for wild animals are certainly not dependent for survival upon humans, at least not upon human *support*. Instead, they are dependent upon humans' putting an end to destruction of natural habitats, or on humans' *restraint*. In fact, just as the ethic of justice would say, it seems that they *do* need only that their space be protected from others' intrusions. While domestic animals depend upon human support, wild animals would most benefit from the disappearance of humans entirely.

Even the argument about the role of emotion in moral argument seems to work better in domestic than in wild contexts. This is evident in "The Caring Sleuth: Portrait of an Animal Rights Activist" (chapter 6, this volume), in which Kenneth Shapiro discusses the crucial role of sympathy in moral considerations about animals. He quotes Helen Jones, founder of the International Society for Animal Rights, who wrote:

> My first awareness of animal suffering was at the age of four or five. My mother took me to a zoo. As we entered we saw a large white rabbit, transfixed with fear, in a cage with a snake. Within a second or two the snake began swallowing the rabbit. . . . My mother never again entered a zoo. I did, many years later, only to collect evidence for a legal case. (157)

Jones experienced a sympathy for the rabbit that many of us share. But in a certain sense this sympathy is odd. After all, snakes *do* eat rabbits, however upsetting it is for us to see a rabbit be eaten, and we certainly cannot legitimately condemn snakes for this behavior, nor can we hope to protect rabbits from this fate. Or, we can only protect rabbits from this fate in places like zoos, when they are rabbits we take into our protection. But it does not seem that our sympathetic reaction to the rabbit in this situation is dependent on the fact that this rabbit is in a zoo. That is, it seems as if the sympathies to which the ethic of care appeals might be more relevant for domestic than for wild animals. As Callicott puts it, in the wild, the fundamental fact of life is eating *and being eaten*, but our sympathies would seem to be out of line with this fact, such that there are good reasons *not* to act on our sympathies for wild animals. This suggests that the fourth argument cited above also works better for domestic animals than for wild animals: at least when it comes to wild animals, a *contextual* approach focusing on particular situations seems less appropriate than an *abstract* approach focusing on the general facts of environmental biology.

From these considerations, it seems possible that the claims on behalf of the ethic of care in *Beyond Animal Rights* apply to domestic but not to wild animals. Thus, even assuming that the main arguments in this work are correct, we are left with the question of what moral approach is most appropriate for our relations to wild animals (as well as how the moral approach for wild animals relates to the moral approach for domestic animals). The fact that the arguments presented against the ethic of justice are *least* successful in the context of wild animals suggests that perhaps our relations to domestic animals should be based on an ethic of care, while our relations to wild animals should be based on the ethic of justice. That is, perhaps in relation to domestic animals, our primary obligation is to meet their needs and to protect them, while in relation to wild animals, our primary obligation is to leave them alone, or to stop interfering with them.

I will first address an objection to this proposal that would be raised by environmental ethicists. Environmentalists would begin by pointing out that the focus on domestic animals I have identified is present not only in the care approach to animal defense theory, but in standard (or "justice") approaches as well, and that *neither* approach works for wild animals. For instance, Mark Sagoff asks, "If the suffering of animals creates human obligation to mitigate it, is there not as much an obligation to prevent a cat from killing a mouse as to prevent a hunter from killing a deer?" (Sagoff 1993:88). Similarly, if nonhuman animals are said to have certain rights, such as a right to life, then we have a corresponding obligation to protect those rights. While it might be appropriate to endeavor to protect domestic animals' rights to life, it would be absurd, not to mention ecologically disastrous, to endeavor to protect wild animals' right to life (Sagoff 1993:88–89).

Environmental ethicists would argue that animal defense theories, whether of the justice or care variety, fail in the context of wild animals because they are individualistic in the sense that it is *individual* beings that are considered morally important. What is needed, they would say, is an approach which is holistic in its focus, in that it is *wholes* such as biotic communities and species that are considered morally important. As Aldo Leopold put it, "a thing is right when it tends to preserve the integrity, stability, and beauty of the biotic community. It is wrong when it tends otherwise" (Leopold 1995:152). Callicott expands on how Leopold's position contradicts animal welfare ethics, writing:

> A central, stark fact lies at the heart of ecological processes. Energy, the currency of the economy of nature, passes from one organism to another, not from hand to hand, like coined money, but so to speak, from stomach to stomach. *Eating and being eaten, living and dying* are what make the biotic community hum. (Callicott 1993:125)

Thus, according to environmental ethicists, in the context of wild animals, advocates of the ethic of care and advocates of the ethic of justice are *equally* mistaken in their moral attention to individual beings.

These considerations suggest that perhaps within the realm of domestic animals, it is appropriate to focus on individual animals, while outside that realm, it is appropriate to think more holistically. In fact, Callicott defends a version of this view in his most recent account of the relationship between animal liberation and environmental ethics (Callicott 1995). He develops an account of "nested communities" that reflect our degree of relationship to various beings and thereby provide the basis for our moral obligations. According to Callicott, we have the greatest moral obligations to those closest to us—to our immediate family—and gradually lesser obligations to those in our more distant communities—such as to neighbors, to citizens, to human beings in general, and to animals in general. One of the ways this account differs from traditional hierarchies which place non-human animals last in our moral consideration is by incorporating Mary Midgley's argument that domestic animals are and have always been members of one of our more intimate communities, the "mixed community" (Midgley 1995). For Callicott, humans' close relationships with domestic animals means that domestic animals have a corresponding moral priority. Humans have "evolved and unspoken" contracts with animals such as pets, farm and work animals, but many of our current practices, such as factory farming, are in clear violation of the trust we have established with these animals, and thus are morally wrong. Callicott holds that killing and eating members of the mixed community is not in itself a violation of this contract, but that the "depersonalization" and "mechanization" of animals in factory farming is. On the other hand, wild animals are not part of the mixed community but are at the outer circle of our nested communities, and thus our obligations to them are of a lower priority. These obligations are derived not from any kind of social contract or trust established between humans and wild animals, but from a description of the *biotic* community, and thus humans are clearly not morally forbidden from killing and eating wild animals either.

I will have something to say about Callicott's position on domestic animals shortly, but first I will challenge the claim that, in relation to wild animals at least, humans are morally bound only by holistic concerns about the health of the ecosystem. This would mean that in relation to members of well-populated species, there would be no moral problem with, say, torturing an animal for the fun of it. Environmentalists do not make a point of this, and, in fact, when the environmentalist Holmes Rolston defends meat eating, he says that "when eating [humans] ought to minimize animal suffering" (Rolston 1993:140). Such a claim is uncontroversial enough that we might not notice that he doesn't say *why* humans ought to minimize animal suffering. In fact, he *can't* provide a reason for this claim within a system that only takes holistic concerns into account. That is, a "moral" approach that focuses *exclusively* on holistic concerns such that suffering becomes morally irrelevant violates some of our most basic moral convictions. As Karen Davis writes in response to Callicott's approach:

> Leopold's plea for humans to think ecoholistically—"like a moun-
> tain"—has been taken by some environmentalists as a mandate to
> exclude from substantive and ethical consideration the individu-
> ated existences that help constitute the mountain. . . . The ontologi-
> cal result is a holism devoid of contents, resembling an empty shell.
> The ethical result is moral abandonment of beings whose suffer-
> ings and other experiences are inconsequential compared to the
> "big realm."   (Davis 1995:199)

In fact, Callicott's account of nested communities as a basis for morality is an attempt to avoid the morally outrageous conclusion that many humans should be eliminated on the grounds that their presence tends to destroy the integrity, stability, and beauty of the biotic community. However, if Callicott succeeds in avoiding this conclusion, it is by *departing* from environmental holism and appealing to widely shared moral convictions about the importance of human beings.

Since Callicott's environmental ethic for human–wild animal relations is too holistic to allow for some of our basic moral convictions, it might seem to follow that human–wild animal relations should be understood in terms of the individualism of the ethic of justice. That is, it might be argued that while we share with wild animals a *biotic* community, we do not share with them a *moral* community of a kind that would be necessary to ground the claim that we have positive responsibilities to them. While environmental critics of justice ethics point out the absurdity of extending the right to life to wild animals, an ethic of justice need not affirm that wild animals have a right to life. Instead, it can affirm that our primary obligation to wild animals is *noninterference*.

While there is something right about this view, I want to show that it also oversimplifies and distorts matters in important ways. Difficulties with this view are revealed by recent discussions among feminist ethicists of the analogous view that the "private sphere" of family and friends ought to be governed by the ethic of care, while the "public sphere" of government and business ought to be governed by the ethic of justice. According to this view, the partialist ethic of care should be confined to the private sphere, and the rights-oriented ethic of justice should be confined to the public sphere. One reason to be wary of this view is that the public/private dichotomy is strongly gender-coded—the private sphere is regarded as feminine and the public sphere as masculine—and serves to reinforce gender divisions. Moreover, the boundary between public and private spheres is itself at issue, as the private and public spheres are not as different from one another as is commonly assumed. For instance, power relations, which are usually considered the distinguishing feature of the political, are also present in personal relations, as evidenced by widespread domestic violence. Also, dependence and vulnerability, which are usually considered distinctive of personal relations, are also present in public relations. Such overlapping features suggest that the private sphere should be not only caring but just, and that the public sphere should be not only just but caring. In fact, when the two ethics are dichotomized, they tend to take on distorted and damaging forms. For instance, an ethic of care which does not value autonomy tends to result in forms of "caring" which are oppressive to either the caregiver or the recipient of care. Likewise, an ethic of justice which does not value caring tends to result in forms of "justice" that are indifferent to individual suffering (Clement 1996).

These conclusions have clear implications for the present discussion. First, just as the public/private dichotomy is gender-coded, so too is the wild/domestic animal dichotomy. Karen Davis has shown that the wild/domestic animal dichotomy is analogous to the public/private dichotomy, such that these dichotomies serve in similar ways to justify the devaluation of women and domestic animals:

> Animals summoning forth images of things that are "natural, wild, and free" accord with the "masculine" spirit of adventure and conquest idolized by our culture. Animals summoning forth images of things that are "unnatural, tame, and confined" represent a way of life that Western culture looks down upon. The contrast can be vividly seen in our literature. Whereas in Herman Melville's *Moby Dick* the hunters of the great white whale conceive of their prey as an awesome, godlike being, in William Golding's *Lord of the Flies* the little boys view the nursing sow, whom they violently rape with a spear, as an object of disgust. (Davis 1995:196)

It might be thought that Callicott does not fit this model because his view of nested communities claims to give domestic animals a higher moral priority than wild animals. However, he clearly does not regard domestic animals with the respect he has for wild animals. Above all, Callicott prizes the natural and the wild, and his deepest moral conviction seems to be that humans ought to overcome their alienation from nature and become more wild.

This leads to a second difficulty revealed by the feminist discussion of the public/private dichotomy. Like that dichotomy, the distinction between domestic and wild animals is not as clear as it is often made out to be. Again, Callicott emphasizes this distinction, regarding wild animals as autonomous beings while arguing that

> barnyard animals, over hundreds of generations, have been genetically engineered (by the old-fashioned method of selective breeding) to play certain roles in the mixed community. To condemn the morality of these roles—as we rightly condemn human slavery and penury—is to condemn the very being of these animals. (Callicott 1995:195)

Against this assessment of farm animals, Karen Davis cites research on chickens which indicates that there is more to chickens than the roles humans have bred them to play. Researchers write: "Domesticated chickens have been shown to retain their ancestral repertoire of behaviors, which undermines the prima facie assumption that they have been rendered docile and servile through breeding for specific traits" (Davis 1995:199). Also, "there is no evidence that genetic selection for egg laying has eliminated the birds' potential to perform a wide variety of behavior" (Davis 1995:204). Callicott's claim that chickens are nothing but what humans have bred them to be seems less the result of careful observations of these animals than a convenient rationalization.

If wild and domestic animals are not completely different, this suggests that our moral stances toward them should not be completely separate, and that when they are, they will tend to be distorted. We can see that this is the case in Callicott's discussion of our obligations toward domestic animals. With his discussion of the mixed community and the trust established between humans and domestic animals, Callicott defends something like an ethic of care toward domestic animals. Yet this ethic is consistent with raising farm animals to kill and eat them, on the grounds that, as a result of selective breeding, farm animals are nonautonomous beings who exist only for this purpose. To the extent that this claim is true, the introduction of justice considerations is important because it reveals that this is a distorted version of the ethic of care. Just as there is a moral problem with caring for persons in a way that undermines their autonomy, there is a moral problem with caring for animals in a way that undermines their autonomy (to whatever extent they can be autonomous). In this way the ethic of justice and its emphasis on autonomy plays an important role in evaluating the ethic of care toward domestic animals.

Just as the ethic of justice has a role to play in an ethic of care toward domestic animals, the ethic of care should play a role in an ethic of justice toward wild animals. First, even if an ethic of justice does not affirm that wild animals have a right to life, there are clearly problems with the individualism of the ethic of justice in the context of wild animals. For instance, for such an ethic, moral claims are based exclusively on characteristics of individual beings, such that environmental concerns about the stability and integrity of the biotic community become morally irrelevant. For instance, an individual member of a well-populated or even overpopulated species is no less valuable than an individual member of an endangered species, or even the *last* members of an endangered species. Taken to this extreme, such individualism seems to threaten the environmental considerations that are essential to the continuance of the individual lives protected. Thus, like the extreme holism of environmental ethics, the extreme individualism of the ethic of justice is morally problematic.

While environmental holists and individualist justice theorists debate whether individuals or wholes should be prioritized, the ethic of care reveals a third possibility. The ethic of care is individualistic in one sense: its moral attention is to *individuals* in virtue of their particular needs. However, it is holistic in another sense: it understands the basic reality to be relationships *between* individuals rather than individuals with their own separate characteristics. Thus, relationships, rather than individuals' characteristics, define the moral realm, but the particularities of individuals dictate the appropriate moral response.

One way in which this middle ground between holism and individualism affects an ethic of justice toward wild animals is the following. In general, we ought to adopt an ethic of noninterference with regard to wild animals because we are unaware of the negative effects our attempts to help animals might have on the natural environment. However, to understand our relationship with wild animals *exclusively* in terms of noninterference suggests that humans are *unnatural* beings who should not in any way be involved in the natural world. The ethic of care helps us avoid this moral distortion by understanding human moral responsiveness to individual animals as arising from the relationship between humans and nonhumans, namely our shared participation in nature. Consider a situation in which an individual encounters a wild animal who is suffering. Should one refuse to alleviate the animal's suffering on the grounds that doing so would be interfering with natural processes that we cannot understand? To do so, I think, would be contrary to one of our most basic moral convictions. This is not to claim that there ought to be public policy devoted to the alleviation of wild animal suffering, only that when an *individual* human being is confronted by the suffering of an *individual* animal, it would be morally unacceptable to say that we have a moral obligation *not* to relieve that suffering.

As part of the "reappraisal of things unnatural, tame, and confined in terms of things natural, wild, and free," Callicott argues that humans should stop attempting to impose artificial moral concepts on nature and instead "reaffirm our participation in nature by accepting life as it is given without a sugar coating" (Callicott 1992:56–57). But what exactly does it mean to *participate* in nature? For Callicott, it seems to mean, first of all, to hunt. As his first elucidation of the idea of participating in nature, he recommends the "posture toward life of tribal peoples in the past. The chase was relished with its dangers, rigors, and hardships as well as its rewards" (Callicott 1992:56). In other words, Callicott assumes that our sympathies toward animals are somehow artificial while our inclination toward hunting is natural.

However, as Brian Luke shows, there are good reasons to believe that the sympathy we feel toward a suffering animal is at least as natural as, or in fact *more natural than* the hunting "instinct" championed by environmentalists (Luke 1995:309). For instance, children's sympathies for animals often lead them to refuse to eat meat when they learn that it comes from slaughtered animals, at least until they are given "good" reasons not to act on these sympathies. More generally, the naturalness of our sympathies for animals is supported by the fact that elaborate social mechanisms are necessary to distance us from or to deny the reality of the animal suffering we cause, even, significantly, the suffering that hunting causes (Luke 1995).

Animal welfare advocates who operate from an exclusively justice approach share environmentalists' distrust of our sympathies for animals. However, contrary to Callicott's view that we need to abandon our sympathies and become more "natural," Singer (1992) and Regan (1983) in effect seek to "tame" us through appeals to reason. Again, the ethic of care reveals a third possibility, in which we recognize the moral importance of our *natural* sympathies toward animals, valuing, like Callicott, participation in nature, but disagreeing with Callicott's account of what is natural and what is artificial. As Luke puts it, instead of "taming ourselves," this involves "going feral" (Luke 1995). I have suggested that, in general, our moral obligations toward wild animals can be understood in terms of noninterference. However, such an approach can easily lead to the morally distorted view that we ought not be involved in nature at all, or that we are unnatural beings, and the ethic of care is necessary as a check against such a distortion.

In this essay I have considered a problem raised by the suggestion that the ethic of care, rather than the ethic of justice, is the appropriate ethic for our interactions with nonhuman animals. The problem is that this suggestion seems to make more sense for domestic than for wild animals, and that in fact, for the most part, the ethic of justice *does* seem to make sense for wild animals. That is, the ethic of care seems to "fit" our relations to domestic animals, while the ethic of justice seems to "fit" our relations with wild animals. However, I have shown that these "fits" are only approximate, and that to develop a moral approach to both domestic and wild animals that does justice to our most basic moral convictions, we need to understand the two ethics not dichotomously, but as working together. This means that while the ethic of care will not work as the exclusive or predominant moral approach to wild animals, a satisfactory moral approach to wild animals must include the ethic of care.

Acknowledgments

I would like to thank Mane Hajdin, as well as the other participants in the 1998 Central SSEA meeting, for their helpful responses to this paper.

Note

1. I do not believe that the following account of the distinction between the ethic of justice and the ethic of care is adequate; it is, however, the account that tends to be presupposed in the recent justice/care debate. The standard versions of these ethics tend to be rather extreme, or ideal-type, versions that are not necessarily defended by any moral philosophers in exactly these forms. Part of what I try to do, here and elsewhere, is to show the problems with these extreme versions of the ethics.

References

Callicott, J. Baird. 1992. "Animal Liberation: A Triangular Affair." In *The Animal Rights/Environmental Ethics Debate: The Environmental Perspective*, ed. Eugene C. Hargrove, 37–69. Albany: State University of New York Press.

——. 1993. "The Conceptual Foundations of the Land Ethic." In *Environmental Philosophy: From Animal Rights to Radical Ecology*, ed. Michael Zimmerman, J. Baird Callicott, Karen J. Warren, Irene J. Klaver, and John Clark, 110–34. Englewood Cliffs, N.J.: Prentice-Hall.

——. 1995. "Animal Liberation and Environment Ethics: Back Together Again." In *Earth Ethics*, ed. James P. Sterba, 190–98. Englewood Cliffs, N.J.: Prentice-Hall.

Clement, Grace. 1996. *Care, Autonomy, and Justice: Feminism and the Ethic of Care*. Boulder, Colo.: Westview.

Davis, Karen. 1995. "Thinking Like a Chicken: Farm Animals and the Feminine Connection." In *Animals and Women: Feminist Theoretical Explorations*, ed. Carol J. Adams and Josephine Donovan, 192–212. Durham, N.C.: Duke University Press.

Donovan, Josephine, and Carol J. Adams, eds. 1996. *Beyond Animal Rights: A Feminist Caring Ethic for the Treatment of Animals*. New York: Continuum.

Leopold, Aldo. 1995. "The Land Ethic; Conservation as a Moral Issue; Thinking Like a Mountain." In *Earth Ethics*, ed. James P. Sterba, 147–56. Englewood Cliffs, N.J.: Prentice-Hall.

Luke, Brian. 1995. "Taming Ourselves or Going Feral? Toward a Nonpatriarchal Metaethic of Animal Liberation." In *Animals and Women: Feminist The-*

oretical Explorations, ed. Carol J. Adams and Josephine Donovan, 290–319. Durham, N.C.: Duke University Press.

Midgley, Mary. 1995. "The Mixed Community." In *Earth Ethics*, ed. James P. Sterba, 80–90. Englewood Cliffs, N.J.: Prentice-Hall.

Regan, Tom. 1983. *The Case for Animal Rights*. Berkeley: University of California Press.

Rolston, Holmes, III. 1993. "Challenges in Environmental Ethics." In *Environmental Philosophy: From Animal Rights to Radical Ecology*, ed. Michael Zimmerman, J. Baird Callicott, Karen J. Warren, Irene J. Klaver, and John Clark, 135–57. Englewood Cliffs, N.J.: Prentice-Hall.

Sagoff, Mark. 1993. "Animal Liberation, Environmental Ethics: Bad Marriage, Quick Divorce." In *Environmental Philosophy: From Animal Rights to Radical Ecology*, ed. Michael Zimmerman, J. Baird Callicott, Karen J. Warren, Irene J. Klaver, and John Clark, 84–94. Englewood Cliffs, N.J.: Prentice-Hall.

Singer, Peter. 1992. *Animal Liberation: A New Ethics for Our Treatment of Animals*. New York: Avon.

Chapter 13

Of Mice and Men

A Fragment on Animal Rights

Catharine A. MacKinnon

Nonhuman animals in man's society are more than things, less than people. If the father of all social hierarchies, or the mother of all social distinctions, is the animate/inanimate division, it is closely followed by the human/animal[1] dichotomy, and then (for present purposes) the male/female line. When the three hierarchies are analyzed together—even, as here, tentatively and incompletely—the ordering of humans over animals appears largely retraced within the human group at the male/female line, which in turn retraces the person/thing dichotomy, to the detriment of animals and women. To unpack and pursue this analysis in the context of theorizing animal rights in law, the ways nonhuman animals are seen and treated by human animals need to be considered in gendered terms. Comparing humans' treatment of animals with men's treatment of women illuminates the way the legal system's response to animals is gendered, highlighting its response to women's inequality to men as well. Interrogating

Talk delivered at Conference on Animal Rights, University of Chicago Law School, April 13, 2001. First published in *Animal Rights: Current Debates and New Directions*, ed. Cass Sunstein and Martha C. Nussbaum (2004). Published by permission of the author.

how animals are treated like women, and women like animals, and both like things, can shed reciprocal light.

Beneath the inquiry lurk large issues. Is the fact that, from the human side, the animal/human relation is necessarily (epistemically and ontologically) a relation *within* human society more problematic than it has been seen to be? Is the inquiry into what can be done for animals in human society and law limited when women's social and legal subordination to men is overlooked—specifically, is missing the misogyny in animal use and abuse detrimental to gaining rights for animals? Under existing law, are animals in any respects treated better than women are? On these questions, my operative suspicion is yes. The resulting further suspicion is that the primary model of animal rights to date—one that makes animals objects of rights in standard liberal moral terms—misses animals on their own terms, just as the same tradition has missed women on theirs. If this is right, seeking animal rights on the "like us" model of sameness may be misconceived, unpersuasive, and counterproductive.

I

People dominate animals; men dominate women.[2] Each is a relation of hierarchy, an inequality, with particularities and variations within and between them. Every inequality is grounded and played out and resisted in unique ways, but parallels and overlaps can be instructive. One prominent similarity between these two hierarchies is ideological: in spite of the evidence that men socially dominate women and people dominate other animals, the fact that relations of domination and subordination exist between the two is widely denied. More precisely, it is widely thought and practiced and said that people are "above" animals, whereas it is commonly thought and practiced but denied that it is thought and practiced that men are "above" women. And while a hierarchy of people over animals is conceded, and a social hierarchy of men over women is often denied, the fact that the inequality is imposed by the dominant group tends to be denied in both cases. The hierarchy of people over animals is not seen as imposed by humans, because it is seen as due to animals' innate inferiority by nature. In the case of men over women, either it is said that there is no inequality there, because the sexes are different, or the inequality is conceded but is said to be justified by the sex difference, that is, women's innate inferiority by nature. Religion often rationalizes both.

In place of recognizing the realities of dominance of humans over animals and men over women is a sentimentalization of that dominance, combined with endless loops of analysis of sameness and difference. We see denial that each hierarchy involves socially organized power, combined with justifications of why one group, because of its natural superiority, should have what is, in substance, power and dominion and sovereignty over the other. The denial often takes the form of the assumption that the groups are equal just different, so their different treatment, rather than being a top-down ranking, is not unequal treatment but merely an appropriate reflection of their respective differences. It is as if we are confronting Aristotle's level line unequally divided, treating unlikes unalike—that is, equality.[3]

The denial of social hierarchy in both relations is further supported by verbiage about love and protection, including in what have been termed "the humane movements." The idea is, love of men for women or people for animals, motivating their supposed protection, mitigates the domination. Or, by benign motivation, eliminates the dominance altogether. One recalls Justice Bradley's concurring language denying Myra Bradwell's petition to be admitted to the bar that permitted persons: "The humane movements of modern society, which have for their object the multiplication of avenues for women's advancement, and of occupations adapted to her condition and sex, have my heartiest concurrence."[4] Difference rationalized dominance despite support for movements for advancement. Organized attempts to prevent cruelty to animals or to treat them "humanely" echo a similar underlying top-down paternalism, one most vivid in some social movements of the past to uplift prostituted women.[5] Neither with women nor animals has redress of abuses of power changed power's underlying distribution. Loving women is an improvement over hating them, kindness to animals is an improvement over cruelty, but neither has freed them nor recognizes their existence on their own terms.

Women are the animals of the human kingdom, the mice of men's world. Both women and animals are identified with nature rather than culture by virtue of biology. Both are imagined in male ideology to be thereby fundamentally inferior to men and humans. Women in male dominant society are identified as nature, animalistic, and thereby denigrated,[6] a maneuver that also defines animals' relatively lower rank in human society. Both are seen to lack properties that elevate men, those qualities by which men value themselves and define their status as human by distinction. In one vivid illustration that condescends to women and animals at once, James Boswell recounts Samuel Johnson saying, "Sir, a woman's preaching is like a dog's walking on his hind legs. It is not done well but you are surprised to find it done at all."[7] Using dogs imitating people as a simile for women speaking in public, a woman engaging in democratic discourse becomes as inept, laughable, unnatural, and imitative as a dog trying to walk upright. Qualities considered human and higher are denied to animals at the same time as qualities considered masculine and higher are denied to women.

In a related parallel, both animals and women have been socially configured as property (as has been widely observed), specifically for possession and use. Less widely observed, both women and animals have been status objects to be acquired and paraded by men to raise men's status among men, as well as used for labor and breeding and pleasure and ease. Compare beauty pageants with dog and cat shows. Men have also appointed themselves women's and animals' representatives without asking and have often defined both as to be protected by them. In law, this has often meant that injuries to animals and women—if seen as injuries at all as opposed to breaches of moral rules—are seen as injuries to their owners, just as seduction of a young woman (which was often rape) was legally considered an injury to her father.[8] In neither case has protection worked.

In a point of overlap and convergence between the two hierarchies, women have been dominated by men in part through the identification of their sexuality with their bodies, and their bodies with nature, meaning with animals. Women are attributed "naturalness," hence proximity to supposedly lower life forms. When your name is used to degrade others by attribution, it locates your relative standing as well, such as when "girl" is used as an insult among boys. Animality is attached to women's sexuality; the most common animal insults for women are sexual insults. Women are called animal names—bunny, beaver, bitch, chick, and cow—usually to mark their categorically lesser humanity, always drawing on the assumption that animals are lower than humans.[9] In pornography, women are often presented as animals and copulating with animals. The more denigrated the woman among women, prominently on racial grounds, the more and lower animal names she is called. This dynamic insults women, reinforces the notion that being like animals is a denigration, and denigrates animals.

Both women and animals are seen as needing to be subdued and controlled. Both are imagined as dangerously powerful, so must be kept powerless; if not locked up and kept down and in place, and killed when they step out, they will take over, overrun civilization, make chaos, end the known world. Both can be subjected to similar treatment, often by the same people in the same course of conduct, including torture, battering, terrorizing, taunting, humiliation, and killing.[10] Nowhere are the powerless as powerful as in the imaginations of those with real, not imaginary, power.

A related ideological parallel is the endless moralism of people with power in contending how good "we" are to be good to "them," surrounded by the resounding silence of the powerless. Consider the repeated retracing of the "As we treat them, so go we" trope.[11] We can tell how civilized we are by how well we treat our—fill in the blank with the unfortunates, the lessers. Take Senator Jennings Randolph in congressional debate in 1963 over the Equal Pay Act: "Emerson wrote that one of the measures of a civilization is the status which it accords women."[12] Or Mahatma Gandhi: "The greatness of a nation and its moral progress can be judged by the way its animals are treated."[13] Treating the low well, raising up women and animals within their limits, shows how civilized and great humans and men are. The ranking of noblesse oblige, who and what matters, in whose eyes, who is great, civilized, and progressing could not be clearer or more self-referential.

Men's debates among themselves over what makes them distinctively human have long revolved around distinctions from women and animals. Can they think? Are they individuals? Are they capable of autonomous action? Are they inviolable? Do they have dignity? Are they made in the image of God? Men know they are men, meaning human, it would seem, to the degree their answer to these questions is yes for them and no for animals and women. In response to this definition-by-distinction, many who seek rights for women and for animals have insisted that they do, too, have these qualities men value in themselves. If men have dignity, women and animals have dignity. If men can think, women and animals can think. If men are individuals, so are women and animals. That women are like men and animals are like people is thought to establish their existential equality, hence their right to rights.

So the question becomes, are they like us? Animal experimentation, using mice *as* men (so men don't have to be) is based on degrees of an affirmative answer.[14] The issue is not the answer;[15] the issue is, is this the right question? If it is the wrong question for women—if equality means that women define the human as much as men do—it is at least as wrong for nonhuman animals.[16] It is not that women and animals do not have these qualities. It is why animals should have to be like people to be let alone by them, to be free of the predations and exploitations and atrocities people inflict on them, or to be protected from them. Animals don't exist for humans any more than women exist for men.[17] Why should animals have to measure up to humans' standards for humanity before their existence counts?

II

Bearing in mind the limitations of dominant standards, following Mari Matsuda's injunction to "ask the other question,"[18] the woman question can be asked of animals in the animal law area. Relatively little attention has been paid by animal law scholars to the sexual use and abuse of animals.[19] Most states have provisions against bestiality, which in substance are laws against doing sexually to animals what is done to women by men on a daily basis. These laws define it as immoral for men to treat animals as they treat women free of legal restraints.[20] To the degree an injured party is envisioned in bestiality laws, though, it is structurally imagined to be the human or the community. Only Utah categorizes the laws against sexual contact by humans with animals under cruelty to animals.[21]

Why do laws against sex with animals exist? Their colonial roots indicate a preoccupation with debasement of the self, a lowering of the human to the animal realm.[22] In contemporary times, these laws are barely enforced, if they ever were. Commercial pornography alone shows far more sex with animals than is ever prosecuted for the acts required to make it. Much as with laws on sodomy (not a random parallel; in some sodomy laws, gay men are *sub silentio* lumped in with beasts). So little is done with it, one wonders what the law is doing there. Moralism aside, maybe the answer is that people cannot be sure if animals want to have sex with us. Put another way, we cannot know if their consent is meaningful.[23] Other than in some feminist work, the question whether the conditions of meaningful consent to sex exist for women has not been seriously asked. Whether it is possible, under conditions of sex inequality, to know whether women fully and freely consent to sex or comply with much sex without wanting to (not to mention whether they consent to other things, like the form of government they live under) is a neglected question of inequality among people. So, too, it is neglected between people and animals, although the substance of the inequalities is not identical. Surely animals could be, and are, trained to make it appear that they enjoy doing what people want them to do, including having sex with people. Pornographers train dogs to sexually penetrate women on signal; other pimps train donkeys to have sex with women in stage shows. Pornographers joke that women would have more sex with animals in their films but that would be cruelty to animals; putting a mouse in a woman's vagina would be cruel to the mouse, ha ha. Now whose status is higher?[24]

Laws against "crush videos" illustrate the comparative public ethos on this point. In this genre of pornography, mice or other (often small furry) animals are "taunted, maimed, tortured and ultimately crushed to death under the heel of a shoe or bare feet of a provocatively dressed woman"[25] to make a fetish film. The sex in the movie centers on the slow killing of the animals, called "pinkies" when they are baby rodents. Congress made crush videos a federal crime recently in a bill providing "punishment for depiction of animal cruelty."[26] It covers any visual or auditory depiction in which a living animal is "intentionally maimed, mutilated, tortured, wounded, or killed" if the conduct is illegal under federal law or the law of the state in which the "creation, sale, or possession" of such materials occurred.[27] There is no such law against depicting cruelty to women—a multibillion-dollar industry with considerable constitutional protection. In movie-making, someone must be on the set to monitor the safety of the treatment of nonhuman animals. No such requirements practically exist for women (or men) in, for example, the making of pornography.

There was some dissent to the federal bill, largely by the American Civil Liberties Union (ACLU), on First Amendment speech grounds, and some opposition to it in committee. The essence of the objection: "films of animals being crushed are communications about the act depicted, not doing the acts."[28] That it often takes the doing of the act to create the communication about the acts depicted is as obvious as the fact that the film itself is not the killing of the animal, although it would not usually exist without it. To the question "whether protecting animal rights counterbalances citizens' fundamental constitutional rights" to speech, the dissenters concluded that they did not.[29] But the bill passed. No prosecutions under it have yet been reported, so no occasion has arisen to consider any issues of freedom of expression further. There still is no equivalent statute prohibiting *a depiction in which* a living human is intentionally maimed, mutilated, tortured, wounded, or killed in order to make the film. The First Amendment protected status of such films, including snuff films, in which a human being is murdered to make a sex film, remains contested even in theory, making it unclear whether such a statute would be found constitutional.

In California, a bill was introduced in February 2000 that would have prohibited both crush videos of animals and torture and snuff films of human beings. For animals, it sought to prohibit an "image that depicts . . . the intentional and malicious maiming, mutilating, torturing, or wounding of a live animal" or the similar "killing of an animal" when the "killing of an animal actually occurred during the course of producing the depiction and for the purpose of producing that depiction."[30] For humans, the bill defined as a felony "the intentional or malicious killing of, or intentional maiming, torturing, or wounding of a human being, and intentional killing or cruelty to a human being actually occurring in the course of producing the depiction and for the purpose of producing the depiction."[31] A massive public First Amendment hue and cry, principally by the ACLU, was raised about the human part of the bill only.[32] No part of the bill passed. However, the makers of a crush video were successfully prosecuted for the underlying acts under the California law this measure had sought to amend, a provision that prohibits malicious mutilation, torture, or killing of a living animal.[33] In the prosecution, the videotape—for which rats, mice, and baby mice were slowly killed "for sexual gratification of others and for commercial gain"[34]—was evidence.

Instructively, the joint crush/snuff bill had a consent provision only for people.[35] Welcome to humanity: while animals presumably either cannot or are presumed not to consent to their videotaped murder, human beings could have consented to their own intentional and malicious killing if done to make a movie, and the movie would be legal. Even that was not enough to satisfy the avatars of freedom of speech. One wonders anew if human rights are always better than animal rights. Many laws prohibit cruelty to animals, but no laws prohibit cruelty to women as such. There are prohibitions on behavior that might be said to be cruel that at times are applied to women, such as laws against battering and torture. And laws against cruelty to animals are not well enforced. But then the laws against battering and torture of people are not well enforced either, especially where women are the victims. Consider the outcry if California's criminal law against negligent and intentional "torture" of animals—defined as any act or omission "whereby unnecessary or unjustified physical pain or suffering is caused or permitted"—was sought to be extended to women.[36] One has to go to Canada's criminal law on pornography[37] to find a law against "cruelty" to women, sexual or otherwise.

Having asked a woman question—sexuality—about animals, it is time to ask the animal question of animals. What is the bottom line for the animal/human hierarchy? I think it is at the animate/inanimate line, and Carol Adams and others are close to it: we eat them.[38] This is what humans want from animals and largely why and how they are most harmed. We make them dead so we can live. We make our bodies out of their bodies. Their inanimate becomes our animate. We justify it as necessary, but it is not. We do it because we want to, we enjoy it, and we can. We say they eat each other, too, which they do. But this does not exonerate us; it only makes us animal rather than human, the distinguishing methodology abandoned when its conclusions are inconvenient or unpleasant. The place to look for this bottom line is the farm, the stockyard, the slaughterhouse. I have yet to see one run by a nonhuman animal.

The overarching lesson I draw for theorizing animal rights from work on women's issues is that just as it has not done women many favors to have those who benefit from the inequality defining approaches to its solution, the same might be said of animals. Not that women's solution is animals' solution. Just as our solution is ours, their solution has to be theirs. This recognition places at the core of the problem of animal rights a specific "speaking for the other" problem. What is called animal law has been human law: the laws of humans on or for or about animals. These are laws about humans' relations to animals. Who asked the animals? References to what animals might have to say are few and far between. Do animals dissent from human hegemony? I think they often do. They vote with their feet by running away. They bite back, scream in alarm, withhold affection, approach warily, fly and swim off. But this is interpretation. How to avoid reducing animal rights to the rights of some people to speak for animals against the rights of other people to speak for the same animals needs further thought.[39]

A related absence is the lack of serious inquiry into animal government, including political organization in the sense of patterns of deference and command, and who gets what, when, how, and why. Ethologists and animal behaviorists have provided observations that might be put into that category,[40] but lawyers have devoted little attention to the emerging rules and forms of governance in animal societies that might illuminate entitlement, remedy, ethics, justice, community. The point of this inquiry would not be to see how "they" are like "us" or different. One point is to see whether, not having made such a great job of it, people might have something to learn. Maybe hierarchy and aggression and survival of the fittest are systematically focused upon by people in animal studies because those dynamics are so central to the organization of human affairs by male humans. How animals cooperate and resolve conflicts within and across species might be at least as instructive. How do they define and distribute what we call rights, or is there some other concept? Do they recognize and redress injuries? While animals aggress, so far as I know there has yet to be an animal genocide. This inquiry would be into animals' laws, not just what the two-leggeds say about the four-leggeds. Inventing what is not known across power lines has not worked well between men and women. I do not know why it would work any better between people and animals.

The question is (with apologies for echoing Freud's infamous question of women), what do they want from us, if anything other than to be let alone, and what it will take to learn the answer. Instead of asking this question, people tend to remain fixated on what we want from them, to project human agendas onto animals, to look for and find or not find ourselves in them. Some see economics. Some see Kant-in-the-making. Some see women. People who study animals often say more about themselves than about animals, leaving one wondering when the road kill will rise up off the page and say: stop making me an object of your analysis. What it would do to the discussion if they spoke for themselves is the question. The animal communicators are working on it.[41] People joke about dolphins' having discursive democracy but miss whether people will ever be able to communicate collectively as well as whales and blackbirds—who seem not to have our collective action problems—do.

Women are doubtless better off with rights than without them. But having rights in their present form has so far done precious little to change the abuse that is inflicted on women daily, and less to change the inferior status that makes that abuse possible. Like women's rights, animal rights are poised to develop first for a tiny elite, the direction in which the "like us" analysis tends. Recognizing rights for chimpanzees and bonobos,[42] for instance, would be like recognizing them for the elite of women who can preach in public—perhaps at the expense of, and surely in derogation of, the rights of that rest of women who are most women. Establishing animal individuality, agency, and rationality as a basis for their rights goes down that road.

Predicating animal rights on the ability to suffer is less likely to fall into this trap, as it leads more directly to a strategy for all.[43] Indeed, capacity to suffer may be closer to women's bottom line than liberal legal approaches to women's rights have yet reached. But women's suffering, particularly in sexual forms, has not delivered us full human status by law—far from it. It has gotten us more suffering. Women's suffering has also been sexualized. That women feel, including pain, has been part of stigmatizing them, emotions in particular traditionally having been relegated to the lower, animal, bodily side of the mind/body split. What will it do for animals to show that they feel?[44] Calculations of comparative suffering weighted by status rankings, combined with the inability to register suffering on the sufferer's terms, have so far vitiated the contribution Bentham's recognition might make. The ways women suffer as women have been denigrated and denied and, when recognized, more often used to make us seen as damaged goods than humans harmed. But fundamentally: Why is just existing alive not enough? Why do you have to hurt? Men as such never had to hurt or to suffer to have their existence validated and harms to them be seen as real. It is because they are seen as valid and real to begin with that their suffering registers and they have rights against its harm.

Women have been animalized, animals feminized, often at the same time. If qualified entrance into the human race on male terms has done little for women—granted we are not eaten, but then that is not our inequality problem—how much will being seen as humanlike, but not fully so, do for other animals? What law resists doing is taking anything they want away from those at the top of hierarchies. It resists effectively addressing the inequality's material bottom line.

III

Rereading Steinbeck's play *Of Mice and Men*[45] in this context—seeing mice as animals in the animal rights and crush video sense, and men as men in the sense of exercising gender dominance—offers insights in hierarchy, power, and love among people and between people and animals. Three interlocking hierarchies structure the play. Lenny, the slow, caring guy who doesn't know his own strength, is above animals. Curly, the boss's son who only wants to have a level conversation with the boys in the bunkhouse, is above his recently wed young wife, initially presented as a sexualized tart. George, Lenny's buddy, the guy's guy, is the smart one: shutting Lenny up, he will speak for him, he will make everything come out right. You know Lenny cares about animals. You question whether Curly cares about his wife. You never doubt that George, with condescension and comprehension, loves Lenny, who returns that love with unquestioning trust, adulation, and adoration.

With his love, Lenny kills the mice he dotes on, then the puppy his heart and hands adore; eventually, by accident and in panic, he kills Curly's wife. Curly's masculinity is desperate; he has to make himself a place among men. He is ultimately responsible for his wife's death, because he set her up for it: he stifled her, made her have to leave, run away, by depriving her of the ability to have her own life. He made Lenny rightly fearful of her making noise, of exposing her plans to flee, of them being together. Curly put her in the position where Lenny, always stronger than he knows, stifles her life out of her because he so loves her silky hair and to keep her leaving from being found out once she starts screaming. She is an animal to him. Once George realizes what Lenny has done, knowing Lenny will be hunted down like an animal and will not survive men's legal system, because he loves him, George kills Lenny himself. As we say of animals, including those who attack humans, he put him down.

On this reading, the play is about men's love: unknowing, gentle, soft, sensual love; sexual and explosive and possessive love; protectionist and "humane" love. Every relationship here is unequal: between humans and animals, between women and men, between some men and other men. It is about unequal love. In Steinbeck's context, one I am calling socially male, loving means death. Specifically, it kills.

Read this way, *Of Mice and Men* is a morality play about loving to death: the relation between affection and aggression. It shows the stifling lethality of protective love in society ordered hierarchically, where no one but George gets to be who he is without dying for it. In the interlocking connections among hierarchies among men, women and men, and people and animals, between love in its male dominant form and death-dealing, each man with the best of intentions kills what he most loves. Men's love did not save Curly's wife, the mice, or Lenny—quite the contrary. The good intentions of the powerful, far from saving the powerless, doom them. Unless you change the structure of the power you exercise, that you mean well may not save those you love. Animal rights advocates take note.

Central dilemmas in the use of law by humans to free women—men's pets, their beasts of burden, their living acquisitions—from male dominance have included analyzing structural power in intimate settings, meeting and changing standards simultaneously, redefining power while getting some, gaining protection without strengthening its arbitrary exercise,[46] and supporting caring and empathy while enforcing accountability. And we supposedly speak the same language. In the effort to use law to free animals from the species domination of human beings, the most socially empowered of whom are men, these and other challenges remain unmet.

Acknowledgments

Special thanks go to Ryan Goodman, Cass Sunstein, Lisa Cardyn, Kent Harvey, and most of all to Carol Adams for their helpful comments, and to the University of Michigan Law Labrary staff, as always, for their resourceful and responsive assistance.

Notes

1. Recognizing that human beings are also animals, and the linguistic invidiousness that elides this fact of commonality, I sometimes here, for simplicity of communication, term nonhuman animals "animals," while feeling that this usage gives ground I do not want to concede.

2. One analysis and documentation of male dominance is Catharine A. MacKinnon, *Sex Equality* (2001).

3. For discussion of this standard approach to equality, and a book full of examples of the problem discussed in this paragraph in the case of women, see id.

4. *Bradwell v. Illinois*, 83 U.S. 130, 142 (1872).

5. See, for example, Mark Thomas Connelly, *The Response to Prostitution in the Progressive Era* (1980), and David J. Pivar, *Purity Crusade: Sexual Morality and Social Control, 1868–1900* (1973).

6. Carolyn Merchant, *The Death of Nature: Women, Ecology, and the Scientific Revolution* (1980); Josephine Donovan, "Animal Rights and Feminist Theory" (chapter 2, this volume); and Carol Adams, *Neither Man nor Beast: Feminism and the Defense of Animals* (1994), have theorized this question.

7. James Boswell, 1 *Boswell's Life of Johnson* 266 (Mowbray Morris, ed., 1922).

8. Lea Vandervelde, "The Legal Ways of Seduction," 48 *Stanford Law Review* 817 (1996).

9. Joan Dunayer, "Sexist Words, Speciesist Roots," in *Animals and Women: Feminist Theoretical Explorations* 11 (Carol J. Adams and Josephine Donovan, eds., 1995).

10. The parallels are documented and analyzed in Carol Adams, *The Pornography of Meat* (2003).

11. This may have begun with Charles Fourier, to whom the insight is often credited, who said something somewhat different: "As a general proposition: *Social progress and changes of historical period are brought about as a result of the progress of women toward liberty; and the decline of social orders is brought about as a result of the diminution of the liberty of women. . . . To sum up, the extension of the privileges of women is the basic principle of all social progress*" (*The Theory of*

the Four Movements 132 [Gareth Stedman Jones and Ian Patterson, eds., 1996] [italics in original]). (The first edition published in the United States was in 1857.) He was making an empirical causal observation that the condition of woman causes social progress and decline, not drawing the moral conclusion that one can tell if one's era is virtuous by how women are treated. Closer to the usual interpretation, Fourier also said that "the best countries have always been those which allowed women the most freedom" (130).

12. 109 Cong. Rec. 8915 (88th Cong., 1st sess., 1963). Probably Senator Randolph was referring to Emerson's statement, "Women are the civilizers. 'Tis difficult to define. What is civilization? I call it the power of a good woman" ("Address at the Woman's Rights Convention, 20 September 1855," in 2 *The Later Lectures of Ralph Waldo Emerson, 1843–1871* 15, 20 [Ronald A. Bosco and Joel Myerson, eds., 2001]), which is something else again.

13. Mahatma Gandhi, quoted in Christopher C. Eck and Robert E. Bovett, "Oregon Dog Control Law and Due Process," 4 *Animal Law* 95, 95 (1998).

14. As James Rachels puts it, "If the animal subjects are not sufficiently like us to provide a model, the experiments may be pointless. (That is why Harlow and Suomi went to such lengths in stressing the similarities between humans and rhesus monkeys.)" (*Created from Animals: The Moral Implications of Darwinism* 220 [1990]). Harlow and Suomi designed horrific aversive experiments in an unsuccessful attempt to create psychopathology in monkeys by depriving infant monkeys of loving mothers. They did, however, succeed in creating monstrous mothers through isolation and rape by a machine. See Harry Harlow and Stephen J. Suomi, "Depressive Behavior in Young Monkeys Subjected to Vertical Chamber Confinement," 80 *Journal of Comparative and Physiological Psychology* 11 (1972). As Rachels points out, if monkeys are sufficiently similar to people to make the experiments applicable to humans, ethical problems arise in using the monkeys, but if the monkeys are sufficiently different from people to make the experiment ethical, the results are less useful in their application to humans. Rachels does not analyze the common mother-blaming theory of child psychopathology the experiments sought to test—an antifemale notion directed equally at humans and nonhuman animals—or the misogyny of an experimental methodology that would, in an attempt to create a bad mother, place female monkeys in an isolation chamber for up to eighteen months after birth, so all they felt was fear, and then impregnate them with a device they called a "rape rack." With their multilayered sexism, these are experiments in the perpetuation of abuse.

15. Elizabeth Anderson productively explores answers in "Animal Rights and the Value of Nonhuman Life," in *Animal Rights: Current Debates and New Directions* 277 (Cass Sunstein and Martha C. Nussbaum, eds., 2004).

16. Deep ecology makes a similar point on the existence of animals on their own terms. See Bill Devall and George Sessions, *Deep Ecology: Living as if*

Nature Mattered (1985); Alan Drengson and Yuichi Inoue, eds., *The Deep Ecology Movement: An Introduction* (1995); and George Sessions, ed., *Deep Ecology for the Twenty-first Century* (1995). However, deep ecology has been criticized as lacking awareness of gender issues. See Val Plumwood, *Feminism and the Mastery of Nature* (1993), and Joni Seager, *Earth Follies: Coming to Feminist Terms with the Global Environmental Crisis* (1993) ("Despite its surface overtures to feminists, the transformation of deep ecology into an environmental force has been characterized by deeply misogynistic proclivities. . . . Despite their putative tilt toward feminism, deep ecologists are unwilling to include gender analysis in their analytical tool kit" [230]).

17. Alice Walker puts it: "The animals of the world exist for their own reasons. They were not made for humans any more than black people were made for whites or women for men" (preface to Marjorie Spiegel, *The Dreaded Comparison: Human and Animal Slavery* 10 [1988]).

18. "When I see something that looks racist, I ask, 'Where is the patriarchy in this?' When I see something that looks sexist, 'Where is the heterosexism in this?'" (Mari J. Matsuda, "Standing Beside My Sister, Facing the Enemy: Legal Theory out of Coalition," in Mari J. Matsuda, *Where Is Your Body? And Other Essays on Race, Gender and the Law* 61, 64–65 [1996]).

19. It figures little to not at all in the following large surveys. Gary L. Francione, *Animals, Property, and the Law* (1995); Pamela D. Frasch, Sonia S. Waisman, Bruce A. Wagman, and Scott Beckstead, eds., *Animal Law* (2000); Keith Tester, *Animals and Society: The Humanity of Animal Rights* (1991); Emily Stewart Leavitt, *Animals and Their Legal Rights: A Survey of American Laws from 1641 to 1990* (1990); Daniel S. Moretti, *Animal Rights and the Law* (1984).

20. See, for example, Wisconsin Statutes, making "sexual gratification" a class A misdemeanor for anyone who "commits an act of sexual gratification involving his or her sex organ and the sex organ, mouth or anus of an animal." §944.17(2)(c).

21. 76 Utah Criminal Code §76-9-301.8, Chapter 9 is "Offenses Against Public Order and Decency," of which Part 3 is "Cruelty to Animals."

22. People in colonial times apparently abhorred intercourse with animals because they thought it could produce progeny. On the race and gender axes, bestiality for white men was considered like interracial sex for white women, both in their unnaturalness and in forfeiting of moral superiority and privileged status for the dominant group member. See Kirsten Fischer, *Suspect Relations: Sex, Race, and Resistance in Colonial North Carolina* 147–48, 156–57 (2002).

23. One of the more thorough and enthusiastic investigations of the subject of sexual contact of humans with animals, Midas Dekkers, *Dearest Pet: On Bestiality* 71 (Paul Vincent, trans., 2000), contains the following observation: "[T]hose wishing to have sexual intercourse with chickens—which have no vagina—use the communal exit of all the waste channels, the cloaca. What is

large enough for an egg is large enough for a penis. Nevertheless this usually proves fatal to the chicken, if for no other reason than because the height of pleasure is achieved only by decapitating the creature just before ejaculation in order to intensify the convulsions of its sphincter." He also reports what a man who has sex with female pigs claims are their sounds and other expressions of desire for his predations (72–73).

24. It is often said that Hitler was a vegetarian, but some people say he ate sausages and squab and the notion he was a vegetarian is Nazi propaganda. It is also said that he was gentle and kind and solicitous to his dogs. Some men who abuse other people also abuse animals. See Carol J. Adams, "Woman-Battering and Harm to Animals," in Adams and Donovan, *Animals and Women*, 55.

25. *People v. Thomason*, 84 Cal. App. 4th 1064, 1068 (Ct. App. 2d 2000).

26. 18 U.S.C. §48.

27. Id.

28. 145 Cong. Rec. H10, 268 (daily ed. Oct. 19, 1999) (statement of Representative Scott).

29. Id.

30. A.B. 1853, sec. 2, Amending Section 597 of the Penal Code at 597 (g) (1). The first conviction is a misdemeanor. The second is a felony. There is an exception for a serious constitutionally protected purpose.

31. A.B. 1853, sec. 1 (a), Amended in Assembly March 20, 2000.

32. The First Amendment double standard posed by those who oppose statutes against the harms of pornography but do not oppose laws against hunter harassment is explored by Maria Comninou, "Speech, Pornography, and Hunting," in Adams and Donovan, *Animals and Women*, 126–48.

33. *People v. Thomason*, 84 Cal. App. 4th 1064 (2002).

34. Id. at 1067.

35. "It does not include conduct committed against a human being to which the human being has given his or her consent" (A.B. 1853, sec. 1 [a]).

36. Cal. Penal Code §599b (West 1999).

37. Canada prohibits as obscene "any publication a dominant characteristic of which is the undue exploitation of sex, or of sex and . . . crime, horror, cruelty [or] violence" (163 [8] Criminal Code [Canada]).

38. Carol J. Adams, "Vegetarianism: The Inedible Complex," 4 *Second Wave* 36 (1976), and *The Sexual Politics of Meat: A Feminist-Vegetarian Critical Theory* (1990).

39. This question is implicit in Cass R. Sunstein, "Standing for Animals (With Notes on Animal Rights)," 47 *UCLA Law Review* 1333 (June 2000).

40. For an argument that, rather than ethology, what is needed is an anthropology of animals that acknowledges them as subjects, see Barbara Noske, *Beyond Boundaries: Humans and Animals* (1997).

41. See, for example, Amelia Kinkade, *Straight from the Horse's Mouth* (2001). One description is contained in the portrayal of Elizabeth in Jane Smiley, *Horse Heaven* (2000).

42. Steve Wise, "Animal Rights, One Step at a Time," in Sunstein and Nussbaum, *Animal Rights*, 19.

43. This of course refers to Jeremy Bentham's famous repudiation of reason and speech as the basis for animal rights and invocation of suffering as its basis: "It may come one day to be recognized, that the number of the legs, the villosity of the skin, or the termination of the *os sacrum*, are reasons equally insufficient for abandoning a sensitive being to the same fate. What else is it that should trace the insuperable line? Is it the faculty of reason, or, perhaps, the faculty of discourse? But a full-grown horse or dog is beyond comparison a more rational, as well as a more conversable animal, than an infant of a day, or a week, or even a month old. But suppose the case were otherwise, what would it avail? the question is not, Can they *reason*? nor, Can they *talk*? but, Can they *suffer*?" (Chapter XVII n.122 *Introduction to the Principles of Morals and Legislation* [1907 (1823) (1780)]).

44. That they do is analyzed and documented in Jeffrey Moussaieff Masson and Susan McCarthy, *When Elephants Weep: The Emotional Lives of Animals* (1995).

45. John Steinbeck, *Of Mice and Men* (1937).

46. For an analysis of protectionism, see Susanne Kappeler, "Speciesism, Racism, Nationalism . . . or the Power of Scientific Subjectivity," in Adams and Donovan, *Animals and Women*, 320, 322.

CHAPTER 14

Empathy and Vegetarian Commitments

LORI GRUEN

Feminist activists and theorists have varied and complicated responses to the moral demand for vegetarianism. For some feminists, the very idea that there should be another restriction on what women do raises hackles. Since vegetarianism is viewed as a restriction on eating, in cultures like our own—in which beauty norms, a glorification of slimness, and eating disorders have significant negative impacts on women, particularly young women—moral arguments against the consumption of meat are met with suspicion, at best. Still other feminists are concerned about the way that universal arguments for vegetarianism fail to adequately take into account traditional values in cultures other than those from which demands for vegetarianism are made. The worries here are that moral requirements that insist that people refrain from eating meat represent a form of value imperialism or cultural chauvinism.[1] At least one feminist has suggested that arguments for ethical vegetarianism are based on a white male health norm and relegate women to a moral underclass. Women may be excused from

This chapter was first published in Steve S. Sapontzi, ed., *Food for Thought: The Debate over Eating Meat* (New York: Prometheus, 2004). Published by permission of the author.

moral requirements to refrain from meat consumption because our bodies are supposedly weaker, but being excused in this way puts women in a position of moral inferiority.[2] Some feminists who adhere to what has been called "an ethics of care" have argued that because non-human animals are not able to enter into reciprocal relations with us, we have no moral obligation to become vegetarians.[3] And some feminists working for environmental and economic justice see the demand for vegetarianism as elitist, classist, and racist and argue that such a demand represents a potential hindrance to building meaningful alliances across class and race lines.[4]

A number of feminists have attempted to address these important concerns while nonetheless maintaining a commitment to vegetarianism.[5] These feminists have argued, among other things, that there are important conceptual and material links between racism, classism, sexism, and speciesism; that cultural traditions often provide the institutional structures for male domination and thus are the appropriate targets of criticism; and that meat-eating itself is a form of partriarchal domination and by consuming animal bodies, women are implicitly supporting their own domination. For these feminists, vegetarianism is one part of a larger project to dismantle the structures of oppression. Feminists should, these scholars and activists maintain, be vegetarians.

Despite how compelling feminist arguments for vegetarianism are in the abstract, many feminists have not been convinced that vegetarianism, even contextual vegetarianism,[6] is an important feminist philosophical and practical commitment. In this essay I want to explore this reluctance to commit to vegetarianism. I will start by speculating about what may be a cause of this reluctance—namely the alienating nature of the demand for vegetarianism. Arguments for vegetarianism have tended to appear as external constraints on behavior. The ethical requirement works from the outside in. Despite allowing for the context in which the agent may find herself, for example that she may have nutritional needs that make a vegetarian diet potentially harmful to her health or that in her culture and climate a vegetarian diet is close to impossible to adopt, the demand does not arise from the agent herself. This distance may be an implicit source of resistance to vegetarianism.[7] I will then offer an alternative argument in favor of contextual vegetarianism that minimizes this alienation by locating the force and authority of the ethical demand within the agent. Here I will build on feminist vegetarian arguments in a largely Humean vein, drawing on the experiences of sympathy, empathy, and compassion.[8]

The standard arguments for vegetarianism, arguments that are most commonly associated with Tom Regan and Peter Singer, maintain that there is no morally relevant distinction between human and non-human animals that can justify humans raising and slaughtering non-humans for food. Regan argues that we should not focus on the differences between humans and non-humans but the similarities. Because both humans and non-humans are individually experiencing subjects of a life who have an individual welfare that matters to them regardless of what others might think, there is no morally important difference between them. Regan argues that subjects of a life "want and prefer things, believe and feel things, recall and expect things. And all these dimensions of our life, including our pleasure and our pain, our enjoyment and suffering, our satisfaction and frustration, our continued existence or our untimely death—all make a difference to the quality of our life as lived, as experienced, by us as individuals. As the same is true of . . . animals . . . they too must be viewed as the experiencing subjects of a life, with inherent value of their own."[9] For Singer, because animals used for food are beings that can suffer and who have an interest in not suffering, we are no more justified in violating their interests than we are in violating the like interests of any being who has such interests. To confine, control, manipulate, transport, and ultimately slaughter animals for food in contexts in which there are other foods available is to disregard their morally important interests in ways that cannot be justified.[10] By carefully reasoning about the capacities that matter morally, being a subject of a life in Regan's case or being an individual who has interests and can suffer in Singer's case, and by carefully documenting the ways that modern first-world food production disrespects animals and violates their rights or interests, both conclude that vegetarianism is the only morally justified option. Both also maintain that it is through reason, not appeals to emotion, by which they come to this conclusion.

Many have suggested that this focus on reason continues a tradition that problematically separates reason from emotion, thought from feeling. Philosophical and psychological investigations into the nature of emotion suggest that a moral psychology that attempts to uphold the dichotomy between reason, and the cognitive capacities with which it is associated, and emotion, which is assumed to be non-cognitive, is mistaken.[11] Feminists have gone further and suggested that this dichotomy represents a value dualism, where appeals to reason are thought to be more important or more legitimate than those based on emotion or feeling. This value dualism is one of the central political tools by which women, who are supposedly less rational and more emotional than men, are thought to be less important and less legitimate and thus inferior to men. In addition, some feminists have argued that women, people of color, queer people, and others who are associated with passion and emotion are linked to animals, a linkage that further undermines all the inferior others' attempts to have their interests considered equally, to be valued appropriately, or to be seen as worthy of respect. This value dualism is part of what has been called a "logic of domination" that operates to reinforce sexism and other forms of prejudicial oppression and supports the exploitation of non-human animals.

Interestingly, both the standard arguments that underlie a moral commitment to vegetarianism and the feminist arguments that are meant as responses to these arguments have features in common, which, I believe, may contribute to the resistance to vegetarianism that some feminists express. Both types of arguments focus on similarity or sameness. Singer and Regan are interested in identifying those features that non-humans share with humans. Pigs are highly sensitive and intelligent animals and these capacities are not valued when pigs are confined in sowing pens, denied access to fresh air, water, and contact with their offspring, and eventually slaughtered. Chickens have elaborate social systems that are confounded when they are forced to live in confined spaces with thousands of other birds. And, of course, the billions of animals who are slaughtered for food each year in the United States are creatures that can and do suffer. We share these capacities and probably others with them, and since we value our intelligence, our relative freedom, our ability to navigate complex social terrain, and our desires to live free from suffering we should also value these things in non-human animals. The feminist arguments also highlight similarities, but usually the similarities are between attitudes toward and treatment of groups, rather than individuals. Women, people of color, queers, non-human animals are all thought to be lower in the hierarchy than white, heterosexual, able-bodied human men. The conceptual tools and institutional structures that maintain the status of these men are employed against women and animals. Oppression of any of these groups is thus linked, and if one is opposed to sexism, racism, heterosexism, etc. she should also oppose speciesism. The best way to oppose speciesism is to become vegetarian, so feminists should be vegetarian.

Yet this focus on similarity tends to obscure the important differences between individuals and between groups. Comparisons cut in both directions. From one perspective making connections between the oppression of women or African-Americans and the treatment of animals, or between the Nazi holocaust and factory farming, or between mentally disabled humans ("marginal cases") and animals can be understood as a

way of undervaluing the former in order to elevate the latter. In addition
to being conceptually problematic, such comparisons can have chilling
political consequences as potential alliances are often undermined.[12] By
focusing on similarities between individuals, groups, or events one often
obscures morally salient differences. Consider the widespread use of the
term "rape" to describe environmental destruction. In describing clear cutting, for example, as the rape of a forest, the very real trauma that women
who are raped must live with when they survive the experience is ignored.
This trauma and the anger, fear, doubt, and other emotions that rape survivors have to deal with are not, indeed, cannot be experienced by trees.
When rape is used to describe anything violent and horrible, the particular violence and horror of a man raping a woman is obscured.[13] Feminist
activism and scholarship has warned of the dangers lurking in categorical
generalizations—the term "woman" although generally meant to include
all females, often represents the particular perspective of some females,
those who are white, heterosexual, middle-class, able-bodied, and otherwise relatively privileged. In making claims about "women" and "animals"
or in focusing on similarities between otherwise quite different individuals, one runs the risk of engaging in problematic overgeneralizations. This
sort of generalizing appears to exclude some individuals who don't recognize themselves in the description. If a moral or political commitment is
spelled out in terms of similarities that miss difference, then many will
find such commitments alienating. One of the important lessons that feminists have learned from the criticisms raised of these generalizations is
how to think harder about understanding "difference" while maintaining
the ability to make meaningful normative claims that do not reduce to a
collection of particular attitudes and experiences.

One of the most important capacities for understanding and respecting difference is the capacity to empathize. Empathy is an ability that
a person with a distinct self-concept has to reflectively engage with the
situation of another. It is important that an empathetic person has a
distinct self so when she is imaginatively engaging with the other, she
doesn't believe herself to be in the other's situation. Only certain beings
have this ability, those who are able to make a distinction between self
and other. While individuals without distinctive self-concepts often
behave as if they are empathizing, they may, for example, respond to the
pain or fear or joy that they see others experiencing, this reaction is different from what I am calling empathy. Rather it involves what has been
called "emotional contagion," the unreflective perception of another's

emotional or mental state, and a spontaneous reaction to it. Empathy, on the other hand, requires reflection.

Empathy is different from the related phenomena called sympathy. Sympathy involves maintaining one's own attitudes and preferences and adding to them a concern for another. Sympathy for another is felt from the outside, the third-person perspective. I can feel sympathy for another's plight, even pity, but remain rather removed from that plight. Sympathy as I am understanding it, more than empathy, has the potential for being condescending, or parentalistic. Because one maintains one's own attitudes, beliefs, even prejudices, one can sympathize with another when sympathy isn't called for. Sympathy, understood in this way, also can be viewed as another form of distance. Empathy, on the other hand, requires some engagement with and understanding of the circumstances of the other. Empathy is thus more suited to situations in which there are significant differences between the empathizer and those with whom she is empathizing. And empathy has more grip than sympathy, it packs a greater motivation punch. Here are some examples of what I think of as empathetic responses:

> The production-line maintenance of animals . . . is without a doubt one of the darkest and most shameful chapters in human culture. If you have ever stood before a stable where animals are being fattened and have heard hundreds of calves bleating, if you can understand the calf's cry for help, then you will have had enough of those people who derive profit from it.[14]

Or consider these remarks from a 19-year-old woman working on a farm as part of a college course.

> The first time I went into the slaughter room I had just haltered and pulled a steer into the waiting line. I could tell that the steer sensed what was going to happen to him. He was doing anything to get away. Then when I walked to the slaughter room I was amazed at the amount of blood. It was an awful feeling to look at that steer with its eyes open and his feet pointing up, so I had to look at the ceiling. Mr. —— told me to cut off the head with a saw. I couldn't do it so I left. I guess slaughtering affects me more that the usual person because I raised calves for 4-H at home and became quite attached to them—but I *don't* butcher them.[15]

These reactions suggest that experiencing empathy for different others requires attentiveness to their experiences as well as reflection on the particular features of the situation, e.g. that people profit from the animals' suffering, that having an attachment to some animal can provide a connection to another animal to whom one is not similarly attached. However, many of us are not in situations in which we bear witness to the pain of animals. We are usually at some distance from the immediate pain, distress, fear, confusion, and suffering of others. Few of us look into an animals' eyes as we slit their throats. So how, from our comfortable distance, do we develop empathy for these animals that will motivate a commitment to contextual vegetarianism? One way for this to happen is to start from our particular experiences in particular contexts with non-human others, as the young woman did with the 4-H calves. Chris Cuomo and I have identified interspecies relationships and friendships as particularly rich sites of information for bridging distance across difference.[16] The bonds we develop with the non-humans in our lives require us to hone our empathetic awareness. We simply cannot know what a non-human needs or wants, what he may be nervous about, when he is annoyed or content, without such an awareness. Because non-humans cannot explicitly tell us what is in their interests, we must develop skills to understand them across our differences. These particular experiences are important opportunities for developing empathy that can help us in navigating other contexts in which our moral responses are required. Once we empathize with the non-humans with whom we have developed friendships, it becomes easier to empathize with others.

Empathetic engagement with different others is a form of moral attention that not only brings into focus the claims that non-humans make on us but also can help widen our moral attention. Features of a particular situation that may be obscured if we were simply to reason abstractly about our duties to animals or their rights come to the fore. When we begin to identify non-human animals as worthy of our moral attention because they are beings with whom we can empathize, they can no longer be seen merely as food. They are creatures with whom we share a way of being in the world. Seen from this perspective, the demand for moral vegetarianism comes from within us. It is not some abstract requirement deduced through careful argumentation. If we desire to see the world better, to understand our reactions to particular situations, and to reflect on the meaning of those reactions, then we cannot help but accept contextual vegetarianism.

These musings on a possible source of resistance to vegetarianism and my view of the importance of empathetic engagement with creatures different from ourselves are not meant to detract from the power of feminist vegetarian arguments or, for that matter, the standard arguments for vegetarianism where either is compatible with the recognition of the importance of empathetic engagement with non-human animals. When billions of animals are still being born to be slaughtered, when the environment is being destroyed by agribusiness, when maldistribution of food leads to the starvation of thousands of children around the world, when the activities of the rich and powerful cause untold suffering to marginalized peoples and animals, one may sensibly be pragmatic. There are many reasons to think hard about what one is contributing to when purchasing the products of modern factory farming and many reasons to stop eating animals.

NOTES

1. The earliest discussion of the topic of cultural imperialism and vegetarianism I am aware of is Jane Meyerding, "Feminist Criticism and Cultural Imperialism (Where does one end and the other begin)," *Animals' Agenda*, November–December 1982, 14–15, 22–23. Chris Cuomo and I touch on the topic in "On Puppies and Pussies: Animals, Intimacy, and Moral Distance," in *Daring to Be Good: Essays in Feminist Ethico-Politics*, ed. Bat-Ami Bar On and Ann Ferguson (New York: Routledge, 1998), 140. See also Val Plumwood's work.

2. This line of thinking has been developed by Kathryn George. There are a number of deep problems with her attempt to reject vegetarianism from a feminist perspective. First, she misrepresents what I call the standard arguments for vegetarianism developed by Tom Regan and Peter Singer. While both Regan and Singer make arguments for vegetarianism, George's claim that these arguments relegate women to a moral underclass by granting women exemptions from moral rules is based on objections to views that Regan, and particularly Singer, simply do not hold. Importantly, the utilitarian argument that addresses animal suffering in meat production is not, strictly speaking, an argument for vegetarianism. If an animal lived a happy life and was painlessly killed and then eaten by people who would otherwise suffer hunger or malnutrition by not eating the animal, then painlessly killing and eating the animal would be the morally justified thing to do. It would not be an exception to the rule; it would be precisely what the theory dictates. In many parts of the world where economic, cultural, or climate conditions make it virtually impossible for people to sustain themselves on plant-based diets, killing and eating animals that previously led relatively unconstrained lives and are painlessly killed would not be morally objectionable. The same would hold for individuals who for dietary reasons would be risking their own suffering if they did not eat animals. Singer's utilitarian position can thus avoid the charges of cultural chauvinism, moralism, and George's attempt to paint this aspect of it with an anti-feminist brush. This has been pointed out to George repeatedly. Second, there are interesting questions about whether in fact women, as a group, have a greater dietary need to eat animals. In the May 1994 issue of the *American Journal of Clinical Nutrition* there is a symposium reporting the numerous health benefits of a vegetarian diet for women, children, and men of various ethnic and racial background, data that directly contradict George's claims. George wants to point out that nutritional research that equates women's bodies with men's bodies is mistaken. This is an important insight, and nutritionists and others in the medical community have become increasingly aware of this. However, one woman's body and nutritional needs is often different

from another's. To lump all women together as if they had the same body "ideal" and suggest that women should not be vegetarian based on this is to be engaged in the same problematic reasoning that ignores differences George accuses others of using. Third, George consistently has ignored the richness and complexity of feminist arguments for vegetarianism, failing to even cite the work of a number of feminists who have addressed this topic. If she were not aware of this work, one might simply think that her scholarship is poor. But she is aware of this work (many of those whom she has repeatedly failed to cite have been in communication with her), so it is unclear what conclusion to draw. For a look at an early set of debates between George and Carol Adams, Josephine Donovan, Greta Gaard, and me, see *Signs: Journal of Women in Culture and Society* 21, no. 1 (1995): 221–61.

3. This is the view of Nel Noddings, *Caring: A Feminine Approach to Ethics and Moral Education* (Berkeley: University of California Press, 1984). For an alternative ethic of care that does include non-humans, see Deane Curtin, "Toward an Ecological Ethic of Care" (chapter 3, this volume).

4. See, for example, Noel Sturgeon, *Ecofeminist Natures: Race, Gender, Feminist Theory, and Political Action* (New York: Routledge, 1997).

5. See the work of Carol Adams, Lynda Birke, Deane Curtin, Josephine Donovan, Greta Gaard, Ronnie Zoe Hawkins, Marti Kheel, Brian Luke, Deborah Slicer, and me, for example. For a comprehensive review, see Greta Gaard, "Vegetarian Ecofeminism: A Review Essay," *Frontiers* 23, no. 3 (2003): 117–46.

6. This is a term originally developed by Curtin, "Toward an Ecological Ethic of Care," 96. Greta Gaard and I develop the idea in "Ecofeminism: Toward Global Justice and Planetary Health," *Society and Nature* 2, no. 1 (1993): 1–35.

7. This is not meant to be an empirical claim, but a philosophical one.

8. For an excellent example of this sort of work, see Josephine Donovan, "Attention to Suffering: Sympathy as a Basis for Ethical Treatment of Animals" (chapter 7, this volume).

9. Tom Regan, "The Case for Animal Rights," in *In Defense of Animals*, ed. Peter Singer (New York: Blackwell, 1985), 22.

10. Peter Singer, *Animal Liberation* (New York: New York Review of Books, 1990).

11. Feminist theorists as well as not explicitly feminist philosophers, neuroscientists, psychologists, and others have made convincing arguments in support of this view of emotion.

12. In "Dismantling Oppression: An Analysis of the Connection Between Women and Animals," in *Ecofeminism: Women, Animals, Nature*, ed. Greta Gaard (Philadelphia: Temple University Press, 1993), 60–90, I discuss an experience I had with a group of radical feminists opposed to pornography. They were displaying a picture of a woman in a meat-grinder, and I approached

them to discuss the parallels between the oppression of women and the treatment of animals in factory farming; they were appalled at the comparison.

13. I discuss this topic in "Thought on Exclusion and Difference: A Response to 'On Women, Animals and Nature,'" *American Philosophical Association Newsletter on Feminism and Philosophy* 91, no. 1 (1992): 78–81.

14. Konrad Lorenz, *On Life and Living* (New York: St. Martin's, 1988), 113, quoted in Brian Luke, "Justice, Caring, and Animal Liberation" (chapter 5, this volume), 131. Though Luke uses the term "sympathy" to describe these forms of "direct responsiveness," I think they are more appropriately instances of empathy, as I am using the term.

15. Harold Herzog, Jr., and Sandy McGee, "Psychological Aspects of Slaughter: Reactions of College Students to Killing and Butchering Cattle and Hogs," *International Journal for the Study of Animal Problems* 4 (1983): 129–30, quoted in Luke, "Justice, Caring, and Animal Liberation," 130.

16. Cuomo and Gruen, "On Puppies and Pussies," 129–42.

CHAPTER 15

On the Backs of Animals

The Valorization of Reason in Contemporary Animal Ethics

CATHRYN BAILEY

And it is stated that the rational soul, which is immaterial, bears the image of its divine maker, has will, is endowed with intellect and is more noble and more valuable of being than "the whole corporeal world." That Adam is soul and Eve is flesh.
> —Susan Griffin, *Woman and Nature: The Roaring Inside Her*

Since all who work on behalf of the interests of animals are more than a little familiar with the tired charges of being "irrational," "sentimental," "emotional," or worse, we can give the lie to these accusations only by making a concerted effort not to indulge our emotions or parade our sentiments.
> —Tom Regan, *The Case for Animal Rights*

Over twenty years have passed since Susan Griffin and Carolyn Merchant offered up their distinctively groundbreaking accounts of the rise of reason and its role in the linked oppressions of women and nature. Since then, feminists have produced numerous analyses of the role of reason in perpetuating that oppression (Bordo, Tuana, Code, etc.). Why is it, then, that some of the most ardent contemporary philosophical defenders of animals continue to argue as if such critiques had not altered the landscape of moral epistemology? Feminist scholar Josephine Donovan has

This chapter was first published in *Ethics and the Environment* 10, no. 1 (2005). Published by permission of Indiana Universty Press.

even gone so far as to detail the limitations of the particular moral philosophies of Tom Regan and Peter Singer, arguing that in their rejection of emotion "they expose the inherent bias in contemporary animal rights theory toward rationalism, which, paradoxically, in the form of Cartesian objectivism, established a major theoretical justification for animal abuse" (chapter 2, this volume, 59).

Regan notes Donovan's criticism but asks, "How could it be otherwise? How, that is, could one conceivably offer a theory of animal rights based on appeals to emotion?" (2001:63). He goes on to defend himself by drawing attention to a passage from one of his early texts:

> "There are times, and these not infrequent, when tears come to my eyes when I see, or read, or hear of the wretched plight of animals in the hands of humans. Their pain, their suffering, their loneliness, their innocence, their death. Anger. Rage. Pity. Sorrow. Disgust. . . . It *is* our hearts, not just our heads, that call for an end to it all." How, I wonder, can one read a passage like this one and criticize me for harboring a masculinist contempt for emotion. (63)

As a person, Regan is as capable of compassion for animals as anyone, much more than most, I would say, but as I argue, he misses the point of the criticism, understanding the problem to be one of an *absence* of emotion rather than a recognition of the continuity between reason and emotion. There are numerous emotionally moving passages in the works of both Regan and Singer, but, as I demonstrate, these are overshadowed by the dazzling work done by reason. In fact, it sometimes seems as if the contemporary philosophical approach to animal ethics serves as much to define and legitimize reason as to help animals, a kind of legitimacy that could only be wrought on the backs of animals.

The Anthropocentric, Sexist Rise of Reason

There is no need to rehearse in detail the feminist critiques of the sexism and anthropocentrism of the premier Western conceptions of reason.[1] From Plato, through Descartes, and culminating in the abstract analytic method that shapes so much contemporary American philosophical discourse, we find evidence of flesh-loathing or what Elizabeth Spelman (1988) calls, "somatophobia." From Plato's denouncement of the body as a cage, and a tomb, through Descartes's deepening of the rift between mind and body, we have long been aware of this tendency. Just as significantly, we have understood that this flight from the body as such has been played out most intensely on certain groups of bodies, "with woman cast in the role of body, 'weighed down,' in Beauvoir's words, 'by everything peculiar to it.' By contrast, man casts himself as the 'inevitable, like a pure idea, like the One, the All, the Absolute Spirit'" (Bordo 1993:5).

This is an association that is raced as well, with nonwhite men, too, caught up in the net of embodiment. Racist mythology about the greater physicality and emotionality of people of color was part of the rationalization for the enslavement of Africans, and part of what continues to justify various oppressive practices. It is expressed in stereotypes about the sexuality of women and men of color, and the supposed natural athleticism of Blacks. It is as apparent in the disproportionate attention to controlling the fertility of women of color as in the racist assumption of criminality of Latinos and Blacks. In short, almost wherever one locates racial stereotype one finds the assumption lurking that people of color are somehow more bodily, more emotional, further away from the reason that is said to distinguish "man" from animal. In fact, Alice Walker has argued that there is an important distinction in the sexist portrayals of Black and White women, "where white women are depicted in pornography as 'objects,' black women are depicted as animals. Where white women are depicted as human bodies if not beings, black women are depicted as shit" (Walker, quoted in Collins 1990:170).[2]

It bears emphasizing that the rise of reason was not incidentally associated with the oppression of women and nonwhite men; rather, that oppression itself was part of what legitimized reason. Reason did not first come into existence and then look for a venue to exhibit itself, rather, what much of philosophy came to define as reason only came into being as result of denying and quashing those attributes regarded as feminine or bodily. In other words, "It is not in order to fit him for the heroic that the Man of Reason is to be trained out of his soft emotions and his sensuousness, but because that is precisely what it is to be rational" (Lloyd 1989:117). The cultural norms of womanhood and those defining what it is to philosophize have been defined in opposition to one another (Tuana 1993:64).

That the rise of reason has been anthropocentric as well hardly needs arguing. After all, we have been reminded again and again that what separates "us" from the animals is reason. Indeed, the level of one's rationality has long been regarded as the very measure of one's level of humanity. When the hierarchy has been drawn with reason/God on top, the white man below, and women and men of color below, who has fallen at the very bottom of the scale? It is no accident that the image poet Delmore Schwartz selects to describe the body is an animal, "The heavy bear who goes with me . . . clumsy and lumbering here and there . . . the hungry beating brutish one" (quoted in Bordo, 1993:1).[3] It is no accident that philosophical conversations about how humans should treat animals often center on the extent to which animals are rational.

Because animals share this assignment as bodily and all that has been associated with it, the very antithesis of reason, white women, men and women of color, and animals have served as a kind of training ground for reason, a place for reason to define itself into existence and show itself off. Against this socially constructed backdrop of clumsy brutes, sometimes childlike, sometimes dangerous, animals, women, and people of color have been made to serve as a kind of foil to the purity and controlled exercise of rationality.

Certainly, this rational "flight to objectivity" offers a comfortable psychological distance, both for the philosopher and the reader (Bordo 1987), as it simultaneously reaffirms the value of reason more generally, not only in the context of these groups, but in all of them. If reason can rise so pristinely from the bloody squalor of the slaughterhouse floor, it shows itself as transcending the horror of such suffering, the ghastliness of it. Reason can best announce its own purity and equanimity against the backdrop of messy, bleeding, shrieking bodies. If reason is a kind of tool of objectivity, then it must be shown in the most apparently challenging context; not for nothing did the Ginsu knife serrate its way through a tin can. Reason promises to take the messy disturbing reality and carve it into a manageable, debatable issue.

Reason and Contemporary Animal Ethicists

In J. M. Coetzee's *The Lives of Animals*, the fictional Elizabeth Costello mocks those philosophers who try to discuss the suffering of animals in abstract terms:

> You say that death does not matter to an animal because the animal does not understand death. I am reminded of one of the academic philosophers I read in preparing for yesterday's lecture. It was a depressing experience. . . . Can we, asked this philosopher, strictly speaking, say that the veal calf misses its mother? Does the veal calf have enough of a grasp of the significance of

the mother-relation, does the veal calf have enough of a grasp of
the meaning of maternal absence, does the veal calf, finally, know
enough about missing to know that the feeling it has is the feeling
of missing? A calf who has not mastered the concepts of presence
and absence, of self and other—so goes the argument—cannot,
strictly speaking, be said to miss anything. In order to, strictly
speaking, miss anything, it would first have to take a course in
philosophy. What sort of philosophy is this? Throw it out, I say.
What good do its piddling distinctions do?   (Coetzee 1999:65–66)

That Costello only slightly exaggerates the tone of many philosophers is
easily confirmed by a quick flip through a journal such as *Environmental
Ethics*. The philosophy Costello describes is, of course, regarded by many
(including some academic philosophers) as a kind of mental masturba-
tion, but by calling up the particular image of the calf and its mother, she
points out, I think, that this is not harmless play. Rather, there is violence
in speaking about an unspeakable act in a way that so clearly privileges
conceptual clarity over empathy.

It is captured well by utilitarian arguments that, instead of emphasizing real suffering, blithely weigh units of pleasure and pain. Such a way
of framing suffering deepens the wound. As Sandra Harding argues, it
suggests that the concerns of the torturer and the concerns of the tortured are somehow equal (1991:159). Interestingly, this is an analogy that
Singer picks up on, pointing out that "you cannot write objectively about
the experiments of the Nazi concentration camp 'doctors' . . . without stir-
ring emotions" (2002:xxii). What Singer doesn't capture, though, is that
the "emotions" are always already present in any description one could
give of such torture. From Harding's point of view, and that of many feminist epistemologists, the whole point is that to use "neutral" language
in a description of such torture would itself be to express an emotionally
charged value. In choosing language that fails to condemn it, somehow
one seems to be assenting to the torture.

Still, even some of the most philosophically sophisticated defenders
of animals have a fear of mucking things up with emotion. Both Regan
and Singer explicitly worry about this in their landmark books *The Case
for Animal Rights* and *Animal Liberation*, respectively. It is telling that the
New York Times Book Review blurbs featured on the jackets of both praise
each for its detachment. We learn that "Singer's documentation is unrhe-
torical and unemotional, his arguments tight and formidable," and that

Regan provides "a lucid, closely reasoned and dispassionate book." And in a certain way, of course, these are selling points, for as Singer notes in one of the prefaces to his book, "The portrayal of those who protest against cruelty to animals as sentimental, emotional 'animal-lovers' has had the effect of excluding the entire issue of our treatment of nonhumans from serious political and moral discussion" (2002:xxi). As we saw above in one of the quotes that opened my essay, Regan's concern is similar as he urges that we make "a concerted effort not to indulge our emotions or parade our sentiments" (1983b:xii). Still, as it turns out, neither author actually excludes emotion from his book, but, rather, presents the emotional as separate from and less important than the rational.

Consider for example, Regan's "Animal Rights, Human Wrongs," an essay that distinguishes itself in an anthology of some twenty-five in the widely read *Ethics and Animals* (Miller and Williams 1983) by being one of few that dwells at any length on the actual treatment of animals rather than hypothetical cases. Regan begins with no fewer than three full pages of attention to these animals. Near his conclusion to this section his imagery is decidedly emotionally evocative:

> A few cases only—the great blue, now floating belly up, its white underside bobbing through the water like an uninhabited ice floe; the infant gibbon, still clutching its mother, their fused bodies barely perceptible on the jungle floor; the furious movements of the rabbit's feet as it seeks relief from the corrosive liquid which, as certain and painful as a knife, moment by moment cuts away at its optic nerve; the dank immobility of the baby calf.   (1983a:22)

Certainly, these images make Regan's piece memorable in a way that few of the others are.

However, these emotionally laden examples are not central to Regan's analysis. Indeed, the language changes sharply once he begins his "serious" philosophical work. Then he concedes that those individual animals add up to statistics, "But numbers prove nothing. They neither establish that something is right nor that it is wrong" (1983a:23). "What is wanted is some rational way to think through and resolve the conflict," he explains. "More particularly, what is wanted are the moral principles that ought to be applied if the conflict is to be resolved equitably" (24). Regan sets out to argue for his rights-based principles and then brings "the results of my argument to bear on how animals are treated in the world at large" (39).

The animals themselves serve as bookends for the "real" work of Regan's article. We are all but instructed to set aside the compassion that Regan evokes for them in the beginning of the essay. There is a similar strategy in Singer's *Animal Liberation*, except that here whole chapters work to impact the reader emotionally.

In this case, Regan's strategy mirrors the common traditional beliefs about the nature and roles of rationality and emotion. One feminist moral philosopher calls this the "bureaucratic model" where "moral agency involves a clear division of labor: reason is responsible for coming to the moral verdicts; it then passes its report on to the will, motivation, or emotion, which then does or does not issue the appropriate response" (Little 1995:1). Emotion has a role to perform, according to Regan, but only after receiving the proper warrant from Reason.

What is especially significant when this "bureaucratic model" is applied to animal ethics is that the separation of rationality from a lower nature is precisely what has been used to define animals as inferior. The "tendency is to view emotion and desire with deep suspicion, as something more to do with the body we have as animals than the mind we have as humans" (Little 1995:3). The hierarchy present in this mode of discourse is played out on the animals themselves. Given the established cultural framework, what is one announcing by one's suspension of emotion if not a transcendence of animal nature? As Regan suggested above, there are worse things for a philosopher than being accused of being "irrational" and "emotional," but, one suspects, not many.

I want to push the point that I am not suggesting that the connection between the valorization of Reason and the denigration of animals is merely symbolic. If Reason sets the parameters of the discourse (and since it is reason, it *will* be a debate of some sort) only Reason can be heard. Only Reason will decide when something of relevance has been said, who has won or lost (and because it is Reason, there must, in some sense, be a winner and a loser). If it is Reason that must ultimately speak and be heard, then what of the animal? According to the history and dictates of Reason, animal "silence" is an indication of *their* lack and so it becomes the philosopher's paternalistic duty to speak for the animal. Rarely is it appreciated by philosophers that the assumption of this as a lack is already an assertion of superiority. This is, I think, analogous to insisting that a discussion about deaf unilingual Italians will only be conducted in spoken English; the scenario is inherently exploitive.

There is a way, too, in which the animals may sometimes serve as a kind of proxy for people. As we have seen, throughout history thinkers of many stripes have been untroubled by valorizing rationality at the expense of various groups of human others, usually women and nonwhite men. However, it may be that as various social justice movements succeed in convincing that it is inappropriate to use certain groups of people in this way, animals become even more oppressed. Although many groups are still widely objectified and dehumanized—for example, prisoners of war, the disabled, lesbians, and gay men—animals have consistently been fair game.[4] Changing societal mores have never come close to placing them outside the bounds, not even to feminists who, for example, routinely protest being treated like "pieces of meat" (Adams 1991:46) or in the Walker quote above, where animals seem to be equated with shit.

Because it is more and more widely recognized (I hope) that it is inappropriate to objectify and denigrate humans in this way, continuing to do it to animals not only reaffirms reason but the lowliness of animals. Only those beneath contempt are left to be the butt of the joke or on the losing end of the comparison. This is also one reason why the Holocaust is thought to be such a sticky analogy to be used to make points about the inhumane treatment of animals. As one of Coetzee's fictional character's protests, the analogy "insults the memory of the dead" (1999:50). It insults their memory, in part, because animals are not valued. Indeed, it is their role to stand in for the lowest, vilest way that a human being can be treated, "like a dog" or, more simply, "like an animal."[5]

Objectifying animal suffering frames it as something distant and debatable. It permits us to maintain a wall of "willed ignorance," a willful refusal to know about animal suffering (Coetzee 1999:20). This is ironic when one considers that philosophy is supposed to open windows of truth. The suffering we inflict upon animals is the white elephant in the living room, with a veil that sometimes falls away. Philosophical discourse can keep weaving new veils, ones that provide the illusion that we are honestly facing the thing when what we are too often doing is debating "piddling distinctions" on a quest for abstract moral principles. At the same time, animal discourse becomes a perfect opportunity for the affirmation of masculinity, for who but a real man can distance himself from the cries of furry animals to have the sorts of measured, mature conversations that the philosophers do? It is, then, the perfect opportunity to showcase the powers of reason itself, and oneself as a manly, rational player, with the added twist that one can still be seen as sensitive because, after all, one is on the side of the animals.

Regan and Singer are certainly not unaware that emotion belongs in animal discourse in some sense. It is the sort of role they envision for emotion that is problematic. In fact, what some feminists would identify as a problem in their work they would likely explain away as symptomatic of their interest in making "fine distinctions." After all, Regan is concerned about animal suffering in a general way, but also about particular cases where human and animal interests may collide, for example, in whaling or animal experimentation: "Then what is needed is not the simple declaration that life is sacred, that all life ought to be revered, and so on" (1983a:24). He is wise to be aware of the limits of such platitudes. There are, of course, numerous particular cases in all areas of ethics where reason has a critical role to play. But, then, few feminist epistemological critiques have ever suggested that reason, even a narrowly construed version, might not have some very limited usefulness, that of a tool. Indeed, I think it is quite clear from the strategies I employ in this very paper that it is not the use of reason per se that I am critiquing. The problems arise when one turns what are actually deep moral issues into "piddling distinctions" precisely by framing them through a narrowly conceived reason. The feelings of the veal calf in the Coetzee example above don't become merely "fine distinctions" *until* the philosophers frame the discourse in a particular way.

The Case of Singer

In a fictional work Singer wrote as a response to Coetzee's two fictionalized lectures in *The Lives of Animals*, it is Singer's fictionalized daughter who first brings the family dog into the discussion: "When I was little I used to wonder who you would save if the house caught on fire, me or Max" (1999:87). It is no accident, I think, that Singer has the girl raise the issue, for if Singer had done it himself, after having been implicitly lambasted by Coetzee's character, Costello, as an overly abstract academic philosopher, what would he be doing except giving confirmation to the critic? Never mind that it is implausible to imagine anyone's daughter, even that of a philosopher, introducing the beloved family dog in this way. Did she really feel that she and Max were in competition for her father's love?

    In any case, what happens next in Singer's fictional vignette is that "Peter kneels by the dog and strokes his neck" (1999:87) (lest we suspect Singer of being one of those insensitive philosophers). Max is then transformed through the discourse into a case for an argument about why it's not such a big deal to kill animals. It is, "Peter" explains, because animals lack a particular kind of consciousness, one that allows them to be, among other things, future-oriented, to care about their death. In fact, fictional Peter addresses the dog, concluding: "I'm sure that you don't think about what you will be doing next summer, or even next week" (87).

Of course, Singer builds in all of the reasonable objections, through the mouth of his daughter, including Costello's objection: "What are you saying—that we could painlessly kill Max, get another puppy to replace him, and everything would be fine? Really, Dad, sometimes you let philosophy carry you away. Too much reasoning, not enough feeling. That's a *horrible* thought" (1999:88). At this, Max licks the girl's feet "consolingly" and Peter replies: "You know very well that I care about Max, so lay off with the 'You reason, so you don't feel' stuff, please. I feel, but I also think about what I feel" (88). We are left to understand that it is feeling that will be legislated by thinking because, after all, unchecked feelings are dangerous.

What neither "Peter" nor Singer seem to appreciate is the checkered past of reason. It is especially telling in how Max is made to exit the story, with fictional Peter's offer to his daughter, "Let's leave Max out of it, since mentioning his name seems to excite him and distress you" (1999:89). This is another show of the philosopher's sensitivity, but it is more than that. It is the dog and the girl, presumably a teen-ager, who show distress about animals, a distress which only highlights the philosopher's objectivity. He defers to her childlike, feminine sensitivity and she gamely agrees to continue the discussion in the land of hypothetical pigs and chickens. Part of what I find fascinating is that even in the immediate wake of Costello's searing criticism of this philosophical approach to animal discourse, Singer, or at least "Peter," creates a forum to show off reason. "Peter" does little more with the concept of feeling than pay lip service to it (he strokes the dog's neck, after all), suggest that it is the stuff of little girls, and lay it aside.

What isn't made clear, though, is why we should worry more about unchecked feeling than unchecked reason. Do we turn our backs on the suffering we inflict on animals because of a failure of rationality or is rationality part of what we often call upon to help justify it? It seems to me that Singer can only get away with addressing emotion in this offhand way because he is riding a wave of philosophical history that has neglected and vilified emotion. Never mind that feminist epistemologists have been quite thoroughgoing in their reconceptualizations of the nature and function of emotion, noting that there are historically specific views of emotion and that, "the modern redefinition of rationality required a corresponding reconceptualization of emotion. This was achieved by portraying emotions as nonrational and often irrational urges that regularly swept the body, rather as a storm sweeps over the land" (Jaggar 1989:130). Never mind that the real power of Singer's own book, the tremendous power that it has had to move people, likely rests much more on its emotionally moving passages than the tedious weighing of animal versus human interests.

Attorney and disability rights leader Harriet McBryde Johnson raises a similar concern about Singer after being invited to speak with him at Princeton. She suggests that Singer's failure to let empathy shape his reasoning negatively affects the direction his arguments take: "Because of this all-too-common prejudice (against disabled people), and his rare courage in taking it to its logical conclusion, catastrophe looms" (2003:79). In many ways, Singer is an easy mark for this kind of criticism. He has, after all, been vilified by all kinds of groups for the unconventional conclusions he has drawn about animals and infants. A writer for *U.S. News & World Report* had this to say, "Most ethicists, arriving at the conclusion that a pig is more valuable than a human baby, would probably re-examine their premises and think about framing a somewhat less repellent argument. But Singer is supremely confident in his coldly abstract line of reasoning" (Leo 1999:1). As it happens, one of the things I admire about good philosophy is its unwillingness to automatically cater to traditionally held values. Where would we be if brave thinkers such as Singer had not challenged peoples' sense of the proper order of things in all sorts of areas? However, I am not so concerned that this "coldly abstract line of reasoning" will offend, nor with the particular conclusions that people like Singer ride this line of reasoning to. My concern is that this message does real damage in terms of reinscribing the kinds of dualisms and hierarchies associated with rationality and embodiment that I have described above.

Johnson makes clear that Singer is a nice enough person. He is pleasant, respectful. She seems to like him. I believe that I would like him, too. But when it comes right down to it, in his philosophical arguments at least, Singer has not only cut reason away from feeling, he seems to use the most potentially emotionally rich occasions as a mere showcase for clever displays of reason. One is left with the sense that all of these feelings are so much dirt on a white carpet with Singer there to whip out reason to vacuum it all up. I can say this and still be in full agreement with Donovan, who claims that it is Singer's "admirable and courageous book *Animal Liberation* that largely galvanized the current animal rights movement" (chapter 2, this volume, 62). It is because Singer is such a great ally to animals in so many ways that the limitations of his method warrant such close consideration.

Like so many philosophers, Regan and Singer are worried about emotion at least partly because they want to reach other philosophers like themselves, a point Regan addresses explicitly. And, of course, these are not trivial concerns. However, in these moments, I am inclined to agree once more with Coetzee's fictional character Elizabeth Costello, in her final engagement with a philosopher:

> On the present occasion, however, I am not sure I want to concede that I share reason with my opponent. Not when reason is what underpins the whole long philosophical tradition to which he belongs, stretching back to Descartes and beyond Descartes, through Aquinas and Augustine to the Stoics and Aristotle. If the last common ground I have with him is reason, and if reason is what sets me apart from the veal calf, then thank you but no thank you, I'll talk to someone else. (1999:66–67)

If we cannot, *as philosophers*, talk to one another about animal suffering in a way that does not risk reinscribing their suffering, what, then, are we doing?

Where Do We Go from Here?

It is telling that when confronted with Donovan's critique, Regan seems to be mystified about the possibility of a theoretically rich role for emotion in moral discourse about animals. "How could it be otherwise?" he asks, than that emotion would fall outside of theorizing about animal rights (2001:63). I don't know if this is because Regan has explored alternative epistemologies and found them wanting or if he has not attended to them. In any case, such alternatives have long been available, for example, Scheler, Schopenhauer, Buber, Weil, etc.[6] Some promising recent alternatives have been formulated by feminists.

As we have seen, the issue isn't one of whether or not philosophers value emotion, but how they conceptualize the nature of emotion and reason and their relationship to one another. To continue to treat emotion and reason as elements that can and should be distinguished in the process of doing moral philosophy ignores the fact that reason and emotion are intertwined in ways that are not always obvious. It is apparent, for instance, in that "what one is attentive to [even as one is engaged in moral reasoning] reflects one's interests, desires, in brief, what one cares about" (Little 1995:4). It is partly because of the interrelatedness of the two that many feminists endorse an "ethics of care," but I find any account promising that emphasizes the continuity of reason and emotion. The stakes for recognizing such continuity in the discourse of animal ethics are especially high because of how this discourse reflects how we understand our relationship to non-human animals. A discourse that assumes that it is the nature of rationality and emotionality to be sharply distinct reflects and reaffirms the view that it is the nature of human and animal to be sharply distinct.

Primatologist Barbara Smuts seems to overcome this dichotomy by beginning with the possibility of relationship with animals, of communion with them. The animal becomes, not the object of study, but a kind of interlocutor. Animal discourse so conceived would demand not so much a deduction of the "correct" moral principles, but an opening of oneself to what is there and that we be present to that being on its own terms instead of through the distancing lens of a very narrowly conceived reason. This is an encounter that can be scientific, as Smuts's work attests, but which is based on a compassionate curiosity rather than a puzzle-solving one.

In at least one essay, Smuts, too, deals with a perennial philosophical concept, but notice how distinctively she approaches it:

> [W]hile we normally think of personhood as an essential quality that we can "discover" or "fail to find" in another, in the view espoused here personhood connotes a way of being in relation to others, and thus no one other than the subject can give it or take it away. In other words, when a human being relates to an individual nonhuman being as anonymous object rather than as a being with its own subjectivity, it is the human, and not the other animal, who relinquishes personhood. (1999:118)

It is not incidental, I think, that Smuts comes to this on the basis of having befriended and lived with various "non-human persons," but I also find echoes of Buber and the phenomenologists.

In similar fashion, following Iris Murdoch, Donovan suggests "the development of forms of attention that enhance awareness of the living environment, that foster respect for its reality as a separate, different, but knowable entity" (1996:181). She calls for an "epistemological awakening" that will "sensitize dominators to the realities of the dominated, that is, to make the dominator-subject see/hear what has been construed as an object" (181). A fuller, richer, more usefully objective picture will be painted by reconceiving the role of reason and emotion and it will be one that does not reinscribe the inferiority of animals. In some ways, what is being recommended is a demand for a higher standard of epistemological accountability, what Sandra Harding calls a "strong objectivity" that "requires that we investigate the relation between subject and object rather than deny the existence of, or seek unilateral control over, this relation" (1991:152).

What does a chicken become to the animal ethicist if it is no longer one more set of "interests" to be weighed or a potential bearer of rights to be ranked? What does the veal calf become if she is no longer a hypothetical case to illustrate concepts related to consciousness and affect? To moral philosophers bound to traditional notions of rationality, what might animals mean if they no longer serve as fodder for pristine discussions about "suffering" or "intelligence"? And without animal discourse, what would become of reason?

Early on, modern reason screamed out its superiority through the "scientific" vivisection of live dogs. The dogs, nailed to boards by their paws, had their vocal cords cut so their screams would not disturb their "experimenters" (Jardine 1999:118). There are less literal ways of silencing animals through reason, though, even when what we mean to do is raise our voices on their behalf. The legislating power of reason so employed may be benevolent in its paternalism, but it is still autocratic, and one could do better than be subject to the whims of an autocrat. This is the master, after all, who draws and redraws the theoretical line between who should live and who should die, a line that continues to have a suspiciously close correlation between who is thought to be able to reason and who is not.

Notes

1. As many of these scholars note, though, this conception has not been the only one; alternatives have always been available even within the Western philosophical tradition.

2. The consequences of the association of women of color with embodiment is explored especially well in Patricia Hill Collins's *Black Feminist Thought*, bell hook's "Selling Hot Pussy," and Dorothy Roberts's *Killing the Black Body*.

3. As Bordo discusses, Schwartz's bear seems to be raced as well.

4. This treatment of disabled people is explored especially well in the chapter "The Flight from the Rejected Body," in *The Rejected Body* by Susan Wendell.

5. I don't mean to suggest that this is the only reason. I, too, think that the Holocaust analogy is generally unwise and inappropriate, but not for the reasons I give here.

6. Several of these alternatives are explored in Donovan's "Attention to Suffering: Sympathy as a Basis for Ethical Treatment of Animals" (chapter 7, this volume).

References

Adams, Carol J. 1991. *The Sexual Politics of Meat: A Feminist-Vegetarian Critical Theory*. New York: Continuum.

Bordo, Susan. 1987. *The Flight to Objectivity: Essays on Cartesianism and Culture*. Albany: State University of New York Press.

——. 1993. *Unbearable Weight: Feminism, Western Culture, and the Body*. Berkeley: University of California Press.

Coetzee, J. M. 1999. *The Lives of Animals*. Ed. Amy Gutmann. Princeton, N.J.: Princeton University Press.

Collins, Patricia Hill. 1990. *Black Feminist Thought: Knowledge, Consciousness, and the Politics of Empowerment*. New York: Routledge.

Donovan, Josephine. 1996. "Ecofeminist Literary Criticism: Reading the Orange." *Hypatia: A Journal of Feminist Philosophy* 11, no. 2:161–84.

Garry, Ann, and Marilyn Pearsall, eds. 1989. *Women, Knowledge, and Reality: Explorations in Feminist Philosophy*. Boston: Unwin Hyman.

Griffin, Susan. 1978. *Woman and Nature: The Roaring Inside Her*. New York: Harper & Row.

Harding, Sandra. 1991. *Whose Science? Whose Knowledge? Thinking from Women's Lives*. Ithaca, N.Y.: Cornell University Press.

hooks, bell. 1998. "Selling Hot Pussy: Representations of Black Female Sexuality in the Cultural Marketplace." In *The Politics of Women's Bodies: Sexu-*

ality, Appearance, and Behavior, ed. Rose Weitz, 112–22. New York: Oxford University Press.

Jaggar, Alison M. 1989. "Love and Knowledge: Emotion in Feminist Epistemology." In *Women, Knowledge, and Reality: Explorations in Feminist Philosophy*, ed. Ann Garry and Marilyn Pearsall, 129–55. Boston: Unwin Hyman.

Jardine, Lisa. 1999. *Ingenious Pursuits: Building the Scientific Revolution*. New York: Doubleday.

Johnson, Harriet McBryde. 2003. "Unspeakable Conversations: Or How I Spent One Day as a Token Cripple at Princeton University." *New York Times Magazine*, February 16, 50.

Leo, John. 1999. "Singer's Final Solution." *U.S. News & World Report*, October 4, 17.

Little, Margaret Olivia. 1995. "Seeing and Caring: The Role of Affect in Feminist Moral Epistemology." *Hypatia: A Journal of Feminist Philosophy* 10, no. 3:117–37.

Lloyd, Genevieve. 1989. "The Man of Reason." In *Women, Knowledge, and Reality: Explorations in Feminist Philosophy*, ed. Ann Garry and Marilyn Pearsall, 111–28. Boston: Unwin Hyman.

Miller, Harlan B., and William H. Williams, eds. 1983. *Ethics and Animals*. Clifton, N.J.: Humana Press.

Regan, Tom. 1983a. "Animal Rights, Human Wrongs." In *Ethics and Animals*, ed. Harlan B. Miller and William H. Williams, 19–43. Clifton, N.J.: Humana.

——. 1983b. *The Case for Animal Rights*. Berkeley: University of California Press.

——. 2001. *Defending Animal Rights*. Urbana: University of Illinois Press.

Roberts, Dorothy. 1997. *Killing the Black Body: Race, Reproduction, and the Meaning of Liberty*. New York: Random House.

Singer, Peter. 1999. "Reflections." In *The Lives of Animals*, by J. M. Coetzee, 85–91. Princeton, N.J.: Princeton University Press.

——. 2002. *Animal Liberation*. 3rd ed. New York: HarperCollins.

Smuts, Barbara. 1999. "Reflections." In *The Lives of Animals*, by J. M. Coetzee, 107–10. Princeton, N.J.: Princeton University Press.

Spelman, Elizabeth V. 1988. *Inessential Woman: Problems of Exclusion in Feminist Thought*. Boston: Beacon.

Tuana, Nancy. 1993. *The Less Noble Sex: Scientific, Religious, and Philosophical Conceptions of Woman's Nature*. Bloomington: Indiana University Press.

Wendell, Susan. 1996. *The Rejected Body: Feminist Philosophical Reflections on Disability*. New York: Routledge.

CHAPTER 16

Caring to Dialogue
Feminism and the Treatment of Animals

JOSEPHINE DONOVAN

In recent years feminists have brought care theory to the philosophical debate over how humans should treat nonhuman animals. Care theory, an important branch of contemporary feminist theory, was originally articulated by Carol Gilligan and has been elaborated, refined, and criticized extensively since it was first formulated in the late 1970s. Since the authors included in the first part of this volume applied care theory to the animal question in the early 1990s, it has established itself as a major vein of animal ethics theory.

This article is an attempt to further refine and strengthen feminist animal care theory. I hope to reposition the discussion to emphasize the dialogical nature of care theory. It is not so much, I will argue, a matter of caring for animals as mothers (human and nonhuman) care for their infants, but of listening to animals, paying emotional attention, taking seriously—*caring about*—what they are telling us. As I note in the conclu-

A much longer and slightly different version of this article was published as "Feminism and the Treatment of Animals: From Care to Dialogue," *Signs: Journal of Women in Culture and Society* 2006, vol. 31, no. 2. © 2006 by the University of Chicago. All rights reserved. Published by permission of the author and *Signs*.

sion of my article "Animal Rights and Feminist Theory" (chapter 2, this volume, 76): "We should not kill, eat, torture, and exploit animals because they do not want to be so treated, and we know that." In other words, I am proposing in this article that we shift the epistemological source of theorizing about animals to the animals themselves. Could we not, I ask, extend feminist standpoint theory to animals, including their standpoint in our ethical deliberations?

Standpoint Theory for Animals

Because it offers a more theoretically sophisticated political perspective than care theory, standpoint theory, a significant vein in contemporary feminist theory, may prove a useful supplement to care theory regarding the ethical treatment of animals.[1] Especially in its original articulation by Georg Lukács, standpoint theory would seem to be particularly apt for the dialogical focus I am proposing here. Lukács, a Marxist, developed the idea in his *History and Class Consciousness* ([*Geschichte und Klassenbewusstsein*, 1923] 1971), in which he posited that the proletariat evinces a particular and privileged epistemology because of its commodification or reification in the capitalist production process. When a subject is treated as an object, Lukács argues, the experience necessarily evokes a critical consciousness born of the subject's ironic knowledge that he or she is *not* a thing. In capitalist assembly-line production, Lukács notes, the worker "is turned into a commodity and reduced to a mere quantity. But this very fact forces him to surpass the immediacy of his condition" (166). Beneath the "quantifying crust," however, lies a "qualitative living core" (169), from which arises a critical, subversive consciousness. Lukács elaborates: "[I]n the proletariat . . . the process by which a [person's] achievement is split off from his total personality and becomes a commodity leads to a revolutionary consciousness" (171). Moreover, "Corresponding to the objective consciousness of the commodity form, there is the subjective element . . . [and] while the process by which the worker is reified and becomes a commodity dehumanizes him . . . it remains true that precisely his humanity and his soul are not changed into commodities" (172).

Feminist standpoint theory has generally—following Nancy Hartsock (1983)—rooted an oppressed group's awakening critical consciousness less in objectification and more in bodily experience and in the practice or memory of nonindustrial craft-based labor (use-value production);[2] however, for the purposes of developing a feminist approach to the animal question, the Lukácian emphasis on reification as the primary element constitutive of the critical standpoint would seem more useful.

In applying the theory to animals, it is abundantly clear that they are commodified and quantified in the production process—even more literally so than the proletariat, whose bodies at least are not literally turned into dead consumable objects by the process, though they may be treated as mechanical means. Where one immediately senses problems, however, in applying standpoint theory to animals is in the question of how their subjective viewpoint is to be articulated. For obviously, unlike human workers, animals are unable to share their critical views with other animals and to organize resistance to their objectification and (in the case of animals) slaughter. However, the fact that workers rarely expressed a proletarian standpoint spontaneously or rose up en masse against their treatment (a perennial problem in revolutionary theory) suggests that the differences between the two cases may not be as great as they might at first appear. Often, as a practical matter, Marxist theorists have fallen back on the idea of an intellectual vanguard leading and educating the proletariat so as to recognize and act against the injustices that are inflicted on it (the most famous example here being V. I. Lenin's idea of the vanguard party). And indeed a central question in feminist standpoint theory has been that of the relationship between the theorists articulating the standpoint and the women on whose behalf it is being articulated (Hartsock 1998:234–38).

In the case of animals, it is clear that human advocates are required to articulate the standpoint of the animals–gleaned, as here argued, in dialogue with them—to wit, that they do not wish to be slaughtered and treated in painful and exploitative ways. And human advocates are necessary as well to defend and organize against the practices that reify and commodify animal subjects.

A Dialogical Ethic of Care for the Treatment of Animals

Ludwig Wittgenstein once famously remarked that if a lion could speak we couldn't understand him (1963:223e). In fact, as I have been proposing here, lions do speak, and it is not impossible to understand much of what they are saying. Several theorists have already urged that humans need to learn to read the languages of the natural world. Jonathan Bate has proposed that we learn the syntax of the land, not seeing it through our own "prison-house of language," in order to develop appropriate environmental understandings (Bate 1998:65, as cited in Simons 2002:77).

Similarly, Patrick Murphy has called for an "ecofeminist dialogics" in which humans learn to read the dialects of animals. "Nonhuman others," he claimed, "can be constituted as speaking subjects rather than merely objects of our speaking" (1991:50).[3] Earlier, phenomenologist Max Scheler spoke similarly about the necessity for learning the *"universal grammar"* of creatural expression ([1926] 1970:11). Indeed, over a century ago American writer Sarah Orne Jewett speculated about the possibility of learning the language of nonhumans, asking,

> Who is going to be the linguist who learns the first word of an old crow's warning to his mate . . . ? [H]ow long we shall have to go to school when people are expected to talk to the trees, and birds, and beasts in their own language! . . . It is not necessary to tame [creatures] before they can be familiar and responsive, we can meet them on their own ground.   (1881:4–5)

There are those, to be sure, who still raise the epistemological question of how one can know what an animal is feeling or thinking. The answer would seem to be that we use much the same mental and emotional activities in reading an animal as we do in reading a human.[4] Body language, eye movement, facial expression, tone of voice—all are important signs. It also helps to know about the species' habits and culture. And, as with humans, repeated experiences with one individual help one to understand that individual's unique needs and wishes. By paying attention to, by studying, what is signified, one comes to know, to care about the signifier.[5] In this way, what Adams (1990) famously termed the *absent referents* are restored to discourse, allowing their stories to be part of the narrative, opening, in short, the possibility of dialogue with them.

The underlying premise here is that one of the principal ways we know is by means of analogy based on homology. If that dog is yelping, whining, leaping about, licking an open cut, and since if I had an open wound I know I would similarly be (or feel like) crying and moving about anxiously because of the pain, I therefore conclude that the animal is experiencing the same kind of pain as I would and is expressing distress about it. One imagines, in short, how the animal is feeling based on how one would feel in a similar situation.[6] In addition, repeated exhibitions of similar reactions in similar situations lead one inductively to a generic conclusion that dogs experience the pain of wounds as we do, that in short they feel pain and don't like it. The question therefore whether humans can understand animals is, in my opinion, a moot one. That they can has been abundantly proved, as Midgley points out, by their repeated success in doing so (1983:113, 115, 133, 142).

Of course, as with humans, there is always the danger that one might misread the communication of the animal in question, that one might incorrectly assume homologous behavior when there is none. To be sure, all communication is imperfect, and there remain many mysteries in animal (as well as human) behavior. Feminist ethic-of-care theorists have explored some of the difficulties inherent in attempting to assess the needs of an incommunicative human and/or the risks of imposing one's own views or needs on her. But as Alison Jaggar summarizes, care theorists maintain that in general such "dangers may be avoided [or at least minimized, I would add] through improved practices of attentiveness, portraying attentiveness as a kind of discipline whose prerequisites include attitudes and aptitudes such as openness, receptivity, empathy, sensitivity, and imagination" (1995:190).

Understanding that an animal is in pain or distress—even empathizing or sympathizing with him—doesn't ensure, however, that the human will act ethically toward the animal. Thus, the originary emotional empathetic response must be supplemented with an ethical and political perspective (acquired through training and education) that enables the human to analyze the situation critically so as to determine who is responsible for the animal suffering and how that suffering may best be alleviated. In her recent book *Regarding the Pain of Others* (2003), Susan Sontag warns that people do not automatically act ethically in response to pictures of other people's pain (she doesn't deal with images of animals). While she characterizes as a "moral monster" the person who through a failure "of imagination, of empathy" (8) does not respond compassionately, she nevertheless argues that various ideologies often interfere with the moral response. Too often, she claims, sympathy connotes superiority and privilege without self-reflection about how one is contributing to the suffering one is lamenting. She therefore urges that a heightened humanist political awareness must accompany the sympathetic response in order for truly ethical action to result. Photos of atrocity "cannot be more than an invitation to pay attention, to reflect" (117) on who is responsible for the suffering and similar questions.

As noted in the introduction, the feminist ethic of care includes a political perspective. To a great extent, as noted by several of the contributors to this volume, getting people to see evil and to care about suffering is a matter of clearing away ideological rationalizations that legitimate animal exploitation and cruelty. Recognizing the egregious use of euphemism employed to disguise such behavior (copiously documented in Joan Dunayer's book *Animal Equality* [2001]) would seem to be an important step in this direction.

But it is not just a matter of supplementing care with a political perspective, for the experience of care can itself lead into political analysis, as Joan Tronto points out in her call for a "political ethic of care" (1993:155). "Care becomes a tool for critical political analysis when we use this concept to reveal relationships of power" (172). In other words, although Tronto doesn't treat the animal question, if one feels sympathy toward a suffering animal, one is moved to ask the question, why is this animal suffering? The answer can lead into a political analysis of the reasons for the animal's distress. Education in critical thinking, these thinkers emphasize, is therefore imperative if an ethic of care is to work.

We also need education, as Nel Noddings proposed (1984:153), in the practices of care and empathy.[7] Years ago, in fact, Gregory Bateson and Mary Catherine Bateson contended that "empathy is a discipline" and therefore teachable (1987:195). Many religions, they note, use imaginative exercises in empathetic understanding as a spiritual discipline (195). Such exercises could be adapted for use in secular institutions like schools (including, especially, high school). Certainly a large purpose of such a discipline must be not just emotional identification but also intellectual understanding, learning to hear, to take seriously, to care about what animals are telling us, learning to read and attend to their language. The burgeoning field of animal ethology is providing important new information that will aid in such study.

In conclusion, therefore, a feminist animal care ethic must be political in its perspective and dialogical in its method. Rejecting the imperialist imperative of the scientific method, in which the "scientific subject's voice . . . speaks with general and abstract authority [and] the objects of inquiry 'speak' only in response to what scientists ask them" (as Sandra Harding [1986:124] characterized the laboratory encounter), humans must cease imposing their voice on that of animals. No longer must our relationship with animals be that of the "conquest of an alien object," Rosemary Radford Ruether notes, but "the conversation of two subjects." We must recognize "that the 'other' has a 'nature' of her own that needs to be respected and with which one must enter into conversation" (1975:195–96). On that basis and in reflecting upon the political context, a dialogical ethic for the treatment of animals may be established.[8]

Acknowledgments

I would like to thank Erling Skorpen, who stimulated my thinking in this direction years ago; Carol Adams for planting the idea of applying standpoint theory to animals; the *Signs* editors and readers for their suggestions; and my dogs Aurora and Sadie, with whom I dialogue daily.

Notes

1. Carol Adams initiated this line of thinking in her 1997 article, "'Mad Cow' Disease and the Animal Industrial Complex" (see esp. 29, 41–42, 44). Adams takes a slightly different tack than I do here, seeing cows as "alienated laborers" whose standpoint has been ignored. See also Slicer (1998). While care theory and standpoint theory derive from different philosophical traditions, they connect in their concern about paying heed to others' misery. And in the original formulation of feminist standpoint theory, Nancy Hartsock (1983) identified as the feminist standpoint the female relational ontology that is at the heart of care theory. Where care theory and standpoint theory differ, however, is that the latter is more of a political theory that seeks to locate the causes of the misery and to confront and eliminate it politically; care theory is more of a moral theory aimed at alleviating misery in an immediate way. Both approaches are necessary, I argue below.

While poststructuralists and postmodernists have critiqued standpoint theory for its alleged essentialism and ascription of privileged perception to the oppressed (proletariat), it remains nevertheless obvious that certain groups are treated as having an essential reified identity which enables their abuse. As Laura Lee Downs aptly asks in the title to her article on the subject, "If 'Woman' Is Just an Empty Category, Then Why Am I Afraid to Walk Alone at Night?" (1993). See also Godfrey (2005). Like women, in being determined as *objects*, animals are forced into an essential identity, which as *subjects* they resist. This critical resistance, which humans know through communication with animals, is the animals' standpoint.

2. Catharine MacKinnon is the exception here. In "Sexuality, Pornography, and Method" ([1990] 1995), she proposes that "sexual objectification" be considered the basis for the emergence of a women's standpoint (135). For a survey of feminist standpoint theories, see Harding (1986:141–51).

3. In the past few years, a number of other literary theorists have begun exploring the possibility of a dialogical "animal-standpoint criticism." I have just completed an article (not yet published), "Animal Ethics and Literary Criticism," that further develops this concept.

4. This is to disagree somewhat with Thomas Nagel, who in "What Is

It Like to Be a Bat?" (1974) argues that we humans cannot apprehend "bat phenomenology" (440); that is, we can only imagine what it would be like for us to be bats, not what it is like for bats to be bats. To an extent Nagel is correct, of course; it is a truism of epistemology that we are limited by our mental apparatus. However, I believe more effort can be made to decipher animal communications and that while we may never fully understand what it feels like to be a bat, we can understand certain pertinent basics of his or her experience, sufficient for the formulation of an ethical response. For an alternative view to Nagel's, see Kenneth Shapiro's "Understanding Dogs" (1989), which argues that we recognize the validity of interspecies "kinesthetic" communication.

Although Val Plumwood proposes a "dialogical interspecies ethic" in her recent *Environmental Culture* (2002:167–95) that would seem to be consistent with what I am proposing here, she inconsistently argues that it is ethically permissible to kill and eat nonhumans under this ethic: one can "conceive [them] both as communicative others and as food" (157). This would seem to defeat the purpose of a dialogical ethic, which is to respond ethically to what the "communicative other" is telling one, namely and invariably that she does not want to be killed and eaten.

5. Here I am modifying classical structuralist terminology.

6. In the *locus classicus* on the subject of knowing another's inner states, "Other Minds" ([1946] 1979), J. L. Austin insists that a primary prerequisite for such communication is that one must have had the feeling oneself (104). Austin, however, like Nagel, abjures the possibility of knowing "what it would feel like to be a cat or a cockroach" (105).

7. Noddings (1991) has, however, stipulated reservations about applying care theory to animals. See also my critique of Noddings's position (Donovan 1991).

8. Other theorists who have advocated and explored dialogical ethical theory include Martin Buber, Simone Weil, Iris Murdoch, and Mikhail Bakhtin. See further discussion in my article "Attention to Suffering: Sympathy as a Basis for Ethical Treatment of Animals" (chapter 7, this volume).

REFERENCES

Adams, Carol J. 1990. *The Sexual Politics of Meat: A Feminist-Vegetarian Critical Theory.* New York: Continuum.

———. 1997. "'Mad Cow' Disease and the Animal Industrial Complex: An Ecofeminist Analysis." *Organization & Environment* 10, no. 1:26–51.

Austin, J. L. (1946) 1979. "Other Minds." In *Philosophical Papers*, ed. J. O. Urmson and G. J. Warnock, 76–116. 3rd ed. Oxford: Oxford University Press.

Bate, Jonathan. 1998. "Poetry and Biodiversity." In *Writing the Environment:*

Ecocriticism and Literature, ed. Richard Kerridge and Neil Sammells, 53–70. London: Zed.

Bateson, Gregory, and Mary Catherine Bateson. 1987. *Angels Fear: Towards an Epistemology of the Sacred*. New York: Bantam.

Donovan, Josephine. 1991. "Reply to Noddings." *Signs: Journal of Women in Culture and Society* 16, no. 2:423–25.

Downs, Laura Lee. 1993. "If 'Woman' Is Just an Empty Category, Then Why Am I Afraid to Walk Alone at Night? Identity Politics Meets the Postmodern Subject." *Comparative Studies in Society and History* 35, no. 2:414–37.

Dunayer, Joan. 2001. *Animal Equality: Language and Liberation*. Derwood, Md.: Ryce.

Godfrey, Phoebe. 2005. "Diane Wilson vs. Union Carbide: Ecofeminism and the Elitist Charge of 'Essentialism.'" *Capitalism Nature Socialism* 16, no. 4:37–55.

Harding, Sandra. 1986. *The Science Question in Feminism*. Ithaca, N.Y.: Cornell University Press.

Hartsock, Nancy C.M. 1983. "The Feminist Standpoint: Developing the Ground for a Specifically Feminist Historical Materialism." In *Discovering Reality: Feminist Perspectives on Epistemology, Metaphysics, Methodology, and Philosophy of Science*, ed. Sandra Harding and Merrill B. Hintikka, 283–310. Dordrecht: Reidel.

——. 1998. *The Feminist Standpoint Revisited and Other Essays*. Boulder, Colo.: Westview.

Jaggar, Alison M. 1995. "Caring as a Feminist Practice of Moral Reason." In *Justice and Care: Essential Readings in Feminist Ethics*, ed. Virginia Held, 179–202. Boulder: Colo.: Westview.

Jewett, Sarah Orne. 1881. "River Driftwood." In *Country By-Ways*, 1–33. Boston: Houghton Mifflin.

Lukács, Georg. (1923) 1971. *History and Class Consciousness*. Trans. Rodney Livingstone. Cambridge, Mass.: MIT Press.

MacKinnon, Catharine A. (1990) 1995. "Sexuality, Pornography, and Method: 'Pleasure Under Patriarchy.'" In *Feminism and Philosophy: Essential Readings in Theory, Reinterpretation, and Application*, ed. Nancy Tuana and Rosemarie Tong, 134–61. Boulder, Colo.: Westview.

Midgley, Mary. 1983. *Animals and Why They Matter*. Athens: University of Georgia Press.

Murphy, Patrick. 1991. "Prolegomenon for an Ecofeminist Dialogics." In *Feminism, Bakhtin, and the Dialogic*, ed. Dale M. Bauer and Susan Jaret McKinstry, 39–56. Albany: State University of New York Press.

Nagel, Thomas. 1974. "What Is It Like to Be a Bat?" *Philosophical Review* 83, no. 4:435–50.

Noddings, Nel. 1984. *Caring: A Feminine Approach to Ethics and Moral Education*. Berkeley: University of California Press.

———. 1991. "Comment on Donovan's 'Animal Rights and Feminist Theory.'" *Signs: Journal of Women in Culture and Society* 16, no. 2:418–22.

Plumwood, Val. 2002. *Environmental Culture: The Ecological Crisis of Reason*. London: Routledge.

Ruether, Rosemary Radford. 1975. *New Woman/New Earth: Sexist Ideologies and Human Liberation*. New York: Seabury.

Shapiro, Kenneth J. 1989. "Understanding Dogs Through Kinesthetic Empathy, Social Construction, and History." *Anthrozoös* 3, no. 3:184–95.

Scheler, Max. (1926) 1970. *The Nature of Sympathy*. Trans. Peter Heath. Hamden, Conn.: Archon.

Simons, John. 2002. *Animal Rights and the Politics of Literary Representation*. Houndmills, Eng.: Palgrave.

Slicer, Deborah. 1998. "Toward an Ecofeminist Standpoint Theory: Bodies as Grounds." In *Ecofeminist Literary Criticism: Theory, Interpretation, Pedagogy*, ed. Greta Gaard and Patrick D. Murphy, 49–73. Urbana: University of Illinois Press.

Sontag, Susan. 2003. *Regarding the Pain of Others*. New York: Farrar, Straus and Giroux.

Tronto, Joan C. 1993. *Moral Boundaries: A Political Argument for an Ethic of Care*. New York: Routledge.

Wittgenstein, Ludwig. 1963. *Philosophical Investigations*. Trans. G. E. M. Anscombe. Oxford: Blackwell.

SELECTED BIBLIOGRAPHY

This list includes only works centrally related to the feminist ethic-of-care tradition in animal ethics.

Adams, Carol J. 1990. *The Sexual Politics of Meat: A Feminist-Vegetarian Critical Theory.* New York: Continuum.

———. 1994. *Neither Man nor Beast: Feminism and the Defense of Animals.* New York: Continuum.

———. 2000. *The Sexual Politics of Meat: A Feminist-Vegetarian Critical Theory.* 2nd ed. New York: Continuum.

———. 2003. *The Pornography of Meat.* New York: Continuum.

Adams, Carol J., and Josephine Donovan, eds. 1995. *Animals and Women: Feminist Theoretical Explorations.* Durham, N.C.: Duke University Press, 1996.

Albright, Katrina M. 2002. "The Extension of Legal Rights to Animals Under a Caring Ethic: An Ecofeminist Exploration of Steven Wise's *Rattling the Cage.*" *Natural Resources Journal* 42, no. 4:915–37.

Allen, Paula Gunn. 1986. *The Sacred Hoop: Recovering the Feminine in American Indian Traditions.* Boston: Beacon.

Benhabib, Selya, and Drucilla Cornell, eds. 1987. *Feminism as Critique: On the Politics of Gender.* Minneapolis: University of Minnesota Press.

Bernstein, Marc H. 2004. *Without a Tear: Our Tragic Relationship with Animals.* Urbana: University of Illinois Press.

Birke, Lynda. 1994. *Feminism, Animals, and Science: The Naming of the Shrew.* Buckingham, Eng.: Open University Press.

Bowerbank, Sylvia. 2004. *Speaking for Nature: Women and Ecologies of Early Modern England.* Baltimore: Johns Hopkins University Press.

Carrighar, Sally. 1973. *Home to the Wilderness.* Boston: Houghton Mifflin.

Cobbe, Frances Power. 1875. *The Moral Aspects of Vivisection.* London: Williams & Margater.

———. 1899. *The Modern Rack.* London: Swann, Sonnenschein.

Code, Lorraine. 1991. *What Can She Know? Feminist Theory and the Construction of Knowledge.* Ithaca, N.Y.: Cornell University Press.

Coetzee, J. M. 1999. *The Lives of Animals*. Ed. Amy Gutmann. Princeton, N.J.: Princeton University Press.

Cole, Eve Browning, and Susan Coultrap-McQuin, eds. 1992. *Explorations in Feminist Ethics: Theory and Practice*. Bloomington: Indiana University Press.

Collard, Andrée, with Joyce Contrucci. 1988. *Rape of the Wild: Man's Violence Against Animals and the Earth*. Bloomington: Indiana University Press.

Collins, Patricia Hill. 1990. *Black Feminist Thought: Knowledge, Consciousness and the Politics of Empowerment*. Boston: Unwin Hyman.

Diamond, Irene, and Gloria Feman Orenstein, eds. 1990. *Reweaving the World: The Emergence of Ecofeminism*. San Francisco: Sierra Club.

Dunayer, Joan. 2001. *Animal Equality: Language and Liberation*. Derwood, Md.: Ryce.

French, Marilyn. 1985. *Beyond Power: On Women, Men, and Morals*. New York: Summit.

Gaard, Greta, ed. 1993. *Ecofeminism: Women, Animals, Nature*. Philadelphia: Temple University Press.

——. 2007. *Home Is Where You Are: Essays on Water, Place, Identity*. Tucson: University of Arizona Press.

Gilligan, Carol. 1982. *In a Different Voice: Psychological Theory and Women's Development*. Cambridge, Mass.: Harvard University Press.

Gilman, Charlotte Perkins. 1976 (1923). *His Religion and Hers*. Westport, Conn.: Hyperion.

Goodall, Jane. 1971. *In the Shadow of Man*. Boston: Houghton Mifflin.

——. 1986. *The Chimpanzees of Gombe: Patterns of Behavior*. Cambridge, Mass.: Harvard University Press.

Griffin, Susan. 1978. *Woman and Nature: The Roaring Inside Her*. New York: Harper & Row.

Murdoch, Iris. 1971. *The Sovereignty of Good*. New York: Schocken.

——. 1993. *Metaphysics as a Guide to Morals*. New York: Viking Penguin.

Murphy, Patrick. 1995. *Literature, Nature, and Others: Ecofeminist Critiques*. Albany: State University of New York Press.

Noddings, Nel. 1984. *Caring: A Feminine Approach to Ethics and Moral Education*. Berkeley: University of California Press.

Noske, Barbara. 1989. *Humans and Other Animals: Beyond the Boundaries of Anthropology*. London: Pluto Press. [Reissued 1997 as *Beyond Boundaries: Humans and Animals*. Montreal: Black Rose Rooks.]

Parham, Barbara. 1979. *What's Wrong with Eating Meat?* Denver, Colo.: Ananda Marga.

Plant, Judith, ed. 1989. *Healing the Wounds: The Promise of Ecofeminism*. Philadelphia: New Society.

Pluhar, Evelyn. 1995. *Beyond Prejudice: The Moral Significance of Human and Nonhuman Animals*. Durham, N.C.: Duke University Press.

Plumwood, Val. 1993. *Feminism and the Mastery of Nature.* London: Routledge.

——. 2002. *Environmental Culture: The Ecological Crisis of Reason.* London: Routledge.

Randour, Mary Lou. 2000. *Animal Grace: Entering a Spiritual Relationship with Our Fellow Creatures.* Novato, Calif.: New World Library.

Rollin, Bernard. 1981. *Animal Rights and Human Morality.* Buffalo, N.Y.: Prometheus.

——. 1990. *The Unheeded Cry: Animal Consciousness, Animal Pain, and Science.* Oxford: Oxford University Press.

Ruddick, Sara. 1989. *Maternal Thinking: Toward a Politics of Peace.* Boston: Beacon.

Ruether, Rosemary Radford. 1975. *New Woman/New Earth: Sexist Ideologies and Human Liberation.* New York: Seabury.

——. 1983. *Sexism and God-Talk: Toward a Feminist Theology.* Boston: Beacon.

——. 1992. *Gaia and God.* San Francisco: Harper.

Sanday, Peggy Reeves. 1981. *Female Power and Male Dominance: On the Origins of Sexual Inequality.* Cambridge: Cambridge University Press.

Seager, Joni. 1993. *Earth Follies: Coming to Feminist Terms with the Global Environmental Crisis.* New York: Routledge.

Shiva, Vandana. 1988. *Staying Alive: Women, Ecology, and Development.* London: Zed.

——, ed. 1994. *Close to Home: Women Reconnect Ecology, Health and Development Worldwide.* Philadelphia: New Society.

Spiegel, Marjorie. 1988. *The Dreaded Comparison: Human and Animal Slavery.* Philadelphia: New Society.

Stein, Edith. 1966 (1916). *On the Problem of Empathy.* The Hague: Martinus Nijhoff.

Taylor, Paul W. 1986. *Respect for Nature: A Theory of Environmental Ethics.* Princeton, N.J.: Princeton University Press.

Thomas, Keith. 1983. *Man and the Natural World: A History of the Modern Sensibility.* New York: Pantheon.

Tong, Rosemarie. 1993. *Feminine and Feminist Ethics.* Belmont, Calif.: Wadsworth.

Tronto, Joan C. 1993. *Moral Boundaries: A Political Argument for an Ethic of Care.* New York: Routledge.

Walker, Alice. 1987. *Living by the Word: Selected Writings, 1973–1987.* San Diego: Harcourt Brace Jovanovich.

Weil, Simone. 1977. *The Simone Weil Reader.* Ed. George A. Panichas. New York: McKay.

Woolf, Virginia. 1963. (1938). *Three Guineas.* New York: Harcourt, Brace.

CONTRIBUTORS

CAROL J. ADAMS is the author and editor of more than twenty books, including *The Sexual Politics of Meat: A Feminist-Vegetarian Critical Theory.*

CATHRYN BAILEY is a professor and the chair of the Department of Philosophy at Minnesota State University–Mankato, where her work focuses on issues in feminist philosophy, especially ethics and epistemology.

GRACE CLEMENT is an associate professor and the chair of the Department of Philosophy at Salisbury University in Salisbury, Maryland. She has written a book, *Care, Autonomy, and Justice: Feminism and the Ethic of Care,* and is currently writing on questions about animal friendship and moral agency.

DEANE CURTIN is a professor and the chair of the Department of Philosophy at Gustavus Adolphus College in St. Peter, Minnesota. He specializes in environmental ethics and globalization, and his most recent book is *Environmental Ethics for a Postcolonial World.*

JOSEPHINE DONOVAN, professor emerita, University of Maine, is the author and editor of eleven books and numerous articles in critical theory, literary history, and animal ethics.

JAMES GARBARINO is Maude C. Clarke Professor of Humanistic Psychology at Loyola University in Chicago. A life-long "dog person," he is the author of twenty-two books, including *Lost Boys* and *See Jane Hit.*

LORI GRUEN teaches in the Department of Philosophy and the Feminist, Gender, and Sexuality Studies Program at Wesleyan University. She is currently working on two book projects: one on empathy and the other on human relations to captive chimpanzee. She maintains a chimp memorial Web site: first100chimps.wesleyan.edu.

THOMAS G. KELCH is a professor of law at Whittier Law School. He focuses on domestic and international animal law, as well as on the intersection of law and moral philosophy relating to animals.

MARTI KHEEL is an ecofeminist author whose articles have been translated into several languages and have appeared in numerous journals and anthologies. She is author of the forthcoming book *Nature Ethics: An Ecofeminist Perspective* and is currently a visiting scholar at the Graduate Theological Union.

BRIAN LUKE is a musician and writer living in Dayton, Ohio. He received a doctorate in philosophy from the University of Pittsburgh in 1992. He is the author of the forthcoming book *Brutal: Manhood and the Exploitation of Animals.*

CATHARINE A. MACKINNON, is Elizabeth A. Long Professor of Law at the University of Michigan. She is a teacher, lawyer, writer, and activist on sex equality domestically and internationally. MacKinnon has been widely published in many languages; her dozen books include *Sex Equality, Toward a Feminist Theory of the State, Only Words, Sexual Harassment of Working Women,* and, in the past two years, *Women's Lives, Men's Laws* and *Are Women Human?*

KENNETH SHAPIRO is founder and coexecutive director of Animals and Society Institute and editor of Human-Animal Studies Book Series. He is the author of three books, most recently *Animal Models of Human Psychology: Critique of Science, Ethics and Policy.*

DEBORAH SLICER teaches environmental philosophy at the University of Montana.

INDEX

Blackwell, Elizabeth, 70, 80n.29
body: alienation from, 96; boundaries
 of, 206; Cartesian attitude toward,
 96; as moral agent, 96; and power,
 221; reclaiming the, 221; separation
 of, from mind, 345–46; of sexed
 female animal, 204, 208
Body in Pain, The (Scarry), 206
Bordo, Susan, 68, 96, 345–46
Boswell, James, 318
boundaries: human–animal, 22, 74,
 202, 251; of men, 206; public and
 private, 309; of women, 213–15, 220
Bradwell, Myra, 318
Brennan, William, 279
Broida, John, 159
Brown v. Board of Education, 237
Browning, Elizabeth Barrett, 85n.78
Buber, Martin, 175, 191, 192, 355, 356
Buddhists, 98
Bueckner v. Hamel, 233, 242

Callicott, J. Baird, 44, 47, 54n.10,
 55n.16, 307, 311, 312–13; on domestic and wild animals, 194n.21, 304,
 305, 308–9, 310; on endangered
 species, 41; on good of the whole,
 41, 42; on kin altruism, 182
calves, 114, 130, 131, 143, 338, 339
capabilities approach, 13–14
capitalism, 7, 67, 188, 261, 361
Capitalism, the Family and Personal Life
 (Zaretsky), 67
Capra, Fritjof, 40
care–justice debate, 4–6, 301, 302
Caring (Nodding), 2
caring attitude, 157–61
caring ethic, 92, 185–87, 199, 230,
 252, 254–57, 356; and animal needs,
 189; attentiveness in, 3, 4; and autonomy, 309, 311; and "caring for,"
 94–95, 96; contextual character
 of, 2, 94, 95, 96, 303; and critical
 thinking, 365; dialogical, 362–65;
 and domestic animals, 305–6; epis-

temology for, 190; feminist, 2, 13,
 102n.16, 186, 221, 365; and moral
 relativism, 4; and ontology of care,
 200; political, 3, 7, 93, 94, 99–100,
 187–88, 364–65; and private sphere,
 309; and reciprocity, 94–95, 334;
 Regan on, 132–33; and rights–care
 debate, 199–200; sympathy as basis
 of, 129–32, 174–92; theorists, theory
 of, 1, 2, 3, 4, 5, 12, 14, 360, 361, 364,
 366n.1; and vegetarianism, 334; and
 women, 2, 103n.22, 155, 159, 161,
 186, 189. *See also* justice ethic
carnivorism. *See* meat eating
Carrighar, Sally, 75, 86n.84
Carter, Janis, 75, 86n.84
Cartesian: attitude toward the body,
 96–97; man, 5; mode, 177, 178;
 objectivism, 2, 59, 68, 69, 345;
 paradigm, 66; view of animals, 63,
 136, 238, 285
"Cartesian Masculinization of
 Thought, The" (Bordo), 68
Case for Animal Rights, The (Regan),
 59, 60, 68, 106, 176, 201, 348
categorical imperative, 60
Cather, Willa, 85n.78
cats, 58, 85n.78, 119, 120, 135, 197n.41
Cavalieri, Paola, 170
Cavendish, Margaret, 69, 70
Cheney, Jim, 108–9, 112, 186–87
Chernin, Kim, 96–97
chickens, 310–11, 336
Child, Lydia Maria, 65, 80n.29
children: abuse of, 10–11, 214, 252,
 256; protection of, 252, 253, 254
Chipko movement, 103n.24
Chrystos, 65
Circe, 71
circuses, opposition to, 76, 287
Cobbe, Frances Power, 8, 59, 80n.29,
 159
Coetzee, J. M., 14, 15, 347, 351, 352, 355
Coleman, Sydney, 55n.22
Colette, 85n.78

CPSIA information can be obtained at www.ICGtesting.com
Printed in the USA
LVOW10s2250221015

459308LV00001B/9/P

9 780231 140393